Music, Technology, Innovation

Music, Technology, Innovation: Industry and Educational Perspectives draws upon cutting-edge practice in the use of technology from both a pedagogical and industry perspective. Situated within the latest research, this edited volume explores technological innovation from a musical perspective, examines current trends within the industry, and carefully considers them from an educational perspective.

Noted throughout history, music education is responsive to industry innovations. However, emerging technologies often begin with over-hyped promises before they move through various phases of development and are then repurposed for learning and teaching. Educators can adopt an innovation and develop a framework that is pedagogically sound and learner-centred. Based on these ideas, the authors together highlight industry innovations that have potential outcomes for engaging students in music learning within research-informed practices, build upon these ideas and identify proactive mechanisms for teaching music education, and work towards developing a framework for understanding these phenomena. The chapters address key topics including the ethics of technology, AI and music, online performance and teaching, gamification, big data, teaching audio production, acoustic ecology, and more. The examination of areas in contemporary innovation can further support the potential to empower teachers and students to understand the opportunities for teaching, sustainability, and growth in music education.

Carol Johnson (PhD) is Senior Lecturer in Music (Online Learning and Educational Technologies) at the Melbourne Conservatorium of Music, The University of Melbourne (Australia), and founded The Virtual School of Music in 2004.

Andrew King (PhD) is Professor in Music and Technology and was Head of the School of Arts (2017–2023) at the University of Hull, UK. He is currently Pro Vice Chancellor at the University of Hull (UK).

Music, Technology, Innovation

Industry and Educational Perspectives

Edited by Carol Johnson and Andrew King

Routledge
Taylor & Francis Group

NEW YORK AND LONDON

Designed cover image: Getty

First published 2025
by Routledge
605 Third Avenue, New York, NY 10158

and by Routledge
4 Park Square, Milton Park, Abingdon, Oxon, OX14 4RN

Routledge is an imprint of the Taylor & Francis Group, an informa business

© 2025 Taylor & Francis

Library of Congress Cataloging-in-Publication Data
A catalog record for this title has been requested

ISBN: 978-0-367-48527-6 (hbk)
ISBN: 978-0-367-48525-2 (pbk)
ISBN: 978-1-003-04147-4 (ebk)

DOI: 10.4324/9781003041474

Typeset in Sabon
by Apex CoVantage, LLC

To my family.
Angela King (1963–2024).

Contents

Tables

Figures

Acknowledgments

As editors, we would like to respectfully acknowledge our authors and their valuable contributions to this book. We would also like to say "thank you" for the patience and consideration across the challenges that had to be overcome during the process of this book writing for many of our authors from 2020 through 2022. We know that many had to overcome various personal and professional challenges due to the COVID pandemic – which is when this writing began. We are grateful to the contributing authors and their perseverance during these challenging times.

We would also like to acknowledge the University of Melbourne Dyason Fellowship that was received to support this book.

Contributors

Fabio Antonacci (PhD) is Associate Professor at Politecnico di Milano, Milan. His research focuses on space-time processing of audio signals for both speaker and microphone arrays (source localization, acoustic scene analysis, rendering of spatial sound) and on modelling of acoustic propagation (visibility-based beam tracing). He is the author of more than 60 articles in proceedings of international conferences and on peer-reviewed journals.

Federico Avanzini (PhD) is currently a full professor with the computer science department, University of Milan. His research interests are in Sound and Music Computing (SMC) and mainly concern algorithms for sound synthesis and processing, 3D sound rendering, non-speech sound in human-computer interfaces, with applications to assistive technologies, virtual musical instruments, digital cultural heritage, and digital learning. He is a principal investigator for EU-, national-, and industry-funded projects, has authored 200+ publications on peer-reviewed international journals and conferences, and has chaired and served in several program and editorial committees. He has been Associate Editor for the international journal Acta Acustica (2014–2021), and is currently a member of the Editorial Board of Milano University Press. He has been President of the Italian Music Informatics Association (2018–2022) and is currently Conference Coordinator of the International SMC Board.

Leah Barclay (PhD) is a sound artist, designer and researcher (Senior Lecturer in Design, University of the Sunshine Coast, Australia) who works at the intersection of art, science and technology. Leah's research and creative work over the last decade has investigated innovative approaches to recording and disseminating the soundscapes of terrestrial and aquatic ecosystems to inform conservation, scientific research and public engagement. Her work explores ways we can use creativity, new technologies and emerging science to reconnect communities to the environment and inspire climate action.

Alberto Bernardini received a Bachor of Science degree in computer engineering from the University of Bologna, Italy, in 2012, a Master of Science degree (cum laude) in computer engineering, and a PhD degree (cum laude) in information engineering from Politecnico di Milano, Italy, in 2015 and 2019, respectively. He was a postdoctoral researcher with Politecnico di Milano, from 2019 to 2021, where he is currently an assistant professor with the Dipartimento di Elettronica, Informazione e Bioingegneria (DEIB). He has authored more than 40 publications in international journals and the proceedings of international conferences. His main research interests include audio signal processing, computational acoustics, and the modelling of nonlinear systems. He is the first author of two international patents. In 2019, he was a recipient of the Dimitris N. Chorafas

Award. He serves as Associate Editor for IEEE Transactions on Circuits and Systems I: Regular Papers and EURASIP Journal on Audio, Speech, and Music Processing.

James Cook joined the Reid School of Music in 2017, having previously been a university teacher in music at the University of Sheffield, a lecturer at Bangor University, a supervision tutor at the University of Cambridge, and an adjunct lecturer at the University of Nottingham. After completing his doctorate on fifteenth-century English mass cycles, supervised by Peter Wright and Philip Weller, James held a number of short-term post-doctoral fellowships followed by a Postdoctoral Fellowship of the Society for Renaissance Studies, during which he worked on the apparent decline in interest in English music in the later fifteenth century. He works mainly on early music and is especially interested in music of the fourteenth to sixteenth centuries – the period that falls neatly between the Middle Ages and the Renaissance. James is also interested in the representation of early music on stage and screen, be that the use of 'real' early music in multimedia productions, the imaginative re-scoring of historical dramas, or even the popular medievalism of the fantasy genre. He was co-founder of the REMOSS (Representations of Early Music on Stage and Screen) study group, which organises regular roundtables and conferences in this area.

Luca Comanducci received a Bachelor of Science degree in music information science from the University of Milan, Milan, Italy, in 2014, a Master of Science in computer science and engineering, and a Ph.D. degree in information technology from Politecnico di Milano, Milan, Italy, in 2018 and 2022, respectively. He is currently working as a postdoctoral researcher at Politecnico di Milano. His research interests include application of deep learning techniques to spatial audio problems, networked music performance, and automatic music generation.

Giovanni Cospito is Professor of Electroacoustic Music Composition, Coordinator of the Department of Music and New Technologies and the School of Electronic Music at the Conservatories of Music of Como and Milano. His research interests span the design and development of technologies for music education, music composition and tools for computer music and live electronics. His artistic activities include music productions and compositions for live electronics, electroacoustic and computer music, at the CSC of Padua, LIMB of Venice, GMVL in Lyon, AGON and LASDIM in Milano, EMS of Stockholm, IRCAM in Paris, TEMPO REALE at Florence, Bourges International Electroacoustic Music Festival, Teatro alla Scala and Milano Musica, the Poket Opera Company in Nürnberg, Dusseldorf and Dresda. He authored several multimedia productions and interactive performances in collaboration with DIST center of Genova, Brera Academy of Fine Arts in Milan, Total Opera in Venice, Carlo Felice Theater of Genoa, Theaters of New Music-Terra delle Gravine, Candiani Venice Center. He is a member of the CEDIM (Center for Electroacoustics and Digital Interactions), of the San Fedele Cultural Foundation-Milan, and he is a director of METAS Association for electroacoustic music, performing arts, soundscape installations and sound design projects.

Stefano Delle Monache (PhD) received his PhD in Science of Design in 2012 from Iuav University of Venice, Italy. His research interests focus on the study and design of behaviours mediated by sound, and span practices, methods and representations for sound-driven design, evaluation of sound in interaction, and interactive sound models for computational artefacts. He has been involved in several EU-funded research projects. He was Marie Skłodowska-Curie Research Fellow at Delft University of Technology, Faculty of

Industrial Design Engineering. His funded project, Participatory Designing with Sounds (PaDS, 2020–2022), contributed to extending knowledge on sound-driven design cognition, to assist designers and other actors to collaboratively create sound-driven designs. He is a member of the Critical Alarms Lab at TU Delft, and co-chair of the DRS Special Interest Group on Sound-Driven Design. Currently, he is a researcher at KTH, Division of Media Technology and Interaction Design, where he is involved in the Sound for Energy project.

Paul Doornbusch (PhD) is an academic, composer, sonologist, researcher and occasional performer who works largely with algorithmic composition systems for traditional instruments and electronics. Currently a guest professor at EPFL Switzerland, prior to that he spent a decade as Associate Dean of the Australian College of the Arts. His work is presented internationally in concerts throughout Europe and Australasia and ranges from compositions involving instruments and electronics to media works. Active as a scholar, Doornbusch has chapters in *The Oxford Handbook of Computer Music*, and he has written articles on algorithmic composition, computer music, mapping and virtual reality for publications worldwide. Doornbusch's book *The Music of CSIRAC* reports on the successful research project to reconstruct and document the music played by Australia's first computer, CSIRAC. This charts a new history of computer music, providing an accessible and cogent overview of a now-pervasive social and technical transformation in how music is mediated.

Nicolas Gold (PhD) is an associate professor in computer science at UCL. His research interests include source code analysis, research ethics, and computing education involving music and making, with particular emphasis on design aspects. He teaches professional practice and ethics in software engineering at UCL, is co-chair of the UCL Computer Science Research Ethics Committee, and has served on the UCL REC. He has contributed to ethics guidance and policy departmentally and in the wider institution. He has also co-authored papers on research ethics in mining software repositories, on the propagation of ethics values by publishing communities, and on post-research ethical duties for research involving affective software. Gold is currently the chair of the ethics committee for the New Interfaces for Musical Expression (NIME) international conference series, a contributing author to its ethics code, and he serves on the UK Research Integrity Office register of advisors. He is also an active musician.

Aristotelis Hadjakos (PhD) is Professor of Music Informatics at the Detmold University of Music. He heads the centre for Music and Film Informatics (CeMFI). His research area is musical human-machine interaction. His specific research interests are digital humanities, digital music scores and tangible music interfaces. He received his doctorate in computer science from the Technical University of Darmstadt and holds diplomas in piano pedagogy and computer science.

Phil Harding (PhD) started in the music industry aged 16 at London's **Marquee Studios** in 1973, where he got to work as an assistant engineer under the guidance of top producers on albums for artists such as **Elton John, Kiki Dee** and **Barry Blue**. As Phil's career progressed, a long list of credits began to accumulate, with artists as diverse as **The Clash, Killing Joke, Toyah, Amii Stewart** and **Matt Bianco** all taking advantage of Phil's fast-growing reputation as a top engineer. During the last decade, Phil has worked with **Lamont Dozier** in Los Angeles mixing **Cliff Richard**'s 'Soulicious' album and published the book '**PWL From The Factory Floor**' with an accompanying '**Phil Harding Club**

Mixes of the 80s' CD. In 2017, he completed a **PhD** doctorate in Music Production at Leeds Beckett University. https://www.philhardingmusic.com/books

Evangelos Himonides (PhD) is Professor of Technology, Education, and Music at UCL, where he leads a number of courses and supervises doctoral and post-doctoral research. He co-directs the International Music Education Research Centre (iMerc) and iMerc Press. He is co-founder of the Music-Education-Technology International Conference (MET), edits the Sempre conference series, is associate editor of *Frontiers in Psychology* and the *Journal of Music, Technology and Education*), and is past associate editor of *Logopedics Phoniatrics Vocology*. Evangelos has developed the free online technologies for Sounds of Intent (2003–2023), Inspire-Music, and the Online Afghan Rubab Tutor. He is fellow of the RSA and Chartered Fellow (FBCS CITP) of the British Computer Society. When time is available, Evangelos likes to handcraft musical instruments in order to raise funds for his charitable work.

Carol Johnson (PhD) is Senior Lecturer in Music (Online Learning and Educational Technology) at the Melbourne Conservatorium of Music in Melbourne, Australia. She is interested in supporting effective practices for teaching and learning in technology-enabled learning (TEL) environments, which include online and blended learning and immersive learning environments. Her main focus in research is on developing approaches for online music pedagogy and practise-based research for the effective adoption of educational technology in higher education music learning. Carol founded The Virtual School of Music in 2004, and her publications highlight evidenced-based teaching practices for teaching music online and provide innovative approaches for teaching online and using educational technology to support students. You can explore her research and publications here: https://carolj.net/

Andrew King (PhD) is Professor of Music and Technology at the University of Hull, UK. He was Head of the School of the Arts from 2017 until 2023 and is a Principal Fellow of the Higher Education Academy. He previously led the music subject area and has led major research projects funded by AHRC, the Arts Council and the Paul Hamlyn Foundation (via PRSF, Sound and Music) in the areas of online music education, psychological well-being and evaluating the impact of composer residencies. His current work examines access and participation in music education examining sustainable models of delivery.

Robert Laidlow (PhD) is a composer and researcher at the University of Oxford. His "gigantically imaginative" (BBC Radio 3) music is concerned with discovering and developing new forms of musical expression through the relationship between advanced technology and live performance. Laidlow's music exploring the intersection of classical music, artificial intelligence, and creativity includes 'Silicon' (2022) for the BBC Philharmonic, 'Post-Singularity Songs' (2023) for Stephanie Lamprea, and 'Tui' (2024) for International Contemporary Ensemble. He is currently a Fellow in Composition at Jesus College, Oxford University. From 2018–2022, he was the PRiSM PhD Researcher in Artificial Intelligence in association with the BBC Philharmonic.

Peter Lee has worked in the field of music education and technology for over 25 years and is one of the original authors of the Auralia and Musition educational music software packages (https://www.risingsoftware.com/). He has worked extensively in the USA, UK and Australia, consulting with teachers and students to better identify appropriate technology solutions for the modern music classroom. The Auralia Ear Training and Musition Theory

Training packages are widely acknowledged as leading software training aids in music classrooms and studios.

Kenny McAlpine (PhD) joined Melbourne Conservatorium of Music in February 2019 as Melbourne Enterprise Fellow in Interactive Composition. He is an award-winning composer, writer, broadcaster, musician, and technologist who has scored for theatre, film, and video games.

Brad Merrick (PhD) is Senior Lecturer in Music and the Arts in the Faculty of Education at the University of Melbourne. He undertakes research across the areas of music education, online learning, music technology, motivation, engagement, and teacher practice. Brad completed his PhD in Music Education at the University of New South Wales, and he has contributed to the *Oxford Handbook of Music Education* and the *Routledge Companion to Music, Technology and Education*. He has published widely and sits on the international and national editorial boards of various journals. Brad is past Chair of the Music in Schools and Teacher Education commission of ISME and is a passionate advocate for music education globally. He currently serves as a member of the ISME International Board and is the current President of the Australian and New Zealand Association for Research in Music Education (ANZARME).

Matthias Nowakowski is a programmer and researcher at the Center for Music and Film Informatics (CeMFI) in Detmold, Germany. He pursued an interdisciplinary education in philosophy, musicology, and media informatics at universities in Cologne and Düsseldorf. Throughout his studies, he was drawn to exploring the complexities of digital musical workflows, aiming to understand their inner workings and potential applications. He could prove this during his time at the Fraunhofer Institute for Digital Media Technology (IDMT) in Ilmenau where he completed his thesis, focusing on deep learning strategies in automatic transcription of electroacoustic music. Currently, he concentrates his research on improving the usability and user experience of music notation software.

Pamela D. Pike (PhD) is the Herndon Spillman Professor of Piano Pedagogy and Associate Dean for Research, Creative Activity and Community Engagement in the College of Music and Dramatic Arts at Louisiana State University. A graduate of the University of Western Ontario, Southern Illinois University, and the University of Oklahoma, Pike has extensive experience teaching piano to students of all ages, both privately and in group settings. In 2002, she founded the "Third-Age Piano Program" for senior citizens to study piano and make music in a group setting. The program has become a model for successful community engagement. She won the 2019 LSU Foundation Distinguished Teaching Award and has received various honors for her teaching in Arkansas and Louisiana. Pike is dedicated to helping pedagogy students develop skills necessary to become successful piano teachers. Graduates of the LSU piano pedagogy program are working in colleges and private studios throughout the United States, Asia, central and south America. In 2020, Pike was named a Yamaha Master Educator.

Ross Purves (PhD) is an associate professor of music education at the Institute of Education, University College London's Faculty of Education and Society. Here he contributes to master's, doctoral and secondary school teacher education programmes. A Senior Fellow of the Higher Education Academy, Ross was previously Deputy Programme Leader and Employability Champion for BA Education Studies at De Montfort University. Before entering higher education, Ross was a course manager for music and music technology in a large 16–19 college and also served as music subject coordinator for a school-led consortium for initial teacher education. Ross's research interests embrace British music education history and the intersections between music, software engineering, design and making. An Associate Fellow of the UCL Centre for Climate Change and Sustainability Education, Ross has also recently begun researching the environmental impacts of music education.

Augusto Sarti (PhD) has a BS/MS and Ph.D. in electrical and electronics engineering from the University of Padua, Italy, in 1988 and 1993, respectively, with research in nonlinear communication systems. Sarti's research interests are in the area of digital signal processing with focus on space-time audio processing, sound analysis, synthesis and processing, image analysis, and 3D vision. His research contributions are in the area of sound synthesis (nonlinear wave digital filters); of space-time audio processing (plenacoustic processing, visibility-based interactive acoustic modeling, geometry-based acoustic scene reconstruction; soundfield rendering, etc.); nonlinear system theory (Volterra system inversion, Wave Digital circuit simulation); computer vision; image analysis and processing. He is currently focusing on geometric space-time audio processing methodologies; music information processing; spatial audio processing and more. https://sarti.faculty.polimi.it/Augusto_Sarti/CV_and_publications.html

Tim Summers (PhD) teaches and researches music at Royal Holloway University of London. His work concerns music in modern popular culture with a particular focus on music in video games. His publications include *Understanding Video Game Music* (2016), *The Legend of Zelda: Ocarina of Time – A Game Score Companion* (2021) and *The Queerness of Video Game Music* (2023), as well as co-editing the *Cambridge Companion to Video Game Music* and *The Journal of Sound and Music in Games*. Both his teaching and research are informed by his experiences of secondary school music teaching. His research seeks to understand the musical experiences and educations that mass media provide for the huge audiences they address.

Chester Thompson is known as the "drummer's drummer". Playing drums in clubs by the age of 13, Thompson's first drum audition, which led to his time with Frank Zappa and the Mothers, was a foreshadow of his exceptional performance and studio career. Thompson is a Grammy award-winning performer. He has performed and/or recorded with Ben E., King (1969), Jack McDuff, Frank Zappa and the Mothers (1973–1975), Weather Report (1975), Genesis (1977 through 1992), Phil Collins (various tours across 1999 to 2007), Santana (1984), Kirk Whalum and many other Grammy award musicians. His expertise in multiple music genres (i.e., Rock, Jazz, Pop, Progressive Rock, and Gospel) position him as an integral part of music history since the 1970s – and he continues to be influential on today's drummers. Whether it is a stadium performance, or a studio recording, his remarkable drumming is second-to-none. Labelled a "drummer's drummer" from his time as drummer with Genesis, Thompson taught applied drum lessons for 20 years at Belmont University (Nashville, USA), and is also a composer and producer. Thompson's accolades include a 2018 Grammy Award for performing on TajMo and 2008 Sabian Lifetime Achievement Award and was inducted into the *Rock and Roll Hall of Fame* in 2010 as a member of the band Genesis. His most recent CD is *Wake-Up Call* (2024) with Robert "Pewee" Hill, Michiko Hill and with special guest appearance by Akil Thompson (guitar). See www.chesterthompson.com

Jason Torrens is a musician, academic, technology expert and audio engineer who works in Higher Education and various musical endeavours. Currently the Senior Program Leader of Entertainment and the Head of Audio Production at Collarts in Melbourne, Australia, Jason has been at the forefront of hybrid and remote learning amongst practical disciplines like Audio Engineering, Music and Music Production. Being a drummer and teacher for over 35 years as well as working in various recording studios and live production environments, Jason has blended this experience of creativity and technology to create ground-breaking educational techniques for inclusive and remote learning, specifically for Audio Production. With qualifications in Music, Audio Production and Higher Education, Jason is currently completing a masters in higher education degree in technology for learning at the University of Wollongong.

George Waddell (PhD) is Performance Research and Innovation Fellow at the Royal College of Music. He is also Area Leader in Performance Science for the BMus programme and an honorary Research Associate in the Faculty of Medicine at Imperial College London. His research focusses on optimising how performers learn and are evaluated, including the development of new technologies to do so. He oversees a range of BMus RCM modules ensuring that students benefit from the latest research, scientific knowledge, and technology in their training. George also works closely with experts across fields to examine parallels in performance practice and to develop and deliver bespoke performance training to a range of professionals. He is a co-author of the research methods textbook *Performing Music Research*, holds a PhD in Performance Science from the RCM, and completed his BMus and MMus in piano performance at Brandon University (Canada) while studying psychology.

Tim Wilson is a music educator, jazz saxophonist and co-author of Auralia & Musition ear training and theory programs. He has taught at Melbourne University, Victorian College of the Arts, Monash University and conducted workshops around the world. His performance credits include Ray Charles, Natalie Cole, Tony Bennett, Melbourne Symphony Orchestra, The Australian Art Orchestra, Robbie Williams, Lalah Hathaway, Michael Buble, and James Morrison. Tim was a finalist at the World Saxophone Competition (BBC Jazz Festival) and the National Jazz Awards. He has released 12 solo albums and was awarded the 2017 Australian Jazz Bell Award for 'Best Australian Instrumental Jazz Album' for his live duo album 'Consider This' with acclaimed pianist Andrea Keller.

Aaron Williamon is Professor of Performance Science at the Royal College of Music (RCM) where he directs the Centre for Performance Science (CPS), a partnership of the RCM and Imperial College London. His research focuses on skilled performance and applied scientific initiatives that inform music learning and teaching, as well as the impact of music and the arts on society. Aaron is the founder of the International Symposium on Performance Science, founding chief editor of Performance Science (a *Frontiers* journal), and the founding chair of Healthy Conservatoires, an international network constituted in 2015 to support health literacy and wellbeing among student and professional performing artists. He is a fellow of the Royal Society of Arts (FRSA) and the UK's higher education academy, AdvanceHE (FHEA), and in 2008, he was elected an Honorary Member of the Royal College of Music (HonRCM).

Introduction

Carol Johnson and Andrew King

By editors

Music, Technology, Innovation draws upon cutting-edge practice in the use of technology from both a pedagogical and industrial perspective. Situated within the latest research, this edited volume explores technological innovation from a musical perspective, examines current trends within the industry, and carefully considers them from an educational perspective.

Noted throughout history, music education can be responsive to industry innovations. However, emerging technologies often begin with over-hyped promises before they move through various phases of development and then are repurposed for learning and teaching. Educators can adopt an innovation and develop a framework that is pedagogically sound and learner-centred. Based on these ideas, the authors highlight industry innovations that have potential outcomes for engaging students in music learning within research-informed practices, build upon these ideas and identify proactive mechanisms for teaching music education, and work towards developing a framework for understanding these phenomena. The examination of areas in contemporary innovation can further support the potential to empower teachers and students to understand the opportunities for teaching, sustainability, and growth in music education.

The focus of the book is about exploring how education music, technology, and innovation in teaching, curriculum, and the creativities surround music creation and performance. There are three parts within the volume: Technology, Performance, and Context; Perspectives and Design for Teaching; and Current Issues. Each part is introduced with a prequel narrative from an industry perspective and followed by standard chapters (i.e., literature review followed by research study with discussion and implications). The themes reflect the key topics for music educators and innovators in higher education as they look to resolve known challenges when adopting new technologies into music teaching, as well as look to the potential for technology to assist in furthering music learning for our next generation of music students.

The changing landscape of pedagogical practice as a result of disruptive technologies will continue its impact upon society and go beyond discipline specificity. Consequently, there are many innovation influences that are impacting the field. Influential factors include pedagogy, audio technologies, key stakeholders, and locations. To effectively understand and surface how music education can better utilize innovation, the book has been addressed thematically. By highlighting research-informed practices and studies of *Music, Technology, Innovation*, a greater understanding of the challenges and opportunities within music education can be reached.

DOI: 10.4324/9781003041474-1

In response to revealing the key considerations within the educational technology domain, the book will lead the reader through the narrative provided by industry experts as well as academic researchers. While this combination of authorship is not often presented side by side, readers are encouraged to consider the different viewpoints arising from the contexts of industry and academe.

Chapter Overviews

This volume opens with a vignette from Chester Thompson, an industry performer with many years of experience on a global stage. It was important to the volume to hear the voices of professionals in this work, since it highlights their perspectives and the ways they have adapted to technology throughout their careers. Using recording technology to learn tunes was something Jazz musicians did from the advent of the gramophone and it continued through the decades, which Green captured from an educational perspective in *How Popular Musicians Learn*. Also, the shift between live performance and studio capture and the impact technological development has on practice and the overall experience in performance venues for musicians and listeners. There are also some important recommendations put forward for young musicians, highlighting the need to balance digital know-how with musical skills – something that also came across from the producer interviews in Chapter 9 of this volume. This performer perspective is an important voice to this section as we go on to consider playing online, performance training, virtual festivals, and finally, how educators go about designing a framework for student studies.

The first chapter begins with a consideration of *technology, performance, and context* with an opening discussion of 'Synchronous Online Ensemble Performance'. This has long been the challenge of online collaboration, since issues around synchronicity can be problematic with latency related to network speeds. Monache, Comanducci, Cospito, Sarti, and Avanzini discuss what is meant by Networked Music Performances (NMP) and report on cutting-edge research from the *Intermusic* project in this area. This chapter considers the nature of ensemble music playing and how it can apply in an online context. These developments are at the forefront of online collaborative musicianship and share some of the same issues discussed by King in Chapter 9 when considering recording studio practice in online environments; several tools have emerged to facilitate online collaboration in real-time. To compliment the considerations for performers and the technical aspects in Chapter 1, we then move on to 'Performing in the Virtual Auditorium'. The recent global pandemic that started in 2020 accelerated the need for other ways for people to engage in music that was performed rather than recorded. McAlpine and Cook shine a light on virtual festivals and the shift from physical to virtual performance and what this entails for our understanding of music practice, stagecraft, and repertoire in Chapter 2. There are also issues concerning engagement with the types of technology, audience, and musician needs, as well as the commercial aspects of the approach.

Beyond the use of the technology for virtual collaboration and the potential for immersive music experiences, there are also the performer's concerns to consider. In Chapter 3, Waddell and Williamon draw attention to self-regulated learning for the development of musical skills in performance. By using technology-enhanced practice methods, learners' interactions can be measured and instant feedback given on their practice sessions. It is the view of the authors that this does not seek to replace effective teaching, merely to improve the practice habits of students and using technology to plug the gap between formal supervised lessons and self-regulated practice. The context for all learning by music students of course needs a framework, which is provided by Johnson in Chapter 4 of this volume. This report of a substantial 12-month study for 'Developing an online music orientation using the framework for teaching music online' provides unique insights to online learning in one of the world's leading conservatoriums. Using a four-stage design process Johnson investigates digital literacy and students' self-regulation in an HE environment. The development of digital literacy is often overlooked, and educators often make assumptions about student pre-requisite skills with digital technology that are not yet embedded when arriving at a conservatorium. It is therefore necessary to consider what these are, take an overview of the design process, and determine what the potential outcomes for the curriculum could be. This first part of the volume has therefore examined some of the design and process challenges and considerations for musicians collaborating in ensembles online; it has addressed technology's potential to provide a practice aid to get the performers onto the stage while also considering the virtual aspects of immersive music festivals. How this is all framed in terms of online delivery, therefore the environment, people, process, and design of learning, is highlighted through a relevant study in an international music school.

The second part of our volume, *Perspectives for Teaching*, begins with the voices of Peter Lee and Tim Wilson working from the position of software development industry experts to support musical development. The duo has many years of experience specifically developing aural and music theory software packages. They discuss shifts in digital computing and how this enabled a different learning environment from the days when students used to listen to cassette tapes for training. What is also emphasized is the collaborative nature of the design process and the need for clear workflow in the various stages, with input from key stakeholders along the way. Their approach relates to what Waddell and Williamon discuss in Chapter 3, in that it recognizes technology as a tool to bridge the gap between more formal musical lessons and therefore act as a practice aid.

How music students engage in online learning requires in-depth study, and this is something Pike demonstrates in Chapter 5, 'Instrumental Learning Online', drawing experience from two studies that examine common findings in synchronous online education and a collective case study of three piano teachers that highlights best practice, how teachers prepare for online lessons, and key lessons for teachers wanting to engage in online music lessons. This research is important since even prior to the global pandemic, there have been issues with students gaining access to music education in remote communities (for example, see King et al., 2019a, 2019b).

Chapter 6 by Merrick provides a broader view of 'Informed Teaching and Practice in Music Education' from a global perspective. This contribution explores teaching with technology, social media, and working with young musicians in Australia. Importance is placed upon curriculum development, emerging technology, and its implications and connecting music technologies to student learning through ICT. This work also draws attention to the need to consider Johnson's approach in Chapter 4 that requires educators to consider the learning environment and structures to support students.

The delivery of traditional teaching and how this can be supported via technology has been an important cornerstone of music academic research. However, emerging fields of study such as game design give opportunities for music educators to think beyond our borders and into other disciplines. Chapter 7, 'Music, Play, Games and Education' by Summers is one such approach that uses music and play through video games and how this may inflect upon teaching. Scaffolding and the role of music interfaces is considered alongside interactivity and music dialogue and cultural participation in informal learning for musical and technical expertise. There is also a suggested lesson plan for teachers wanting to follow this approach in their own practice. In Chapter 8, Sarti, Antonacci and Bernardini explore how music-makers reach beyond the outcomes of previously achieved acoustical properties of musical instruments to harness technology as an aid in further tapping into the listener's emotional state as elicited by their music. Describing the dramatic historical shifts of music technology on the listener's experience (e.g., the development of digital reverberation rather than sole dependence on environmental acoustics; change of listener consumption habits from dependence on a physical store to retrieve music to retrieval automation through algorithmic search of music content metadata), the authors identify how technology can be used to influence our musical perceptions. Implications from this research has particular significance in the application of music in immersive technologies and how adjustments of spatial acoustics as a form of expressivity can further influence the listener and their sense of environmental space.

The 'State and practice of music education software design' chapter aligns with the industry voices we heard at the start of this section. Nowakowski and Hadjakos stress the necessity of understanding the historical perspective in terms of new developments and the importance for music education. This approach provides a helpful context for music education software developers and highlights key empirical papers in the domain. Voices from industry are again highlighted in Chapter 10 in 'Audio Education: Perspectives from Industry'. This interview-based study contains insights into professional projects, technology, and collaboration online in the recording industry, tools, and workflow, as well as recent developments in the field of Artificial Education. For many music production students, the industry professionals represent their goal in terms of a career path. However, there is often a dichotomy between experienced audio professionals utilizing analogue workflow methods in a digital domain with students who are approaching from the standpoint of only ever engaging in digital approaches. This chapter shares some insights into the domain of pedagogical recording studio practice whist also setting out implications for the curriculum. Staying with audio production teaching, Chapter 11, 'Strategies for Teaching Audio Production Online', is put forward by Torrens and Doornbusch. This autoethnographically informed approach in Australia examines the challenges and opportunities of a group of staff members teaching audio production online. This is achieved by considering not only the curriculum but also the skill of the instructor in delivering in this way.

The final part of this edited volume, Environments and People, begins with an authoritative voice not only from industry but also academia. Dr. Phil Harding achieved a great deal of commercial success as an audio engineer and producer and has also entered the world of academia, writing extensively on the music industry. In this vignette, Harding gives perspectives of collaborating with people in the professional studio, the technological developments during their career, as well as the commercial aspects of the music industry alongside the environment for audio professionals. There are some important insights for educators and students about sustaining a career in the industry over several decades.

People are an important part of any conversation about music, technology, and education. Gold and Purves address the issue of ethical choices in the shifting landscape of music education as a result of technological development. AI in music education, as discussed in several of the chapters, will become a more dominant force within industry practice and education over the next decade. Important questions are raised here about musical innovation and ethical risks concerning making music *easier*. These include an awareness of issues for educators, sustainability of technological development, and cultural inclusivity. This environment we now find ourselves in requires careful navigation for the future of music. Environments are an important part of our next chapter, 'Acoustic Ecology: exploring the role of sound and technology in understanding climate change'. Barclay shares an important narrative the possibilities of this domain in 'addressing the major challenges of environmental conservation and ecological engagement'. The interdisciplinary approach of many composers, sound artists, and researchers is drawn out in this contribution, and the possibilities to use the arts to engage communities and industry are highlighted in this important work.

Generative AI and music then become the specific focus of Chapter 14, after emerging in various guises during the volume. Laidlow explores this topic through the lens of AI and musical creativity by using four case studies of musical compositions by the author. The approaches used include symbolic-generative machine learning and audio-generative machine learning in their practice, and they share unique insights into this new world. There is a lot for music educators to learn from this chapter, especially considering potential future approaches to composition. The final chapter of this edited volume innovation highlights a collaboration between Himonides, Purves, and Gold. Together, they explore literature on using LEGO to learn coding and music, but also work at the intersection of construction, coding/electronics, and music. Following the rehearsal of the evidence-based experiences are shared findings presented from a short-scale, exploratory funded case-study with participatory research components. Pupils engaged in creative exploration of instrument making, collaborative project management, musical performance, and rehearsal of instrument making principles within both the acoustic and digital domains.

We close the book with our 'Final Considerations' for music, technology, and innovation in music education. Our current period in history places us with many potential creative opportunities for the use and development of music technology in music education. Bringing together the threads of innovation and technology across the book, we provide some commentary on the potential growth for technology in the music classroom and the enlargement of the music classroom environment with immersive technologies and their potential contributions.

References

King, A., Prior, H., & Waddington-Jones, C. (2019a). Connect resound: Using online technology to deliver music education to remote communities. *Journal of Music, Technology & Education*, *12*(2), 201–217.

King, A., Prior, H., & Waddington-Jones, C. (2019b). Exploring teachers' and pupils' behaviour in online and face-to-face instrumental lessons. *Music Education Research*, *21*(2), 197–209.

Part 1

Technology, Performance and Context

Industry Perspective

Chester Thompson

The first major artist I played with was Frank Zappa back in the 1970s. From there I went into a band called Weather Report, did quite a lot of freelancing recording after that, and then ended up in a band called Genesis, which led to also doing Phil Collins' solo tours as well. Most of the need for technology happened during the Genesis period. Being a drummer throughout the 1970s, I've experienced the emergence of new music technologies that allowed for the development of many hallmarks in musical styles. Across the years of my music career, technology became more advanced and integrated for those of us recording in the music studio and playing live music performances. Innovation in technology has allowed many of us musicians to advance many aspects of our performances – and the listening experience of our audiences.

I started my performance career back in the '60s – 1962, to be exact. I started out playing in local bands with cover songs, and then eventually writing songs with other bands. Basically, I played just purely drum set. None of what we use today for music technology really existed when I started playing. Back then, you just played your instrument. Even overdubs in the recording studio were pretty new at that point. We tracked almost everything live in the studio. (It wasn't until a few years later that a lot of the professional studios became able to overdub.) For the most part, recording music meant you played it down until you got it right – and that was it. Even in my own drum performances, there wasn't really any sort of trickery or anything other than just playing the songs down.

In my practice time, I learned cover tunes by listening to recordings. We bought singles, the actual 45 RPM singles. If it was a complicated part, you would play the recording at 33 RPM (revolutions per minute). Even though it changed the pitch, it allowed you to hear the actual parts that were being played. You just had to put them back in the right key.

From 1973 to 1975, I played with Frank Zappa. Zappa was ahead of his time both musically and technologically. I remember when I played with him that he had a big old eight-track recorder – a big reel-to-reel. It was like one inch or something – I think he eventually maybe got into a 16-track recorder – but he would actually take this thing on the road. He recorded every rehearsal, every concert. He recorded everything with every band – every rehearsal, every concert. He built his famous vault under his driveway at his home, and all of those tapes lived there. Sometimes in rehearsal, he would use a recording to play back a section if it wasn't clear what needed to be done. We used the big one-inch eight-track machine in rehearsal to listen to the parts, and then cleaned up whatever needed to be cleaned up for performances.

DOI: 10.4324/9781003041474-2

I was with the band Genesis from 1976 until 1992. When I started touring with Genesis, we just played everything straight down. At first, it was all prog rock (progressive rock) and every song had different movements. In one case, one song was around 19 minutes – a kind of hallmark of that style. As they got into more pop material, the length of songs changed – to both shorter and more accessible songs.

Phil Collins (Genesis' lead singer and drummer) incorporated drum machines when they first came out. He created percussive loops that would go along with the songs. This meant that when I played, I had to have that loop playing in my monitors to play in sync with the song. It also meant that monitors had to be loud enough for me to be able to play along with the loop and hear the rest of the band in the monitors. That was probably the beginning of performing with live drum loops. There were other songs, too, like "Land of Confusion" (from "Invisible Touch," 1986), that required me to play with a loop originating from a synthesized bass.

There were a lot of "firsts" with this band from a music technology point of view. Playing live, from beginning to end, in a song with something that wasn't just a drum machine loop was another first. From a musical viewpoint, the keyboard player actually played live along with the loop. Yet, it was such a distinct synthesized sound that we used it almost as sort of a click (i.e., electronic metronome). The line was doubled live, as well as coming through the system.

Moving from the Studio to Live Performance

The technological innovation of drum sounds can be heard on "In the Air Tonight" (from "Face Value," 1981). This has probably become the best-known drum fill. It was really, really heavily processed in the studio; it was two or three kinds of compression as well as reverbs and gated reverb, in fact. They created that sound and the sound of the snare. All the drum sounds were very affected.

Moving this song to its live concert form, we initially tried having the sound engineer manipulate it live while he was also mixing the rest of the band. It was understandably a little overwhelming for the sound engineer. So, we decided to sample those drum sounds directly from the multi-track tape. At that time, I had a really good sampler, made by the German company Dynacord.

There was a lot to be done prior to the live concert performance of this song and others to get the Genesis sound from the 1980s. To prepare for the live performances, I went after hours into a studio in England near where we rehearsed and sampled the snare drum parts and then loaded it into the sampler. I triggered these parts from my snare drum – it was a little tricky adjusting the timing live.

Overall, getting everything in sync took a little doing. The sampling proved to be the simpler way to make the Genesis sound in a live situation – otherwise, you would likely have required two different people trying to mix sound while covering all the sampling that needed to happen. Time was taken in the studio to play with sounds and effects and all of that. For example, the natural snare was basically blended with the sound of the sampled snare in the live concerts. Eventually, two or three tom sounds were triggered from the acoustic drums as well. Other effects developed in the studio used cymbals as well. For example, they recorded a cymbal sound (i.e., basically a cymbal hit) and then reversed the actual sound wave. So, instead of a cymbal sound growing to a crescendo, it started with the louder part first. It sounded like something was sucked into nothing.

The tricky part about this cymbal sample was that it wasn't triggered in time with the song. I had to figure out when to trigger the sample to start it so it ended at the proper time. From a playing perspective, it wasn't about the timing of hitting it but ending it. I had to start it so that it actually ended on the right beat. For example, if the song is in 4/4 with a 16th beat feel where I'm playing a broken-up 16th pattern on the hi hat and I wanted the sample to end on beat one, I would probably hit it on third 16th note of beat two of the prior measure. It was about thinking about the sample ending, not its beginning. It was always pretty wacky because it was definitely not playing within the groove. The outcome sounded like part of the groove, but initiating the sample trigger required careful musical calculation.

Together these, and other kinds of technology, made the Genesis sound that everyone expected from the recordings.

Innovations in technology for performance went beyond the creation of sample sounds that we used in live concerts. Early on, we used monitor wedges on stage, but this meant I had a lot of sound coming from both my drums and the wedges. One of the main reasons we moved to in-ear monitors was because the Front of House (FOH) engineers and members of the group preferred it as it meant a lot less stage volume.

When the technology of in-ear monitors came out, the initial appeal was that it would quiet down all the stage monitors and eliminate a lot of the bleed from those monitors going into the instrument mics. The plus side was that you could hear a much cleaner version without all the stage ambience going on around you. The negative side was that there was a bit of a coldness when using in-ear monitors – it isolated you from hearing the audience sound. However, for it to be effective for drums, the monitors had to totally seal out that outside noise. This made in-ear monitors quite practical. They block out about 18 decibels of sound from the stage, yet they feed in a really good blend as far as the track and the drums and whatever else is needed. In-ear monitor technology was also directly connected to being able to accurately play along with the loops and affected sounds. Each band member could now have a separate monitor mix, feed in specific loops, and each of us could hear ourselves at an individual level. At the time, it was quite revolutionary for live music performance.

When we were using analog, there was always a separate sound console, or board, for mixing stage monitors. It meant a sound engineer was on stage to mix the stage monitors, in addition to an engineer for FOH. They both fed sound signals back and forth to each other while the band played. One big challenge was that the sound levels had to be adjusted for each different stadium. When automated sound boards came out, this allowed for pre-sets to be created at rehearsals the day before and then recalled for the next show. The scene pre-sets were about 80 to 90 percent ready before the next show started. There would still be some tweaking to get it exactly where you wanted it for the live show, but the automation of pre-set levels saved a lot of time for everyone.

Because everything's digital these days, consoles can recall the exact sound you had before. But in those early days, the combination of the automated boards and the in-ear monitors made sound checks a lot more efficient than they had been without the automation. For the most part, what could easily take an hour, hour and a half, could be done in under an hour, and much more efficiently between the automated boards and the in-ear monitors.

From a signal perspective, we still had analog sound coming into the microphones to keep the quality of sound fidelity for a live show. The analog sound was then converted to digital at the sound board. Within the board, the digital signal was then converted back to analog when it was sent to the speakers. Over several years, the quality of components got better and better, which meant the sound was better and better.

Technology Innovations for Performance Venues

It's not unusual to perform in stadiums made of concrete – they are often built for sports rather than concerts. Adoption of technology has helped make the stadium concerts better fidelity. One of the challenges of playing in a large stadium is that sound takes time to travel to the back of the stadium. For example, I would hit the snare drum on stage but there might be a quarter of a second, or half a second, delay before I heard that beat coming back to me. This often happened acoustically, without amplification. This can get really challenging for live performances because once you put music into the sound system and out to the stadium, you have the delay multiplied.

Technology and the skills of the sound engineers obviously had to grow with the size of venues and the sound required by particular bands. Because the sound is being reflected off the stadium's back wall, there would be delay towers near the back, so people heard what they were supposed to hear coming from the stage. The sound from the delay tower would have to be a little louder than the "slap back" coming off the back wall. The acoustic challenges also meant that the speakers at midway and back of the stadium required set up for synchronicity. These speakers were set with a specific time delay to match the sound coming from the stage. This wasn't something that you would think about as a concert-goer, but you would hear the sound delay if the speakers were not set for synchronicity. Technology had to be used to create a quality sound experience for the audience at those large venues.

Recommendations for Musicians Starting Out

When I learned to play, songs were very imperfect, which made them very "warm" as opposed to being purely "clean." A clean sound can be perceived as cold and sterile. But you need to be able to play both in this generation. The pretty serious players still look to Jazz to really learn how to hone their musical craft.

For musicians starting out today, they still have to learn to play their instrument well. I would recommend practicing with a metronome. A lot. Many shows today, especially the big-name pop groups, have the whole band playing along to loops and various bits that have already been recorded. Many of the pop singers are incredible dancers, and it's almost impossible to be dancing with that amount of energy and have a clear vocal at the same time. It might mean that the audience is actually hearing a vocal track and the person is singing along with a track. A performance scenario like this requires the band to be locked in with that vocal track. As a musician, you need to have solid time. A metronome can help develop and solidify that skill. You will spend quite a bit of your career having to lock in and be in sync with automated music and cues. The accuracy required is at a much higher level.

From a live performance perspective, companies like Ableton were well-prepared for the use of tracks in live performance. Their software Live can be recorded in sections, as opposed to a linear recording. You can record the verse separately, or the chorus separately, and either of those sections could be triggered at any time. This means that if something gets out of sync, the person running the software can hit a button and the band could catch up to the music. With everyone hearing the band through in-ear monitors, you hear the sync update and know where to go musically. Being able to shift and play any section means you have to not only know your instrument, but the details of the music itself. Learn to listen what to others are playing and be able to adapt your playing to what is needed.

There is a new breed of drummer out there today. They use loops and recordings to create incredible performances in multiple time signatures. I toured with Marco Minnemann, who literally could play six time signatures at once. He did this by creating an ongoing pattern between sounds – simultaneously playing with four limbs playing individual time signatures and creating the other parts with other sounds, such as the bell of the cymbal, etc. He developed the skills to play like this from practicing with a metronome. Playing with a metronome can help develop an amazing sense of time and consistency which is a requirement for musicians today.

When we look at music education and technology, I don't think we can separate them anymore. Schools and higher education programs have music technology subjects which highlight the importance of musicians needing to be both fluent on their instrument and with technology. Musicians need to know how to use basic music software programs to record digital and analog (e.g., ProTools software); it opens up possibilities in ways that never existed before.

But creativity still wins out over anything. And that, combined with technology to create things that probably weren't possible before . . . it's just a wonderful horizon.

1 Synchronous Online Ensemble Performance

Stefano Delle Monache, Luca Comanducci,
Giovanni Cospito, Augusto Sarti and Federico Avanzini

Introduction

From the workplace to the free time, in pliable forms of augmented, mixed and virtual realities, computer systems and applications for remote collaboration and social interaction are pervasively shaping our lifestyle. Geographically displaced (i.e., non-co-located) music-making over computer networks, such as the Internet, is a peculiar form of social activity which has been attracting the interest of both academy and industry for decades (Barbosa, 2003).

Broadly speaking, a Networked Music Performance (NMP) can be defined as the "practice of conducting real-time music interaction over a computer network" (Gabrielli & Squartini, 2016, p. 4). The original NMP vision was to have "a group of musicians, located at different physical locations, interacting over a network to perform as they would, if located in the same room" (Lazzaro & Wawrzynek, 2001). The possible bias implicit in this definition soon became clear as the NMP acronym now includes a plethora of networked musical practices and applications, ranging from remote music teaching, rehearsals and concerts (Mills, 2019), to ubiquitous computer music and the internet of things (Keller et al., 2019).

The general characteristic of any NMP environment, either as a limit or a creative constraint, is to be found in the presence of a mediation technology layer – the networked audio-visual capturing and display. Consequently, this layer unavoidably affects the mental and the physical representations of the sonic articulations. Typically, the temporal dimension is considered to be the main component affecting the musicality and interactivity quality of the performance (Bartlette et al., 2006). The inherent network delay depends on the physical distance between the connected places, the available network bandwidth, and the efficiency of the signal processing. Aspects of the delay tolerance threshold largely depends on the type of the music activity (e.g., a lesson, a rehearsal, a concert), the expertise of the players and the demands of the music genre being played (Rottondi et al., 2016).

Indeed, the experience itself of real-time, synchronous interaction may not happen precisely at the same time for all musicians across a network when compared to the synchronous interaction that takes place when performing in the same room. When a computer network accommodates a lesson or a computer music performance it typically shows a higher temporal flexibility in system response compared to the performance requirements of a chamber music ensemble. The continuity of the time dimension must be preserved (Sora et al., 2017), in order to keep a common ground for social coordination and music problem-solving (Slette, 2019).

DOI: 10.4324/9781003041474-3

Besides the significant impact of latency on the NMP experience (Delle Monache et al., 2019), the overall spatial coherence plays a major role as it is rendered through the networked medium. Spatial coherence not only preserves a certain degree of the auditory and visual spatial acuity and congruence (Nordahl & Nilsson, 2014), but it also involves the design of the physical rooms and staging where the remote music activity takes place (Alpiste Penalba et al., 2013; Konstantas et al., 1999).

In this chapter, we consider social and cultural aspects and look at the specific use case scenario of chamber music ensembles engaged in remote rehearsal practice as we analyse the interaction and collaboration in NMP. The chapter provides an overview of the most relevant research approaches to NMP within the areas of aesthetics and music creativity, perception and coordination in the workspace of music ensembles, approaches to music education and the supporting technologies to cope with temporal disruptions and audio-visual immersion. We further discuss two studies that explore technology strategies to support the social and musical coordination of duos and duets (i.e., the basic chamber music configurations). The first study investigates the use of binaural audio rendering combined with large screens as a means to improve the audio--visual immersion of NMP environments and ultimately enhance the overall scenario coherence. The second study explores the strategic use of adaptive beat tracking as a mechanism to help instrumentalists cope with the disruptive effects of network delays and interruptions.

In the next section, we reflect on the methodological aspects of design orientation within NMP research and briefly describe the conceptual framework of Delle Monache et al. (2019), which situates the context of the two studies discussed later in this chapter's section on exploring supportive strategies in NMP immersion, spatial coherence and music coordination (see p. 20).

A Conceptual Framework for NMP Research

The design and understanding of any NMP environment and practice represents a typical *wicked* problem – that is, a problem which is inherently ill-structured, complex and entangled, has no unique nor final solution whose acceptance is not true or false but rather good or bad (Farrell & Hooker, 2013). In this respect, we contend there is a need for a design turn in NMP research that takes in full consideration the cultural situatedness of the musical expression.

Put in Human-Computer Interaction (HCI) terms, the inquiry of remote music-making practices moves along the continuum between a design-oriented research and a research-oriented design (Dahl, 2016). According to Fallman (2007), in a design-oriented research approach, research is the locus and design is the means and new knowledge is the main result. The designed artefact, usually in the provisional form of sketches and prototypes, represents the experimental playground. Problem-setting, or exploring formulations outside the established paradigms, is also an integral part. Research-oriented design instead is concerned with the actual production of the artefact (i.e., the performance), which represents the primary outcome. Research represents the means, and knowledge is essentially embodied in the design outcome.

Given these premises, we conceptualise the practice of conducting real-time music interaction over a computer network in a research framework to take in equal account the several components of NMP. The framework (NMPF), shown in Figure 1.1, generalises actors and roles, yet it is situated in the chamber music learning practices scenario (Comanducci et al., 2018). Essentially, a performance, which is a taught lesson or a performed music composition (i.e., a rehearsal or a concert), occurs when two or more subjects musically

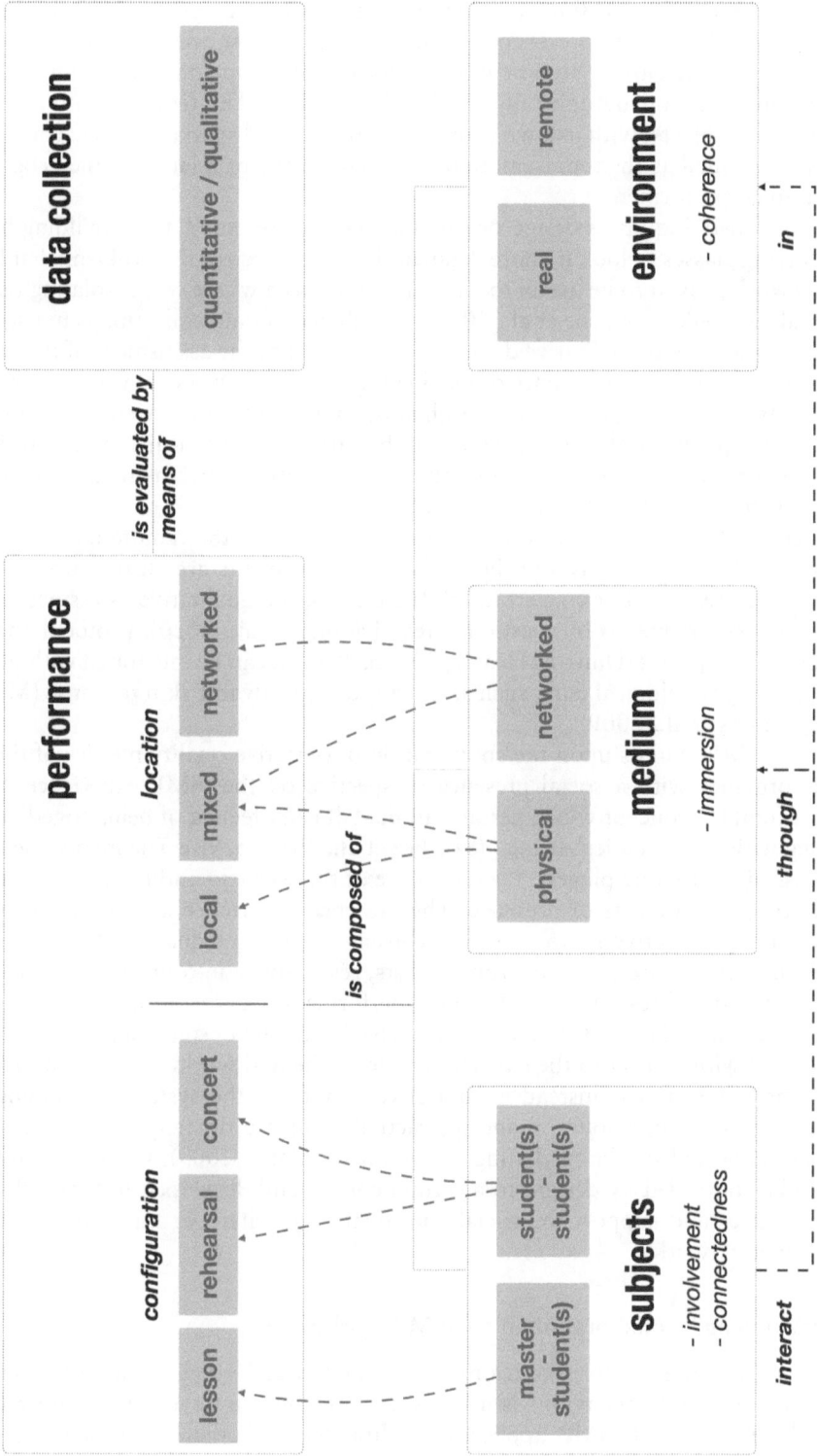

Figure 1.1 The conceptual framework for NMP research in the chamber music practice and learning scenario.

interact together through a medium in an environment. When the performance is a taught lesson, it involves the remote presence of a master and at least one student. Mixed performances consider the case of two or more co-located instrumentalists playing together in remote rooms (e.g., a geographically displaced ensemble). The real environment is the space hosting the subjects, with its own acoustic properties and spatial staging. The remote environment is defined as the representation of the environment relative to the geographically displaced co-performer.

Whether the NMP inquiry is design-oriented or research-oriented, these building blocks act as magnifying glasses to look in more detail at the *wickedness* of the problem(s) at hand. Such a framework proved to be useful to tackle the NMP as a whole while isolating its constituent variables (Delle Monache et al., 2019). The choice of data collection is not secondary; both quantitative and qualitative data are instrumental to the assessment of the quality of the performance and the experience of playing together while physically apart. Since the score represents the common ground of any chamber music performance configuration, the evaluation of the quality of the performance can be carried out by means of content-based analysis of the remote recordings and objective quality metrics, such as tempo trends and misalignments, from the shared score (Rottondi et al., 2016).

Consequently, the performance configuration largely affects the remote music-making: Motivations, goals, expectations and the performance recipients are clearly different in a networked lesson, rehearsal or concert. In all these cases, the qualitative assessment of the players' experience, by means of questionnaires (Tsioutas et al., 2020), protocol analyses and ethnographic inquiries (Duffy & Healey, 2017b, 2017a), can be integrated with quantitative analyses of physiological data, such as heart rate and galvanic skin response (Meehan et al., 2003; Olmos et al., 2009).

Finally, the NMPF builds upon the combination of objective quality metrics of the networked performance with a social presence perspective on the NMP experience. Social presence is a complex concept which pertains to the "illusory feeling of being together with and engaging with a real sentient being" (Skarbez et al., 2017, p. 96): The involvement and connectedness of the remote players, the coherence of the scenario and the overall system's immersion are key constructs of presence. The presence experience is considered to be a prerequisite of any collective performance. Involvement, connectedness and coherence reflect the psychological state of the instrumentalists, respectively in terms of 1) the focused allocation of attentional resources on the music performance, 2) the optimal state of social engagement and musical flow, 3) the overall perceived consistency and congruity of the experience at hand with respect to the expectations from the real world (i.e., the co-presence situation). The immersion is instead an objective quality of the system's technology, in terms of sensory breadth, resolution and interactivity which ultimately provide the set of valid actions supported by the mediating environment (Slater, 2009). Coherence and immersion can be controlled by design, to a certain extent, and developed to best reflect the user characteristics and support the social coordination in chamber music performances over a computer network.

Social Interaction and Collaboration in the NMP Workspace

Ensemble music-making is a form of teamwork characterised by rich social dynamics. Understanding the ensemble behaviour is a necessary prerequisite to set the design requirements of any user-centred NMP application. Ultimately, whether in co-presence or in remote places, the complex network of interpersonal and collective negotiations, occurring between the members of a chamber music ensemble, is aimed at achieving the shared goal of communicating musical structures and expressive intentions.

The nature of expressive ensemble performance is multifaceted and depends on several intertwined factors. This includes the timing and its deviations within and between parts as a function of the tempo and the musical structure, the music style and genre which exploit an expressive use of more or less wide asynchronies, leader-follower(s) relations and agogics (Keller, 2014). In this respect, it has been argued that the ensemble cohesion and performance quality rest upon the quality of the social inter-action within the group, rather than the technical aspects of playing music (Volpe et al., 2016).

Davidson and Good (2002) investigated the social processes of a students' string quartet involved in rehearsing and performing Mozart's String Quartet in G, K156 and Britten's Rhapsody. Davidson stressed the conversational nature of the musical work "constituted by the score and players' culturally situated knowledge and abilities" (p. 200). The score represents the common ground, and the social coordination unfolds around the content and the process, which is updated on a moment-by-moment scale. Seddon and Biasutti (2009) found that six degrees, or modes, of communication are implied in the intersubjective engagement and creativity of a string quartet. The instrumentalists consolidate their ideas through rehearsal, specifically by means of verbal or non-verbal instruction, cooperation and collaboration.

Further, Slette (2019) investigated the collaborative workspace of a chamber music trio specific to how its members manage to build a shared conceptual space within which articulating knowledge, negotiating problems and finding solutions can achieve the best possible performance. Put in NMP terms, a chamber music ensemble would be involved in musically problem-solving the experience of remote playing. Slette points out the central role of performing-while-listening, that is, an aural awareness and attentiveness in ensemble rehearsals, which much resonate with the key constructs of involvement and focused attention earlier discussed: Negotiations can be cooperative, or carried out mostly individually, or collaborative, or collectively coordinated, whereas the sharing of knowledge resources can be complete or partial. The problem negotiation is complete when it is collaborative and the knowledge resources are fully shared (e.g., the trio found itself singing all together a complex polyrhythm instead of playing it). On the contrary, a shared problem space is hardly maintainable when the negotiation is personal; that is, the cooperation is salient and yet the solution, if any, leans on the individual knowledge of a single member (for instance, because he imposes his own idea).

Consider also that the social negotiation of the musical meaning in the NMP environment can be well approached from a perception-action loop perspective. Keller (2014) situates the ensemble cohesion and the construction of a shared performance goal in the human ability to engage in joint action and develop mental representations of each other's tasks: Anticipatory auditory and motor imagery leads to forward and inverse representations, which means respectively causal representations between motor commands (i.e., musical gestures) and their effect (i.e., the musical articulation), and inverse representations from the music outcomes to the motor commands that produced them.

Joint action is coordinated, synchronised actions performed by a number of individuals together and characterised by shared goals. In musical joint action, anticipatory mechanisms support motor learning and control, and when a score is implied, the forward representations of each instrumentalist are paired with the inverse representations of each other player and vice versa, to allow corrections on the basis of the anticipated relation between the parts of the score. According to Keller (2008), attention plays a major role in modulating the sensory feedback required to enact effective anticipatory mechanisms, and metric frameworks and tempo act as pivots to facilitate the allocation of attentional resources to one's own actions and those of the co-performers while monitoring the ensemble performance as a whole. Finally, internal timekeepers or timing mechanisms mediate between anticipatory imagery and attention and allow adaptive behaviours in the form of motor alignments (i.e., phase adjustments) and period corrections to tempo changes.

It has been shown by Repp and Keller (2008) that the performer's adaptive strategy (i.e., phase or period correction) to computer-controlled tempo changes varies with the degree of cooperativeness of the computer, or whether it is aimed at reducing or increasing asynchronies. Taken together, their heuristic framework well depicts the situation of remote chamber music practicing in the computer-mediated environment, wherein the presence of varying network delay and jitter inherently hinder the social negotiation of the music performance. This problematic situation sets the rationale for the exploration of strategies for adaptive beat tracking in the networked music performance, as is discussed further at page 29.

A certain amount of asynchrony is always present in any music performance; its acceptability typically responds to the aesthetic demands and expressiveness of the music genre. For instance, in small chamber ensembles, the levels of asynchrony tend to be between 25*ms* and 50*ms* (Rasch, 2000).

However, the common grounding around the score is not only a matter of purpose (that is, the shared goal of music rehearsing and performing) but also a function of the medium of communication and the affordances of the medium to accomplish the task (i.e., from face-to-face conversations to telepresence). The immersion of the medium, or the set of valid actions supported, varies according to several dimensions including: co-presence, the visibility and the audibility of the actors involved, the co-temporality and the simultaneity of the actions performed (Clark & Brennan, 1991).

Bartlette et al. (2006) investigated the effect of various network latencies on the coordination of two duets (clarinets and strings) involved in performing (at first sight) respectively duets #2 and #5 from Mozart's K. 487 collection for basset horns. A latency threshold of 86*ms* one way was found to be the breaking point above which a mean asynchrony, between the two parts, higher than 50*ms* led to poor coordination and poor ratings of the musicality of the performance.

Several other studies investigated the latency acceptability in networked music performance. Although the accepted threshold is set in the range of 20 to 60 *ms* (Rottondi et al., 2015), it must be said that the music tasks or repertoire used in the experiments are not homogeneous. For example, Chafe et al. (2010); Farner et al. (2009); Chafe et al. (2010) and Farner et al. (2009) made use of rhythmic hand-clapping tasks, whereas Rottondi et al. (2015) made use of pop music repertoire and various instruments. While most of these works use a similar framework in terms of evaluation measures (Rottondi et al., 2016), the different application scenarios do not define a common acceptable latency threshold for all music genres.

Therefore, rather than aiming at finding a general set of rules applicable to all the possible NMP-related scenarios, it is more reasonable to approach the NMP research in a culturally situated framework.

The Rise of NMP Applications

The interest in network-based collaborative music making has been growing steadily through the years. Whereas several platforms were already available in the early 2000s (Barbosa,

2003), the increasing availability of fast network connections and the interest in the distance collaboration of musicians created a fertile ground for the development of platforms aimed at various targets and scopes.

A Taxonomy of Network-based Music Environments

Barbosa (2003) proposed a taxonomy based on three types of network-based music applications: Musical Composition Support Systems, Shared Sonic Environments and Remote Music Performance Systems.

Musical Composition Support Systems are platforms designed for asynchronous online collaboration, such as composition, recording and production. *Splice* and *Faust Music On-Line* (FMOL) (Jordà Puig, 1999) are examples of support systems for musical composition.

Shared Sonic Environments are applications aimed at exploring the distributed and shared nature of the Internet, typically to synchronous improvisation. Examples of such applications include Auracle (Ramakrishnan et al., 2004) and Public Sound Objects (Barbosa & Kaltenbrunner, 2002).

Remote Music Performance Systems include tools for synchronous collaboration with strict latency requirements. JackTrip is one such system. It allows for bidirectional low-latency uncompressed audio transmission (Cáceres & Chafe, 2010), yet it does not support video transmission in its current version, which may be desirable in certain musical interactions. LOwLAtency (LOLA) allows users to obtain very low-latency performances; however, it requires the use of high-end hardware which may be not available to non-professional musicians (Drioli et al., 2013). An open-source free alternative is Ultra-Grid (Holub et al., 2006), which achieves slightly worse performance outcomes; however, it is certainly suitable for NMP applications with looser latency requirements. Finally, an updated list of resources for synchronous and asynchronous online music collaboration is maintained by Fasciani (2020).[1]

NMP Approaches to Music Education

To date, the original vision of having a "group of musicians, located at different physical locations, interacting over a network to perform as if they would, if located in the same room" (Lazzaro & Wawrzynek, 2001, p. 157) is increasingly becoming a real possibility. Several projects demonstrated the feasibility of online synchronous concerts (Carôt et al., 2020; Drioli et al., 2013). The Online Orchestra project examined the technology, collaboration and compositional processes over the network, and made use of tailored, scalable and off-the-shelf solutions to enable rehearsal of large ensembles (Rofe et al., 2017). However, music education represents one major and promising area of application of NMP technologies. Distance learning is not a novelty anymore and several institutions are shifting towards blended approaches to music teaching, especially in music higher education (Johnson, 2017). In this application area, the technology requirements for synchronous and asynchronous online interaction intertwine with the requirements for effective music pedagogy and teaching practices (Duffy & Healey, 2012; Lisboa et al., 2020; Lock & Johnson, 2018). See also Chapter 4 by Johnson in this book.

Iorwerth and Knox (2019) discussed the communication and creativity issues of domestic NMP as a means to overcome the geographical barrier of providing music curricula in remote areas. King et al. (2019) examine this from a behavioural and technological framework perspective as part of a major study that was rolled out in England in 2018 called "Connect Resound". Similarly, Riley et al. (2016) evaluated the effectiveness of three video-conferencing systems, namely GARR's LOw LAtency (LOLA) system developed in Italy (Drioli et al., 2013), Polycom[2] and Skype, in supporting synchronous teaching in a classical masterclass, a jazz lesson and an old-time fiddle session.

Duffy and Healey (2017b) instead analysed the master-student communication in one-to-one, co-present and video-mediated woodwind lessons. Their research highlights the importance of the music stand and the score as an interactional pivot for turn-taking and spatial coordination. Along this rationale, CidReader is an open source, multipurpose, collaborative PDF reader for real-time sharing of navigation and annotation on sheet music, recently proposed to support online, collaborative music-making and problem-solving, especially during the rehearsal.[3]

The Opera Singing eLearning project (Alpiste Penalba et al., 2013) developed a distance teaching framework for opera singing, focusing in particular in exploring various user-centred staging designs, and assessing their effectiveness in terms of perceived quality of modular configurations of visual displays and electroacoustic acquisition and rendering.

More recently, the 2017–2020 EU project INTERMUSIC[4] (Interactive Environment for Music Learning and Practicing) demonstrated the use of blended learning approaches in synchronous and asynchronous music teaching and practice. With the goal of developing an integrated music higher education shared among European institutions and conservatoires, it focused on designing both the platform and several pilot courses, namely in chamber music practice, music theory and composition and vocal training.[5]

This literature tackles the NMP teaching environment with a realistic, though video-mediated, approach that attempts to make the NMP learning experience the most faithful and coherent possible with its own co-present counterpart. Alternatively, Xiao and Ishii (2016) proposed an embodied approach to the design of remote lesson interfaces that stresses the qualitative and first-person perspective in music motor learning. For instance, with MirrorFugue, remote pianists can learn music fingering by interacting with the hands of the remote performer, projected on the locus of interaction (i.e., the piano) rather than displayed on a monitor (Xiao & Ishii, 2010).

The degree of immersion and coherence, as well as social coordination and affordances, are key factors for the effectiveness of an NMP environment.

Exploring Supportive Strategies in NMP Immersion, Spatial Coherence and Music Coordination

In this section, we report on two studies aimed at exploring technological strategies to improve the immersion of an NMP environment tailored to chamber music practising and rehearsal, enhance the perceived coherence of the remote music interaction and support the social coordination. The two studies were carried out in the scope of the EU INTERMUSIC project[6] (Comanducci et al., 2018; Delle Monache et al., 2019).

We situate the two studies within the NMPF, as illustrated in Figure 1.1. The first experiment explored the effectiveness of two basic spatial configurations of audio-visual display through: 1) monoaural reproduction of the close take of the instrument on a pair of loudspeakers, coupled with the screen-based frontal view of the remote performer; and 2) binaural audio rendering on headphones coupled with large screens that provide near-life-size lateral view of the remote performer (see Figure 1.3). The main hypothesis was that improving the immersion of the NMP system and enhancing the scenario coherence would provide a stronger impression of the real and remote environments surrounding the instrumentalists,

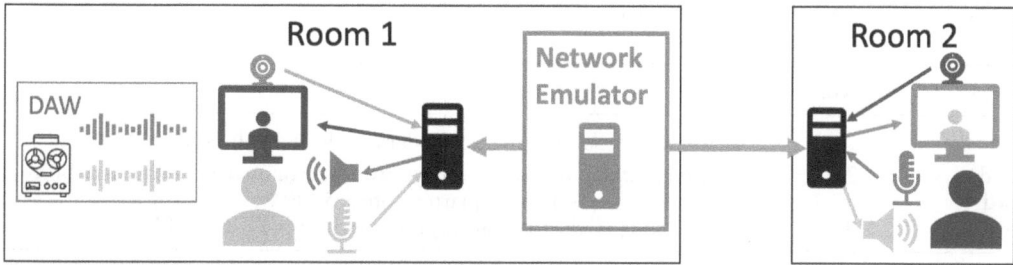

Figure 1.2 The setup shared by the two studies, wherein two musicians perform together through a network emulator.

ultimately leading to a more effective and higher user experience (Nordahl & Nilsson, 2014; Skarbez et al., 2020).

The second experiment explored the use of adaptive metronomes over the network to support the social coordination of the remote performers. Specifically, we use an adaptive metronome that tracked the tempo of the musicians in order to provide a sort of augmented version of the master/slave latency compensation strategy (Carôt & Werner, 2007). Following this strategy, the follower musician tries to compensate for the latency by using the performance of the other leader musician as his reference tempo. To ease this process, the adaptive metronome tracks the tempo of the leader, which is then passed to the follower.

The two studies took place at the Music Conservatoire of Milano, in two acoustically treated studios located on two different floors of the building. Each study used a direct network connection using the LOw LAtency – LOLA – software/hardware environment (Drioli et al., 2013) and a network emulator, as shown in Figure 1.2. The baseline two-way processing time was estimated in a network delay of *25ms*, which can be seen (acoustically) as two musicians playing *4m* apart. Instruments were monitored using cardioid condenser clip microphones (Audio-Technica ATM350), which offered well-balanced response and reduced the pickup of environmental sounds other than the instruments.

Grounding NMP Explorations in the Chamber Music Repertoire

Taking in account the situatedness of the expressive intentions of any remote performance over a computer network calls for careful consideration of the experimental stimuli. The quality and synchronicity of any chamber music performance is not limited to a temporal matter. Rather, the emerging musical structures are the result of subtle combinations of rhythm, melody and markings of dynamics, articulation and agogics. Following our previous work (Delle Monache et al., 2019), we make instrumental use of Béla Bartók's exercises in meaningful rhythm-melody-expression relationships. According to Genovefa (1962), the "44 Duos for 2 Violins" (Bartók, 1992) represent pedagogical pieces, specifically addressed to train motor responses to aural problems, rhythmic and structural features, interpretation and music memory. In particular, a group of four duets was used as experimental stimuli in the two studies.

The rationale of the selection reported in Table 1.1 is to have the maximum of variation in musical content with a minimal focus on the technique difficulties. The peculiar musical aspects of Bartók's "44 Duos for 2 Violins" makes them a valuable stress test to conceptualise the critical aspects of teaching and practising chamber music over a computer network.

Table 1.1 The group of four duets arranged in a continuous sequence and used as stimuli in the studies.

Order	No.	Title
1st	7	*Walachian Song* – Allegro moderato, dotted half note = 60 BPM
2nd	25	*Hungarian Song No. 2* – Allegretto leggero, quarter note = 108 BPM
3rd	33	*Harvest Song* – Lento, quarter note = 58 BPM
4th	9	*Play Song* – Allegro non troppo, quarter note = 120 BPM

The tension between folk and art music in Bartók's compositions manifests in continuous fluctuations in rhythm, from objective structures to subjective internalisations (i.e., the parlando-rubato style) (Puglia, 2019). Hence, the stimuli require a focused attention to the musical interaction, a constant management of the rhythm, and effective communication strategies during the performance.

Study 1: Audio-visual Immersion and Scenario Coherence in NMP Chamber Music Rehearsal

Music playing and music teaching rely on a significant repertoire of non-verbal forms of communication. In chamber music ensembles, the typical semi-circular seating arrangement and the availability of the shared score set the spatial template around which the instrumentalist negotiates the performance.

In the design of the NMP scenario, it becomes crucial to consider the appropriate system's immersion, either with a realistic or a functional approach to the set of sensorimotor and effective valid actions that need to be supported. In addition, the scenario should behave coherently – that is, in a reasonable and predictable way (Skarbez et al., 2020). While chamber musicians do not need to stare at each other when performing, they do support their mutual understanding through glances, peripheral vision and musical gestures (Badino et al., 2014; Jensenius & Wanderley, 2010). In terms of the relative audio-visual quality and low latency necessary to preserve sensory acuity and sensitivity to timing, Cooperstock (2005) proposed the notion of a shared reality to describe the optimal state of co-presence in distributed musical performances.

In this respect, although the remote duo represents the most basic configuration to study, feeding back a coherent virtual proximity represents one of the most demanding aspects of this NMP scenario. Therefore, we explored the use of an immersive Augmented Reality (AR) set-up aimed at this goal. Specifically, we wanted to assess the relevance of dynamic, spatial audio-visual cues in supporting the embodiment of the interaction between the duo. To address the visual cues, we employed a 2D screen, and we used binaural audio to spatially render the sound of the remote performer. To this end, the instrumental sound has to be processed through a pair of Head-Related Transfer Functions (HRTFs). These filters account for the acoustic transformations produced by the listener's head, pinna, torso and shoulders, on a sound coming from a specified direction (Xie, 2013). As such, HRTFs depend on the relative position of listener and sound source. Having a set of HRTFs measured over a discrete set of spatial locations allows users to spatially render a dry sound by convolving it with the desired filter pair and present the resulting stereo signal through headphones.

The overall embodiment of the interaction through headphone-based binaural audio requires the use of a head-tracking system in order to adapt the rendering to the listener's head motion. Moreover, in order to elicit the perception of the remote performer being there, the reverberation of the environment must be added back to the sound. Finally, headphones are intrusive and can be uncomfortable to wear for long periods of time, thus the acceptability of this device by the musicians has to be assessed carefully.

Set-up

The study compared two different conditions, with different degrees of immersion. The first condition (set-up C_1, see Figure 1.3, left frame) uses a 24-inch screen for visual rendering. It was positioned in front of the performer, at a distance of approximately $1.70m$ from the seatback, and projected the remote performer from a frontal angle. Sound was rendered though a pair of loudspeakers positioned at the sides of the monitor.

The second condition (set-up C_2, see Figure 1.3, right frame) resembles that of a face-to-face situation. It uses a 50-inch screen for visual rendering, positioned at the side, and projected the remote performer from a corresponding lateral view. The overall angle between the two musicians approximately reproduced that of a face-to-face performance. Sound was rendered through a pair of open headphones (Sennheiser HD-650), which gave the advantage of providing minimal acoustic insulation and allowed for environmental sounds to be heard along with the sound of the remote performer. Together, this aided the naturalness of the augmented reality scenario. The headphones were augmented with a custom-made head-tracker based on an Arduino Nano board and a triaxial MEMS gyroscope/accelerometer (MTU6050). It used an open-source library[7] to read three rotational degrees of freedom (Yaw, Pitch, Roll) from the device.

Both the incoming audio and the head-tracker data were fed into a Pure-Data (PD)[8] patch, running on a laptop which performed all of the audio processing. The sound was spatialised in real-time using interpolated HRTFs that followed the positional data read by the head-tracker. In this way, a rotation of the performer's head produced a corresponding and opposite rotation in the rendered acoustic field. Moreover, the binaural sound was passed through a reverberation stage in which the acoustic characteristics of the listening

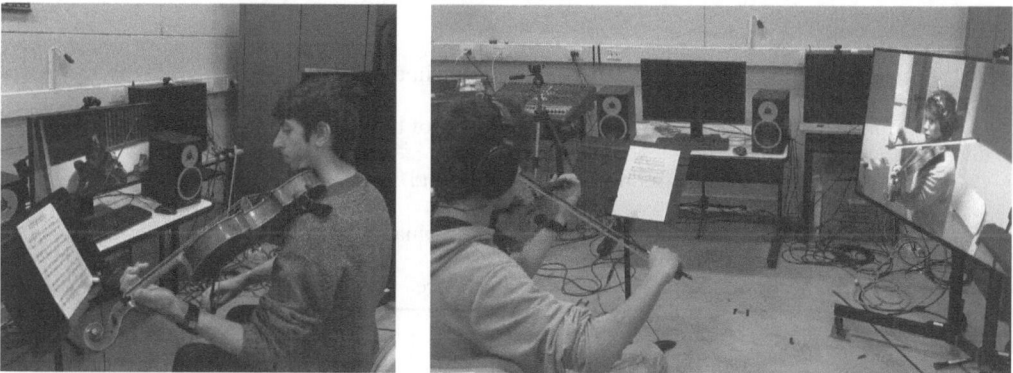

Figure 1.3 Exploring audio-visual spatial configurations in NMP. Left: stereo sound through loudspeakers and frontal view. Right: binaural sound on headphones and lateral view.

Table 1.2 Mean value and standard deviation of the answers to the questionnaire. Top: post-condition questions. Bottom: general questions on the overall experience, administered after the second repeat.

Post-condition questions	Mean		Std	
	C1	C2	C1	C2
1. Involvement and connectedness				
1.1 The sense of playing in the remote environment was plausible.	5.90	5.05	1.21	1.47
1.2 I had a sense of playing in a shared environment, rather than playing "from outside".	5.45	4.50	1.67	1.40
1.3 I was aware of things and people around me while I was playing.	5.85	4.65	1.63	1.56
1.4 I could actively survey the musical environment using vision.	5.70	4.90	1.52	1.48
1.5 I could actively survey the musical environment using audition.	6.15	5.40	1.18	1.60
2. Coherence				
2.1 The musical interaction in the remote environment seemed natural.	5.45	4.30	1.23	1.66
2.2 The distance between me and my co-performer seemed natural.	5.25	4.60	1.65	1.87
2.3 I was able to anticipate the musical outcome in response to my performance in the remote environment.	5.50	4.31	1.00	1.45
2.4 I was able to anticipate the musical outcome in response to the performance of my co-performer in the remote environment.	5.35	4.60	1.03	1.66
2.5 I coped easily with the performance in the remote environment.	5.90	5.80	1.33	1.40
3. Interface awareness and quality				
3.1 I could concentrate on the music performance rather than on the equipment required to perform.	5.90	5.80	1.33	1.40
3.2 The control and display devices were frustrating.	1.85	2.85	1.18	1.66
3.3 The visual display quality interfered with the performing.	2.85	2.80	2.08	1.32
3.4 The auditory display quality interfered with the performing.	3.05	3.70	1.31	2.02
4. Quality of immersion				
4.1 The visual representation made me feel involved in the remote environment.	5.35	4.85	1.14	1.18
4.2 The auditory representation made me feel involved in the remote environment.	5.60	5.25	1.19	1.41
4.3 I could rely on eye contact to manage the performance.	5.90	4.50	1.41	1.43
4.4 I could rely on the gestures of the co-performer to manage the performance.	5.75	4.95	1.52	1.76
4.5 I could rely on the breath to manage the performance.	5.35	4.50	1.46	1.82
4.6 I could rely on the sound dynamics to manage the performance.	5.70	5.10	1.17	1.07
Post-experiment questions				
5. Quality of the musical experience				
5.1 I could adjust quickly to the experience of playing in the remote environment.	6.05		1.15	
5.2 I felt proficient in remote music playing at the end of the experience.	5.65		1.27	
5.3 The configuration with the reduced-size monitor and loudspeaker was plausible	5.8		1.32	
5.4 The configuration with near-life-size monitor and binaural audio through headphones was plausible.	5.25		1.62	
5.5 Wearing the headphones hampered the performance.	3.9		2.24	

environment were added back to the sound. We employed two different PD externals for binaural rendering – namely, [earplug~] and [+binaural~] – which offered similar functionalities but used different HRTF sets. As for reverberation, we employed the external [convolve~], which implemented a partitioned impulse response convolution reverb effect, and we measured the responses of the two studios using the software REW.[9]

Procedure

The experimental procedure was aimed at comparing the two set-ups described earlier, by letting several duets rehearse together in each of the two conditions. Each duet completed a questionnaire after each condition and at the end of the entire experiment. Therefore, a within-subject experimental design was used, in which all the duets were exposed to both experimental conditions (the two set-ups). The post-condition and post-experiment questionnaires are reported in Table 1.2, along with the standard deviation and mean scores of the answers, on a seven-point Likert scale (ranging from completely disagree to completely agree).

Specifically, each experimental session with a duet worked as follows:

- The participants received the musical score two weeks before the experiment, in order to prepare the pieces;
- The day of the experiment, the duet was welcomed into one of the two studios and briefed about NMP in the context of the INTERMUSIC project. Each instrumentalist was instructed about the experiment. They would perform the same exercise twice (see "Grounding NMP Explorations in the Chamber Music Repertoire"), in two different conditions, and they would answer to various questions about their experience;
- Then the duet was allowed to perform a short (10 minutes at most) face-to-face rehearsal in the same room, and afterwards one of the performers was taken to the second studio;
- Before initiating the actual experiment, the performers wore two wristbands for physiological data recording (Empatica E4);
- The participants underwent a short preliminary listening test in order to choose their preferred HRTF set.

This preliminary step was included in the experimental protocol because it is known that HRTFs are highly individual and different listeners may have different preferences for HRTF sets, in terms of localisation accuracy, externalisation and immersion (Geronazzo et al., 2018). Specifically, [earplug~] works with a single HRTF sets whereas [+binaural~] offers the choice between two sets. In the preliminary test, the participants were thus exposed to the three sets, in randomised order, and could choose their preferred one to be used throughout the experiment.

Table 1.3 Statistical comparison of the key constructs of the questionnaire.

Construct	C1	C2	Wilcoxon signed-rank test	
1. Involvement and connectedness	M = 5.8	M = 4.9	$z = -2.023$	$p = 0.0431$
2. Coherence	M = 5.5	M = 4.6	$z = -2.023$	$p = 0.0431$
3. Interface awareness and quality	M = 4.5	M = 4.5	$z = 0.000$	$p = 1.000$
4. Quality of immersion	M = 5.6	M = 4.9	$z = -2.201$	$p = 0.0277$

During the actual experiment, the order of conditions (the two set-ups, C_1 and C_2) was randomised across duets, in order to compensate for possible learning effects and other biasing factors. At the end of the experiment, and after the completion of the questionnaires, the experimenter collected spontaneous comments, ideas and suggestions by both performers.

Results

A total of 10 duos performed the experiment (8 violin, 1 viola, 1 flute). The participants were all students of the music conservatoire of Milano (female = 13, male = 7, age M = 19.55, SD = 4.4, musical experience M = 11 years, SD = 4.5). A whole experimental session, including welcome and debriefing, had a duration of approximately 30 minutes.

From the visual inspection of the answers to the questionnaire in Table 1.2, it emerges that the participants could make sense of C_1 for the purpose of rehearsing the Bartók pieces. Indeed, all the mean answers are well under or above the score of 4, which represents the neutral or undecided attitude towards the questions' statement. Apparently, the C_2 rehearsal configuration was perceived as rather puzzling. Table 1.3 shows the statistical comparison of the participants' answers, grouped according to the key constructs introduced in Section 2. The Wilcoxon signed-rank non-parametric test shows a statistical significance for 1) the involvement, that is, the focused allocation of attentional resources to the musical task, 2) the coherence, that is, the reasonableness and predictability of the scenario behaviour and 3) the quality of immersion, that is, the set of valid and effective actions supported by the system's interactivity and resolution.

The interface quality construct takes into account the obtrusion of control and display devices in terms of external distraction factors potentially affecting the selective attention of the musicians. In general, this construct provides a clue of the mastery of the interface, in terms of spatial staging, and its acceptance may increase through practice and familiarity. The NMP interfaces in C_1 and C_2 are judged mostly as neutral, and the overall scores do not show a statistical significance. However, a more in-depth inspection of the answers to the single questions shows that the headphones and the lateral screen were experienced as potentially more distracting than the frontal loudspeakers and screen staging (Q3.2, Wilcoxon signed-rank, $z = -2.323$, $p = 0.0202$). Taken together, the C_2 interface resulted in a less familiar experience, which is understandable if one considers the typical frontal set-up of video-conferencing systems.

Figure 1.4.: Distribution of the answers to the questionnaire, reported in Table 1.6. Top: post-condition questions. Bottom: post-experiment questions. The duos felt more comfortable in condition C1 and they adapted quickly to the NMP environment. The lower plausibility of C2 can be partially ascribed to the intrusiveness of headphones.

The overall picture is reported in Figure 1.4. In particular, Figure 1.4b stresses the motivation and aptitude of the participants towards the NMP rehearsing (Q5.1), their confidence in the NMP environment (Q5.2), and the plausibility of the set-ups (Q5.3, Q5.4). Although Q5.3 and Q5.4 box plots have the same median, it is clear that there is a lower consensus around the plausibility of C_2. In this respect, the distribution of the answers in Q5.5 shows that the perceived intrusiveness of the headphones was very subjective.

Finally, a closer look at the quality of immersion shows that the main difficulty experienced by the instrumentalists was not related to the resolution of the audio-visual rendering (Q4.1, Q4.2), but rather to the reduced availability of eye contact (Q4.3, Wilcoxon signed-rank, $z = -2.675$, $p = 0.0075$), bodily gestures (Q4.4, Wilcoxon signed-rank, $z = -2.446$, $p = 0.0144$) and breath information (Q4.4, Wilcoxon signed-rank, $z = -1.959$,

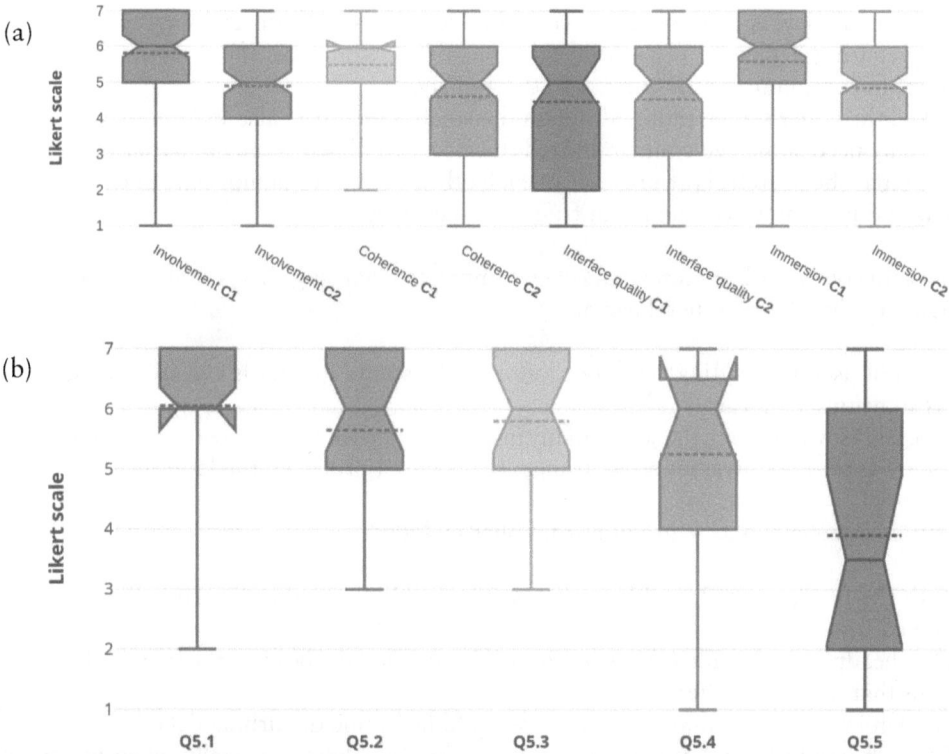

Figure 1.4 (a) In C1, the immersion and the coherence were perceived as more functional to the re-hearsal requirements, and the participants' involvement was more focused. The quality of the interface is comparable, yet the physical configuration of control and display devices in C2 was experienced as more frustrating (see Q3.2, in Table 1.6).

(b) The participants were motivated to adapt to both conditions. The *head-tracking* head-phones design represented a major obstacle.

p = 0.0501) as communication means to manage the rehearsal in C_2. Consequently, the lower quality of immersion in C_2 affected the perceived coherence of the C_2 rehearsal sce-nario and the involvement of the participants, thus suggesting breaks in the music experi-ence. Taken together, we can conclude that there is a familiarity issue in the experience of binaural audio representations through headphones, combined with the poor and contra-dictory design solution regarding the lateral view of 2D screens.

In fact, in the post-experiment debrief, almost all the participants reported the unnatural-ness of having the screen on their side for a variety of reasons. A compilation of participant statements include:

- "The position of the screen would actually depend on the repertoire; when playing in duo it is better to be frontal. Perhaps a remote quartet would benefit from the laterali-sation of the screen; moreover I would expect a different position based on the type of neighbour instrument";
- "If the lateral position is not coherent, I prefer the frontal view";

- "The frontal view is certainly more comfortable in duo, and especially when rehearsing and preparing a piece", yet "the spatial metaphor would be effective for the performance, to communicate the concert to the audience";
- "I liked the wider screen more, although the small screen was also ok";
- "We only need some eye-contact; indeed the visual feedback is only a matter of glance";
- "The screen helps to feel the presence of each other, even if we do not stare at each other";
- "It would feel unnatural to play in front of a dark screen".

Alternatively, we collected several other comments regarding the experience of binaural audio monitoring the remote rehearsal:

- "I am not used to play[ing] with headphones; the sound quality is even too high, and it feels somehow unnatural";
- "Especially I was missing the sound of my instrument; I wish I had more open headphones";
- "Listening to one's own sound is strange; that's why I preferred the loudspeakers".

Positive statements on the use of headphones included:

- "With the headphones I could concentrate more, the immediate surroundings resulted softened";
- "With headphones I could clearly listen [to] the attacks, the bow on the strings. These are details that mark the difference!";
- "Though in binaural audio condition, we could feel some disturbing delay";
- "The best would be to have the 3D audio on loudspeakers, especially when playing in quartet; I would like to have the sound coming from the various positions of the other members";
- "Ideally, I'd like to feel the sound of my co-performer as in the binaural reproduction, and feel my own sound as it was with the loudspeakers".

In conclusion, the experiment provided relevant design implications. Besides the lack of familiarity with the use of headphones in chamber music practice, the cross-modal consistency of the audio-visual representations should be carefully considered. Further, potentially more engaging and realistic representations, such as those elicited in AR audio solutions, do not necessarily lead to better designs; that is, it might be the case that the specific user requirements of the situation under scrutiny can be fulfilled with simplified and functional approaches. In practice, the basic NMP set-up with a frontal view and listening of the remote performer resulted in a viable solution to effectively prepare and rehearse a chamber music piece for duo over a computer network. We do not however expect this finding to be valid for other ensembles, music genres or other performance configurations without further exploration.

Figure 1.5: Electrodermal activity recorded during two whole experiments. The dotted vertical lines delimit the performances under the two conditions C1 and C2.

Finally, Figures 1.5a and 1.5b represent the physiological data of the whole experimental sessions of two participants, respectively a violinist and a flautist, captured with the Empatica E4 wristbands. Whereas a thorough analysis is outside the scope of this chapter, Figure 1.5 shows the Electrodermal Activity (EDA), which measures the variation in the electrical characteristics of the human skin, and has been already used to assess the stress level of musicians in virtual environments (Meehan et al., 2003). The dotted vertical lines represent the time frames of the performances under the two conditions C_1 and C_2. From a methodological

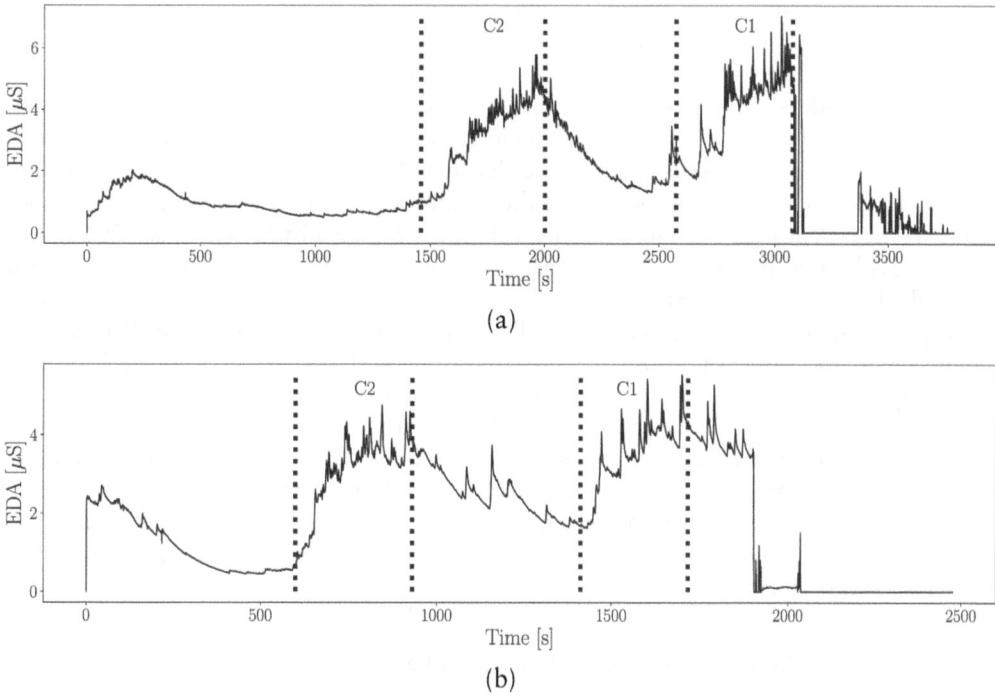

Figure 1.5 (a) The experimental session of a violinist.
(b) The experimental session of a flautist.

perspective, the clear rise of EDA levels during C_1 and C_2 suggests that the use of physiological data can be a viable tool to approach the emotional impact of different NMP setups, together with qualitative survey questionnaires (Skarbez et al., 2020; Slater, 2004).

Study 2: Adaptive Beat Tracking

Metronomes are devices that produce a tick at a regular interval, which can be specified by the user and is usually measured in Beats Per Minute (BPM). They have been used for decades by musicians for practice to train for consistency of a steady tempo. While often used during recording in the context of music production, metronomes are less commonly used during the performance, especially in the chamber music context. We believe that the adoption of a metronome could prove useful in a NMP scenario, as it could provide a stable reference tempo to the musicians and help them to cope with the latency.

The use of adaptive metronomes has already been explored in the NMP literature. A user-adjustable metronome approach was tested for different music genres by Bouillot (2007). Alternatively, Cáceres et al. (2008) reported a remote concert organised between Stanford University, USA, and Peking University, China, where the metronome pulse was regulated by the Round Trip Time of the underneath network connection. Hupke et al. (2019b) proposed a global metronome technique, which takes advantage of the Global Positioning System (GPS) to generate a synchronised audio signal in order to guide the tempo of the musicians during the performance (Oda & Fiebrink, 2016). This technique was tested through rhythmic hand-clapping experiments (Hupke et al., 2019a) under different network delay conditions – similarly to what is done in the literature relative to the effects of the latency on the musicians' performances.

The approach that we propose is, to the best of our knowledge, the first investigation that deals with adaptive metronomes – that is, metronomes that can modify the interval of the produced regular pulse, following the tempo of the performance of a musician (Battello et al., 2020). A beat tracker is a technique that is able to determine the beat onsets contained in an audio recording to determine the tempo in BPM of the recorded performance. In this work, we consider the multipath beat tracker proposed by Giorgi et al. (2016) since it can be easily used in an adaptive scenario. This means that, while beat tracking is usually applied to the overall audio recording in order to determine a single tempo value, in an adaptive application it is done for smaller parts of the audio recording. It repeatedly updates the tempo value and thus tries to follow along with the tempo of the performance.

The technique proposed in this study is inspired by the master/slave approach to NMP latency compensation by Carôt and Werner (2007). In this approach, the leader dictates the tempo of the performance and the co-performer, the follower, modifies its tempo according to the leader. In this study, we use the beat tracker to follow the tempo of the lead musician, and we use it to regulate the tempo of the follower. We hope that in this way, the adaptive metronome can be used as an additional tool to cope with the asynchronicity inherent to any networked performance.

Adaptive Beat Tracking Metronome Technique for Latency Compensation

A schematic representation of the method is shown in Figure 1.6. We denote as $s_L^{in}(t)$ and $s_F^{in}(t)$ the signals relative to the recordings of the leader and follower, respectively, and $s_L^{out}(t)$ and $s_F^{out}(t)$ as the signals received by the leader and follower, respectively.

While the audio signal received by the leader simply corresponds to the delayed version of the follower's recording

$$s_L^{out}(t) = s_F^{in}(t)(t{-}d)$$

where d is the latency of the network, the signal received by the follower

$$s_F^{out}(t) = s_L^{in}(t{-}d) + s_M(t)$$

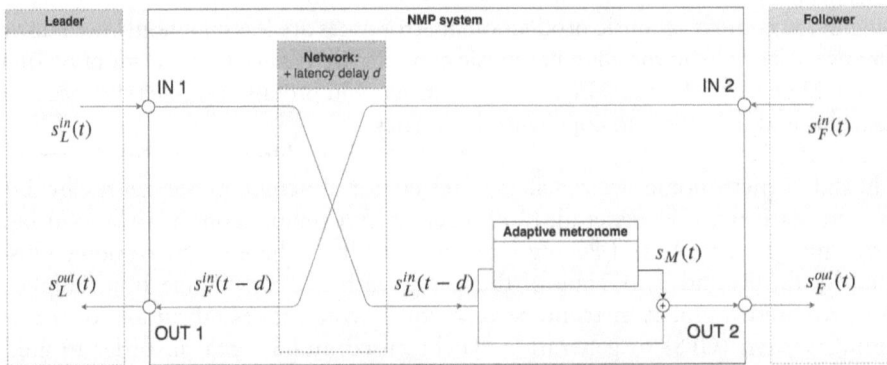

Figure 1.6 schema_metodo_gs.eps – Schematic representation of the adaptive metronome technique.

instead corresponds to the sum of the delayed signal of the leader's performance and the metronome signal $s_M(t)$ obtained by tracking the tempo of $s_F^{in}(t)(t\text{-}d)$

We define τ_t as the target tempo of the performance, while τ_d is the tempo detected by the beat tracker. The detection is not operated at every instant, but it considers an interval of time of β beats, where β is a parameter that can be tuned by the user. Since abrupt tempo changes may result in discomfort to the musicians (Bos et al., 2006), the parameter β must be set with care, as values that are too low will not give the beat tracker enough time to correctly detect the leader's tempo; excessively high value would sacrifice the adaptive characteristics of the metronome. The initial tempo of the metronome τ_d is initialised to the target tempo τ_t and is then updated every β beats

$$\tau_M(\eta\beta) = \begin{cases} \tau_d \ if \ |\tau_d - \tau_t|\varepsilon\tau_t \\ \tau_M((\eta-1)\beta)otherwise \end{cases}$$

where ε defines the maximum acceptable difference between the detected tempo and the target tempo as a percentage value of τt, and η is a positive natural number. In this way, if the difference between the target tempo and the detected one $|\tau_d - \tau_t|$ is smaller than the selected threshold $\varepsilon\tau_t$, then the metronome tempo is modified accordingly; otherwise, the previously detected value is used. A schematic representation of the adaptive metronome technique is depicted in Figure 1.7.

Set-up and Conditions

The aim of the study was to provide a first understanding of the viability of using adaptive metronomes in the context of NMP. In order to do this, we considered two one-way latency levels of 25 *ms* and 60 *ms*, thus taking into account low and high levels of delay. The two latency conditions were tested both with and without using the adaptive metronome technique, devising a total of four conditions for each couple that took part in the experiment, as reported in Table 1.4.

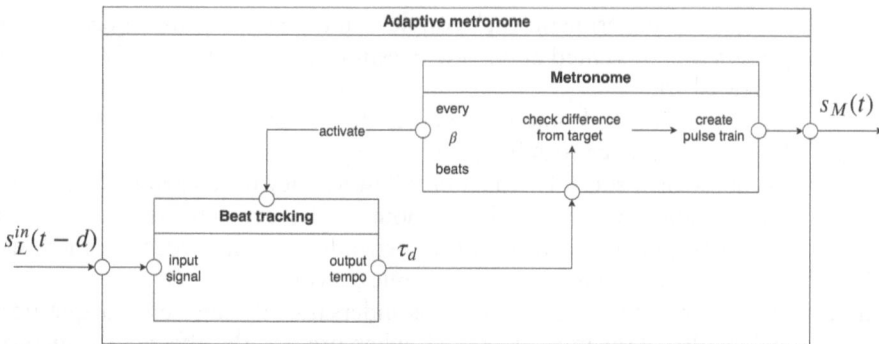

Figure 1.7 schema_metronomo_gs.eps – Schematic representation of the adaptive metronome architecture.

Table 1.4 Experiment conditions, study 2.

Condition label	C1.0	C1.1	C2.0	C2.1
One-way latency [ms]	25	25	60	60
Adaptive metronome	No	Yes	No	Yes

The two musicians were located in two different and acoustically isolated rooms and interacted by means of microphones, loudspeakers, screens and cameras. Since the visual perception was not the main issue considered in this experiment, we used a simple video set-up, i.e., the musicians were placed in a frontal position with respect to a 144 Hz Asus ROG video monitor.

The acquisition and transmission devices were connected to two Windows computers, powered with Intel/Nvidia components and equipped with PCIe audio cards and Gigabit ethernet connections to a common LAN. The workstations communicated via LOLA, which is optimised both for low-latency audio and video transmission. A server was inserted in the communication chain, acting as a Network Emulator in order to be able to add an arbitrary fixed latency level through the Linux command "tc". The signals acquired by the two microphones were recorded for analysis through a Digital Audio Workstation from the perspective of the room, where the follower musician was playing; the signal of the leader musician was also processed by an additional computer where the beat tracking technique was performed in order to generate the tempo of the adaptive metronome. The follower musician could listen to the metronome signal by means of open headphones, which also allowed him to be able to listen to the feedback of the other musician's performance reproduced by the speaker.

The parameters of the metronome were set as $\beta = 8$ and $\varepsilon = 0.1$; therefore, the metronome performed the beat tracking on the leader and updated its tempo every 8 beats, while the maximum allowed difference from the target tempo was 10.4 BPM.

Procedure

The objective of the experiment was that of analysing first if the use of the metronome could be helpful in attenuating the impact of the latency during the performance. This was performed by making the duets following the conditions defined in the previous section. The order of the conditions was randomised for each different duo.

Each experimental session with a duet worked as follows:

- At the beginning of the experiment, each couple of musicians was introduced to the procedure, the project was presented and a few questions about the musical expertise of the participants were asked;
- The musicians could read and practice together the musical score in order to feel comfortable with the performance for about 10 minutes;
- The musicians choose their role (i.e., leader or follower), they were separated, and the audio and video communication were tested first without any latency in the two different rooms;
- The musicians began playing each repetition depending on the order assigned, without any knowledge about the latency condition while playing;
- At the end of each repetition, the musicians independently answered a questionnaire regarding the difficulty of the interaction and, when present, the effect of the metronome;
- At the end of the experiment, the musicians were reunited in room 1 and a brief interview was conducted about their sensations and the preferences.

Results

The experiment was aimed at validating the effectiveness of the adaptive metronome technique. Although limited in terms of participants, the experimental results provided useful insights on the applicability of the technique in NMP contexts.

A total of four duets participated to the experiment (1 saxophone, 1 guitar and 2 oboes). The task was to perform one of the Bartók exercises under the four conditions reported in Table 1.4. That is, two main conditions of one-way network latency ($C_1 = 25$ ms, $C_2 = 60$ ms), each experienced with the use of the adaptive metronome or not.

We compared the rhythmic trends of the performances in the four conditions, by computing the asymmetry and the tempo trend (Rottondi et al., 2016). The asymmetry αFL represents the average time that the follower lags behind the leader. The tempo slope κ represents the tendency to accelerate or decelerate during the performance.

Table 1.5 shows the average asymmetry values in the four conditions. With a network latency of $25ms$ (C_1), the use of the adaptive metronome seems to slightly worsen the duets' synchronicity ($C_{1.1}$). One hypothesis is that the latency is small enough to enable a natural synchronisation between the musicians; the metronome appeared to be perceived as a distraction factor. Instead, when there is a higher latency (C_2), the synchronicity of the duets worsens. In this case, the use of the adaptive metronome may allow a small decrease in the asymmetry and thus foster a higher synchronicity.

As an example, Figures 1.8a and 1.8b show the tempo trends of the guitar duet. Of interest in this case, the adaptive metronome seems to effectively support the players in keeping the tempo even when the introduced latency is not excessively high, such as in C_1. As shown in Figure 1.8a, without the use of adaptive metronome the musicians progressively

Table 1.5 Asymmetry results.

Condition label	C1.0	C1.1	C2.0	C2.1
$\lvert\alpha(F\ L)\ \rvert$[ms]	25	29	42	37

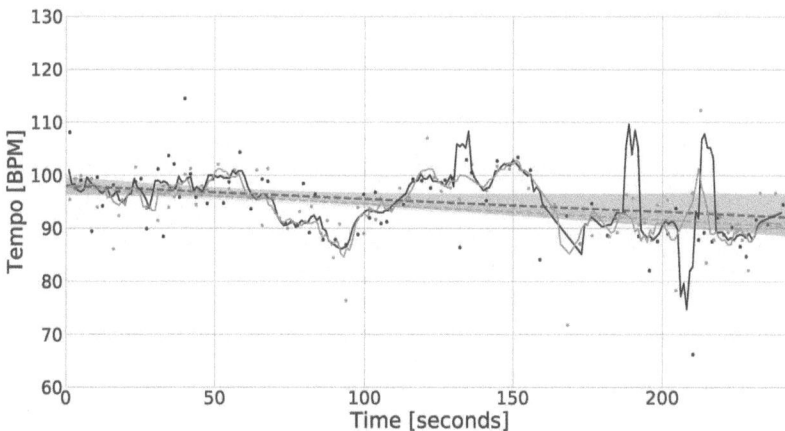

(a)

Figure 1.8 (a) Guitar duet, condition C1.0; (b) Guitar duet, condition C1.1; (c) Guitar duet, condition C2.0; (d) Guitar duet, condition C2.1. *Tempo trend analysis: black plots refer to the follower, grey plots to the leader,* • *is the BPM trend* $\bar{\delta}(n)$, ----- **is the BPM tempo slope,** κ is the BPM smoothed trend.

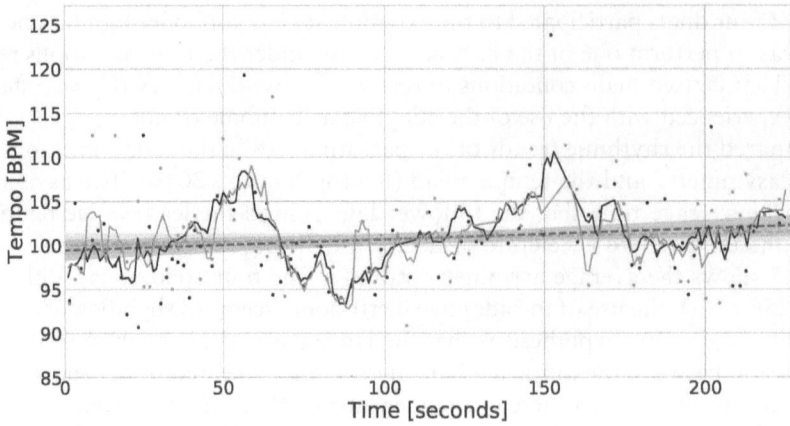

(b)

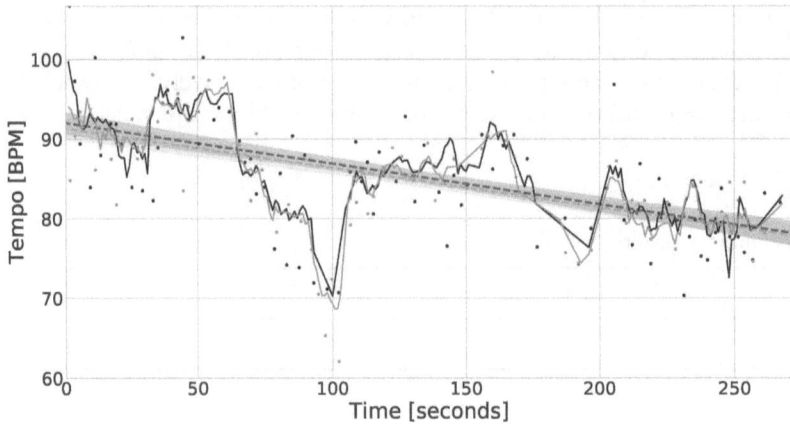

(c)

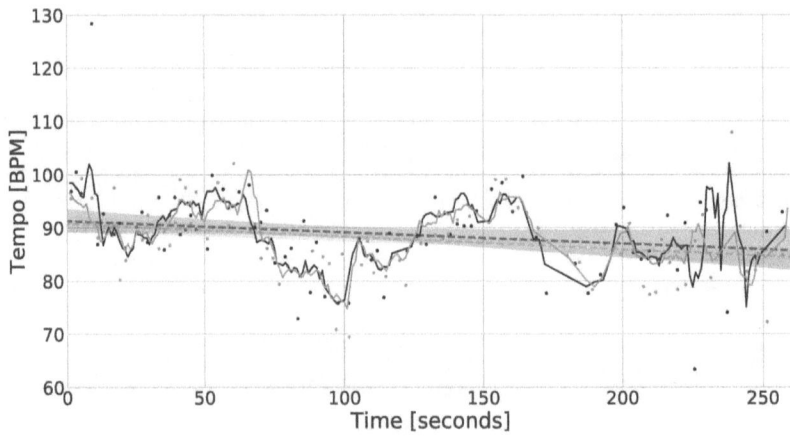

(d)

Figure 1.8 (Continued)

decelerated from a tempo of 100 BPM to a tempo of almost 90 BPM. Instead, when using the metronome, they apparently maintain a more stable tempo around 100 BPM, thus remaining closer to the target tempo of $tt = 104$ BPM.

In Figure 1.8c and Figure 1.8d, we compared the tempo trend of the guitarists in conditions $C_{2.0}$ and $C_{2.1}$: The musicians clearly struggle more at keeping the target tempo. In $C_{2.1}$, the supporting rationale of the metronome is more evident.

We also administered a short five-point Likert scale questionnaire (see Table 1.6), together with the mean score of the answers. Q.1 and Q.2 were addressed to all the participants (i.e., leaders and followers), whereas Q.3 and Q.4 on the adaptive metronome were addressed to the followers only. The mean answers to Q.1 depict a discomfort increasing with the latency rather than with the presence of the metronomic support. The difficulty of performing in Q.2 is apparently depending on both factors; that is, the followers likely struggled to allocate attention to both the metronome's tick and the part played by the leader.

Taken together, the adaptive metronome is a candidate as a viable tool to aid remote performers in coping with the inherently unavoidable network latency. In the post-experiment debrief, the participants commented positively on the use of the metronome, which was not perceived as excessively intrusive. This exploration provides room for the development of an extension of the presented method to the scenario in which the tempo of several musicians is tracked simultaneously. In other words, it suggests the opportunity to devise a method that, similarly to what a human conductor does, merges the information relative to the tempo of each musician and gives back a specific tempo indication (in this case the metronome signal), thus acting as some sort of virtual conductor.

Conclusions

The NMP overview offered in this chapter, along with the two studies on the coherence and immersion of technology-based design solutions to support the social coordination of chamber music duets, carries some relevant methodological implications. We showed that when the NMP research is situated in a specific cultural context, with its own expectations and idiosyncrasies (i.e., duets rehearsing chamber music for the purpose of learning

Table 1.6 Questions and mean answers per condition on a 5-point Likert scale.

Questions	Mean			
	C1.0	C1.1	C2.0	C2.1
Q.1 How much were you stressed/dissatisfied during the performance?	1.375	1.5	2.75	2.75
Q.2 Was it difficult to perform?	1.875	2.25	2.875	4
Q.3 Did the metronome increase your confidence during the performance? (follower only)	–	3.25	–	2.75
Q.4 Could you exploit both the metronome's tick and the co-performer's part as reference guidance during the performance? (follower only)	–	2.75	–	3

a piece), the apprehension of the socio-technological environment makes the assessment of the system much more complex. As technology development advances together with the understanding of the perceptual and cognitive mechanisms involved in the face-to-face and remote, collaborative music-making spaces (Carôt et al., 2020), we believe that, for the future development and effective introduction of NMP solutions in music-making and teaching, it would be beneficial to have a tighter collaboration between scientists, engineers, designers, pedagogists and musicians. In this respect, grounding the research in the design discipline does not mean to abandon the scientific methods, but rather to integrate them in a designerly way of knowing. As we showed in the two experimental studies, the assessment from the duets experience does not provide general results that are valid per se on the effectiveness of the technology. Rather, we looked at the particular issues of real-time networking technologies and computer systems for music collaboration becoming issues of interior design (e.g., the remote classroom and staging), sound-driven design (e.g., dynamics and agogics as interpersonal communication tool) and interaction design (e.g., peripheral vision, foot tapping, breath).

Acknowledgements

This study was conducted in the scope of the INTERMUSIC project, which received the financial support of the Erasmus+ National Agency under the KA203 Strategic Partnership action, grant no. 2017–1-IT02-KA203–036770.

Notes

1 https://stefanofasciani.com/?p=1550
2 https://www.hp.com/emea_middle_east-en/poly/video-conferencing.html
3 The tool is being developed and maintained by Enrico Pietrocola (https://enricopietrocola.com/software).
4 http://intermusicproject.eu/
5 https://intermusic.lmta.lt/
6 The Consortium is composed of the Music Conservatoire "G. Verdi" of Milano (Coordinator), the Polytechnic University of Milan, the RDAM Royal Danish Academy of Music of Copenhagen, the LMTA Lithuanian Academy of Music and Theatre of Vilnius, the AEC Association Européenne des Conservatoires.
7 https://www.i2cdevlib.com/devices/mpu6050#source
8 https://puredata.info/
9 https://www.roomeqwizard.com/

References

Alpiste Penalba, F., Rojas-Rajs, T., Lorente, P., Iglesias, F., Fernández, J., & Monguet, J. (2013). A telepresence learning environment for opera singing: Distance lessons implementations over internet2. *Interactive Learning Environments, 21*(5), 438–455.

Badino, L., D'ausilio, A., Glowinski, D., Camurri, A., & Fadiga, L. (2014). Sensorimotor communication in professional quartets. *Neuropsychologia, 55*, 98–104.

Barbosa, Á. (2003). Displaced soundscapes: A survey of network systems for music and sonic art creation. *Leonardo Music Journal, 13*, 53–59.

Barbosa, Á., & Kaltenbrunner, M. (2002). Public sound objects: A shared musical space on the web. In *Proceedings of Wedelmusic02, Second international conference on web delivering of music* (pp. 9–16). IEEE Computer Society.

Bartlette, C., Headlam, D., Bocko, M., & Velikic, G. (2006). Effect of network latency on interactive musical performance. *Music Perception, 24*(1), 49–62.

Bartók, B. (1992). *44 duos for 2 violins* (Vol. 1–2). Universal Edition.

Battello, R., Comanducci, L., Antonacci, F., Sarti, A., Delle Monache, S., Cospito, G., Pietrocola, E., & Berbenni, F. (2020). An adaptive metronome technique for mitigating the impact of latency in networked music performances. In *Proceedings of the 27th conference of of open innovations association (FRUCT)* (pp. 10–17). FRUCT Oy.

Bos, P., Reidsma, D., Ruttkay, Z., & Nijholt, A. (2006). Interacting with a virtual conductor. In R. Harper, M. Rauterberg, & M. Combetto (Eds.), *Entertainment computing – ICEC 2006. Lecture notes in computer science* (vol. 4161, pp. 25–30). Springer.

Bouillot, N. (2007). nJam user experiments: Enabling remote musical interaction from milliseconds to seconds. In *Proceedings of the 7th international conference on new interfaces for musical expression* (pp. 142–147). Association for Computing Machinery.

Cáceres, J.-P., & Chafe, C. (2010). Jacktrip: Under the hood of an engine for network audio. *Journal of New Music Research, 39*(3), 183–187.

Cáceres, J.-P., Hamilton, R., Iyer, D., Chafe, C., & Wang, G. (2008). To the edge with China: Explorations in network performance. In *Artech 2008: Proceedings of the 4th international on digital arts* (pp. 61–66). Universidade Católica Portuguesa.

Carôt, A., Sardis, F., Dohler, M., Saunders, S., Uniyal, N., & Cornock, R. (2020). The world's first interactive 5G music concert: Professional quality networked music over a commodity network infrastructure. In S. Spagnol & A. Valle (Eds.), *Proceedings of the 17th sound and music computing conference* (pp. 407–412). Axea sas/SMC Network.

Carôt, A., & Werner, C. (2007). Network music performance-problems, approaches and perspectives. In *Proceedings of the "music in the global village" conference, Budapest, Hungary* (Vol. 162, pp. 23–10).

Chafe, C., Cáceres, J.-P., & Gurevich, M. (2010). Effect of temporal separation on synchronization in rhythmic performance. *Perception, 39*(7), 982–992.

Clark, H. H., & Brennan, S. E. (1991). Grounding in communication. In B. Resnick, J. M. Levine & S. D. Teasley (Eds.), *Perspectives on socially shared cognition* (pp. 127–149). American Psychological Association.

Comanducci, L., Buccoli, M., Zanoni, M., Sarti, A., Delle Monache, S., Cospito, G., Pietrocola, E., & Berbenni, F. (2018). Investigating networked music performances in pedagogical scenarios for the IN-TERMUSIC project. In *Proceedings of the 23rd conference of open innovations association (FRUCT)* (pp. 119–127). FRUCT Oy.

Cooperstock, J. R. (2005). Interacting in shared reality. In *Proceedings of the 11th international conference on human-computer interaction*. Lawrence Erlbaum Associates, Inc (LEA).

Dahl, L. (2016). Designing new musical interfaces as research: What's the problem? *Leonardo, 49*(1), 76–77.

Davidson, J. W., & Good, J. M. (2002). Social and musical co-ordination between members of a string quartet: An exploratory study. *Psychology of Music, 30*(2), 186–201.

Delle Monache, S., Comanducci, L., Buccoli, M., Zanoni, M., Sarti, A., Pietrocola, E., Berbenni, F., & Cospito, G. (2019). A presence-and performance-driven framework to investigate interactive networked music learning scenarios. *Wireless Communications and Mobile Computing, 2019*.

Drioli, C., Allocchio, C., & Buso, N. (2013). Networked performances and natural interaction via LOLA: Low latency high quality A/V streaming system. In P. Nesi & R. Santucci (Eds.), *Information technologies for performing arts, media access, and entertainment. ECLAP 2013. Lecture notes in computer science* (vol. 7990, pp. 240– 250). Springer.

Duffy, S., & Healey, P. G. (2012). Spatial co-ordination in music tuition. In *Proceedings of the annual meeting of the cognitive science society* (vol. 34, pp. 1512–1517). Cognitive Science Society, Curran Associates, Inc.

Duffy, S., & Healey, P. G. (2017a). Co-ordinating non-mutual realities: The asymmetric impact of delay on video-mediated music lessons. In *Proceedings of the 39th annual conference of the cognitive science society*. Computational Foundations of Cognition.

Duffy, S., & Healey, P. G. (2017b). A new medium for remote music tuition. *Journal of Music, Technology and Education, 10*(1), 5–29.

Fallman, D. (2007). Why research-oriented design isn't design-oriented research: On the tensions between design and research in an implicit design discipline. *Knowledge, Technology & Policy*, *20*(3), 193–200.

Farner, S., Solvang, A., Sæbo, A., & Svensson, U. P. (2009). Ensemble hand-clapping experiments under the influence of delay and various acoustic environments. *Journal of the Audio Engineering Society*, *57*(12), 1028–1041.

Farrell, R., & Hooker, C. (2013). Design, science and wicked problems. *Design Studies*, *34*(6), 681–705.

Fasciani, S. (2020). *Network-based collaborative music making*. Retrieved August 1, 2020, from https://stefanofasciani.com/?p=1550

Gabrielli, L., & Squartini, S. (2016). *Wireless networked music performance*. Springer.

Genovefa, S. M. (1962). The pedagogical significance of the Bartók Duos.*American String Teacher*, *12*(3), 22–29.

Geronazzo, M., Spagnol, S., & Avanzini, F. (2018). Do we need individual head-related transfer functions for vertical localization? The case study of a spectral notch distance metric. *IEEE/ACM Transactions on Audio, Speech, and Language Processing*, *26*(7), 1247–1260.

Giorgi, B. D., Zanoni, M., Böck, S., & Sarti, A. (2016). Multipath beat tracking. *Journal of the Audio Engineering Society*, *64*(7/8), 493–502.

Holub, P., Matyska, L., Liška, M., Hejtmánek, L., Denemark, J., Rebok, T., Hutanu, A., Paruchuri, R., Radil, J., & Hladká, E. (2006). High-definition multimedia for multiparty low-latency interactive communication. *Future Generation Computer Systems*, *22*(8), 856–861.

Hupke, R., Beyer, L., Nophut, M., Preihs, S., & Peissig, J. (2019a). Effect of a global metronome on ensemble accuracy in networked music performance. *Audio Engineering Society Convention, 147*.

Hupke, R., Beyer, L., Nophut, M., Preihs, S., & Peissig, J. (2019b). A rhythmic synchronization service for music performances over distributed networks. *Fortschritte der Akustik: DAGA, 45*.

Iorwerth, M., & Knox, D. (2019). The application of networked music performance to access ensemble activity for socially isolated musicians. In *Proceedings of the web audio conference 2019–diversity in web audio*. Norwegian University of Science and Technology.

Jensenius, A. R., & Wanderley, M. M. (2010). Musical gestures: Concepts and methods in research. In R. I. Godøy & M. Leman (Eds.), *Musical gestures: Sound, movement, and meaning* (pp. 24–47). Routledge.

Johnson, C. (2017). Undergraduate online music course offerings rising exponentially: A research study. In *10th international conference for research in music education* (pp. 24–27). Bath Spa University.

Jordà Puig, S. (1999). Faust music online (fmol): An approach to real-time collective composition on the internet. *Leonardo Music Journal*, *9*, 5–12.

Keller, D., Schiavoni, F., & Lazzarini, V. (2019). Ubiquitous music: Perspectives and challenges. *Journal of New Music Research*, *48*(4), 309–315.

Keller, P. (2008). Joint action in music performance. In F. Morganti, A. Carassa & G. Riva (Eds.), *Emerging communication: Studies on new technologies and practices in communication: Vol. 10. enacting intersubjectivity: A cognitive and social perspective on the study of interactions* (pp. 205–221). IOS Press.

Keller, P. (2014). Ensemble performance: Interpersonal alignment of musical expression. In D. Fabian, R. Timmers & E. Schubert (Eds.), *Expressiveness in music performance: Empirical approaches across styles and cultures* (pp. 260–282). Oxford University Press.

King, A., Prior, H., & Waddington-Jones, C. (2019). Connect resound: Using online technology to deliver music education to remote communities. *Journal of Music, Technology & Education*, *12*(2), 201–217.

Konstantas, D., Orlarey, Y., Carbonel, O., & Gibbs, S. (1999). The distributed musical rehearsal environment. *IEEE MultiMedia*, *6*(3), 54–64.

Lazzaro, J., & Wawrzynek, J. (2001). A case for network musical performance. In *Proceedings of the 11th international workshop on network and operating systems support for digital audio and video* (pp. 157–166). ACM. http://doi.org/10.1145/378344.378367

Lisboa, T., Jónasson, P., & Johnson, C. (2022). Synchronous online learning, teaching, and performing. In *The Oxford handbook of music performance*. Oxford University Press.

Lock, J. V., & Johnson, C. (2018). Playing together: Designing online music courses using a social constructivist framework. In C. Johnson & V. C. Lamothe (Eds.), *Pedagogy development for teaching online music* (pp. 183–201). IGI Global.

Meehan, M., Razzaque, S., Whitton, M. C., & Brooks, F. P. (2003). Effect of latency on presence in stressful virtual environments. In *IEEE virtual reality, 2003. Proceedings* (pp. 141–148). IEEE Computer Society.

Mills, R. (2019). Telematics, art and the evolution of networked music performance. In *Tele-improvisation: Intercultural interaction in the online global music jam session* (pp. 21–57). Springer.

Nordahl, R., & Nilsson, N. C. (2014). The sound of being there: presence and interactive audio in immersive virtual reality. In K. Collins, B. Kapralos & H. Tessler (Eds.), *The Oxford handbook of interactive audio*. Oxford University Press.

Oda, R., & Fiebrink, R. (2016). The global metronome: Absolute tempo sync for networked musical performance. In *Proceedings of 13th international conferences new interface musical expression, 2016* (pp. 26–31). Queensland Conservatorium Griffith University.

Olmos, A., Brulé, M., Bouillot, N., Benovoy, M., Blum, J., Sun, H., Lund, N., & Cooperstock, J. R. (2009). Exploring the role of latency and orchestra placement on the networked performance of a distributed opera. In *PRESENCE 2009: 12th annual international workshop on presence* (pp. 1–9). International Society for Presence Research (ISPR).

Puglia, J. (2019). *On Bartók's violins duets*. Retrieved August 1, 2020, from https://www.research-catalogue.net/view/558604/558605

Ramakrishnan, C., Freeman, J., & Varnik, K. (2004). The architecture of auracle: A real-time, distributed, collaborative instrument. In *Proceedings of the 2004 conference on new interfaces for musical expression* (pp. 100–103). National University of Singapore.

Rasch, R. A. (2000). Timing and synchronization in ensemble performance. In J. A. Sloboda (Ed.), *Generative processes in music: The psychology of performance, improvisation, and composition* (pp. 70–90). Clarendon Press/Oxford University Press.

Repp, B. H., & Keller, P. E. (2008). Sensorimotor synchronization with adaptively timed sequences. *Human Movement Science*, 27(3), 423–456.

Riley, H., MacLeod, R. B., & Libera, M. (2016). Low latency audio video: Potentials for collaborative music making through distance learning. *Update: Applications of Research in Music Education*, 34(3), 15–23.

Rofe, M., Murray, S., & Parker, W. (2017). Online orchestra: Connecting remote communities through music. *Journal of Music, Technology & Education*, 10(2–3), 147–165.

Rottondi, C., Buccoli, M., Zanoni, M., Garao, D., Verticale, G., & Sarti, A. (2015). Feature-based analysis of the effects of packet delay on networked musical interactions. *Journal of the Audio Engineering Society*, 63(11), 864–875.

Rottondi, C., Chafe, C., Allocchio, C., & Sarti, A. (2016). An overview on networked music performance technologies. *IEEE Access*, 4, 8823–8843.

Seddon, F. A., & Biasutti, M. (2009). Modes of communication between members of a string quartet. *Small Group Research*, 40(2), 115–137.

Skarbez, R., Brooks Jr, F. P., & Whitton, M. C. (2017). A survey of presence and related concepts. *ACM Computing Surveys (CSUR)*, 50(6), 96.

Skarbez, R., Brooks Jr, F. P., & Whitton, M. C. (2020). Immersion and coherence: Research agenda and early results. *IEEE Transactions on Visualization and Computer Graphics*, 1–1.

Slater, M. (2004). How colorful was your day? Why questionnaires cannot assess presence in virtual environments. *Presence: Teleoperators & Virtual Environments*, 13(4), 484–493.

Slater, M. (2009). Place illusion and plausibility can lead to realistic behaviour in immersive virtual environments. *Philosophical Transactions of the Royal Society B: Biological Sciences*, 364(1535), 3549–3557.

Slette, A. L. (2019). Negotiating musical problem-solving in ensemble rehearsals. *British Journal of Music Education*, 36(1), 33–47.

Sora, C., Jordà, S., & Codina, L. (2017). Chasing real-time interaction in new media: Towards a new theoretical approach and definition. *Digital Creativity*, 28(3), 196–205.

Tsioutas, K., Xylomenos, G., Doumanis, I., & Angelou, C. (2020). Quality of musicians' experience in network music performance: A subjective evaluation. *Audio Engineering Society Convention*, 148.

Volpe, G., D'Ausilio, A., Badino, L., Camurri, A., & Fadiga, L. (2016). Measuring social interaction in music ensembles. *Philosophical Transactions of the Royal Society B: Biological Sciences*, *371*(1693), 20150377.

Xiao, X., & Ishii, H. (2010). Mirrorfugue: Communicating hand gesture in remote piano collaboration. In *Proceedings of the fifth international conference on tangible, embedded, and embodied interaction* (pp. 13–20). Association for Computing Machinery. https://doi.org/10.1145/1935701.1935705

Xiao, X., & Ishii, H. (2016). Inspect, embody, invent: A design framework for music learning and beyond. In *Proceedings of the 2016 chi conference on human factors in computing systems* (pp. 5397–5408). Association for Computing Machinery. https://doi.org/10.1145/2858036.2858577

Xie, B. (2013). *Head-related transfer function and virtual auditory display*. J. Ross Publishing.

2 Performing in the Virtual Auditorium
Performance Practice in Second Life

Kenny McAlpine and James Cook

This chapter explores the fundamental shift in performance practice that is currently taking place as musicians, audiences, and venues explore the emerging virtual music landscape. Drawing on a practice-led research project, *Space, Place, Sound and Memory*, with singers and acoustic instrumentalists creating pre-recorded and live content for virtual performance, we explore the impact of moving from performing in physical space to virtual spaces on musicians' practice and sense of self-efficacy. In particular, how do we capture acoustic performance in the real world and translate this into the virtual world? How do musicians self-regulate when the visual and acoustic cues that they normally use to regulate their timing, tuning, and intonation are no longer there?

Through the process of staging a series of multi-participant virtual performances and installations, the project also poses some critical lines of future enquiry. What are the opportunities and barriers to access? How should audiences visualise virtual performance and their participation with it, and how does the conviviality of live music change when the shared experience is no longer physical? Finally, pulling together all of these strands, what does this mean for the design and staging of virtual performances in virtual auditoria? Can what we lose in the transition to the virtual be reintroduced by design? The chapter concludes by suggesting some next steps.

Introduction

Historically, festivals have served a panoply of fundamental human and cultural needs. Combining diversity and international reach with a very particular local flavour, many festivals embody the notion of 'glocalization' (Roudometof, 2016), and they reinforce a sense of community and identity whilst at the same time giving license to subversion, challenge, and the unfamiliar (Gordziejko, 2015).

Festivals have both positive and negative impacts on their host cities and communities, but frequently the economic impact is often the only real measure of success. In part, this is because it is often the most directly observable impact and the easiest to metricise.[1] Indeed, as Hall (1992) notes,

> Economic analysis of events provides one aspect of why events are held and the effects that they have on a region. However, while many of the economic impacts . . . are quite tangible many of the social are not.
>
> (p. 10)

DOI: 10.4324/9781003041474-4

Well-planned cultural festivals are often strongly and positively connected to the host communities through employment, volunteerism, and participation (Gibson et al., 2010). Getz (1997), for example, discusses how the buy-in of the host community is a vital aspect of running a successful event, but adds that the successful organisation of a festival must factor in all of the local benefits and costs, the cultural meanings of the event, and the political factors that sit behind it. Simply focusing on economic impacts cannot hope to capture the complex and comprehensive set of benefits and disadvantages associated with festivals (Carlsen et al., 2007).

Consider the *Edinburgh International Festivals* (EIF), for example. Launched in 1947 during the period immediately after World War II, the EIF were used to aid reconstruction and drive economic regeneration (Waterman, 1998), and to reconstruct and reinforce a sense of European identity by supporting the revival of culture and the arts (Harvie, 2003).

As the EIF have grown in both scale and reputation, they have brought substantial economic growth, they have contributed to the events infrastructure of Scotland and the capacity of the country to showcase and contribute to the global cultural dialogue, and they have played an important role in easing the transition of the Scottish economy from one that was strongly dependent on manufacturing and heavy industries to one increasingly based on services and tourism (Harvie, 2003).

This model, that of using cultural events as a driver for economic transition and regeneration, has been applied in different locales to similar effect. For example, in the late 1970s, Melbourne's (Australia) metropolitan planning authority, the *Melbourne and Metropolitan Board of Works*, published two reports voicing concerns about the effects of economic change on inner Melbourne. It further highlighted a crisis in manufacturing that was rapidly leading to deindustrialisation, economic stagnation, and rising unemployment. In response, the city followed a strategy of utilising its cultural infrastructure and tradition of mass spectatorship at cultural festivals and sporting events to drive economic development and in the process revitalise the urban economy (O'Hanlon, 2009).

And yet despite, or perhaps because of, their success, the EIF have been the focus of ongoing criticism. Harvie (2003) notes the continual charges of elitism as evidence of a reinforcing and propagation of cultural power that caters to a small, class-privileged audience. She further highlights the derogatory treatment of Scottish culture, noting that the official Festival programming, which represented a largely foreign import grafted onto an Edinburgh setting, reinforced the notion that "while Edinburgh's natural and historical features made a lovely, apparently internationally worthy, and auspicious site, its current cultural practice, including theatre, was to be understood implicitly as provincial and unworthy of a place amongst an international elite" (p. 17)

Those tensions have continued through to the city residents. Edinburgh hosted over 2.4 million international visitors in 2018 (Edinburgh City Council, 2019), many of whom came for the EIF in August, and in 2019 the combined audience for festival events in the city topped 4 million for the first time (Ferguson, 2019a). The EIF's immense scale and the influx of visitors each year creates logistical problems and cultural tensions that make life in the city challenging for the six weeks of festival season.

The scale and intensity of this influx places great strain on the city's infrastructure, not least its short-term rental accommodations. Residents have begun to voice concerns that their neighbourhoods and locales are losing their character—a situation that is replicated worldwide in similar metropolitan cities, including New York, Berlin, and Melbourne (Rae, 2019).

Brännäs and Nordström (2006) suggest that the overall effect of festivals is to maximise the tourist draw—but of course there are physical limits. Edinburgh was recently cited, alongside other global destinations that include the Taj Mahal and the Peruvian mountain citadel of Machu Picchu, as destinations "that can no longer cope with their own popularity" (Ferguson, 2019b).

The continued growth and sustainability of large-scale festivals is an active issue, the resolution of which is open for debate. On the one hand, while the economic, social, and cultural impact of festivals is not uniformly positive, the local, regional, national, and international impacts are often significant enough that the benefits outweigh the costs. On the other hand, those same festivals can be disruptive, exclusionary, and can push local infrastructures to the breaking point. Balancing these factors – positive and negative – was already a challenge. The 2020 festival season, of course, accentuated them to catastrophic effect.

COVID-19

The impact of COVID-19 has been significant. Social distancing measures, curfews, periods of societal lockdown, and the enforced closure of non-essential businesses have all contributed to what is widely anticipated to be the biggest global recession since the Great Depression (Rappeport & Smialek, 2020).

More broadly, COVID-19's impact on the creative and performing arts has been devastating. Many of our biggest and best-loved institutions have had no option but to close their doors and cancel programming, and some face an existential threat. It has ravaged the associated performers, suppliers, freelancers, and independent owner-operators who form the majority of the creative workforce. Writing for *The Age* in July 2020 during the first-wave of the COVID-19 pandemic, Sonia Harford (2020) notes,

> Australia's multibillion-dollar arts sector has been pummelled by the economic downturn, with estimates of job losses ranging from about one quarter to as high as 75 per cent. [Government subsidy] helps many organisations retain staff, but the mainstage companies are heavily dependent on box-office income and theatres have gone dark.

This acute impact has been severe, but the ongoing impact is also likely to be felt for many years to come. Many of the micro-businesses that form the contemporary festival eco-system – the hundreds of venues, the thousands of performers, producers, designers, technicians, and other creative professionals, and the skilled trades, catering, equipment hire, accommodation, and marketing companies who rely on festivals to generate a significant proportion of their annual income – will not survive the current crisis. This will impact the ability of festivals to bounce back.

For example, in a written submission to the UK Parliament, the *Edinburgh Festival Fringe Society* (2020) notes that the cancellation of the 2020 Edinburgh Fringe has led to a direct revenue gap of £1.5M for the Fringe Society. More broadly, however, most Fringe venues are not in receipt of public funding and ineligible for Government-funded COVID-19 support. In the absence of door sales and ancillary spending, conservative estimates place the revenue deficit for these venues at around £21M.

In the same submission, the Society notes that

> a catastrophic year, brought on by COVID-19, could lead to the loss of Edinburgh's infrastructure as the world's leading festival city, and the pivotal role the Fringe plays for the UK creative Industries . . . [The] Society and the Fringe itself, the largest non-curated performing arts festival in the world, will face significant costs with existential consequences.
>
> (p. 1)

At the time of writing this chapter, there is considerable uncertainty as to what the future holds for society at large, never mind the creative sector or the festivals sector more specifically. Different international regions have employed very different lockdown exit strategies and very different approaches to balance population health and wellbeing, healthcare and social services, and the economy. This has led to very different regional infection and transmission profiles, with the consequential impact that international travel, particularly between areas of high and low COVID-19 infection rates, is likely to remain heavily restricted until a reliable vaccine is available. Even with accelerated approaches to development and testing, this could still be some time off (Eyal et al., 2020).

This current challenge highlights the broad susceptibility of festivals to external factors and underlying market forces. The high costs and low profit margins combined with the volume of attendees and the associated health and safety regulations and risk management (Getz & Page, 2016) suggests a very challenging environment for festivals for some years to come. While short-term financial intervention by government may provide immediate support during the 2020 season, this is not sustainable and is unlikely to support the recovery of the sector in the medium- to long-term. One thing seems certain: the traditional notion of the festival, a large-scale physical gathering of people from multiple geographic regions, will not be viable for some time to come. Other strategies, including online and virtual festival streams are likely to play an important role here (Davies, 2020).

Shifting large-scale events online – particularly when that shift requires fundamental changes to the commercial infrastructure and to the established modes of practice of performers – is not trivial. It raises a number of immediate questions, not least how this shifts our negotiated understanding of performance space, practice, stagecraft and repertoire, and the value that we attribute to these when they are taken out of the physical auditorium and into virtual space.

Virtualised Venues

It was within this context that our project team from the Melbourne Conservatorium of Music at the University of Melbourne and the Reid School of Music at the University of Edinburgh developed the project *Space, Place, Sound and Memory*. This project investigated both the technical development of virtual performance spaces, and the impacts of these on hosting and organising live events.

The project consisted of two main phases. The first employed an iterative design approach that applied the findings of earlier work on the real-time modelling of acoustic spaces for video games and other interactive media (Horsburgh et al., 2011) to design, build and evaluate two virtual heritage performance spaces. The first space, St. Cecilia's Hall, now forms part of the estate of the University of Edinburgh and is home to the Russell Collection of Historic Keyboard Instruments. The second, the Chapel at Linlithgow Palace, is a site of international archaeological interest managed and maintained by Historic Environment Scotland, the executive public body that is responsible for investigating, caring for, and promoting Scotland's historic environment.

These sites were selected in part because of their historical significance. In keeping with the spirit of festivals, St. Cecilia's Hall was designed to be Scotland's first purpose-built concert hall and a significant venue for introducing audiences to leading international performers of the day (Blackie, 2002). We know from surviving records that King James IV had '*chapele geir*' and '*organis*' in the royal chapel at Linlithgow (Dickson & Paul, 1902). Further, from the point of view of methodological rigour and operationalisation, both venues are spaces for which there exist detailed historical records and archaeological information about the construction and nature of the spaces as they were in the past. This provided a mechanism by which we were able to reconstruct the historic environments digitally from accurate models of the spaces as they currently appear: a modern physical reconstruction of the historic space in the case of St. Cecilia's Hall, and little more than a stone shell in the case of the Chapel at Linlithgow Palace (see Figure 2.1).

To begin the virtual reconstruction, the team carried out a detailed site survey to create a quantitative record of the physical acoustics of the spaces that would serve as a direct point of comparison with the virtually-reconstructed environments. Using a binaural microphone and the sine sweep method (see Frey et al., 2013), detailed Binaural Room Impulse Responses (BRIRs) were recorded at both sites and from a variety of sound source and listener locations.

In the case of Linlithgow Palace, the lack of a roof and any interior fixtures or fittings in the physical space precluded any useful recordings being made. St. Cecilia's Hall, however, provided a useable and valid point of acoustic reference.

Originally built in 1763 and named for the patron saint of music, St. Cecilia's Hall is the oldest purpose-built concert hall in Scotland—and one of the oldest in Europe. At its heart is its concert room, wherein regular concert meetings for the Edinburgh Music Society were held until 1798. Following the disbandment of the Society in 1801, the hall was sold to a Baptist congregation, and was later used as a Freemasons' lodge, a warehouse, a school, and a ballroom. As its function changed, the interior was drastically remodeled. As such,

Figure 2.1 The chapel at Linlithgow Palace is currently a stone shell. There is no roof and no interior fixtures or fittings survive.

when the building was purchased by the University of Edinburgh in 1959, the elliptical concert room bore little resemblance to its original concert hall appearance (Blackie, 2002).

In 2016, St Cecilia's Hall underwent a £6.5m restoration and renovation in order to improve the concert hall and return it to its original condition, or as close to its original condition as contemporary public access building regulations allow (see Figure 2.2).

The contrast between the pristine, contemporary performance space, which was built to replicate closely the original layout of a historic venue, and the architectural records of the original space provided us with a systematic approach to investigating and modelling the acoustics. We had a measurable control case, the sampled acoustic of St. Cecilia's Hall, against which a modelled virtual reality (VR) acoustic of the same space could be compared (see McAlpine et al., 2021). This process provides some procedural validation for the notion that we might then remodel the spaces as they were according to architectural records and have some confidence that the modelled spaces provide an accurate representation of their acoustics.

Working with our project partners, the physical locations were scanned using LIDAR (LIght Detection and Ranging), a type of laser telemetry used for accurate distance measurement and surveying of physical spaces. Working with specialists from Historic Environments Scotland, the project team used LIDAR to create detailed architectural scans of the two sites to create two very high-resolution point clouds that represent the spaces as they currently are (see Figure 2.3).

This gave us an accurate virtual architectural framework that allowed us to strip back the modern elements of construction – or, in the case of Linlithgow Palace, those elements of its

Figure 2.2 The £6.5m reconstruction of St. Cecilia's Hall captures the geometry of the space, but makes concessions to modern safety regulations and comfort.

deterioration – and recreate *in virtuo* the original performance spaces. This process took place in close consultation with Historic Environments Scotland's architectural historians, who were able to advise on the design and material qualities of the interior fixtures and fittings. This included the virtual plasterwork, wood panelling, and drapes and hangings (see Figure 2.4), all of which have a material impact on the quality of the acoustic and the liveness of the space.

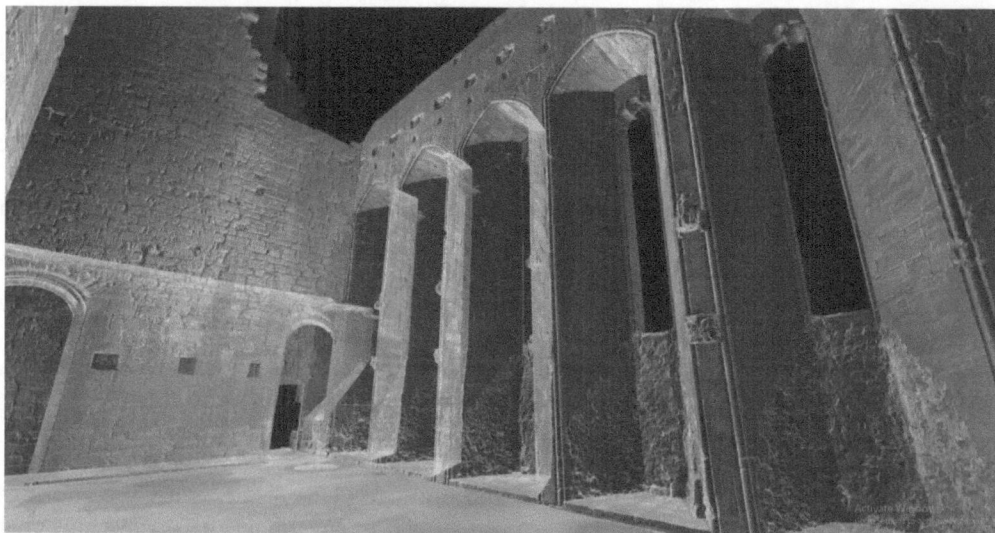

Figure 2.3 Scanning the Chapel at Linlithgow Palace created a detailed point cloud, a dense cluster of spatially-indexed data points that captures digitally, and with phenomenal accuracy, the dimensions and layouts of the physical site.

Figure 2.4 Virtual reconstruction of the interior of the Chapel at Linlithgow Palace in panoramic view. The layout and the qualities of the materials were selected in consultation with architectural historians from HES.

Curating the Space

Once the two virtual auditoria were constructed, our plan was to host a series of themed events to create a virtual micro-festival. *Hearing Historic Scotland* was hosted virtually in 2018 using the virtual acoustic spaces as venues to perform and celebrate historically informed performance. This enabled audiences to experience first-hand the music, performance practice and acoustics, and other immersive elements of performance at the venues as they would have sounded in their heyday.

Early music performance was a fully immersive, perhaps even overwhelming, multi-modal sensory experience. Audiences – if, indeed, "audiences" is the correct term for this very different listening context – were not bound by the social conventions of music performance that we adhere to today; they would have had much more agency to move around the space and experience the shifting qualities of sound in a changing acoustic.

Indeed, fifteenth-century liturgical music was explicitly constructed as a multimedia spectacle (Kirkman & Weller, 2017). As the audience moved through the sacred space unencumbered by pews, they would have been able to explore a richly decorated world of wall paintings and sculptures: decorative, instructive, and devotional. As many contemporary accounts attest, these sculptures, lit by the play of flickering candlelight, would be transformed into living stone. Sight and sound worked reciprocally to full effect, and even the faculty of scent would have been brought in to play by censing with a thurible.

How then can modern performance seek to recapture these aspects? Certainly, it is possible live, although even here we can never recapture the absolute 'authenticity' of a performance: even if the space, place, performers, and music are entirely accurate, the audience will still be consciously aware that they are watching a re-enactment. It is something that is far harder to achieve in recorded performance. Whilst historically informed performance practice may capture a sense of the sound of the past when heard via CD, it will necessarily stop short of giving a sense of presence, participation, multi-modal immersion, and the broader aspects of space and place.

This is something that VR can address, at least in part. By drawing on the abilities of VR to embody music performance in a virtual environment that encourages a sense of presence and agency in the listener, we contend that it is possible to bring together the experiential aspects of live performance with the reproducibility and accessibility of a recording. In the same way that the architectural and acoustic spaces of historic performances were mechanical structures for creating immersive sensory experiences, modern VR technology provides a digital mechanism to do likewise.

Our intention in this practice-led phase of the project, then, was to employ reflective practice in operational (or near-operational) conditions to better understand those considerations that might inform the staging of events in virtual space that intricately and intimately connect audiences, performers, and repertoire. These can broadly be grouped into three key elements, which we have dubbed 'the three Ps': programming (i.e., in terms of the selection of repertoire), performance, and production.

Programming

Broadly speaking, programming a virtual festival is similar to programming a physical one. It should embody and project the values of the event, and it must balance artistic and cultural intent with the operational costs involved with hosting and promoting it. De Valck (2014) presents a case study review that discusses the tensions of festival and event programming in an increasingly commercial context. She suggests that in practice, a negotiated set of principles that balances these competing tensions is effective.

As noted, the intention of our virtual micro-festival was to place listeners at the heart of a virtual experience that recreated the sound and performance context of each venue as it would have appeared in its heyday, the late 18th century in the case of St. Cecilia's Hall, and the early 16th century in the case of Linlithgow Palace. Consequently, programming had to strike a balance between three elements. First, it had to be consistent with the repertoire that would have been performed in those spaces at those points in time. Second, it had to function consistently as a liturgical setting in the case of Linlithgow Palace Chapel and as an entertainment programme in St. Cecilia's Hall. Finally, the programme, considered as a whole, had to function coherently to address a contemporary audience and serve as a showcase for the virtual spaces.

Balancing these principles when programming the virtual concert in St. Cecilia's Hall was relatively straightforward. Edinburgh Music Society kept very detailed programme notes for all of the concerts that it held. With the help of Dr Jenny Nex, Curator of Musical Instruments Collections at Edinburgh University, we were able to select a representative concert programme featuring music that had been performed in the hall in 1769. The programme included an ensemble piece, Thomas Erskine's *6th Earl of Kellie Overture XIII*, and two pieces for voice and harpsichord, J. C. Bach's *Blest with Thee, My Soul's Dear Treasure*, and the Scottish traditional song *The Lass of Peaty's Mill*.

Programming for the Chapel of Linlithgow Palace was more challenging. The virtual model relates to the building as it was under the rule of James IV of Scotland—this being the period for which the architectural historians have the most detailed information. Unfortunately, specific knowledge of the repertory performed for James, and indeed more widely within his country at this period, is scant. We do know, however, from surviving records that the King spent many important occasions at Linlithgow, particularly at Easter, by far the most important religious occasion for the medieval Christian.

For our reconstruction, we focused on a documented Easter visit in 1512. It was during this visit that his son, the future King James V, was born on Easter Saturday. On the following morning, after the King had heard Mass, James V was baptised in the chapel. While we will never know what music was performed on this occasion, we do know that the Scottish Chapel Royal followed the Sarum Use, originating at Salisbury Cathedral (Baxter, 2001). Accordingly, we constructed a programme around Easter chants, some of them augmented by means of the improvised contemporary practice of faburden (Aplin, 1980), which we know was employed in Scotland around that time.

Performance

Performing historic repertoire in a way that is faithful to the approach, manner, and style of the musical era in which a work was originally conceived is always challenging. It requires detailed historic and historiographic research, a high level of performance practice that is often at odds with contemporary techniques, and a degree of educated guesswork. When that nuanced approach to performance is then recast in a virtual setting, it introduces a number of complicating factors – including acoustics and real-time ensemble feedback – that must be addressed if a high level of performance is to be attained.

To perform the selected repertoire, the project team drew upon the expertise of two ensembles, each of whom brought expertise in historically informed performance. To perform the 18th-century concert repertoire for St. Cecilia's Hall, we formed a small chamber ensemble predominantly of players from the Royal Conservatoire of Scotland. The internationally acclaimed Binchois Consort, conducted by Professor Andrew Kirkman, performed the 16th-century programme for Linlithgow Palace.

Both ensembles were already extremely well-versed in crafting performances of historic repertoire. They took into account everything from historic tunings (Duffin, 2006) to the localised Scottish pronunciation of Latin as derived from an analysis of the spelling used in historic documents from that period. A full discussion of this approach is beyond the scope of this chapter, but Mateos-Moreno and Alcaraz-Iborra (2013), for example, present a broader overview of the methods that underpin such work, and Cook et al. (2023) give a detailed account of our approach for the Linlithgow Palace reconstruction.

The notion of live performance in a virtual space does require some interrogation, however. Performing in virtual space presents a very different performing context for musicians, and it requires additional performance skills. Indeed, arguably virtual performance deconstructs some of the assumptions that have traditionally underpinned audience and performer perceptions of live performance and the social codes and conventions that have developed alongside them (Auslander, 2008).

If we take the point of view that 'liveness' is an emergent quality that results from the 'in-the-moment' interaction and interplay of environment, musicians, instruments, audience, and repertoire, then changing one or more of those elements necessarily changes the pathways to it. If, for example, we can find alternate ways to engineer those interactions, liveness no longer requires audiences and performers to be co-located, either physically or temporally.

At the very least, and unless a performance is situated entirely within the virtual domain, performance in virtual spaces must incorporate some form of interface between the physical the virtual (see, for example, Mazalek & Nitsche, 2007), for a discussion of the broader challenges around intuitive interfaces for virtual performance spaces and Young (2001), who discusses this with specific reference to distributed music performance in digital space).[2]

The choice of programming for our micro-festival dictated acoustic instrumentation, primarily voice, harpsichord, string, wind, and brass chamber ensemble. Accordingly, we made the decision to pre-record both sets of ensembles performing live in a studio setting, using multiple microphones to provide scope for rebalancing and mixing, a common approach in both studio and live recordings and in live sound reinforcement. This approach also correlates strongly with the broadcast practice of transmitting work that is 'recorded-as-live' to balance the need for editorial control and risk management with the energy and dynamic of being 'in-the-moment' (Russo, 2004).

In order to produce as natural a reconstruction of the acoustics as possible, the music was performed and captured in the anechoic chamber at Edinburgh University—a space that is specially constructed to have no natural acoustic of its own (see Figure 2.5). This approach enabled us to create performances as though they were properly situated in our reconstructed space without also overlaying the natural acoustic of a studio or other venue.

While this approach was designed to provide audiences with the most natural acoustic in virtual space, it did not provide the ensembles with a natural performance space. Anechoic chambers are claustrophobic, hot, and they offer very little in the way of feedback to the performer. This raises an immediate question: how does one approach professional-standard performance in such an environment?

The acoustics of a space are typically used by performers, and by singers in particular, for tuning and intonation (see, for example, Ternström, 1991), and they play an important role in animating a performance and in shaping the resultant sound. This was particularly

Figure 2.5 The anechoic chamber at the University of Edinburgh is constructed around a suspended floor and wall- and ceiling-mounted diffusion baffles to absorb and scatter reflected sound and create an unnaturally dry acoustic.

relevant for our 16th-century repertoire as the vocal polyphony of the high Middle Ages was designed for the particular acoustics of the church space, something which is replicated by few modern concert halls.

This meant that many of the performance cues that the musicians normally used for balance, intonation, tuning, and timing – particularly of entries and exits – were missing. This made it a challenge to craft performance decisions which reflect the intended reconstructed acoustic, rather than the artificially dry acoustic as it is found in the chamber. Indeed, one criticism commonly directed at live recordings made anechoically is that they sound flat and lifeless—and this was a situation that we were actively striving to avoid.

To address this, we initially planned to feed all performers a headphone mix with the modelled acoustic applied. However, the singers, who were used to singing and playing in an open space with a large, natural acoustic and without headphones, found this distracting and it impacted the quality of performance. Working with the musicians and the sound engineer, it became clear that the most effective way of capturing performance was to allow the musicians time to acclimatise to the sound of the chamber and recalibrate the acoustic cues that they used for performance validation.

Interestingly, the initial urge of the performers was to subconsciously push the tempo in an attempt to substitute the lost animation of the acoustic with that of outright pace. Once the ensemble directors had controlled that tendency to push, it was surprising how quickly and how strongly the focus of the musicians shifted onto each other, giving a much more intense focus on sound production than one usually experiences in either live performance or studio recording. Absence of any acoustical distraction, or perhaps scope for evasion, forces a focus on intonation and blend that, while exposing and intimidating, is ultimately very productive. While there was an inevitable sense of performers 'walking on eggshells' since every error is instantly and vividly present, there was also a degree of listening that is unusually concentrated.

Production

The production, or to be more precise, the reproduction of the performances in virtual space also raised open-ended questions about how best to situate and visualise performers and audiences, and the degrees of autonomy and agency that we give to each.

To begin, consider the most pervasive assumption that is made about technical sound production. It is an assumption that is so pervasive, in fact, that it rarely even enters our consciousness. It concerns the position of the notional listener, or the point of audition. For ease we shall refer to this position by reference to the assumption that typically underpins it, to wit, that they inhabit 'the best seat in the house'.

In most instances, the goal of production is to provide an idealised listening experience that may not be an accurate representation of the sound on-stage. Taken to extremes, this can result in some interesting audio-visual anomalies that, nonetheless, we do not consciously register unless they are pointed out to us. At the opening ceremony of the 2008 Beijing Olympics, for example, child singer Yang Peiyi, who had recorded "Ode to the Motherland", was replaced by Lin Miaoke, who mimed to Peiyi's recording. Peiyi's face was considered "not suitable" for the Olympics opening ceremony (Branigan, 2008).

For the same opening ceremony, A/Prof Kenny McAlpine produced studio recordings of Mains of Fintry Pipe Band to very strict technical production specifications, so that these could be broadcast through the loudspeakers of the Beijing National Stadium as the band paraded and performed on the track below. This was done to ensure that everyone in the stadium came away with a pristine listening experience, but it was not representative of the sound trackside. In its own way, this is a constructed, if not a virtual, reality.

By convention, the production of late medieval and early classical music has dictated that the notional 'best seat' is located some distance from the source of the sound. It allows for that kind of reverberant bloom that creates a warm and pleasing halo around the performance and that smooths out the consonants and sibilants.

Unfortunately, that warm, pleasing halo obscures many of the details of the music— particularly the intelligibility of the vocal lines and the contrapuntal complexity of the late medieval polyphony. What the listener gains in the perceived quality of sound as they move further from the source, they lose in detail and intelligibility. Virtual spaces provide listeners with the opportunity to make their own judgements, experiencing performances in new ways and developing new perspectives on familiar repertoire and listening experiences that may change their relationship with the music.

Having to address this notional point of audition consciously in virtual space forced the project team to think not only of the effect that acoustic space may have had on the reception of the music, but also of how situating performances in virtual space might afford opportunities to break with the social conventions of modern concertgoing and explore the effects of acoustic space and its relationship with the listener experience more broadly.

In order to develop and test these ideas – those of exploring acoustic space and the listener experience as an element of performance – the project team staged a series of virtual performances of *Hearing Historic Scotland* to more than 200 participants as part of the Manchester Science Festival in 2018.

Here, we designed a listening experience around synchronised head-mounted VR displays and offered participants the opportunity to experience the concert programmes with varying degrees of interactive control. Our baseline user experience was to provide audents with a fixed seating position in the auditorium in which they were asked simply to sit and listen, something akin to replicating a traditional concert-going experience. Note that this still gave listeners some degree of agency, since they could rotate and move their heads to help localise the sound sources and they could leave the performance at any time.

We then augmented this by providing listeners with the opportunity to 'time-travel'—switching at will between the present-day and the past in both of the virtual spaces. This allowed listeners to compare directly contemporary and historic acoustics using the same source material, something that would be impossible to do in a physical space.

Next, we gave listeners the opportunity to move between a number of pre-configured listening positions in the space. The positions allowed them to hear the effect of proximity and relative location to the music. Finally, we enabled listeners to wander freely around the space during the performance which allowed them to audition dynamically the relationship between acoustics, repertoire, and performance.

We analysed the user experience through a combination of observation and post-event interview. An overwhelming preference amongst the interviewees for some degree of control and interaction over and above the baseline experience was revealed. The majority of those interviewed expressed a strong preference for the maximum degree of freedom within the virtual environment. However, direct observation of user behaviours in the space suggested that as the level of agency increased, the attentional focus of the users shifted from active to passive listening, and they became much more interested in exploring the visual and architectural detail of the spaces.

There may well be a novelty effect at play here – many of those interviewed were experiencing immersive virtual reality for the first time – but nevertheless this raises an important question for organisers of events in virtual space: how do you balance the potential of using virtual spaces to present work to audiences in new ways with the need to direct audiences' collective attentional focus towards the work itself? This is a manifestation of what Sloboda et al. (2009) describe as a paradox of modern music listening: "musical engagement is increasingly passive [yet] music use has never provided more opportunities for active agency" (p. 431).

This notion of attentional focus raises one further immediate question: Where should attentional focus be directed? In a physical venue, particularly in classical performance, many listeners close their eyes to direct all of their conscious attention on the listening experience. This happened infrequently in the virtual venues, where listeners appeared to be much more visually focused on the details of the environment. As noted earlier, this may be a partial consequence of the novelty effect, but it also suggests that most audents, particularly those new to virtual performance, would benefit greatly from clear visual framing of performances.

It may seem obvious, but having no visualisation of the performers at all created a disembodied listening experience and makes it difficult for listeners to localise the origin of the performance accurately or even the size of the ensemble. Conversely, however, providing an explicit visualisation of the physical performance will not necessarily enhance the audients' connections between what they see and what they hear. Feeding listeners a video stream of the performers in the anechoic chamber, for example, created a mild sense of cognitive dissonance between the very different performance context that was being visualised, the associated acoustic that this implied, and the modelled acoustic that could be heard colouring the performances. That served to take listeners out of the moment, both in terms of the audio-visual contract, and also in terms of them feeling present in the virtual performance space.

This points towards a much deeper issue around embodiment and representation in virtual performance spaces, an issue that is gaining significant traction in virtual theatre (see, for example, Parker & Martini, 2011) and in virtual dance (Essid et al., 2013). The nuance of this work is much too detailed to explore in any depth here. However, in broad terms, when staging an event or festival in virtual space, organisers must make curatorial judgements in a way that provides a sense of continuity and consistency across all of the events that might fall under a festival umbrella. That is especially true as audiences are taken out of the familiar territory of physical venues and into a virtual space. Asking audiences to learn and adapt to unfamiliar performance contexts and to respond to unfamiliar performance codes and conventions again pulls focus away from the event itself.

In providing some form of visualisation of the virtual performers, consideration should also be given to the function of that visualisation. Is it being used primarily and singularly to provide a point of visual focus, in which case a static avatar might suffice, or should it also serve to provide some sort of embodiment of the performance itself – representing intricate fingerwork or musicianship, for example – in which case there is a need to consider both degrees of movement and how to capture and render the original detail of performance virtually? In both instances, the question arises: how representational should the visualisations be? The more heavily stylised or abstract these are, the more the audients are removed from the familiar physical experience of performance, but conversely, the more accurately rendered they are, the greater the likelihood of uncanniness (Mori et al., 2012) creeping in and impeding the experience.

And, if these issues are true of the performers, then they are equally true of the audiences. Part of the attraction of live events and festivals is the sense of conviviality and community that they bring—of being part of a throng, a collective and emergent dynamic that is greater than the sum of its constituent parts (Wood & Kinnunen, 2020). This is particularly relevant for immersive virtual experiences using head-mounted displays: the technology is physically isolating, and so conviviality, if it is to be a part of that experience, has to be designed in (McKenna, 2020).

Future Work

Following the staging of *Hearing Historic Scotland* in 2018, the project team have continued to develop the underlying technologies and methods across a range of different performance contexts and venues and at scale. In the first instance, this has involved developing an interactive visitor exhibit for Historic Environments Scotland that is situated at Linlithgow Palace and allows visitors to experience the physical site before donning headsets and stepping into the past to see and hear the environment.

In 2019, audience numbers at Linlithgow Palace fell just short of 100,000 (Dent, 2019), and were drawn from a broad and international demographic, which provides us with an opportunity to test the technology and the audience response to staged virtual performance at significant scale. It also enables us to investigate and explore different enterprise models beyond ticketing that could support either semi-permanent virtual events, as is the case with a visitor exhibit, or one-off special events, by examining the impact on footfall and the potential of virtual events for driving trade across Historic Environments Scotland's onsite retail and hospitality venues.

In 2021, the project team released a full commercial CD of early Scottish music – *Music for the King of Scots: The Pleasure Palace of James IV* – with Hyperion Records.[3] It used the post-production tools derived from the VR acoustic models described earlier. The CD repertoire was collated and edited by Dr James Cook and Professor Andrew Kirkman using the approach outlined here, and performed anechoically by the Binchois Consort, with Hyperion carrying out the engineering and post-production. This provides an opportunity to test our acoustic models under the most stringent of critical listening conditions, and to test the commercial viability of the virtual performance paradigm in the market.

In addition to a CD release, a companion app, again derived from the original VR models, will allow consumers to download additional recorded content and remix it at different points in time and space. We plan to investigate the impact of this as an approach to developing audiences and new modes of listening; of monetising the existing back catalogue, and of maximising the commercial potential of newly recorded content.

The project team are also developing new themed events that are designed to extend the degrees of control and liveness beyond those described here, in part to explore further the impacts of situating live performance in virtual space, but also to explore how repertoire changes in response to this shifting context. With that in mind, the team have tentatively begun work on a contemporary live virtual opera and an improvised performance with the Glasgow Improvisers Orchestra.

Conclusions

Our experience demonstrates that there is significant scope and – as a result of COVID-19 – a pressing need for development in this area. For the foreseeable future, physical distancing is likely to dictate the operational logistics of physical events. Streamed events are relatively easy to stage and can be supported by advertising; however, much like watching a performance on television, they create a degree of disconnect and passivity between the viewer and the performance and do little to recreate the festival experience. The common solution to this challenge at present is to stream to public hubs – to cinemas and theatres – which, in the wake of COVID-19, is likely to remain a much less convivial experience in the short term.

Situating performances in VR offers real potential to address those issues, but it also presents some open, and arguably bigger, challenges: limited take-up of the technology, the need for significant audience and musician development, and the underlying funding and revenue models that will support virtual events at scale.

There are, however, areas in which physical and virtual staging overlap. Programming, for example, remains broadly similar. Here virtual festivals really change only the context of the event and require programmers to consider and account for new dimensions as they structure their events.

More broadly, however, there are significant areas of practice, and here we come back to those micro-businesses who support the festival ecosystem – the lighting and sound engineers, the choreographers, the makeup artists, and the set designers – who, with support in translating their physical skills to the virtual domain, could transform the immersive experience of virtual performance by drawing on centuries of established practice.

Unquestionably, audiences are eager to see a return to the physical festival, but as the last years have shown, virtual festivals have their place and are likely to form an increasingly important part of festival strategy and planning. The challenge is to make that virtual experience virtual only in the sense that they are distributed and mediated by technology.

Notes

1. Indeed, it is common in all areas of systematic review to gather and use data that are easy to collect. In academia, a number of international initiatives, such as the San Francisco Declaration on Research Assessment (DORA), have been created to improve the gathering and responsible use of metrics, both qualitative and quantitative.
2. This may well be the case when an autonomous artificially intelligent virtual agent generates a performance on a virtual synthetic instrument in a virtual environment (Mandelis & Husbands, 2003).
3. Catalogue number CDA68333.

References

Aplin, J. (1980). The fourth kind of faburden: The identity of an English four-part style. *Music & Letters*, *61*(3/4), 245–265. https://doi.org/10.1093/ml/61.3-4.245

Auslander, P. (2008). *Liveness: Performance in a mediatized culture*. Routledge. https://doi.org/10.4324/9780203938133

Baxter, J. R. (2001). Music, ecclesiastical. In M. Lynch (Ed.), *The Oxford companion to Scottish history* (pp. 431–432). Oxford University Press. https://doi.org/10.1093/acref/9780199234820.001.0001

Blackie, J. (2002). *A new musick room: A history of St. Cecilia's Hall*. Friends of St. Cecilia's Hall and the Russell Collection of Early Keyboard Instruments.

Branigan, T. (2008). Olympics: Child singer revealed as fake. *The Guardian*. https://www.theguardian.com/sport/2008/aug/12/olympics2008.china1

Brännäs, K., & Nordström, J. (2006). Tourist accommodation effects of festivals. *Tourism Economics*, *12*(2), 291–302. https://doi.org/10.5367/000000006777637458

Carlsen, J., Ali-Knight, J., & Robertson, M. (2007). Access – a research agenda for Edinburgh festivals. *Event Management*, *11*(1–2), 3–11. https://doi.org/10.3727/152599508783943237

Cook, J., Kirkman, A., McAlpine, K. B., & Selfridge, R. (2023). Hearing historic Scotland: Reflections on recording in virtually reconstructed acoustics. *Journal of the Alamire Foundation*, *15*(1), 109–126. https://doi.org/10.1484/J.JAF.5.133797

Davies, K. (2020). Festivals post Covid-19. *Leisure Sciences*, *43*(1–2), 184–189. https://doi.org/10.1080/01490400.2020.1774000

Dent, S. (2019). *Another record-breaking year for Scottish heritage sites*. Historic Environments Scotland. https://www.historicenvironment.scot/about-us/news/another-record-breaking-year-for-scottish-heritage-sites/.

De Valck, M. (2014). Supporting art cinema at a time of commercialization: Principles and practices, the case of the International Film Festival Rotterdam. *Poetics*, *42*(1), 40–59. http://doi.org/10.1016/j.poetic.2013.11.004

Dickson, T., & Paul, J. B. (1902). *Accounts of the lord high treasurer of Scotland* (Vol. IV, p. 347). H.M. General Register House.

Duffin, R. (2006). *How equal temperament ruined harmony (and why you should care)*. W.W. Norton.

Edinburgh City Council. (2019). *Edinburgh by numbers 2019*. https://www.edinburgh.gov.uk/downloads/file/25200/edinburgh-by-numbers-2019

Edinburgh Festival Fringe Society. (2020). *Impact of Covid-19 on DCMS sectors*. https://committees.parliament.uk/writtenevidence/2942/pdf/

Essid, S., Lin, X., Gowing, M., Kordelas, G., Aksay, A., Kelly, P., Fillon, T., Zhang, Q., Dielmann, A., Kitanovski, V., & Tournemenne, R. (2013). A multi-modal dance corpus for research into interaction between humans in virtual environments. *Journal on Multimodal User Interfaces*, *7*(1–2), 157–170. https://doi.org/10.1007/s12193-012-0109-5

Eyal, N., Lipsitch, M., & Smith, P. G. (2020). Human challenge studies to accelerate coronavirus vaccine licensure. *The Journal of Infectious Diseases*, *221*(11), 1752–1756. https://doi.org/10.1093/infdis/jiaa152

Ferguson, B. (2019a). Edinburgh festival fringe audience breaks three million barrier for the first time. *The Scotsman*. https://www.scotsman.com/arts-and-culture/edinburgh-festivals/theatre-and-stage/edinburgh-festival-fringe-audience-breaks-three-million-barrier-first-time-542031

Ferguson, B. (2019b). Edinburgh named one of the world's most serious "overtourism hotspots". *The Scotsman*. https://www.scotsman.com/arts-and-culture/edinburgh-festivals/edinburgh-named-one-worlds-most-serious-overtourism-hotspots-544625

Frey, D., Coelho, V., & Rangayyan, R. M. (2013). *Acoustical impulse response functions of music performance halls*. Morgan & Claypool Publishers. https://doi.org/10.2200/S00488ED1V01Y 201303SAP012

Getz, D. (1997). *Event management and event tourism*. Cognizant Communications Corporation.

Getz, D., & Page, S. J. (2016). *Event studies; theory, research and policy for planned events* (3rd ed.). Routledge. https://doi.org/10.4324/9781315708027

Gibson, C., Waitt, G., Walmsley, J., & Connell, J. (2010). Cultural festivals and economic development in nonmetropolitan Australia. *Journal of Planning education and Research*, 29(3), 280–293. https://doi.org/10.1177/0739456X09354382

Gordziejko, T. (2015). Belonging and unbelonging: The cultural purpose of festivals. In C. Teoksessa, C. Newbold, C. Maughan, J. Jordan & F. Bianchini (Eds.), *Focus on festivals; contemporary European case studies and perspectives*(pp. 265–275). Goodfellow Publishers. https://doi.org/10.239 12/978-1-910158-15-9-2636

Hall, C. (1992). *Hallmark tourist events: Impacts, management and planning*. John Wiley and Sons Ltd.

Harford, S. (2020). As the arts sector crumbles, students hold onto their dreams. *The Age*. https://www.theage.com.au/culture/theatre/as-the-arts-sector-crumbles-students-hold-onto-their-dreams-20200727-p55ftq.html

Harvie, J. (2003). Cultural effects of the Edinburgh International Festival: Elitism, identities, industries. *Contemporary Theatre Review*, 13(4), 12–26. https://doi.org/10.1080/1048680032000118378

Horsburgh, A. J., McAlpine, K. B., & Clark, D. F. (2011). A perspective on the adoption of ambisonics for games. *Audio engineering society conference: 41st international conference: Audio for games*. Audio Engineering Society. https://www.aes.org/e-lib/browse.cfm?elib=15759

Kirkman, A., & Weller, P. (2017). Music and image/image and music: The creation and meaning of visual-aural force fields in the later Middle Ages. *Early Music*, XLV(1), 55–75. https://doi.org/10.1093/em/cax005

Mandelis, J., & Husbands, P. (2003). Musical interaction with artificial life forms: Sound synthesis and performance mappings. *Contemporary Music Review*, 22(3), 69–77. https://doi.org/10.1080/0749446032000150898

Mateos-Moreno, D., & Alcaraz-Iborra, M. (2013). Grounded theory as a methodology to design teaching strategies for historically informed musical performance. *Music Education Research*, 15(2), 231–248. https://doi.org/10.1080/14613808.2013.788139

Mazalek, A., & Nitsche, M. (2007). Tangible interfaces for real-time 3D virtual environments. In *Proceedings of the international conference on advances in computer entertainment technology*(pp. 155–162). https://doi.org/10.1145/1255047.1255080

McAlpine, K., Cook, J., & Selfridge, R. (2021). Hearing history: A virtual perspective on music performance. In J. Paterson & H. Lee (Eds.), *3D audio* (pp. 207–227). Routledge. https://www.routledge.com/3D-Audio/Paterson-Lee/p/book/9781138590069

McKenna, B. (2020). Creating convivial affordances: A study of virtual world social movements. *Information Systems Journal*, 30(1), 185–214. https://doi.org/10.1111/isj.12256

Mori, M., MacDorman, K. F., & Kageki, N. (2012). The uncanny valley [from the field]. *IEEE Robotics & Automation Magazine*, 19(2), 98–100. https://doi.org/10.1109/mra.2012.2192811

O'Hanlon, S. (2009). The events city: Sport, culture, and the transformation of inner Melbourne, 1977–2006. *Urban History Review/Revue d'histoire urbaine*, 37(2), 30–39. https://doi.org/10.7202/029575ar

Parker, J. R., & Martini, C. (2011). Puppetry of the pixel: Producing live theatre in virtual spaces. *2011 IEEE consumer communications and networking conference*(pp. 327–331). https://doi.org/10.1109/CCNC.2011.5766483

Rae, A. (2019). From neighbourhood to "globalhood"? Three propositions on the rapid rise of short-term rentals. *Area*, 51(4), 820–824. https://doi.org/10.1111/area.12522

Rappeport, A., & Smialek, J. (2020). I.M.F. predicts worst downturn since the great depression. *New York Times*. https://www.nytimes.com/2020/04/14/us/politics/coronavirus-economy-recession-depression.html

Roudometof, V. (2016). *Glocalization: A critical introduction.* Routledge. https://doi.org/10.4324/9781315858296

Russo, A. (2004). Defensive transcriptions: Radio networks, sound-on-disc recording, and the meaning of live broadcasting. *The Velvet Light Trap, 54*(1), 4–17. https://doi.org/10.1353/vlt.2004.0018

Sloboda, J. A., Lamont, A., & Greasley, A. (2009). Choosing to hear music. In *The Oxford handbook of music psychology* (1st ed., pp.431–440). Oxford University Press. https://doi.org/10.1093/oxfordhb/9780199298457.013.0040

Ternström, S. (1991). Physical and acoustic factors that interact with the singer to produce the choral sound. *Journal of Voice, 5*(2), 128–143. https://doi.org/10.1016/S0892-1997(05)80177-8

Waterman, S. (1998). Carnivals for elites? The cultural politics of arts festivals. *Progress in Human Geography, 22*(1), 54–74. https://doi.org/10.1191/030913298672233886

Wood, E. H., & Kinnunen, M. (2020). Emotion, memory and re-collective value: Shared festival experiences. *International Journal of Contemporary Hospitality Management, 32*(3), 1275–1298. https://doi.org/10.1108/IJCHM-05-2019-0488

Young, J. P. (2001). Networked music: Bridging real and virtual space. *Organised Sound, 6*(2), 107–110. https://doi.org/10.1017/S1355771801002059

3 Enhanced Performance Training

George Waddell and Aaron Williamon

Introduction

Technology can be a tool to transform, modernize, and optimize the ways in which people learn. The domains of musical performance and music performance education see particular benefit from technology's potential (Purves, 2012). The suite of electronic keyboards and computers (or, more recently, tablets) has become ubiquitous within primary, secondary, and post-secondary music classrooms, along with professional-grade recording equipment and software packages allowing each developing musician to compose, record, edit, and play back their creations. With every passing year the role that technology plays, and is expected to play, is ever widening, enhancing how musicians learn, create, record, experience, analyze, archive, communicate, share, assess, and teach (Himonides & Purves, 2010).

Within the domain of one-to-one teaching, and particularly within the Western classical tradition, technology use has generally been more restrictive, mostly limited to the key tools of audio and video recording, tuners, and metronomes, as well as standard tools of planning time, scheduling lessons and performances, and communicating with colleagues and teachers, the majority of which can now be accessed on mobile smart devices within the spaces where musicians practice and learn (Waddell & Williamon, 2019). However, recent advancements in audio and video capture and analysis, motion capture, artificial intelligence, and enhanced feedback (see Ramirez-Melendez & Waddell, 2022, for a review) offer exciting possibilities for how musical performance can be understood, taught, and shared.

Technology, however, is only a tool and not an automatic solution. For new technology to be adopted and beneficial it must be both useful and easy to use (Davis, 1989), and it must be responsive to the specific challenges, techniques, and traditions of centuries of musical practice as well as the needs of the 21st-century musician. Therefore, strong pedagogical frameworks are required to guide the development, choice, and use of new technologies to enhance the training of musical performance.

A relatively recent development in the understanding of maximally efficient and effective skill developed is that of self-regulated learning, defined by the individual's having control over the processes, motivations, and behaviours by which they learn skills and acquire knowledge (Zimmerman, 1989, 1990). Such learning does not exclude the need for externally driven instruction, such as that provided by an expert teacher, though effective pedagogy will enhance and encourage self-directed study rather than stifle it. The process of self-regulated learning is generally understood as comprising three main components: (1) *forethought*: the thoughts and beliefs that prime, prepare, and motivate the learning process; (2) *performance/volition control*: that which takes place during learning, affecting efficiency and concentration; and (3) *self-reflection*: how the learner responds to the period

DOI: 10.4324/9781003041474-5

of learning that was undertaken (Zimmerman, 1998). This final reflective phase is crucial, allowing the learner to identify areas for improvement, to monitor progress, to target and define future goals, and to build a sense of control and self-efficacy (Paris & Winograd, 1990).

Enhancing one's belief in the ability to perform specific skills has been found to be a strong predictor of effective learning and performance among musicians (McCormick & McPherson, 2003; McPherson & McCormick, 2006; Ritchie & Williamon, 2012). Indeed, Zimmerman's (1998) three self-regulated components of *forethought, performance control*, and *self-reflection* have been found to map closely to the activities undertaken in effective musical development. Jørgensen (2004) proposed one such model encompassing the three categories of learning and practice strategies:

- *planning and preparation strategies*: that which takes place before practice, including activity selection and organization, setting goals and objectives, and time management;
- *executive strategies*: that which takes place during practice, for rehearsal, distribution of practice over time, and preparing for a public performance;
- *evaluation strategies*: that which takes place after practice, for process and product evaluation (pg. 86).

These three are then accompanied by a fourth overarching category of *metastrategies*, which represent the knowledge of individual strategies within each category and the ability both to gauge their efficacy and to choose the most appropriate approach for a particular challenge or situation. Thus, *metastrategies* is a higher-order category encompassing strategies of planning, execution, and evaluation. Furthermore, the three component strategies can operate in a cyclical pattern (see e.g., Hatfield et al., 2017, who posit a similar framework of *forethought, performance*, and *self-reflection*) in which the evaluation of one's practice – including monitoring development, identifying areas for improvement, and expanding *metastrategy*-level understanding of the efficacy of practice – drives the planning stage for continued learning. Thus, a cycle of self-regulated learning is established, fostering effective and efficient learning (see Figure 3.1).

While self-regulated learning has primarily been studied within general educational domains, a growing body of research demonstrates the value of musicians taking control of their learning process (Ritchie & Williamon, 2013; Hatfield et al., 2017; McPherson et al.,

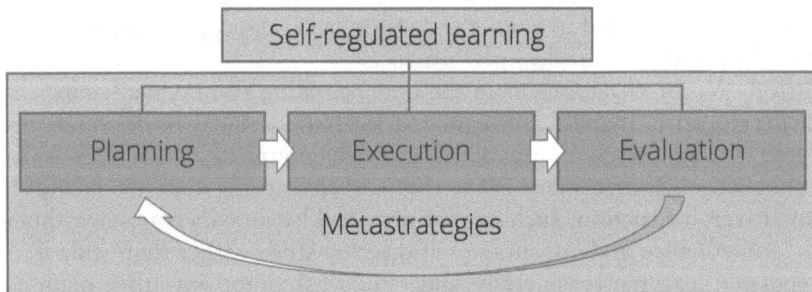

Figure 3.1 A model of self-regulated learning as a cycle of *planning, execution*, and *evaluation* practice strategies guided by overarching *metastrategies*, adapted from Zimmerman (1998) and Jørgensen (2004).

```
                    ┌─────────────────────────────┐
                    │    Self-regulated learning   │
                    └─────────────────────────────┘
         ┌───────────────────┬───────────────────┐
  ┌──────────────┐   ┌──────────────┐   ┌──────────────┐
  │   Planning   │   │   Execution  │   │  Evaluation  │
  └──────────────┘   └──────────────┘   └──────────────┘
         │                   │                   │
  ┌──────────────┐   ┌──────────────┐   ┌──────────────┐
  │  Activity    │   │  Rehearsal   │   │ Aural and    │
  │  selection   │   │  strategies  │   │ visual models│
  └──────────────┘   └──────────────┘   └──────────────┘
         │                   │                   │
  ┌──────────────┐   ┌──────────────┐   ┌──────────────┐
  │ Goal setting │   │ Distribution │   │ Error        │
  │              │   │ over time    │   │ detection    │
  └──────────────┘   └──────────────┘   └──────────────┘
         │                   │                   │
  ┌──────────────┐   ┌──────────────┐   ┌──────────────┐
  │    Time      │   │ Performance  │   │ Self-guidance│
  │ management   │   │ preparation  │   │              │
  └──────────────┘   └──────────────┘   └──────────────┘
```

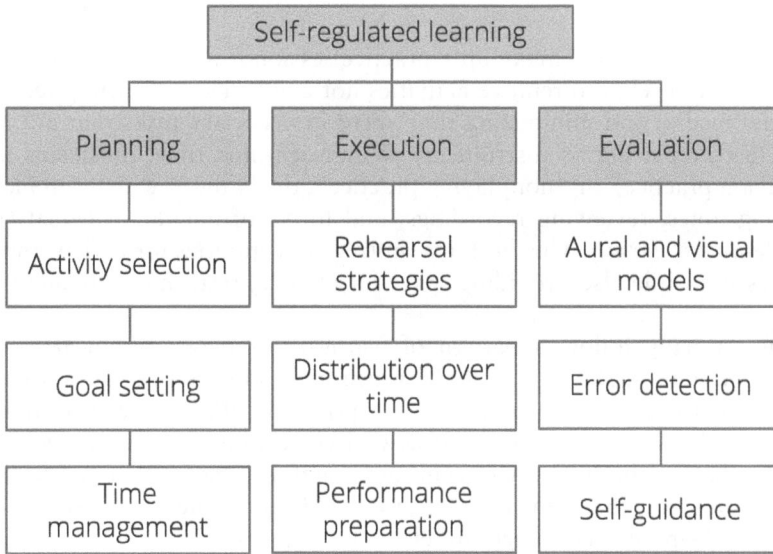

Figure 3.2 Sub-components of the three cyclic self-regulation processes, adapted from Jørgensen (2004).

2019). In outlining his music-specific model, Jørgensen (2004) set out sub-categories within each overarching strategy that target the specific challenges faced, approaches taken, and tools used by musicians in their practice (see Figure 3.2).

Returning to the theme of technology-enhanced approaches to music performance training, these components of self-regulated learning provide a useful framework to consider effective strategies for incorporating technology into music practice. Thus, the remainder of this chapter summarizes the individual components of *planning, execution*, and *evaluation* and how they can serve as a guide to design, choose, and employ new technologies in music learning. What follows does not include a review or outline of specific technologies or applications currently available, as such an approach would quickly become out-of-date. Instead, the challenges and approaches are presented as a framework by which musicians and teachers can evaluate their own technology choices to use in their practice, and for developers, researchers, and engineers to design the next generation of performance- and practice-enhancing hardware and software.

Technology-Enhanced Practice Planning

Planning how practice time will be used is critical to the self-regulation process as it ensures the efficient and effective use of time and that short- and long-term goals are met. While new technologies, particularly those employing audio-, video-, and motion-capture, offer ever-expanding opportunities for musicians to capture and absorb information about their practice, the principles of self-regulated learning also demand that this information be used to decide how future time in the practice room will be spent. Thus, effective technologies should take an active role in guiding students and teachers through this process. This includes helping musicians choose what activities will be undertaken, what their goals are, and how to manage their time.

Activity Selection

Choosing what activities will make up a practice session is a key component of effective planning. The first level is to remove activities not conducive to learning (e.g., spending time on social media) and minimizing time spent in necessary tasks that are not related to learning (e.g., repairing an instrument). Within learning time, musicians may spend time in "playing practice" or "nonplaying practice", the latter of which can include score study, making notes, reviewing recordings, and forms of mental rehearsal (Jørgensen, 2004; see *Mental rehearsal*). This both maximizes opportunities for review and reflection within the session while also providing space for physical rest, thus reducing risk of pain or injury.

Musicians normally follow a pattern of warm-up exercises, technical exercises and études, and repertoire (Duke et al., 1997). Warm-ups and exercises can be chosen to address specific challenges in the repertoire to be practiced. Within the repertoire, research suggests that students primarily work on new pieces without having strategies to review former works (Jørgensen, 2004). Musicians are therefore faced with a constant stream of decisions regarding how their time in practice should be most effectively used. Technologies can theoretically help these challenges in several ways:

Challenge: reducing 'non-learning time'
Approach: Use technologies that monitor time spent learning by tracking active practice time (including silent practice) and engagement with the practice system. Where technologies are integrated with a mobile device or laptop, incorporate data on time spent on non-musical activities via the device (e.g., using e-mail or social media applications) and allow learners to review what proportion of their practice time is spent on such activities. Crucially, develop or choose technologies that require minimal time to set up, calibrate, operate, and pack up, otherwise they risk themselves becoming contributors to "non-learning" time.

Challenge: encouraging "nonplaying practice" to balance effective learning with physical rest
Approach: Use technology to expand the tools available to allow non-playing time, including approaches to mental rehearsal (see *Mental rehearsal*) and for reviewing performance (see *Technology-enhanced practice evaluation*). When providing or using tools to aid in time management (e.g., calendar- or diary-based software), distinguish between 'playing' and 'non-playing' activities and encourage musicians to actively build the former into the practice schedule (e.g., by highlighting extended periods of practice where no 'non-playing' time has been incorporated).

Challenge: choosing and sequencing practice activities
Approach: Use or provide a practice-planning interface that allows musicians to plan and structure a practice session with warm-ups, technical exercises, and repertoire-based components. Include a catalogue of salient items in each category appropriate to the learner at their particular stage, chosen by the teacher or student if not suggested by the technology itself, so that items can be quickly selected for efficient planning.

Challenge: choosing appropriate technical exercises and encouraging specific skill development
Approach: Develop intelligent practice planning technologies that – as effective teachers do – suggest technical and warm-up exercises salient to the repertoire being practiced in

the session. With enough sophistication, technologies incorporating automatic performance review (see *Technology-enhanced practice evaluation*) would be able to identify technical skills found challenging by the learner and would recommend exercises to reinforce the techniques in question.

Challenge: practicing and maintaining former repertoire
Approach: Have practice planning technologies keep an active record of a musician's cumulative repertoire, including the last point at which a work, movement, or passage was practiced or performed. Recommend review sessions on repertoire that have been untouched over a certain time threshold, customizable by the learner based their need to balance learning new works with maintaining a wide performable catalogue.

Goal Setting

At the conservatoire level, practice sessions are often started without setting clear goals for the time period (Jørgensen, 2004). While related to activity selection, specific goals provide focus to sections of time devoted to a particular exercise or piece of repertoire. Musicians' use of goal setting has been found to predict frequency of self-observation and degree of concentration and self-control (Hatfield et al., 2017). These goals might be technical, focusing on developing a particular skill or executing a specific task, or musical, focusing on the achievement of a particular artistic aim that may require technical experimentation to achieve. In either case, the goal should define not just *what* is to be practiced but *why*, and should set clear and specific goals that are relevant to their stage of development. Learners should also regularly review and revise their goals over time.

Challenge: encouraging goal setting and monitoring
Approach: Develop and use technologies that allow for specific practice goals to be logged alongside periods of practice. Allow goals to be registered for different time periods, whether daily, weekly, monthly, yearly, etc. Encourage learners to determine in the practice evaluation stage whether goals have been met and allow them to revise goal wording and timelines and mark goals as completed. Allow learners (and their teachers) to set up sequences of goals, triggering the next when a particular stage has been completed. Where possible and appropriate, tie goals to specific outcomes measurable through technologies that can monitor and analyze performance (e.g., performing an exercise at increasingly faster tempi with consistent intonation, rhythmic accuracy, tone quality, etc. (see Giraldo et al., 2019; Ramirez-Melendez & Waddell, 2022) to ensure that goals are being met to measurable standards before progressing to the next stage.

Time Management

There is no standard answer as to how much time should be spent in practice. Practice time and frequency tends to increase with experience (Sloboda et al., 1996), though quantity of practice for a specific performance has been found to be a poor predictor of its ultimate quality; here, the nature and quality of practice (based on the principles of self-regulated learning) are stronger predictors (Williamon & Valentine, 2000). There is also evidence of musicians' tendency to unevenly mange practice time over longer periods; surges in practice time tend to take place preceding examinations (Hallam, 2001) and both before and after lessons (Lehmann & Ericsson, 1998). As excessive practice can trigger injury and exhaustion, it stands to reason that efficient practice should be the goal. Musicians should not fill a predetermined amount of practice time; rather they should spend what time is needed to achieve specific goals as part of a purposefully planned schedule. Practice time is also often limited by practical constraints, so considering one's daily schedule and availability of practice space or equipment is key.

Challenge: ensuring adequate time is scheduled to achieve practice goals
Approach: When using digital calendars or diaries to set practice goals (e.g., a task for an upcoming lesson or repertoire for an upcoming performance or examination), require musicians to estimate how much time will be needed to complete a given goal. Furthermore, allow musicians to track practice time constraints (e.g., gaps in their academic or social calendars, availability of practice rooms or equipment, appropriate time for mental and physical rest, etc.), automatically syncing with existing personal or institutional calendars where available. Within these constraints, technologies should help musicians work backwards from upcoming milestones to ensure that practice time is evenly distributed to avoid the need for potentially damaging or demotivating practice 'crunches' ahead of key performances. With enough information regarding practice availability, ongoing repertoire, and key performance milestones, intelligent practice planning software might be able to suggest a balanced distribution of time over longer periods.

Challenge: discouraging over-practicing for the sake of 'filling time'
Approach: Where practice goals are logged and recorded alongside time spent practicing, technologies that provide motivating feedback should acknowledge, reward, and encourage goal completion rather than arbitrary daily or weekly time-based quotas. Where possible, musicians should be praised for spending as little time as possible in successfully achieving a given goal, with planning based on performance outcomes rather than time quotas. Signs of over-practicing might also be seen within practice execution itself (see *Distribution over time*).

Challenge: using time efficiently and planning time accurately
Approach: Use technologies to provide an overview of the relative amount of time spent on particular activities, skills, repertoire, goals, etc. Where technologies have a record of the anticipated time it will take to complete a goal, as well as a record of how much time was spent working on the goal and when it was deemed completed, they can build a record of the musician's ability to predict their own pace of learning. This information should then be fed back to the musician to allow them to evaluate their accuracy and plan future goals and practice schedules accordingly, affording more time for elements that have historically taken them longer and being more stringent in allocating time to goals that they know they can achieve quickly. Developing such metacognitive knowledge of their own abilities helps the learner move towards the *metastrategies* of taking control of their self-regulated learning.

Technology-Enhanced Practice Execution

Rehearsal Strategies

Once the activities, goals, and timeframe of a practice session have been planned, the musician must still employ appropriate rehearsal strategies and techniques to achieve the planned outcome. Jørgensen (2004) described four common strategies used in musical rehearsal.

Mental Rehearsal

Mental rehearsal comprises 'nonplaying' practice in which musicians employ imagery, score reading, and audiation to reflect upon the music to be played. In particular, they hone their mental model of their ideal or intended version of the performance with which they can compare what they actually execute in practice and performance. Mental rehearsal also provides an opportunity for physical rest within practice. Transitions from mental rehearsal to physical rehearsal can be fluid and can be used to develop other primary skills such as concentration, memory, and the management of performance anxiety (Connolly & Williamon, 2004).

Challenge: encouraging mental rehearsal
Approach: In addition to allowing and encouraging musicians to actively plan time for mental rehearsal in their practice (see *Activity selection*), let technologies help make space and provide tools for such practices. Musicians can use technologies to examine and mark up digital scores, to review and reflect on audio and video recordings of themselves and others, or to take physical breaks within practice *execution* time itself to transition seamlessly and deliberately to *planning* and/or *evaluation* phases. Where the musician is using technology to guide them through their planned practice schedule (see *Distribution over time*), allow the software to prompt them to imagine how they wish the passage or piece to sound or feel before physically executing it.

Rehearsing the Whole Piece versus Smaller Parts

Musicians may choose to practice exercises and repertoire from beginning to end without pause, play through while stopping to address issues, or concentrate on individual parts of the score. Each offers advantages; rehearsing the whole work allows for sections to be understood in the context of the whole and develops fluid transitions between components; rehearsing parts can allow for the efficient addressal of challenging sections, improve memorization (Chaffin et al., 2010), and result in technically stronger performances (Williamon & Valentine, 2002). Thus, musicians should employ a combination of these techniques. The choice of where sections begin and end differs between pieces and individuals, often driven by the musical and structural features of the work.

Challenge: approaching parts of a piece
Approach: Just as technology might help a musician oversee and plan to practice a range of repertoire (see *Activity selection*), a similar approach can be taken to breaking down a piece into components. A simple approach would allow users to enter the number of bars within a piece of repertoire, triggering the software to suggest a series of goal-based practice sessions in which they execute each bar (or grouping of bars) to a particular level of proficiency before moving to the next selected in various orders. A sufficiently detailed catalogue of repertoire, or sufficiently intelligent analytical ability of the technology, might be able to automatically offer sections to rehearse based on the work's structure and identify closely related sections across the work to practice side-by-side to maximize learning efficiency, or at least allow the musician to mark such structural points accordingly (perhaps in a phase of mental rehearsal, as discussed earlier). Such technology could then track the degree to which certain parts of the work have been played – either through the

planned practice schedule or analysis of audio in the practice session – and highlight areas that have been given proportionally less attention across a period of practice (particularly if a major performance milestone for the repertoire in question is imminent). Where metrics of performance quality are being automatically measured (e.g., accuracy of pitch and rhythm), a system could recognize cases where repeated play-throughs of an entire work were being undertaken without focus on particularly error-prone sections, then prompt the appropriate sectional work needed to address them.

Rehearsing Challenging Parts

In their practice, musicians will identify exercises, techniques, or pieces (and component parts) of repertoire that they find particularly challenging. Common strategies to approach learning this material include repetition, incorporating technical studies into practice that address the core skills and techniques in question, breaking the section into component parts, and slow practice.

Challenge: addressing challenging parts

Approach: Combining a practice planning application with record of what repertoire, and what sections therein, are being played with a system that can automatically assess standard metrics of performance quality would allow for the rudimentary flagging of works or sections that are particularly challenging. Such a system could highlight these parts for practice, employing goal-based strategies including further sectional work (e.g., breaking a section down into bars) or slow practice. As described earlier (see *Activity selection*) the system might also suggest relevant technical exercises as part of the warm-up in anticipation of the challenging parts to be learned in the practice period. Crucially, the technology's ability to identify over-practicing (see *Time management*) would be particularly salient here in identifying when the repetition of challenging parts was not leading to marked improvement, prompting the musician to consider a change in rehearsal strategy before the barrier leads to inefficient use of time or unnecessary risk of frustration or physical injury.

Fast versus Slow Rehearsal

While slow practice is a common strategy in approaching unfamiliar works and ensuring accuracy in those well known, executing a work at a different speed to the intended final performance can activate a different set of physical movements (Winold & Thelen, 1994). This must be weighed against the advantages of having more time to perceive and classify mistakes, thus an alternation between the two approaches is usually recommended.

Challenge: balancing fast and slow rehearsal

Approach: Use systems of scheduling part rehearsal and setting practice goals that also let the musician set tempo goals. When using automatic performance analysis, have technologies recognize and record tempi of practice and, where mistakes regularly occur, prompt slower practice. The staged goals discussed earlier (see *Goal setting*) can employ increasingly fast tempi, not allowing progression until the system identifies one or more performances of appropriate consistency and accuracy. Use motion-tracking to highlight the physical differences between fast and slow practice, allowing the musician to learn to regulate their tempo while generally maintaining movement patterns.

Distribution Over Time

Planning how time will be used in a practice session, or how practice will be distributed over hours or days or weeks, only provides its full value if that plan is executed. In the flow of practice, it can be easy to lose track of time or to forget one's good intentions coming into a session. At the same time, rigorous adherence to a plan without adjusting to the challenges and successes of a session is equally efficient. Musicians should be able to alter their plans within rehearsal depending on the quality and outcomes of their practice.

Challenge: adhering to a practice schedule

Approach: The same tool used to plan practice is now used to execute practice. Through aural and/or visual notifications, the musician can be notified of the next item on the agenda or when a planned period has elapsed. When moving to a new task, a particularly useful system would bring forward the tools needed to execute it, such as a score, a metronome, a reminder to take a break, a mental rehearsal guide, a recording, or a motion tracking application.

Challenge: allowing the flexibility to adapt a practice schedule

Approach: Rather than forcing a musician to change tasks, a flexible practice execution guide could simply notify the musician when a planned transition point has arrived. Depending on their preference, the student might decide in advance how intrusive they want any notification to be (e.g., a loud noise versus a subtle visual reminder), depending on whether they prioritize keeping their strict schedule versus maintaining their focus on a task not yet completed. Once notified, the musician could then decide whether to advance the system to the next task or remain on their current priority. Meanwhile, the system would track the planned schedule and compare it to the realized schedule, allowing the potential for the musician to build an awareness of the accuracy of their predicted time per task (as in *Time management*). At this point, the musician could be invited to review their plans for future practice sessions and adjust them accordingly, or to allow an intelligent software system to do this for them.

Performance Preparation

Performance is fundamentally different than practice, often involving new, larger, and contextually richer spaces with different acoustic responses, the presence of audiences and/or judges, different attire, a higher degree of risk associated with errors and memory lapses, and higher levels of physiological arousal and anxiety (Chanwimalueang et al., 2017). Musicians should practice for these situations, learning how they react mentally and physically to the demands of live performance and developing appropriate strategies to counteract them.

Challenge: preparing for performance

Approach: Technologies offer the opportunity to prepare for the challenges of performance through recreating and simulating particular contexts and stressors, such as spaces where musicians can practice waiting backstage before walking out to face the lights and their (virtual) audience or audition panel (Williamon et al., 2014). Other aspects of musical activity might also be simulated, such as the act of evaluating a live performance as a music judge or examiner (Waddell et al., 2019). Augmented and virtual reality technologies, as well as acoustic simulation, offer further potential to allow musicians to experience and prepare for the sounds and sights of different performance spaces. Recordings of audio, video, motion capture, and physiological reactions to performance conditions can help musicians understand how their performances change in such heightened settings (Chanwimalueang et al., 2017).

Technology-Enhanced Practice Evaluation

Performance capture technology, whether measuring audio, video, motion, or physiology, offers musicians the unprecedented ability to self-review their own practice. Despite this potential, and the core role self-reflection plays in the self-regulated learning cycle, Jørgensen (2004) found in one study that 79% of conservatory students did not regularly review the results of their practice. Waddell and Williamon (2019) found that nearly half of student and professional musicians sampled kept no record of what took place in the practice room, and only 20% kept any kind of daily record. They also found that, while approximately one-half of musicians audio- or video-recorded themselves each week, those recordings were viewed much less frequently. A gap remains, therefore, in finding ways to help musicians process and find value in the potentially overwhelming amount of information generated from a single performance, never mind a series of practice sessions over days, months, and years.

Aural and Visual Models

Musicians tend to compare their practice with internal and external models of performance. These may be mental models of how a technique should sound or feel, or audio and video recordings of peers, teachers, and masters performing the same works. Experienced musicians are expected to transition from imitating the performances of others to developing their own models for performance, though research highlights how even experts can benefit from this practice of imitation (Lisboa et al., 2005). The challenge lies in having access to appropriate models of practice and translating third-person perspectives of viewing another musician with the first-person, embodied perspectives of one's own body executing the movements, bridging the gap between the movements they think they are performing and what they are actually performing. There is also the challenge of reviewing hours of recorded practice which, through normal means, takes as long to review as it does to execute.

Challenge: changing visual perspectives
Approach: While audio and video recordings (or even simple mirrors) provide baseline tools to allow musicians to understand their motions and sounds in relation to others', new technologies will allow musicians to see, understand, and compare their own and others' performances in ways undreamt of in previous decades. Motion capture sensors and advanced visualizations will allow musicians to review performances from any angle, highlighting important symmetries and subtleties of their instrument and body and making direct comparisons with similar recordings by their peers, teachers, or experts. Specific motions of the body or instrument can be extracted and highlighted, isolating underlying components of performance and revealing hidden patterns of movement (see Ramirez-Melendez & Waddell, 2022). Augmented and virtual reality technologies will allow musicians to see their teachers' own limbs in front of them at their instrument, allowing for a direct translation from sight to movement.

Challenge: choosing which recordings to review
Approach: Automatic analysis of recorded performance could highlight areas of inconsistency of sound or movement, or where progress is not being made. Rather than reviewing

an hour of footage, technology could guide the musician to the key moments to review, intelligently linking them to (or making annotations on) the musical score. Technology can also be used to provide expert commentary and feedback on recorded performance, including time-based annotations on the timeline or video player, or by a continuous evaluation recorded in real time by one or more viewers through which dips in perceived enjoyment, quality, or effectiveness are immediately linked to the relevant musical moments that caused them (e.g. see Waddell et al., 2018).

Error Detection

A key component of practice is recognizing and addressing errors, requiring not only an awareness of what constitutes a mistake but also what constitutes an accurate execution. Musicians must monitor a wide variety of factors for errors at any given time, including pitch, rhythms, dynamics, intonation, tempo, and articulation, each interrelated and tied to the technical demands of the instrument. If attention is drawn to one factor (e.g., correct pitches), then errors in other areas may go unnoticed. Musicians may not even be aware that they are committing an error, either by missing an indication in the score, incorrect memorization, or inability to hear or feel the mistake. Even when errors are correctly identified they may not be immediately addressed, leading to their continued and learned execution.

Challenge: monitoring errors
Approach: Where sound- or movement-based models of the correct execution of particular tasks (or a threshold within which accuracy can be defined) exist, develop systems that can identify them and notify the musician. Such feedback could be written directly to a musical score, as a teacher might mark feedback (e.g., see Ramirez-Melendez & Waddell, 2022). Care should be taken to avoid an overly narrow definition of accuracy which could risk stifling expressive freedom and artistic creativity. Where 'errors' are less well defined (e.g., inconsistencies in tone quality), provide feedback tools that allow musicians to understand the relative consistency and variety of the sounds or movements produced so that they and their teachers can judge what is appropriate for the musical moment (e.g., see Giraldo et al., 2019).

Challenge: monitoring errors across multiple parameters
Approach: Use technologies that can track multiple parameters at once but will selectively display the information to musicians to avoid an overload of information. A musician might then choose to focus on one aspect (e.g., a consistent dynamic) then, once that is achieved, go back to see whether consistency of other factors (e.g., rhythm or intonation) was maintained.

Challenge: correcting errors
Approach: Where objective errors or inconsistencies can be identified (e.g., a wrong note, a limb in an objectively inefficient position), use feedback systems that clearly and intuitively highlight the issue and what the correct action should be. This could be an indication on a digital score, a markup on a visual display of the body, or a text or spoken instruction. Advances in wearable haptic devices that mimic human touch might allow musicians to feel responsive feedback in the practice room, just as a teacher might nudge an arm or tap a shoulder to draw attention to a limb out of place (e.g., van der Linden et al., 2010). When using staged goals to organize practice (see *Goal setting*), have the

technology disallow or discourage progression to the next bar, section, or tempo until the error has been consistently resolved.

Self-guidance

In addition to simply reviewing their practice, musicians should adjust their strategies accordingly with the practice session. This might include slowing down or switching from whole-piece to sectional practice if too many errors are noticed. Musicians should also monitor their physical and mental state, adjusting their practice distribution, use of non-playing practice, or taking breaks to maximize efficiency and prevent injury. Their review of practice efficacy should inform how they plan for and execute future practice sessions. Musicians should also provide themselves with constructive encouragement when goals are met and tasks completed to maintain motivation to practice and continue their development.

Challenge: using feedback to guide practice execution

Approach: Applying the systems described in the preceding sections, technology can be used to provide immediate feedback to musicians within their practice and encourage them to take immediate action to address it.

Challenge: using feedback to plan future practice

Approach: A unified practice technology system will allow musicians to plan how they will practice, to execute their practice with respect to that plan, and, while reviewing the results of their practice, to seamlessly access the planning functions so that they can immediately adjust their next session (or period of sessions) based on what they have just learned. This entails not just *what* will be practiced (e.g., which bars, exercises, or repertoire), but *how* it will be effectively practiced (e.g., through goal setting, predicting time allocation, setting tempo- or section-based strategies, etc.), activating the knowledge and use of Jorgensen's (2004) *metastrategies* as the musician takes full control of the self-regulated learning cycle.

Challenge: using feedback to motivate practice

Approach: Effective technology-enhanced feedback will help musicians see subtle short- and long-term progress they might not have noticed, to celebrate milestone goals and achievements that might be taken for granted within the context of the many more steps to learn, and to feel in control of their development as they grow as musicians.

Challenge: monitoring and responding to mental and physical state

Approach: Within practice time, a practice execution system might prompt musicians to take a moment to consider their physical and mental state and whether a break would be of use. The musician might be asked to respond to a quick self-report of such states, through which an algorithm could learn to recognize patterns in practice length, timing, and strategy that correspond to decreased mental and physical fitness to practice, highlighting these trends in the planning stage and suggesting alternate planning strategies as appropriate. A sufficiently advanced system, using some combination of wearable sensors tracking such factors as motion, muscle activity, and neurological function, might even provide direct measurement of mental and physical exertion and notify the musician accordingly to avoid unnecessary fatigue and injury (Elshafei & Shihab, 2021).

Conclusion

When considering the role technology can play in how musical performance practice is planned, executed, and evaluated, it becomes apparent that many of the roles are those served by an experienced and effective music teacher. Indeed, a primary role of the teacher is to teach not just the skills to be learned, but how to practice them. As violin pedagogue Ivan Galamian stated, "children do not know how to work alone. The teacher must constantly teach the child how to practice" (reported in Applebaum & Applebaum, 1972, p. 351). In a survey of 100 instrumental teachers across ability groups, Barry and McArthur (1994) found that the majority of teachers always or almost always discussed the importance of practice strategies with their students, providing specific instruction of how to practice and emphasizing the use of techniques following the concepts of self-regulated learning. These included slow practice with gradually increasing tempi, analyzing a new work before learning it, completing daily practice in multiple shorter sessions rather than one long one, and setting goals for each practice session. However, most teachers reported sometimes, rarely, or never having observed or required a record of their students' practice behaviour, whether via recordings or written notes from the students or their parents. Fewer than one-third of the teachers reported that their students almost always practiced effectively. Thus, there remains a gap in intentions and outcomes in having students optimize their practice habits, driven perhaps by the fact that the teacher cannot be expected to be always in the practice room with their student. And there are also potential students who, due to such restrictions as geography or finance, will not have access to a teacher (or a teacher of adequate skill, expertise, or effectiveness) in the first place.

It is here that technology can help fill the gap. Not by replacing effective teachers but by expanding their influence to the spaces and times where they are not present, and enhancing communication between them and their students by providing methods of capturing, storing, interpreting, and communicating data in ways of which no human is capable. By the mid-2000s, teachers were developing strategies to incorporate recording and edited playback, video conferenced demonstrations and collaborations, and web-based instructional videos into their teaching (Anderson & Ellis, 2005), and calls for more professional development were made following the demonstrated benefits teacher workshops based around music technologies (Bauer et al., 2003). By 2003, the UK government reported that 24% of secondary classrooms made substantial use of technology and, as a result, 30% of secondary teachers reported a substantial positive effect on teaching (DfES, 2005). In 2010, an independent review on *Music Education in England* for the Department for Education recommended that:

> further work should be undertaken to develop a national plan for the use of technology in the delivery of Music Education – and to ensure that the workforce is up-to-date with latest developments. This review should examine how technology could enable better teaching of music (particularly in rural communities) as well as ways in which new methods of creating music that embrace technological innovation are taught in the classroom.
> (Henley, 2011, p. 30)

Further study has found that technology use continues to grow, with the greatest barriers being a lack of availability, technical competence, and staff support (Gall, 2013). This mirrors data from the European Commission (2013) which showed a substantial increase in numbers of computers and quality of broadband access in European schools in 2006–2012, and while fewer than half of teachers were making use of ICT in more than 25% of their classes, a second survey published in 2019 found that this had increased to 71%, 58%, and

65% among European primary schools, lower secondary schools, and upper secondary schools, respectively (European Commission, 2019). According to the teachers surveyed, the greatest obstacle to the expansion of digital education was a lack of tablets, laptops, and notebooks available in the classroom. The percentage of European students owning their own digital technologies remained stable across the 2012 and 2019 studies, with only half of students reporting access to devices, the majority of which were smartphones. Thus, challenges of affordability and accessibility remain, though recent work is tackling these using online tools and networks. For example, the *Connect Resound* project (King et al., 2019a) used existing technologies and platforms (e.g., microphones, cameras, Skype) to deliver music education opportunities to primary schools that lacked or had little instrumental music provision across four regions of England. While the digital learning environment brought with it some of the standard challenges often associated with digitally delivered versus in-person tuition (e.g., variable video/audio quality and internet connectivity, time-lag that precluded synchronous playing), these could be overcome by careful pedagogical activity selection and technology enhancements, such as allowing students and teachers to choose between multiple camera views. Crucially, students showed good levels of concentration, motivation, and progress, and teachers expressed an intention to continue working in the digital environment despite the limitations (King et al., 2019b). As technology affordability and network connectivity continues to improve, so will such opportunities for distance learning in communities traditionally lacking access to quality music tuition (see Lisboa et al., 2022 and Chapter 13 of this volume for a review). The technology-enhanced (and self-regulated) individual practice activities described in this chapter can then be incorporated into a framework of taught lessons, whether in person or online, to provide a well-rounded and fully supported approach to music performance training.

As technologies continue to evolve, so too should their use within music education, practice, and performance. Waddell and Williamon (2019) found a general desire among student and professional musicians to engage with new technologies to enhance their musical practice, provided that those technologies were deemed to be easy to use and useful. So long as the ongoing exponential increase in technology's capability and ubiquity continues, and so long as the principles of self-regulated learning are kept at the core of the development and adoption of new systems, technology may offer ever greater possibilities to expand access to, engagement with, and enjoyment of the many benefits of music performance.

References

Anderson, A. J., & Ellis, A. (2005). Desktop video-assisted music teaching and learning: New opportunities for design and delivery. *British Journal of Educational Technology, 36*(5), 915–917.

Applebaum, S., & Applebaum, S. (1972). *The way they play, Book I*. Paganiniana Publications, Inc.

Barry, N. H., & McArthur, V. (1994). Teaching practice strategies in the music studio: A survey of applied music teachers. *Psychology of Music, 22*(1), 44–55.

Bauer, W. I., Reese, S., & McAllister, P. A. (2003). Transforming music teaching via technology: The role of professional development. *Journal of Research in Music Education, 51*(4), 289–301.

Chaffin, R., Lisboa, T., Logan, T., & Begosh, K. T. (2010). Preparing for memorized cello performance: The role of performance cues. *Psychology of Music, 38*(1), 3–30.

Chanwimalueang, T., Aufegger, L., Adjei, T., Wasley, D., Cruder, C., Mandic, D. P., & Williamon, A. (2017). Stage call: Cardiovascular reactivity to audition stress in musicians. *PLoS ONE, 12*(4), e0176023.

Connolly, C., & Williamon, A. (2004). Mental skills training. In A. Williamon (Ed.), *Musical excellence: Strategies and techniques to enhance performance* (pp. 221–245). Oxford University Press.

Davis, F. D. (1989). Perceived usefulness, perceived ease of use, and user acceptance of information technology. *MIS Quarterly*, 319–340.

Department for Education and Skills (DfES). (2005). *Support for parents: The best start for children.* Stationery Office.

Duke, R. A., Flowers, P. J., & Wolfe, D. E. (1997). Children who study piano with excellent teachers in the United States. *Bulletin of the Council for research in Music Education*, 51–84.

Elshafei, M., & Shihab, E. (2021). Towards detecting biceps muscle fatigue in gym activity using wearables. *Sensors*, 21(3), 759.

European Commission. (2013). *Survey of schools: ICT in education.* Publications Office of the European Union.

European Commission. (2019). *Executive summary of 2nd survey of schools: ICT in education.* Publications Office of the European Union.

Gall, M. (2013). Trainee teachers' perceptions: Factors that constrain the use of music technology in teaching placements. *Journal of Music, Technology & Education*, 6(1), 5–27.

Giraldo, S., Waddell, G., Nou, I., Ortega, A., Mayor, O., Perez, A., Williamon, A., & Ramirez, R. (2019). Automatic assessment of tone quality in violin music performance. *Frontiers in Psychology*, 10, 334.

Hallam, S. (2001). The development of expertise in young musicians: Strategy use, knowledge acquisition and individual diversity. *Music Education Research*, 3, 7–23.

Hatfield, J. L., Halvari, H., & Lemyre, P.-N. (2017). Instrumental practice in the contemporary music academy: A three-phase cycle of Self-Regulated Learning in music students. *Musicae Scientiae*, 316–337.

Henley, D. (2011). *Music education in England: A review by Darren Henley for the department for education and the department for culture, media and sport.* Department for Education.

Himonides, E., & Purves, R. (2010). The role of technology. In S. Hallam & A. Creech (Eds.), *Music education in the 21stcentury in the United Kingdom: Achievements, analysis and aspirations* (pp. 123–140). Institute of Education.

Jørgensen, H. (2004). Strategies for individual practice. In A. Williamon (Ed.), *Musical excellence: Strategies and techniques to enhance performance* (pp. 85–104). Oxford University Press.

King, A., Prior, H., & Waddington-Jones, C. (2019a). Connect resound: Using online technology to deliver music education to remote communities. *Journal of Music, Technology & Education*, 12(2), 201–217.

King, A., Prior, H., & Waddington-Jones, C. (2019b). Exploring teachers' and pupils' behaviour in online and face-to-face instrumental lessons. *Music Education Research*, 21(2), 197–209.

Lehmann, A. C., & Ericsson, K. A. (1998). Preparation of a public piano performance: The relation between practice and performance. *Musicæ Scientiæ*, 2, 67–94.

Lisboa, T., Jónasson, P., & Johnson, C. (2022). Synchronous online learning, teaching, and performance. In G. E. McPherson (Ed.), *The Oxford handbook of music performance* (Vol. 2). Oxford University Press.

Lisboa, T., Williamon, A., Zicari, M., & Eiholzer, H. (2005). Mastery through imitation: A preliminary study. *Musicae Scientiae*, 9, 75–110.

McCormick, J., & McPherson, G. (2003). The role of self-efficacy in a musical performance examination: An exploratory structural equation analysis. *Psychology of Music*, 31(1), 37–51.

McPherson, G. E., & McCormick, J. (2006). Self-efficacy and music performance. *Psychology of Music*, 34(3), 322–336.

McPherson, G. E., Osborne, M., Evans, P., & Miksza, P. (2019). Applying self-regulated learning microanalysis to study musicians' practice. *Psychology of Music*, 47(1), 8–32.

Paris, S. G., & Winograd, P. (1990). How metacognition can promote academic learning and instruction. In B. J. Jones & L. Idol (Eds.), *Dimensions of thinking and cognitive instruction* (pp. 15–51). Lawrence Erlbaum Associates, Inc.

Purves, R. (2012). Technology and the educator. In G. E. McPherson & G. F. Welch (Eds.), *The Oxford handbook of music education* (Vol. 2, pp. 457–475). Oxford University Press.

Ramirez-Melendez, R., & Waddell, G. (2022). Technology enhanced learning of performance. In G. E. McPherson (Ed.), *The Oxford handbook of music performance* (Vol. 2). Oxford University Press.

Ritchie, L., & Williamon, A. (2012). Self-efficacy as a predictor of musical performance quality. *Psychology of Aesthetics, Creativity, and the Arts*, 6, 334–340.

Ritchie, L., & Williamon, A. (2013). Measuring musical self-regulation: Linking processes, skills, and beliefs. *Journal of Education and Training Studies*, 1, 106–117.

Sloboda, J. A., Davidson, J. W., Howe, M. J. A., & Moore, D. G. (1996). The role of practice in the development of performing musicians. *British Journal of Psychology*, 87, 287–309.

van der Linden, J., Schoonderwaldt, E., Bird, J., & Johnson, R. (2010). Musicjacket – combining motion capture and vibrotactile feedback to teach violin bowing. *IEEE Transactions on Instrumentation and Measurement, 60*(1), 104–113.

Waddell, G., Perkins, R., & Williamon, A. (2018). Making an impression: Error location and repertoire features affect performance quality rating processes. *Music Perception: An Interdisciplinary Journal, 36*(1), 60–76.

Waddell, G., Perkins, R., & Williamon, A. (2019). The evaluation simulator: A new approach to training music performance assessment. *Frontiers in Psychology, 10*(557), 1–17.

Waddell, G., & Williamon, A. (2019). Technology use and attitudes in music learning. *Frontiers in ICT, 6*(11), 1–14.

Williamon, A., Aufegger, L., & Eiholzer, H. (2014). Simulating and stimulating performance: Introducing distributed simulation to enhance musical learning and performance. *Frontiers in Psychology, 5*, 25.

Williamon, A., & Valentine, E. (2000). Quantity and quality of musical practice as predictors of performance quality. *British Journal of Psychology, 91*(3), 353–376.

Williamon, A., & Valentine, E. (2002). The role of retrieval structures in memorizing music. *Cognitive Psychology, 44*(1), 1–32.

Winold, H., & Thelen, E. (1994). Coordination and control in the bow arm movements of highly skilled cellists. *Ecological Psychology, 6*(1), 1–31.

Zimmerman, B. J. (1989). A social cognitive view of self-regulated learning. *Journal of Educational Psychology, 81*, 329–339.

Zimmerman, B. J. (1990). Self-regulated learning and academic achievement: An overview. *Educational Psychologist, 25*, 3–17.

Zimmerman, B. J. (1998). Developing self-fulfilling cycles of academic regulation: An analysis of exemplary instructional models. In D. H. Schunk & B. J. Zimmerman (Eds.), *Self-regulated learning: From teaching to self-reflective practice* (pp. 1–19). Guilford Press.

4 Developing an Online Music Orientation Using the Framework for Teaching Music Online

Carol Johnson

Introduction

In higher education music departments, online learning was yet to be a commonly used teaching approach prior to the global 2020 COVID-19 pandemic (Johnson, 2021). With online music learning requiring teachers and students to have and use digital literacy skills (e.g., creating, recording, and sharing of audio and video files), it is understandable that the online music environment can be deemed more technologically complex than its face-to-face teaching counterpart.

In today's context, music students learning in both face-to-face classes and fully on-line environments are required to interact with content in a Learning Management System (LMS) and to have a developed technology competency for creating and uploading multimedia files and assets for their class assignments. However, as evidenced during the emergency remote learning required by the pandemic, tertiary music students and teachers met the transition to online music learning with challenges due to the increased requirements of technology use (Habe et al., 2021; Schiavio et al., 2021). Teachers found themselves having to increase their own abilities to teach with digital technologies (e.g., video conferencing applications, notation software, recording software, etc.), and supporting their students with technology helps and guides (Ritchie & Sharpe, 2021). While some instructors reported an increase of sharing teaching strategies and resources (Merrick & Johnson, 2020), the memories of remote teaching for many music instructors are reminders of how music learning took a backseat as we recall how the necessity of post-secondary music students' digital literacy skills were realized.

Digital literacy skills provide students with abilities to create, engage, adapt, and share digital artifacts. With minimal digital literacy skills, a student may not be able to fully utilize communication tools in an online class (e.g., limited to a text-based reflection versus a video reflection in a discussion area), and thereby feel a lack of connection or presence with their peers and instructor. A traditional, face-to-face student orientation program limits students' flexibility in attendance and their ability to revisit resources to help prepare for their upcoming studies in a music department or conservatoire. However, providing students with a fully online orientation module (i.e., no face-to-face component) can support students entering a music program with the practical knowledge and skills to successfully navigate the technologies that are commonly used within the program. By building on the knowledge and research-informed practices for developing engaging online orientations, this project set out to design a seven-day online orientation module for music students through Design-Based Research (DBR) methodology.

DOI: 10.4324/9781003041474-6

The research questions that informed the iterative development of the final design framework for the 100% online orientation were: 1) What are essential skills and attributes for music students in the online learning environment? and 2) What activities and resources help support students form self-regulation skills for online learning? Highlighting the practical outcomes from this study, this chapter explores the use of an online orientation developed specifically for music students as an innovation for supporting digital literacy and preparation for students to use technologies in their music learning.

Background Context

To date, the use of online learning for music has been explored around the world. While many higher education music instructors found online music teaching a different teaching approach at the start of the COVID-19 pandemic, there were various music scholars who had been exploring this field since the early 2000s. Furthermore, institutions such as Finland's Sibelius Academy began using forms of distance learning back in 1996 Ruippo (2003). Another early exploration in online music learning involved the Canadian MusicGrid project in the province of Quebec led by Masum et al. (2005).

More recent research by King, Prior and Waddington-Jones explores the implementation of the 2014 Connect ReSound project pilot and its second phase that included a larger national four-region sector of England in 2017. Action research, including interview data, from this longstanding project with 110 students provides insight into a "standard technical set-up" (King et al., 2019, p. 205) when teaching group tuition using the Skype application, identification of technological issues (i.e., time lag and technological problems), and key pedagogical items to consider when teaching tuition online. Further detail on the student learning outcomes resulting from remote community tuition across rural areas in the project are further explored in a comparison between students using a face-to-face tuition model and the online tuition model (King et al., 2019). As the technology for online music tuition became more available across the globe, the feasibility of online music tuition into regional areas of Australia was explored by researchers Stevens et al. (2019) in the iMCM project. Their research considered the potentials of video conferencing technologies for online music tuition using Australia's then-new National Broadband Network (NBN) that brought Internet to rural Australia. Highlighting its potential for future implementation, the researchers also presented necessary technical and pedagogical considerations for such innovations to be successfully adopted in a broader context. While the 2020 pandemic flung many music conservatoires into online teaching, the 2017–2022 Erasmus+ INTERMusic Project (Delle Monache et al., 2024) was well-positioned to share its research knowledge on the challenges and benefits of networked music performance and its experiences of asynchronous music teaching across multiple European conservatoire settings. Together, this brief global overview of online music learning projects highlights that while the technologies may not have been perfected, there was a shared desire to innovate music teaching through online learning technologies.

However, successful innovations in technology-enabled learning environments involve not only technology and teachers. A key consideration as more music departments and faculties move toward regularly using online learning in their programs is the proactive preparation of students with the necessary digital literacy skills and self-regulation skills required when learning online.

Higher Education Orientations

There is an increased need for students to have digital literacy skills (i.e., use of university-specific technology platforms, online communication skills, academic integrity skills, etc.) and basic self-regulation skills (i.e., time management, etc.). The adoption of online classes continues to increase in higher education, yet we cannot assume our online students have the digital literacy skills and self-regulation skills required for learning online. To bridge this divide, research supports the positive outcomes of online student learning success and student retention through the use of online orientations (Lock et al., 2019).

Traditional lecture-style orientations can leave students overwhelmed with the amount of information given during these sessions (Hansen et al., 2009). By incorporating an online orientation that is housed within a learning management system, students have the opportunity to visit and revisit orientation content within a flexible and accessible online learning experience.

While the research literature on the development of online orientations is still nascent, studies have begun to confirm the positive outcomes from the use of daily 15- to 20-minute activities across seven- or ten-day orientation modules (Lock et al., 2020). The brief time commitment prompts online students to take part in low-stakes online activities, reflect on their technology skills, and learn how to prepare to be successful online learners. Seven-day orientation models filled with short 15- to 20-minute daily content learning and activities have been studied previously and found to be positive support mechanisms for education students (Lock et al., 2019; Lock et al., 2017).

The overall goal of an online orientation is to support students (i.e., both face-to-face and online) with flexible and accessible information for accessing university- and discipline-specific resources while providing practical activities to engage students in developing their digital-based skills (e.g., how to create a video, upload a video, take part in a synchronous session). Further, an online orientation can help a student be successfully introduced to the nature of general online learning as they learn to skillfully use an LMS and explore possible technical issues they may encounter while using the LMS. Supported by low-stakes activities, an online orientation can surface students' self-awareness for technology skills needed for their academic discipline within a non-graded environment.

Designed with a particular student audience in mind (e.g., music students), online orientations can help students gain specific digital literacy and technology skills (Cho, 2012). Together, an online orientation provides students with practical digital literacy skills that positively contribute to the development of their personal time management strategies and self-efficacy (e.g., confidence and motivation) in digital technology use.

Key Considerations for Online Music Orientations

As music educators who include technology in our teaching, we can easily assume that our students have the technology skills required for today's music classroom. Prensky (2012) highlighted this assumption when he termed students as "Digital natives" (p. 69). Yet, as noted by Keengwe et al. (2008), our students may use technology for personal purposes (e.g., apps to chat with their friends), but they are not "producers" in terms of using technology to build their learning and knowledge.

Breaking the assumptions of what we think our music students know about technology is an important first step when considering how to create effective online music learning scenarios. Once our assumptions are identified, we are better positioned to provide clearer expectations of the technology our students will encounter in their music learning. The focus of an online orientation is crafted in engaging and low-stakes (i.e., non-graded) learning opportunities that utilize required learning technologies – students learn about their new music school or department while simultaneously becoming acquainted with the technologies they will soon encounter in their music classes.

The use of online orientation is becoming more prevalent in faculties across tertiary institutions. There are two main considerations when developing an online orientation: the overarching design process when creating an innovative work, and the design of the online learning area. Together, these two processes work concomitantly to create and inform a learning experience that produces a design concept as its end result (e.g., an online orientation program).

Adopting an Iterative Design Approach

An iterative design approach that has been used to implement innovation in learning is McKenney and Reeves' (2012) Design-Based Research. Starting with a design prototype, the researcher collects feedback and evaluation from the main stakeholders to use in the next redesign phase of the innovation. Exploring additional literature-informed ideas, the researcher continues to revise the innovation. This iterative cycle (see Figure 4.1) is continued until the design is finalized through to the final new concept.

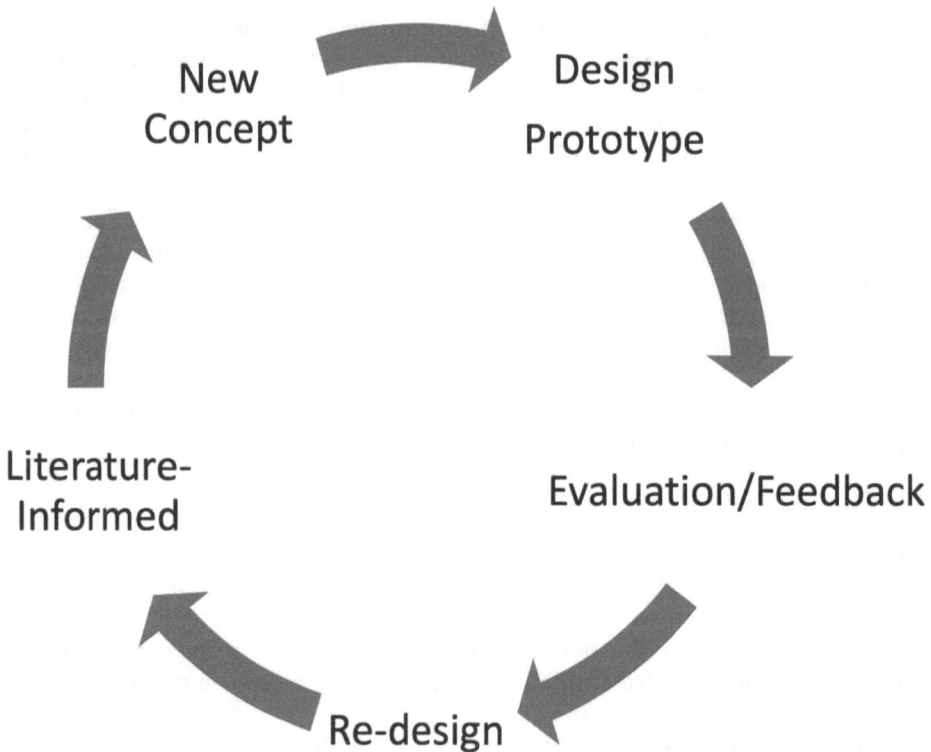

New Concept → Design Prototype → Evaluation/Feedback → Re-design → Literature-Informed → New Concept

Figure 4.1 Design-Based Research Iterative Cycle adapted from the work of McKenney and Reeves (2012).

Frameworks are approaches that can provide guidance for an experience or pathway (Miles et al., 2014). One of the benefits of using Design-Based Research is that it allows for the incorporation of established frameworks to inform both the design prototype and the iterative design approach itself. Given the limited research in online orientations for music students at the tertiary level, it is prudent to construct a prototype through design-based research and a researched-informed framework that is focused on online music learning.

The *Framework for Teaching Music Online* (Johnson, 2022) was developed to support the transformation of tertiary music teaching into the online environment. Centered on the foundations of teaching philosophy, the three main elements of the framework (i.e., design, communication, and assessment) form an iterative process that prompts the instructor to consider how an online course is developed from start to finish. When using the research-informed framework, an instructor is guided through a "continuous cycle of development" (p. 28) that supports social constructivist learning. Specifically, the framework looks to help instructors create online learning experiences that address teaching presence, cognitive presence, and social presence as outlined in the Community of Inquiry framework (Garrison et al., 2000).

Evidencing its function as an iterative design cycle (see Figure 4.2), the three main elements of communication, assessment, and design of *Framework for Teaching Music Online* (Johnson, 2022) provide the course designer with opportunity to construct a learning design that addresses the specific needs of the students within that faculty. For example, when considering the types of assessment design and feedback to use in the online orientation, there is a need to approach the discipline of music through the lens of authenticity. That is, students should be comfortable with using technology tools that can record a music performance or be able to reflect on their own performance abilities as a musician. This has relevance to the orientation, as it suggests students will need to have a familiarity with technological tools

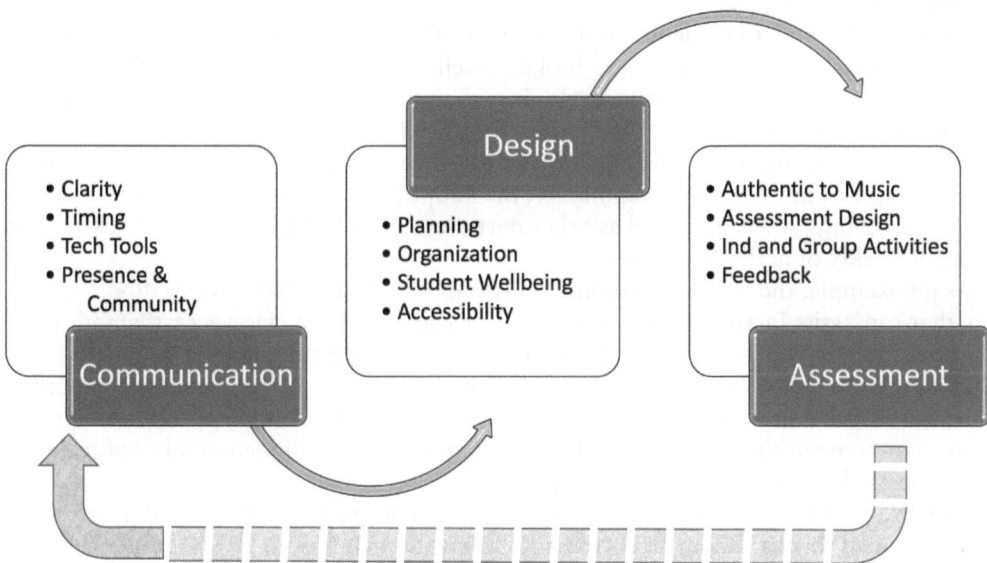

Figure 4.2 Iterative design cycle for the framework for teaching music online.

for recording, as well as sufficient skills for self-reflection. Therefore, surfacing literature regarding authenticity (Koh, 2017) and self-regulation (McPherson, 2022) is paramount for the construction of a supportive online orientation design prototype.

Incorporating Student Voice

Working in tandem with both the Design-Based Research cycle and the Framework for Teaching Music Online, the need to surface student voice as a feedback mechanism on the content and activities is made apparent. That is, the DBR process identifies an evaluation interrogation that ensures the stakeholders (i.e., students) have a voice in the content and activities chosen for inclusion. Further, the design component in the Framework reiterates the need to ensure that the learning content is presented in a way that supports student wellbeing (e.g., flexible access and low-stakes learning activities). The communication component also ensures that the learning is crafted in such a way that the students can develop community through their learning, and that the timing of the content (e.g., amount of participation and activity content required each day) is appropriate for a low-stakes workshop.

Focus on Authenticity, Well-being, and Self-Regulation

As noted in Johnson's (2022) framework, the areas of authenticity, well-being, and self-regulation are key considerations when designing for online music learning. It is of value to explore these aspects when transitioning from a face-to-face teaching environment to an online environment. Briefly, one could use the eight components of authentic assessment as outlined by Koh (2017) to address fundamental areas that ensure learning is authentic to the discipline of music (i.e., authenticity of design). Purposeful alignment with these eight components ensures that assessments developed for an online music class are not only an activity that the student will encounter in their future music career but also something that is assessed in multiple ways over time and through transparent and reliable rubrics or evaluation systems.

Secondly, the area of student and instructor well-being in an online music teaching and learning scenario should not be overlooked. Well-being may be approached in terms of instructor workload hours when developing an online music course, or alternately the amount of reading and activity time required by students to complete their weekly learning modules. Supports for student well-being can include the use of weekly student cohort chats for developing a sense of community, the adoption of video use in discussion areas to support teaching presence, as well as other purposefully embedded informal check-ins with students weekly or across the semester.

As an example, the online environment can support students with translation technologies that can assist in addressing unique student learning needs. However, the addition of more technology components can be disruptive even when offered as a supportive tool. That is, the number of technologies tools required or used in an online class can support student well-being or detract from it. Therefore, implementing design approaches that align to alleviate some of these challenges may include identifying a limited number of technologies to be used across courses or degree program.

Thirdly, the online environment can support students' self-regulation skill development when designed through thoughtful content organization (Johnson, 2017) and need for students' job or family life flexibility (Damon & Rockinson-Szapkiw, 2018). Studies have also identified how integral online music learning can to support disaster planning (i.e., flooding, earthquakes, or other large-scale disruptions) in education (Klingenstein & Hagen, 2013). Together, research identifies that online music learning can support students to engage with "the multiplicity of strategies and the use of self-directed learning to engage with resources, people, and to develop new skills [that] aligns with expected behaviour of people with higher self-efficacy beliefs" (Ritchie & Sharpe, 2021, p. 6) as found in music conservatoires.

Building an Online Orientation for Musicians

The development of an online orientation brings together the knowledge of online learning instructional design, as well as a focused regard for the unique context of the discipline of focus. In their research within online music orientations, Johnson and Binns (2018) identify four key areas to consider when designing and online music orientation. These four key areas include: orientation purpose and objectives; audience; design construction; and content topics. Their visualization of each key area as a square of equal importance to the outcome of the orientation design suggests that an online orientation would limit student learning outcomes if one of these key areas were missing. However, research specific to online music orientations has yet to surface in the literature to support or deny the relevance of these areas within the development of an online music orientation. Therefore, this research project explored the following research questions: 1) What are essential skills and attributes for music students in the online learning environment? and 2) What activities and resources help support students form self-regulation skills for online learning?

Design-Based Process

This study uses the iterative process of Design-Based Research (DBR) to develop a low-stakes, seven-day online orientation learning experience specifically designed for music students in a music conservatorium. As outlined earlier, each iterative phase (see Figure 4.3) is positioned to respond to the survey and interview data gathered directly from students. A design-based research approach (McKenney & Reeves, 2012) supports the use of an iterative approach that not only promotes a final product implementing informed design and redesign by stakeholders but also surfaces a practical design process that can be used by others.

There were four main parts to the design-based project (see Figure 4.3): 1) Scoping review and prototype development; 2) Initial implementation and redesign; 3) Second implementation and redesign; and 4) Final implementation. The findings identified key student engagement activities and technology supports within an asynchronous online class and affirms the assistive support of a four-part iterative online music course design process.

In this research, a four-phase iterative re-design loop, or revision, allowed the researcher to create a prototype (in this case a seven-day fully online orientation), and

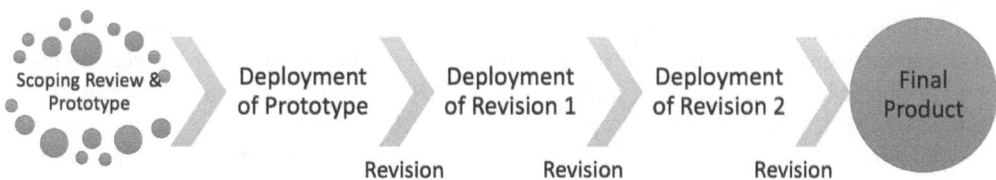

Figure 4.3 Design-based process.

three additional phases that were informed by survey and interview responses from participants who had completed the online orientation module across its various stages. In addition, the prototype and redesign phases of the online modules were designed by adhering to the Framework for Teaching Music Online (Johnson, 2022). This particular focus on the instructional design is addressed in the second section of the chapter. An external online learning expert reviewed the final design for confirmation of design completion.

Students in the conservatorium's Bachelor of Music degree program were invited to participate in the online orientation study via an invitation through the students' regular newsletter. A $50 AUD gift card was given to the 24 students participating at various stages across the project. This study was approved by the university's ethics process.

After taking part in the prototype iteration and/or the three subsequent iterations, students were invited to participate in the study and complete an anonymous 11-question online survey (including three open-ended responses) and take part in 10- to 15-minute semi-structured interviews. For each iteration, statistical survey data was analyzed using quantitative analyses of mean and correlations (Creswell, 2012) and the qualitative responses from both the surveys and interview responses were each thematically and descriptively coded using Miles et al.'s (2014) first and second coding methods.

Scoping Review and Prototype Development

The initial development consisted of completing a scoping review of the literature for online orientations in music (Johnson & Binns, 2018). After the scoping review, a prototype of the online orientation was created with additional ad hoc student input.

The scoping exercise (Johnson & Binns, 2018) outlined four key points for consideration when developing an online orientation for music students: 1) the need for the online orientation to be aligned towards a specific purpose and learning objectives; 2) create the orientation to support your specific student audience, and learning culture; 3) identify the approach to design construction; and 4) include content topics that address relevant issues and common online activities for music students.

Examining the four areas arising from the scoping process resulted in establishing parameters for the online orientation. The purpose of the online orientation was to support the development of music students' digital literacy skills and self-efficacy for using digital technology. This purpose guided each iteration of the development process. The student audience consisted of both undergraduate and graduate music students and therefore meant the orientation would be designed for music performance, music psychology, music performance teaching, and musicology students. All these students were required to use the university Learning Management System (LMS) software, and had common requirements for technology use (e.g., university email, online library resources, text- and video-based computer files, etc.) in their academic and music-based classes.

The online orientation prototype was developed by a researcher with expertise in online music class design. Specifically, the module aligned to the foundations of Universal Design for Learning (Meyer et al., 2014) and was guided by the Framework for Teaching Music Online (Johnson, 2022). Content topics included in the prototype were based upon previous face-to-face orientations with the activities focused on basic functions required for communication (e.g., using Zoom and discussion boards) and assignment activities (e.g., uploading to Dropbox) within the LMS.

Prototype Implementation

The prototype (i.e., Orientation 1.0) offered to participants consisted of a seven-day module that briefly addressed a new topic on each day (see Table 4.1). These topics were based on the parameters identified from the scoping activity and provided participants with an overview about the music campus offerings, identified ways students could develop community and connection during their studies, highlighted general approaches for student well-being, introduced the library and the importance of academic integrity, and provided an overview on how technology is used to support music studies.

The activities for the entire week included: discussion posts, creation of a master calendar activity, taking part in a synchronous video conference, locating a journal article, a self-reflection quiz on personal technology skills, and locating grades and feedback. This allowed one activity to be completed each day, with opportunities to make small additions to the main calendar activity, which was to be submitted on the final day of the orientation.

Participant Feedback

Five participants took part in the online orientation across the third week of Y1 semester 1. They actively participated in the discussion forum activities and submitted examples of the calendars they created for themselves for the final activity. In the prototype, two synchronous sessions were held across the module: one on Wednesday at 12 noon and the other on Saturday at 12 noon. Only one person attended the Wednesday synchronous session held in a Zoom room. No one attended the Saturday synchronous session.

Five out of five participants completed surveys and interviews regarding their experiences with the content and activities within the module. (See Appendix A for Interview Questions.) Feedback in interviews identified the need for minor text edits and clarification of activities (e.g., use of locating a journal article, content on academic integrity, etc.), and requested the inclusion of more information on campus maps, student services, more photos, highlighting more music apps used in classes, and having other options for synchronous video conference times to maximize participation.

Survey feedback identified a positive agreement for module organization and design, and there was unanimous agreement by participants that the module content and activities were a helpful support for preparing students. Specifically, students found the following information beneficial: to use the LMS and increase knowledge on how to use the technology tools, complete an online library search for a research publication, and upload a document to the assignment area. All five participants completed the final calendar creation activity and submission. Participants expressed that at the completion of the orientation module, they

Table 4.1 Initial online orientation content topics.

Day	Topic
Day 1	Welcome and Planning your Semester
Day 2	Preparing for Successful Music Making: Manage Expectations
Day 3	Collaboration and Community
Day 4	Learning at the University Level
Day 5	Using Technologies to Support your Learning
Day 6	Academic Integrity and Assessments
Day 7	Reflections and Moving Forward

had gained additional technology skills through the calendaring activity. This activity was found practical and useful to map out weekly assignments and organize practice routines in a manageable manner.

All comments from the survey responses and the interviews were used to revise the prototype. Once all changes were incorporated, another invitation was posted on the student newsletter for participants to take part in the revised online orientation module.

Revision 1

Between the initial implementation of the prototype and the first revision, the university transitioned to a new LMS. The online orientation allowed students to engage in activities in the new LMS as a pilot before the LMS became fully integrated across all classes. From this perspective, participants in this iteration noted that the online orientation was helpful in orienting them to the new LMS.

The revision (i.e., Orientation 2.0) incorporated more high-quality videos and graphics, as requested by the participants in the previous cohort. The videos were made by the university's videography team. A total of 10 music performance and academic staff were asked to be in the videos, welcome the students, and address a particular topic that was both part of the orientation topics and aligned with their research area. Given the maximum time per day was 10 to 15 minutes of time to watch videos, read text, and complete activities, a maximum of two short (i.e., two- to three-minute) videos were included per day. There was one exception, which was kept to five minutes due to its content regarding library skills and media retrieval.

The shift to the new LMS also made available better website design on the daily landing pages, improved visual placement of text and graphics, and the opportunity to have daily announcements automated to serve as topic overviews and reminders of any upcoming orientation activities.

Participant Feedback

Another invitation was sent out via the student newsletter for interested students to take part in completing the online orientation module version 2.0. There appeared to be momentum growing for students to take the orientation, as 19 students enrolled in the online orientation and completed the activities and tasks. Upon completing the orientation module, students were again invited to complete another round of surveys and interviews. Ten participants completed interviews.

The main challenges students voiced were that they had not encountered the new LMS before; however, it was found that the stepped-out format of the orientation decreased their anxiety about the LMS transition in their upcoming semester for all classes. These challenges addressed the need for students to locate and learn to use the email function within the new LMS.

Overall, interviews identified that the orientation organization was "quite clear" and that the academic integrity section was "very helpful" and "the information about referencing was most helpful." The clarity of design helped students easily navigate the orientation area. The calendar activity was noted by all participants to be a practical activity and enjoyable. Students wanted to integrate on a regular basis for developing their weekly practice routines and organizing their class assignments across the semester.

The academic integrity section was noted as a helpful resource that students needed. One student noted that the highlighting of collusion was effective but wanted to see more offerings for writing workshops and learning how to write for academia.

Students in years other than first year identified that they would have liked to have had the information in the online orientation available to them in their first year. Specifically, the introduction of technologies that students could use, or have available to use, for their music classes was identified as being helpful for those entering first-year classes. Access to the orientation was requested to stay open beyond the orientation week, and across the full length of their program.

Students noted that they found the apps identified in the technology section to be helpful and beneficial for not only their music studies, but their entire campus experience. Specifically, students noted they tried out the apps identified in the orientation module and added many of the apps (e.g., campus map app, metronome app, etc.) to their mobile devices.

Some students noted that because the content topics were only 15 minutes in length, this allowed them to complete two days of content in one sitting. A consensus of how long the orientation should be (i.e., seven days or extended to two weeks) was not achieved. Overall, students identified that they would complete the tasks in the time frame presented as the time commitment was reasonable and easily achievable.

Revision 2

From the 10 interviews and survey responses collected, no major issues were identified. However, the interviews identified minor changes that would create an orientation that was even more finely tuned. These revisions included touch pointing on each web page to ensure hyperlinked text for easier navigation. For example, instead of assuming students would click on an item in a navigation bar, a hypertext link was coded into activity directions, and for words like "Day 1", "Day 2" or "Calendar Activity" for quick linking.

To ensure all links were active and had not changed across the revisions, each link in the orientation LMS shell was verified, and visibility on computers and mobile devices and different operating systems was confirmed. During this update, it was noted that large topic titles for each day were not practical when viewing on mobile devices. Therefore, daily title topics were shortened as outlined in the suggested curriculum outline (see Figure 4.4). Finally, fine-grained aspects, such as outlining specific music software available in the campus computer lab and music recording devices available for student rental, were added to the technology section to provide additional knowledge sharing from the broader faculty (i.e., not limited to the conservatorium) level.

After the third version was completed, another invitation was posted on the student newsletter inviting participants to take part in the online orientation module (i.e., version 3.0).

Final Iteration (Version 3.0)

At this point in the project, all first-year students were given access to the online orientation to support the orientation week that took place prior to the start of a new semester. As per

Day 1	Day 2	Day 3	Day 4	Day 5	Day 6	Day 7
Welcome	Wellbeing & Self-Regulation	Community & Networks	Music Research	Technology Skills	Academic Integrity	Self-Reflection

Figure 4.4 Suggested curriculum topic outline for online music orientation.

Table 4.2 Curriculum design outline for online orientation.

DAY 1	DAY 2	DAY 3	DAY 4	DAY 5	DAY 6	DAY 7
Topic: Welcome	**Topic:** Well-being and Self-Regulation	**Topic:** Community & Networks	**Topic:** Music Learning	**Topic:** Technology Skills	**Topic:** Learning at the Uni level	**Topic:** Self-Reflection
Activity: Discussion Board Introduction	**Activity:** Create a Master Calendar	**Activity:** Join a Synchronous Video Conference	**Activity:** Locate "feedback" in the LMS	**Activity:** Technology Skills Personal Survey	**Activity:** Self-Reflection Quiz	**Activity:** Submit Calendar Screenshot
Video 1.1 Welcome from Leadership Video 1.2 How to Plan your Semester	Video 2.1 Video Tour of Orientation Video 2.2 Supporting your Well-Being	Video 3.1 Building Collaborative Networks Video 3.2 Extending your Community	Video 4.1 Addressing Academic Integrity	Video 5.1 Using Tech in your Learning Video 5.2 Technology Resources Available	Video 6.1 Library Resources	Video 7.1 Finishing Well

the prior iterations, an invitation was posted on the student newsletter inviting participants to take part in a survey or interview following their completion of the orientation (version 3.0).

Only two students opted to complete an interview for this third and final iteration. Comments from these interviews reiterated that the orientation was helpful to students in learning to connect to various communities within the conservatorium, as well as learn about technologies and skills that were expected to be used during upcoming classes. One participant suggested that all students should have to take part in the online orientation, but that it might be challenging to mandate.

Again, the benefit of the calendar activity was identified, along with the usefulness of having the videos and activities short enough that students could complete each as a daily task or together in one sitting. Participants also noted that they did not feel the need to take part in the synchronous session due to already knowing how to use the technology; however, it was described as a helpful activity for students who do not yet know the technology. Locating a day and time to have a synchronous session was deemed to be different for those in various classes and programs and perhaps was best crafted as a choice of two times in the week. The Wednesday and Friday allocation of times were identified as logical.

An external review by an online learning expert was completed on the final iteration. The review outlined that the orientation provided students with activities that were appropriately scaffolded and appropriate for a basic orientation. Further, the review identified that the learning design incorporating Universal Design for Learning (UDL) as exemplified by the use of text, audio, video, and graphics across the entire module along with low-stakes activities engaged the students through multiple approaches.

Results and Discussion

There are three key findings that arise from the design-based research approach. These include key content topics for curriculum map, approaches for information delivery, and participatory learning.

The main finding is the development of the online orientation curriculum map (see Table 4.2). This seven-day curriculum content and activity map addresses the main content areas (i.e., well-being and self-regulation, community and networks, music research, technology skills, academic integrity, and self-reflection). Students found that they were building a community through the process of feedback that promoted student voices (Ung & Rossiter, 2018); the online orientation supported student community and network building. Overall, the content aligns with the objectives of an online music orientation as surfaced in the research of Johnson and Binns (2018).

The content also addresses the need for students to be familiar with the technology and learning tools used in this specific disciplinary program (Johnson & Lock, 2018). Furthermore, the content supports the unique skills required for the specific discipline (see Myers & Ishimura, 2016) and the institutional organization and culture (Labrecque, 2006).

Secondly, there were three learning approaches integrated within the instructional design for successful online orientation development: Authentic Learning, Universal Design for Learning, and Community of Inquiry. Students were given hands-on experience with the common technology tools that they would be required to use in their music practice and overall music learning during their studies. The activities (e.g., using a video conference tool, locating a music research article, and creating a calendar of assignments and practice routines) were authentic learning opportunities; these are common activities within the music classes, as well as common activities for real-world musicians. In addition, the foundations of Universal Design for Learning (Meyer et al., 2014) were used to support multiple approaches for student learning and engagement. Examples of this included the multiple use of text videos and graphics within the learning content, and the opportunities for students to submit their learning activities in multiple formats (i.e., video, text, and/or audio). Finally, delivery of information was set up to support a Community of Inquiry (Garrison et al., 2000). For example, social presence was supported through activities of community building. The clear design and organizational structure of the course content adjusts the element of teaching presence. The use of reflection multiple times across the seven-day orientation further supported cognitive presence.

The third, and final, overarching finding is the activation of participatory learning in an online music orientation. The use of learning through low-stakes activities as evidenced in the research of Lock et al. (2020) was found to be beneficial for the students to take part in the orientation. While not all students who completed the orientation participated in the research, participants in the research identified the low-stakes activities useful and pertinent to their studies. Furthermore, students in their advanced study years indicated that it would have been helpful to have this form of orientation for their first year. The use of discussions, self-reflection surveys, video conference use, and calendar creation were identified as useful approaches within a music studies program. This further underscores an authentic assessment approach (Koh, 2017) and the opportunity for encouraging participatory learning. Finally, the use of explicit expectations and communication organization throughout the learning content and instructor communication was found to encourage learner participation. The use of timely instructor feedback and interaction is further iterated in the research of Lock et al. (2020). Together, these themes outline effective design approaches to consider when developing an online music orientation.

Significance and Future Research

Through the identification of particular content items and module design, online orientations for music students will be more effective tools for addressing self-regulation skills and digital literacy skills for the post-secondary music student. The resulting themes suggest not only how the development of student creativity in higher education can be supported, but it addresses how online orientations can incorporate participatory learning to engage students in low-stakes learning mechanisms.

A key consideration that arises from this research is the importance of supporting the online music orientation project with the personnel to complete the project. This includes the use of a video production team, production assistant, and graphic designer. Finally, the opportunity to have an external expert advisor is a benefit for both the online orientation creator and the students who will be recipients of the orientation learning. The results from this study can be used to support student preparedness in online music courses such as both music performance-based tuition and service-learning classes as described by Pike in her chapter on Instrumental Learning Online (see page 88).

There is opportunity for further research to explore the extent to which each of these specific items can influence a learner's study across the years of their music program, and for the teachers to be involved in long-term training to better position and support the future potential of online music learning. For example, using a longitudinal study, one could explore the impact of online orientations on both student and teacher technology uptake and its consequential influence on their future music performance and music research. In addition, research into which technology tools should be included in the online orientation would be advantageous: for example, investigating the extent to which the use of video recording in practice sessions may impact what technology tools would be most beneficial.

Conclusion

The creation of an online orientation for music students can be a beneficial learning experience for students in their tertiary learning journey. Through use of a Design-Based Research methodology (McKenney & Reeves, 2012) and the inclusion of the Framework for Teaching Music Online (Johnson, 2022), a final design product was surfaced. This curriculum design outline addresses key content topics that support the digital literacy and self-regulations skills of the tertiary student. Together, the use of learning design that includes authentic activities, Universal Design for Learning, and Community of Practice supports student participation and overall engagement in the orientation. As the higher education music sector continues to explore online learning, taking up an online orientation could further support students in their learning journey.

Acknowledgments

This Teaching and Learning project was funded by a University of Melbourne Teaching and Learning Initiative grant.

References

Cho, M. H. (2012). Online student orientation in higher education: A developmental study. *Educational Technology Research and Development*, 60(6), 1051–1069. http://doi.org/10.1007/s11423-012-9271-4

Creswell, J. W. (2012). *Educational research: Planning, conducting, and evaluating quantitative and qualitative research* (4th ed.). Pearson.

Damon, M., & Rockinson-Szapkiw, A. J. (2018). Online and face-to-face voice instruction: Effects on pitch accuracy improvement in female voice majors. In C. Johnson & V. C. Lamothe (Eds.), *Pedagogy development for teaching online music* (pp. 21–44). IGI Global.

Delle Monache, S., Comanducci, L., Sarti, A., & Avanzino, F. (2024). Synchronous online ensemble performance. In C. Johnson & A. King (Eds.), *Music, Technology & Innovation*. Routledge.

Garrison, D. R., Anderson, T., & Archer, W. (2000). Critical inquiry in a text-based environment: Computer conferencing in higher education. *Internet and Higher Education*, 11(2), 1–14.

Habe, K., Biasutti, M., & Kajtna, T. (2021). Wellbeing and flow in sports and music students during the COVID-19 pandemic. *Thinking Skills and Creativity*, 39, 100798.

Hansen, E., Clark, C., McCleish, J., & Hogan, J. (2009). Getting to know you: Development of an RN-to-BSN online orientation. *Journal of Nursing Education*, 48(11), 638–641. http://doi.org/10.3928/01484834-20090828-04

Johnson, C. (2017). Teaching music online: Changing pedagogical approach when moving to the online environment. *London Review of Education*, 15(3), 439–456.

Johnson, C. (2021). A historical study (2007–2015) on the adoption of online music courses in the United States. *International Journal on Innovations in Online Education*, 5(1), 1–20. http://doi.org/10.1615/IntJInnovOnlineEdu.2021037316

Johnson, C. (2022). *A framework for teaching music online in higher education*. Bloomsbury Publications.

Johnson, C., & Binns, G. (2018). Designing online orientations for higher education music students: A proposed framework. In *Open oceans: Proceedings ASCILITE2018: 35th international conference on innovation, practice and research in the use of educational technologies in tertiary education*. http://ascilite.org/past-proceedings/

Johnson, C., & Lock, J. (2018). Making multimedia meaningful: Outcomes of student assessment in online learning. In E. Langran & J. Borup (Eds.), *Proceedings of society for information technology & teacher education international conference* (pp. 1542–1549). Association for the Advancement of Computing in Education (AACE). https://academicexperts.org/conf/site/2018/papers/52476/

Keengwe, J., Onchwari, G., & Wachira, P. (2008). Computer technology integration and student learning: Barriers and promise. *Journal of Science Education and Technology, 17*(60), 560–565. https://doi.org/10.1007/s10956-008-9123-5

King, A., Prior, H., & Waddington-Jones, C. (2019). Connect resound: Using online technology to deliver music education to remote communities. *Journal of Music, Technology & Education, 12*(2), 201–217.

Klingenstein, B. G., & Hagen, S. L. (2013). A case study in online delivery: Boarding the bullet train to an online music degree. In J. Keengwe (Ed.), *Research perspectives and best practices in technology integration*. IGI Publications.

Koh, K. (2017). Authentic assessment. *Oxford Research Encyclopedia of Education.* http://doi.org/10.1093/acrefore/9780190264093.D13.22

Labrecque, K. (2006, April). *Online orientation programs for new students.* For submission to PACRAO. https://view.officeapps.live.com/op/view.aspx?src=http%3A%2F%2Fwww.pacrao.org%2Fdocs%2Fresources%2Fwritersteam%2FOnlineOrientationProgramsforNewStudents.doc

Lock, J., Johnson, C, Hanson, J., Liu, Y., & Adlington, A. (2019). Designing an online graduate orientation program: Informed by UDL and studied by design-based research. In S. Gronseth & E. Dalton (Eds.), *Universal access through inclusive instructional design: International perspectives on UDL* (pp. 250–257). Routledge.

Lock, J., Johnson, C., Liu, Y., Hanson, J., & de Gannes Lange, S. (2017, October 20). Are we designing for online learning success?: A study of an online orientation program. *COHERE (Canada's collaboration for online higher education research).* Presentation proposal for COHERE (Canada's Collaboration for Online Higher Education Research), October 20, 2017, Toronto, ON.

Lock, J., Liu, Y., Johnson, C., Hanson, J., & Adlington, A. (2020). Learning with each iteration of a graduate student online orientation program: A design-based research study. In G. Parchoma, M. Power & J. Lock (Eds.), *The quest for the finest blends of text and voice in blended and online graduate education.* Athabasca University Press. Open Access. https://doi.org/10.15215/aupress/9781771992770.01

Masum, H., Brooks, M., & Spence, J. (2005). MusicGrid: A case study in broadband video collaboration. *First Monday, 10*(5).

McKenney, S., & Reeves, T. C. (2012). *Conducting educational design research.* Routledge.

McPherson, G. (2022). Self-regulated learning music microanalysis. In G. McPherson (Ed.), *Oxford handbook of music performance* (Vol. 1, pp. 553–575). Oxford University Press. https://doi.org/10.1093/oxfordhb/9780190056285.001.0001

Merrick, B., & Johnson, C. (2020). Teaching music online in higher education: 2020 conference report. *Journal of Music, Technology & Education, 13*(1), 95–108. https://doi.org/10.1386/jmte_00018_1

Meyer, A., Rose, D. H., & Gordon, D. (2014). *Universal design for learning: Theory and practice.* CAST.

Miles, M. B., Huberman, A. M., & Saldaña, J. (2014). *Qualitative data analysis: A methods sourcebook* (3rd ed.). Sage.

Myers, A., & Ishimura, Y. (2016). Finding sound and score: A music library skills module for undergraduate students. *Journal of Academic Librarianship, 42*(3), 215–221.

Prensky, M. (2012). *From digital natives to digital wisdom: Hopeful essays for 21st century learning.* Corwin.

Ritchie, L., & Sharpe, B. T. (2021). Music student's approach to the forced use of remote performance assessments. *Frontiers in Psychology, 12*(641667), 1–9. https://doi.org/10.3389/fpsyg.2021.641667

Ruippo, M. (2003). Music education online. *Sibelius Academy, 2*, 1–8.

Schiavio, A., Biasutti, M., & Philippe, R. A. (2021). Creative pedagogies in the time of pandemic: A case study with conservatory students. *Music Education Research, 23*(2), 167–178. https://doi.org/10.1080/14613808.2021.1881054

Stevens, R. S., McPherson, G. E., & Moore, G. A. (2019). Overcoming the "tyranny of distance" in instrumental music tuition in Australia: The iMCM project. *Journal of Music, Technology & Education, 12*(1), 25–47.

Ung, E., & Rossiter, I. (2018). University Library develops app designed for students, by students. *Incite, 39*(7/8), 30–31.

Appendix A
Online Orientation Interview Questions

1) When did you take part in the online orientation?
2) Was the orientation easy to navigate? If not, what design aspects should be changed?
3) How has participating in the online orientation helped you with preparing you for your conservatorium classes and studies?
4) Would you say that being part of the online orientation helped you develop community with other conservatorium students?

   a. If so, what are 2 or 3 ways the orientation helped you develop community?

5) Would you say that being part of the online orientation helped you develop technology skills that you will use or have used in conservatorium classes?

   a. If so, what are 2 or 3 ways the orientation helped you develop these technology skills?

6) Did you have any initial expectations about taking the online orientation? (Yes/No). If yes, how were these expectations met?
7) Did you find it challenging to initially use the technology required to take the orientation? What were the most helpful activities for you in the orientation?
8) Thinking about the content given each day, was there any particular topic you thought was missing and should have been included? What was that and why?
9) Thinking about the activities given each day, were there too many activities? If yes, what were the most important activities to include in the orientation?
10) What, if any, recommendations would you give for re-designing future iterations of the orientation?

Part 2

Perspectives for Teaching

Industry Perspective

Peter Lee and Tim Wilson

As co-founders of the music education software "Auralia" and "Musition", our company story goes back to high school in Melbourne, Australia. In the 1990s, our high school music teachers created cassette-based resources to assist with our music theory and music listening skills. Whilst useful, this method wasn't easily accessible, and the resources could typically only be used once. The different learning needs of individual students were also hard to manage. To pass our music classes, a fellow student (Hamish Moffatt) and I (Peter Lee) developed a little ear training program called 'Auralia'. Early versions of the software would play us intervals, chords, and scales so we could learn how to identify these musical elements as required by the new Victorian Certificate of Education (VCE) syllabus (our end of high school exam curriculum). Being able to practice independently and focus on specific learning areas and personal weaknesses made a huge difference to our development. We passed our music classes with flying colors and founded Rising Software. Shortly thereafter, Tim Wilson joined the team, contributing heavily to new versions of Auralia and the initial development of our theory program, Musition.

While we aren't all full-time professional musicians today, music is still part of each one of our lives. Tim is a saxophonist who has recently performed with Lalah Hathaway, Robbie Williams, as a featured soloist with the Melbourne Symphony Orchestra, and recorded live for ohjazz.tv. Hamish still plays some gigs here and there but is more focused on software development. And Peter still loves to sing classical music and listen to his eclectic mix of CDs (with a large emphasis on pre-1920s!). The merging of technology into our music learning didn't take us away from music; in fact, it ensured that we stayed connected. Today we get to explore music through the creative elements of music playing, curriculum, and music learning. Our love for music and creativity has shaped where we are today as a company and as individuals.

Our involvement with the development of Auralia and Musition certainly shifted our musical journeys and brought with it a deeper awareness of music pedagogy and processes for learning and design development. We travelled around Melbourne with a computer in the back of our parents' car visiting schools, and began to sell a few licenses here and there. As the software evolved, there was a growing interest in the curriculum-aligned ear training and music theory drills that it offered. The programs slowly grew in popularity, and we tentatively stepped into the international arena, attending the NAMM show in the United States with boxed software, hiring a small booth, and working with distributors and resellers.

Our software was then picked up for distribution by Sibelius as part of their educational suite. This helped enormously, giving Auralia and Musition excellent exposure to entirely

DOI: 10.4324/9781003041474-7

new audiences. Subsequent partnerships with other organizations, including MusicFirst and Wise Music, have also been key parts of our journey into the music technology market.

Critical development at that stage involved offering customers a product that was built for multiple platforms – Windows and Mac. Many may recall that Sibelius users at the time were already familiar with having dual platform software – so our cross-platform journey and usability meant we could reach a similar group of customers through Sibelius distribution.

Shifts in Digital Computing

During the 2000s, huge shifts were happening in terms of computing. From our original 1990s computer programming in Visual Basic with distribution on floppy disks, and then to CD-ROMs, the global access to the Internet in the 2000s meant that people could start to work remotely, communicating and collaborating over long distances in a simple manner. This was a profound shift. In terms of music education, the Internet meant that students could access music technology away from school. This freed up computer technology labs, as well as valuable teaching time, and facilitated a much more adaptable learning environment.

The rise of the Internet also enabled accessibility for music educators and students. In particular, the adoption of the web browser meant we could take our software beyond the computer desktop and onto smartphones, tablets, Chromebooks, and beyond. Whilst there are additional challenges in designing apps to run through a browser, it does mean technology can be adapted to suit the unique ways that people choose to consume their software. This means more flexibility and more effective use of time; every person gets to use the platform they are familiar with.

As a niche software company, the development and management tools that emerged during this time also helped us to maintain, improve, promote, and support Auralia and Musition in a way that was not previously possible.

Collaboration

Collaboration is one of the key elements of effective technology design and teaching. In the field of educational technology, you can build a piece of software on your own, but to build a software company in a specialized field, you need to be able to work with a broad network and facilitate conversations to best understand the needs of your audience.

Collaboration is also about workflow. This is about you as the educator being able to assign your students specific tasks, whether they be 10 melodic dictation questions, a four-part writing exercise, or an extended listening response.

The collaboration goes beyond student to student, or instructor to student; it means that educators can interact with the software to create new questions to suit their students as required, as well as integrating or modifying the provided content. Today, educators and students can interact with the software as they sit on the bus or train, completing exercises and reviewing student work on their phones.

Learning becomes profoundly different; efficient workflow leads to more effective use of time. Students can finish an exercise and have it automatically assessed. Gone are the days of completing a four-part writing exercise only to receive feedback from the tutor four to five days later. The doors of learning design, and the opportunities within, have opened wide.

Shaped by (and for) Music Learning

With Auralia and Musition, students can work with content that is appropriate to their learning levels and needs. At the same time, the educator can easily review and examine all student work. From an overall summary of student work through to the detail of the individual notes that a student has entered on a staff; the opportunity to efficiently interact with students and provide specific feedback is very powerful. The design of the software is now more than ever focused on finding creative ways to address the changing (and varied) curriculum needs of music educators, identify effective research-based delivery models and processes, and present the content in a format that is engaging to music students.

But let's be honest: for many students, the desire to complete homework is no different with or without technology. Some students may be motivated to complete more exercises than they've been told, and others may stick to standard assignments (or elect to bypass homework altogether). The tools support all types of learners, allowing students to practice as much as they feel necessary, with unlimited questions and the ability to explore areas not necessarily covered in their core curriculum.

Our work with Auralia and Musition is often driven by the conversations we have with experts in music education, curriculum design, perception, cognition, and technology. We work with high schools and universities in many countries, and we are lucky to interact with people from many different backgrounds. Having prior musical experience is key to being able to design our technology to meet the needs of music learners and to extend the proverbial arm of music instructors through our software.

Together, as cofounders, our musical knowledge, technical skills, and composition and performance backgrounds provide a unique and comprehensive way of being able to address our customer needs through our product development. Our software can respond to student and instructor challenges; we originally developed the programs based on a genuine musical need, and we continually collaborate with teachers, instructors, and students to ensure their relevance.

Designed to Fill a Learning Gap

An ideal learning scenario in music is to have a one-to-one relationship with the music teacher. Whether it's cost, time, or geography, connecting with the music teacher on a one-to-one basis all the time, is close to impossible! Auralia and Musition are not meant to replace a traditional teacher, but simply to provide a support and delivery mechanism. We try to fill the gap in learning feedback and allow people to use their time as effectively as possible.

The software is specifically designed to support any method of teaching. Whilst we include a robust set of curriculum materials, our solution has always been about supporting existing pedagogy, providing tools for teachers to reinforce and extend their teaching methods.

The innovation of music technology for learning means that we can help develop the craft of music making in ways that are flexible, engaging, and effective.

The idea of students being self-directed is now pervasive and is accepted by teachers everywhere, especially since COVID. Staying connected to their teachers and using materials relevant to their school curriculum during this process completes the loop. The innovation of the Internet and personal and portable devices truly allow students to have meaningful learning experiences beyond the classroom walls.

Looking Toward the Future

As we look to the future of Auralia and Musition, there is no shortage of ideas or things to do.

Current AI developments feel like the wild west of innovation in our time. AI is raw, rapidly evolving, and with many reactionary ethical and policy decisions being made as the technology itself unfolds. To some extent, we are only just starting to wrap our heads around the possibilities it may offer, as well as the many implications and potential outcomes for music creation and education.

On some levels, the days of specialized, technical skillsets may be limited, and the modern musician/educator/technologist may need to be able to think more broadly, know how to frame the right questions, and understand larger systems architecture to generate creative outcomes and solutions.

5 Instrumental Learning Online

Pamela D. Pike

This chapter reports on two studies. The first highlights the common findings and practices in synchronous online music instruction, based on a survey of peer-reviewed literature. The second reports on a collective case study of three piano teachers with varying levels of experience in the online lesson environment, teaching private and group piano online for six weeks. Data were triangulated through researcher notes, online lesson videos, lesson plans, student and teacher written surveys and a focus group interview with the teachers. The constant-comparison method identified common themes from each case and across the cases. Discussion relates to the previously and newly identified best practices for online learning, the strengths and weaknesses of current teacher preparation for online instrumental teaching and suggestions for preparing future music educators to teach music online, should they choose to engage in online instrumental instruction.

Introduction and Context for Instrumental Learning Online

Online educational programs grew out of a convergence of distance learning programs (stemming from Europe in the 1840s), technologically facilitated learning via computer mediation, e-learning and electronically assisted learning and the capacity of the Internet to be used for synchronous and asynchronous education (Holden & Westfall, 2008). In general education, Holden and Westfall argue that symmetrical interactions, where "the information flow is evenly distributed between learners and instructors" (p. 11), are equally important for learner outcomes in both the asynchronous and synchronous environments. Symmetrical interactions may include two-way interactions between student-student, student-teacher or student-content (Bernard et al., 2009). As such, symmetrical interactions tend to be more effective because they require the learner to engage with and apply new content during more interactive learning. Talent-Runnels et al. (2006) also note that student-student and student-teacher interactions are particularly effective in online courses.

An important strand of recent literature on online learning at the tertiary level addresses effective instructional design (e.g., Simonson et al., 2019), high-impact practices in online education (Linder & Hayes, 2018) and best practices in supporting the autonomous individual learner in formal online environments, often through varied or new technologies (e.g., Moore & Anderson, 2003; Pauling, 2008). Although adults are considered to be more autonomous than children and many appreciate the convenience of learning at their own pace in asynchronous learning environments (Talent-Runnels et al., 2006), in reality adult learners need appropriate scaffolding and support from highly trained instructors to facilitate their learning and maintain motivation (Wlodkowski, 1999). Indeed, even when inequalities in technology exist among online learners, instructors who know their subject matter

DOI: 10.4324/9781003041474-8

deeply have thought about what students need to learn and structure the learning sequence appropriately help students overcome these disparities (Larreamendy-Joerns & Leinhardt, 2006). Larreamendy-Joerns and Leinhardt (2006) note that in their "performance-tutoring" educational view, where highly structured tasks requiring detailed and timely feedback take place, the online learning platform can be very effective.

Music educators acknowledge there is potential for online learning to grant access to musical information, education and music-making opportunities (Bennett, 2010; Mercer, 2009). Recent studies demonstrate how the Internet is used to facilitate informal music learning and communities of practice (Kruse & Veblen, 2012; Waldron, 2009, 2012; Waldron & Veblen, 2008, 2009), asynchronous or synchronous music instruction (Pike, 2020a) and professional music development (Johnson, 2017; Pike, 2018). Instructional design of online courses (see page XX of Johnson's chapter) is of paramount importance since music learning involves multi-sensory and multiple modalities of learning, in addition to systematic and careful development of complex physical and technical skills. Unlike the experience of quickly moving classes and lessons online during the first months of 2020, instructional design of effective online courses is different than traditional courses and must be planned carefully for online music classes (Johnson, 2022, 2017). The focus of Chapter 8 furthers this exploration in how to frame online music classes for supporting student engagement and learning.

Throughout the world, preservice and in-service teaching are typical components of undergraduate music education programs that prepare students to teach in classroom settings. Instrumental pedagogy programs are less common than music education or performance programs and, in many ways, have fewer curricular elements in common across institutions and may vary depending upon the instrument. However, the National Association of Schools of Music (NASM), a North American accrediting body, recommends that students who earn a Bachelor of Music in pedagogy experience at least two semesters of a supervised teaching internship (NASM, 2020, p. 108). Internship experience is acknowledged as a high impact educational practice (Kuh, 1993) and has been used successfully in instrumental pedagogy curricula, in the synchronous online environment (Pike, 2015a, 2018). Other efficacious projects for meeting supervised teaching standards in online instrumental pedagogy include service-learning projects (Pike, 2017a) and shorter teaching practica, distributed across the music program or curriculum (Pike, 2017a).

Study 1: Best Practices in Online Instrumental Teaching

Method

A search of the research literature was conducted to identify peer-reviewed quantitative, qualitative and practitioner-based articles about online instrumental music teaching. Dissertations and theses were excluded from the search since only blind peer-reviewed articles were considered for this study. The following databases were used: Music Periodicals Database (formerly the International Index to Music Periodicals), EBSCO, JSTOR, APA PsychInfo and Google Scholar. From these searches, non-English manuscripts, reviews or non-empirical reports and articles relating to nonformal, informal or asynchronous online music instruction were eliminated as the purpose of this literature review was to identify teaching behaviors and practices observed in synchronous online instrumental instruction. The reference lists of eligible articles were scoured to identify additional suitable articles that had not appeared during the database searches.

Once obtained, articles were read to identify effective teacher strategies, skills and practices employed in the online environment. Then, each of these studies was read and open coded, using the constant comparison method to identify broad categories of information. Subsequently, axial coding of the initial themes (Scott & Medaugh, 2017) permitted the researcher to create a concept map of emergent themes with respect to teacher practice explored in the research (Creswell, 2012).

A Synthesis of Themes from Peer-reviewed Literature

EFFICACY OF ONLINE INSTRUMENTAL MUSIC LEARNING

In the field of music performance, much work is exploring the possibilities of synchronous online collaborations. Such future collaborations require high-speed Internet2 connections and specialized software to create low-latency audio-visual streaming (LoLa) environments, often only found on the campuses of universities and conservatories. This is discussed more in depth in Chapter 6 regarding audio setup. In terms of large ensemble or general music instruction, music educators (Bennett, 2010 Mercer, 2009; Orto & Karapetkov, 2011) have studied the potential for using high-end video-conferencing platforms such as Polycom, because developers created a music mode and many educational institutions have access to the platform. Challenges of delivering music education using standard technological setups and platforms have also been discussed (King et al., 2019b).

In the realm of synchronous instrumental pedagogy, national institutions in Canada and the United States have done preliminary work using Internet2 and video-conferencing options available to larger organizations (Webster, 2012). Practical research into more accessible online instrumental music lessons, which exemplify the teacher-student and performance-tutoring interactions that are effective online, includes a small number of studies exploring instrumental tuition using specialized technology such as Yamaha Disklavier acoustic pianos, developed in 2011, which enable the instruments to communicate directly with each other and produce the sound on each instrument through MIDI signals (Yamaha, n.d.). Internet MIDI, a software program created by Timewarp Technologies, permits any MIDI-enabled acoustic or digital keyboard to communicate with another, at a more accessible price point. Studies exploring the use of Internet MIDI during synchronous online piano lessons show that students can effectively acquire specific skills (such as sight reading) during synchronous online instruction (Pike & Shoemaker, 2013). Further, they can learn piano as beginners (Pike, 2015b, 2017a) and teacher training in the online environment is feasible (Pike, 2015a, 2015b, 2017a, 2020c).

Although online music software that enables better sound quality for instruments other than the piano is surely being developed, to date, most studies report on instrumental lessons that take place using video-conferencing software. Issues with respect to transmitting high-fidelity musical sound across platforms designed for speaking have been noted (see Chapter 6). The most common challenge is hearing tone quality, dynamic contrasts or musical nuance accurately (Stevens et al., 2019). Platforms that provide better video images, such as Zoom, do allow better sound by enabling "original audio", which permits a wider range of frequencies. Using high-quality external microphones and speakers can improve the sound considerably and carefully placed video cameras permit excellent viewing of the entire body and playing apparatus (Dumluvwalla, 2020; King et al., 2019b). To date, many of the published studies of online instrumental lessons use Skype, which is widely available and free, as their video-conferencing platform (e.g., King et al., 2019b; Kruse et al., 2013).

Researchers recommend leaving the online studio equipment set up in order to expedite lesson preparation and create consistency between lessons (Stevens et al., 2019).

DIFFERENCES IN ONLINE MUSIC INSTRUCTION

There are differences between the private lesson experience in the face-to-face (F2F) and online settings. Most researchers report that it is more challenging to see and interpret student body language online (e.g., Dammers, 2009; Duffy & Healy, 2017). It can be difficult to see student movements or gestures, and there are changes in spatial cues and even loss of peripheral vision in string or woodwind lessons, where the teacher and student typically share a score (Duffy & Healy, 2017). Teachers' inability to annotate students' scores (Duffy & Healy, 2017; Pike, 2015a), physically manipulate students' body positions (Duffy & Healy, 2017; Pike, 2015a, 2017a) or help with assembly of instruments (King et al., 2019b) have been cited as problems, though these can be leveraged to enable more student autonomy (King et al., 2019b; Pike, 2015a, 2015b).

Changes in communication during the lesson are frequently cited. Less experienced teachers tend to talk more in online lessons and use their language imprecisely (Pike, 2015a). More expert online instrumental teachers talk less and provide musical demonstrations more frequently than some F2F teachers (Orman & Whitaker, 2010; Pike, 2020c). Back-channeling and side coaching, typical F2F lesson behaviors where teachers and students talk and gesture while the other plays, are not possible online (Pike, 2020c) or happen less frequently (Duffy & Healy, 2017). Possibly the most important communication difference in online lessons is the inability of teacher and student to play together in real time due to latency (e.g., King et al., 2019b; Stevens et al., 2019). While fewer researchers have studied online lessons with young children, Comeau et al. (2019) compared Suzuki lessons taught to five- and six-year-old students. They found that the teacher directed comments to the parents in the online lessons as opposed to directing comments to the students, even when parents were in the room, during F2F lessons. Fortunately, musical and nonmusical interactions during online instrumental lessons improve with experience (Stevens et al., 2019).

POSITIVE ATTRIBUTES OF EFFECTIVE ONLINE INSTRUMENTAL TEACHING: INSTRUCTOR AND STUDENT BEHAVIORS

An important attribute of synchronous instrumental lessons is access to qualified teachers (Dammers, 2009; Pike, 2020b). Teachers who have highly developed information and communication technology (ICT) skills are more successful instructors in the synchronous online environment (Ruippo, 2003). Prior to commencing lessons, effective teachers introduce students to the technology, demonstrate appropriate set up of cameras, monitors and/or computers to enable the best view of the student and have prepared contingencies, should there be a technological glitch during a lesson (Dammers, 2009; Pike, 2020c). One study revealed that although the length of online and F2F lessons is identical, the duration of in-lesson playing and educational activity is longer in the online environment since students arrive online ready to play, rather than wasting time setting up books and instruments, which bookend F2F lessons (Comeau et al., 2019). Additionally, both teacher and students engage in less off-task behavior in online lessons (Comeau et al., 2019; Dye, 2016; Orman & Whitaker, 2010).

To date, most published research explores student and teacher behavior during online lessons. Behaviors recorded by researchers that are comparable with teacher traits in F2F lessons include: asking questions to test student knowledge (King et al., 2019a), asking questions to direct student listening and self-evaluation (Pike, 2020c), providing information, instructions or practice directions (Comeau et al., 2019; King et al., 2019a; Pike, 2020c), giving evaluative feedback (King et al., 2019a; Pike, 2020c), demonstrating or modeling (Comeau et al., 2019; King et al., 2019a; Pike, 2020b, 2020c) and students playing or singing (Comeau et al., 2019; Dammers, 2009; Dye, 2016; Orman & Whitaker, 2010; Pike, 2020b, 2020c). Among researchers who report the percentage of lesson time devoted to students playing or singing (i.e., performing), teachers who are newer to the online medium talk more, model less and have the students play less than their F2F counterparts (Dye, 2016; King et al., 2019a; Pike, 2015a). More experienced online instrumental teachers appear to engage students in performance just as much as or more than comparable F2F lessons (Dammers, 2009; Pike, 2020c) and eye-contact and focus are increased in the online environment (King et al., 2019b; Orman & Whitaker, 2010). In their small study, Comeau and colleagues (2019) found that while the overall duration of teacher talk was similar between F2F and online lessons, the online teacher interrupted the playing less frequently to talk, though this may have been attributable to differences in learner personality.

INTRODUCING INSTRUCTORS TO ONLINE LESSONS AND TRAINING THEM TO TEACH ONLINE

Teachers who are new to teaching online express initial concern or trepidation about the ability to teach effectively online, but they quickly overcome such fears and accommodate for differences in the environment (King et al., 2019a, 2019b; Pike, 2017a). In general education, providing online teachers with teaching experiences each semester that gradually culminate in extended preservice teaching is effective (Dell et al., 2008). To date, little has been published about preparing instructors to teach instruments online. Pike (2015a) guided undergraduate piano pedagogy students through a series of online video critiques prior to an online peer-teaching practicum. Subsequently, she used directed readings, video observations with written reflections and class discussions for four weeks to prepare graduate piano pedagogy students for a service-learning online teaching internship (Pike, 2017a).

Once pedagogy students begin teaching online, access to video recordings for reflection and timely feedback from faculty are imperative, as poor teaching is magnified online (Pike, 2017a, 2017b, 2020a). As the technology becomes more transparent during online lessons, focus groups and debriefings with pedagogy students may help to avail them of beneficial pedagogical technology tools (Pike, 2020c). Novice teachers need help with creating and delivering a suitable curriculum online, which includes practice and feedback with learning objectives, scaffolding of concepts and fixing mistakes from a distance (Pike, 2015a, 2017a). Practice with providing concise demonstrations, demonstrating adequately and empowering students to become more autonomous should also be explored in instrumental pedagogy classes to prevent common pitfalls in online teaching (Comeau et al., 2019; Duffy & Healy, 2017; Johnson, 2017; Pike, 2017a).

Discussion: Training Future Online Instrumental Teachers

The result of the literature study suggests there are ample opportunities for exploring the training and approaches for future online instrumental teachers. As online technology improves and becomes more ubiquitous in daily life and in schools, and online learning is an accepted form of music instruction, particularly in smaller schools and communities where expert teachers do not live, tertiary music educators must respond by training future educators to teach online. Secondary and tertiary institutions and music organizations will likely be charged with improving access to music-making opportunities for students of all ages. For potential students who are bound by place, without access to high-quality instrumental tuition, having a cadre of teachers trained to work with students online will permit timely implementation of new ventures and projects as funding becomes available. Based on the related literature, there is a need to create and study a pilot online teaching curriculum within the framework of a typical instrumental pedagogy program at both the undergraduate and graduate levels. By sharing subsequent findings and testing these more broadly in several countries and on various instruments, we can begin to codify an online instrumental pedagogical practice for teacher training.

The following strategies might be included in such a curriculum: engaging in critical readings and examination of scholarly articles; planning online instrumental curricula and adapting teaching techniques for online lessons; finding new ways to observe and listen to student performance during lessons (and asynchronously); practicing giving concise feedback that is effective online; modeling and demonstrating effectively; and preparing potential students to work in the online lesson medium. Novice online teachers could be encouraged to develop online teaching skills through peer-teaching experiences, which highlight teaching flaws and deficiencies, before engaging in longer-term online service-learning and internship teaching projects. Key effective practices suggest that online teaching should be recorded and followed up with timely written reflections from the teaching intern and supervising instructor. Ideally, peer reflections and focus groups can debrief interns about the teaching, student learning and technology usage. Such student-student and teacher-student interactions permit optimal student engagement and learning. Institutional support, including adequate faculty load and student credit for online teaching preparation, technology support and facility maintenance will be critical for successful online pedagogy projects and programs. Blending online experiences into traditional pedagogy programs is critical, since tertiary students need to know how to teach online both before and immediately upon graduation.

In short, researchers have identified the efficacy of teaching instrumental music online, and they have surfaced some important differences from face-to-face lessons. Positive attributes of online lessons have emerged, including encouraging student outcomes. Effective instructor behaviors and skills in the online medium have been identified, yet there is a need for more systematic and effective instructor preparation for teaching synchronous online instrumental lessons.

Study 2: Training Teachers for Teaching Online

The purpose of this second study was to explore the experiences of teachers during a six-week online piano teaching practicum. For this collective case study, three experienced piano teachers who were enrolled in the final semester of a graduate-level piano pedagogy course sequence, were recruited and agreed to teach piano students online. They were each assigned three sections of group piano and three individual students to teach remotely. The teachers and students were chosen through convenience sampling, as the teaching assignments reflected their graduate teaching duties. Following a short period of study and training for online teaching, the instructors prepared lesson plans (with the assistance of the researcher) and asynchronous tutorials (videos and Power-Points) together. They loaded all prepared tutorials, practice assignments, self-reflection assignments and evaluation rubrics into the Learning Management System (LMS) and taught piano online for six weeks.

Methodology

Data gathered during the study included: written reflections from the teachers, weekly focus groups with the researcher where online teaching concerns and opportunities were explored, individual meetings with the researcher to discuss their experiences and brief written student evaluations at the end of the online learning experience. Data were triangulated through the aforementioned lesson plans, asynchronous tutorial materials, written reflections, transcripts and notes from individual and group interviews and student evaluations. From these, the constant comparison method (Creswell, 2012) was used to identify and code themes for each individual teacher case. Member checks were performed to ensure accuracy of interpretation of the data (Creswell, 2012; Stake, 2005). Then, the cases were compared to categorize the themes using an axial coding strategy, a typical approach with the constant comparison method (Scott & Medaugh, 2017).

Participants

The teachers for this project were graduate teaching assistants who were teaching as part of their graduate teaching assistantship, so there was no additional teaching load. However, the preparation burden did increase in the online environment. All students and teachers agreed to participate in the project and institutional research protocols were followed. The teachers had varying levels of experience and comfort with the online medium for music instruction but were eager to teach piano online. Pseudonyms are used throughout this chapter to maintain the anonymity of the study participants.

Angela had never experienced online music instruction, either as a student or as a teacher, though she was keen to learn. She was technologically savvy and not intimidated by the prospect of teaching piano online. Candace had never taken online piano lessons, though she participated in an eight-week online teaching internship using Disklavier acoustic pianos five years earlier. During the prior internship, Candace spent one month preparing to teach online by reading specified articles, participating in class conversations about the distance teaching research, observing and discussing online teaching and writing detailed reflections of five synchronous online piano lesson videos (Pike, 2017a). Throughout the teaching first internship, Candace prepared thoroughly and learned to talk less, explain concepts succinctly, prioritize teaching skills and activities during the lesson, react to real-time student technical problems and create asynchronous materials for her students to use outside of the lesson. She assimilated many of these teaching skills into her face-to-face teaching during the intervening years. However, during that time she neither used asynchronous online materials with her traditional students nor taught synchronously online. Initially, Ann was resistant to the idea and efficacy of synchronous online teaching, but she was curious to learn more about it. In order to experience online lessons firsthand, she took 10 weeks of online piano lessons (using digital pianos and Internet MIDI) during the semester prior to this research project (Pike, 2020c). During her 10 weeks as a synchronous online piano student she overcame pre-lesson apprehensions, learned to use the teaching technology, improved her piano skills, experienced typical lesson behaviors and acknowledged learning benefits due to appropriate pedagogical use of the music technology.

The online students in the study were undergraduates at the university, and all had studied with their teachers previously. The teachers were assigned to classes and students with whom they were familiar so that they would not have to develop rapport in the online environment, which can be challenging for novice teachers online (Duffy & Healy, 2017; Pike, 2015a, 2017a). Because they understood the various learning styles of the students and the dynamics of each group already (Pike, 2017b), they could focus on adapting and developing online teaching strategies during the study.

ASYNCHRONOUS AND SYNCHRONOUS TEACHING TOOLS

Each teacher participated in online teaching modules in prior pedagogy classes (these are embedded throughout the pedagogy curriculum) wherein they attended online teaching webinars, observed online teaching videos, read related literature and created asynchronous technique videos and PowerPoint tutorials. Immediately before their online teaching practicum, they wrote lessons plans and shared them with the researcher and one another for feedback. They created portals for their students in Moodle (version 3.1), the campus-wide LMS. They each created and shared asynchronous playing videos to demonstrate and explain piano skills including technique, harmonization, sight reading and to introduce new repertoire. The researcher provided feedback on the initial asynchronous videos and online workspaces so that new ideas could be implemented in future videos and PowerPoint tutorials. The researcher was available to help troubleshoot throughout the study, but the teachers were empowered to problem solve and find creative solutions together.

While the ideal synchronous learning environment for pianists includes digital instruments or MIDI-enabled acoustic pianos that can communicate directly with each other via specialized software (Pike, 2015b), for this study, the teaching did not employ such sophisticated technology. The reasons for this decision were twofold: first, there was no funding to purchase the requisite software for each student participating in the online lessons, and second, most students who enroll in online lessons will not have access to specialized piano software, so this created a more realistic online teaching environment. Thus, during the study the teachers met with their students synchronously using the Zoom video-conferencing platform, which was freely accessible to the teachers and students.

The technology used for the online lessons was relatively modest and readily available to everyone involved. The teachers each taught from high-quality digital keyboards since they had access to these throughout the day. The students used either portable keyboards, digital pianos or acoustic pianos, depending on which instrument was available during their class or lesson time. Two of the teachers connected to Zoom through iPad Pro tablets and the third used a Macbook Pro computer. The students connected to Zoom via three convenient devices: laptops, tablets or mobile phones. No one used external speakers to improve the sound. The teachers worked with each class and individual synchronously once per week for six weeks. Since the sound quality was not optimal, students submitted video recordings of repertoire and many other assignments via the LMS Kaltura feature, YouTube links or Dropbox. Evaluative feedback was provided to students verbally during synchronous meetings and in written form. Additionally, students were encouraged to evaluate their own playing prior to submitting their videos.

Discussion and Findings: Common Themes

Eight themes were identified from the case study. These themes highlight common experiences of the teachers, though two of the themes touch on aspects of student engagement and learning that emerged from the study. Each of these themes is explored in more detail here.

PREPARATION FOR ONLINE TEACHING

Although each of the teachers in this study had prepared at least one asynchronous tutorial per semester (for at least two semesters) and had read reviews and articles about the use of software and useful apps for online teaching in pedagogy classes, each reported that they would have liked more training in this area prior to the online teaching experience. The tutorial and technology assignments in their prior pedagogy classes were authentic-context learning activities (Paul et al., 2001), intended to be applicable to future real-world online teaching. However, perhaps because these weren't applied in a learning context immediately upon creation, the teachers appeared not to have recognized the previously developed competency.

Interestingly, although this online teaching was intended to serve as a capstone to each teacher's online teaching preparation, and the teachers taught relatively well in this medium, the teachers each lamented about the relative lack of online teaching exposure before the six-week study (recall that two had experienced several weeks of online teaching or learning). They seemingly missed the purpose of the intensive online practicum, which was to gain needed supervised experience through regular online instruction and reflective pedagogical practice (Pike, 2017a, 2018).

COMMUNICATION AND STRATEGIC PLANNING

Experienced online educators recognize the importance of careful preparation of the LMS, design and management of all course content prior to the teaching experience (Johnson, 2017; Lock, 2020) and the need to communicate regularly and strategically with students between synchronous learning experiences (Merrick, 2020). Although these topics were explored and discussed in pedagogy classes and in the weeks leading up to the online teaching venture (as well as during the study), the teachers underestimated the importance of pre-teaching planning. Perhaps because they had taught the curriculum previously, they did not appreciate fully the many differences in online curriculum design and instruction, including the numerous communication interventions that were needed. Their lived experience of teaching online, in both group and private settings, for six weeks drove this point home for the teachers. Each noted how they had underestimated the extent and frequency of using various kinds of communication tools to ensure optimal student engagement. During the course of the study, they created more tutorials, assignments, learning memos (Pike, 2020c) and text or email messages than they had planned prior to beginning the online teaching.

PRIORITIZE MEANINGFUL ACTIVITIES FOR THE STUDENTS AND ENSURE ENGAGEMENT

Each teacher noted that the online environment forced her to reassess the curriculum, including course design, learning objectives and student outcomes (Johnson, 2022). The teachers remapped the content, changing lesson pacing and sequencing of the learning activities. They used between-lesson practice assignments to ensure ongoing practice and engagement with the piano and to motivate students to process and practice the new skills on their own. Grading the additional assignments was reported as time-consuming but valuable for student learning outcomes.

TUTORIALS AND ASYNCHRONOUS SUPPORT

Because the teachers had taught the group piano curriculum and repertoire used in this study previously, they were able to readily identify specific content requiring additional explanation. Thus, they were strategic when creating the asynchronous tutorials. They created tutorials for concepts with which students typically struggled and they homed in on critical technical skills that students needed to develop throughout the learning sequence. Most of the tutorials they created were short videos that included verbal explanations and playing demonstrations. In hindsight, they recognized that more PowerPoint tutorials, including both text and voice narration, would have helped some students and engaged more reflective observer-type students (Kolb, 2015; Pike, 2017b). They acknowledged that more tutorials would have been useful and they needed to improve strategies to increase asynchronous student engagement with the valuable content.

ENERGY, TIME COMMITMENT AND TEACHER LIMITS

All three teachers were astonished at the amount of physical, mental and emotional energy it takes to teach an instrument online, despite having read about or witnessed this during previous online teaching and learning experiences. In line with previous research (Dumluvwalla, 2020; Kirk, 2020; Pike, 2020a, 2020b), the poor piano sound quality resulting from the video-conferencing platform required extra effort to discern subtle visual cues on the screen and additional preparation was physically and emotionally draining. While participants felt that they had come to know each of their students better as pianists, musicians, learners and human beings, they identified as exhausted at the end of their experiences. Perhaps if they had not been taking their own graduate classes on top of the online teaching, they would have found suitable strategies for decompressing, relaxing and coping with the fatigue of online teaching (Cornett, 2020). Because their own teaching and learning loads had not changed from earlier in the semester–only teaching in the online setting had changed–they were able to attribute the fatigue to the additional responsibilities of teaching piano online.

PEER SUPPORT AND COMMUNITY-BUILDING DURING THE TEACHING

Sharing of asynchronous resources, co-creation of some materials and collaborative preparation prior to and during the project was evident. While each teacher created different video tutorials for the course, they jointly agreed upon the objectives and overall structure of each tutorial. Once the initial design for each tutorial had been planned, they met to offer feedback and suggestions and even helped each other film some of the videos. The quality and content of the tutorials improved as a result of the co-constructed knowledge generated in these peer-peer, socio-constructivist interactions and collaborations (Johnson, 2017; Palloff & Pratt, 2005).

Additionally, the teachers met regularly, without the researcher, to discuss their individual synchronous online student-teacher experiences and to share ideas to improve their teaching practice. These peer-peer meetings were beneficial from an educational standpoint because the learning was symmetrical, where they learned from and with each other (Holden & Westfall, 2008; Pike, 2015a) and they were creating a community of practice. There were emotional benefits of these meetings, too. Meeting to reflect upon shared challenges and opportunities that they were experiencing in the online medium alleviated feelings of isolation and promoted connectivism (Irwin & Coutts, 2020 Vas et al., 2018). It is doubtful that a teacher going through this intensive online teaching experience alone, without peer support, would have attained the deep teaching and personal meaning that these teachers reported.

POSSIBILITY OF DEEPER STUDENT LEARNING

Although the purpose of this research was to explore the experience of the teachers during the six-week online piano teaching study, student evaluations, comments and grades were gathered to triangulate the data. The teachers and researcher noted that the students covered less material during the six-week online teaching experience than they normally do during the same six-week period in F2F lessons. Yet, consistent with previous research (Pike, 2015b), the teachers reported that the learners were fairly autonomous, assignments were prepared more thoroughly and accurately and the learning of core concepts and competencies appeared to be deeper. Overall, individual and mean student grades during the six-week online teaching period were reported as being higher than they had been earlier in the semester. The teachers speculated that the students took more time and care with preparing recorded repertoire and playing assignments and that the asynchronous listening assignments improved students' ability to self-assess, evaluate and improve their practicing–hallmarks of deep and reflective learning (Dillon & Greene, 2003).

PEDAGOGY PROJECTS FOR PREPARATION

Since creating authentic-context learning activities (Paul et al., 2001) that gradually lead to the online teaching experience (Dell et al., 2008) is important for teacher development, the teachers were asked to comment on possible pedagogy projects that might be useful for future teaching interns. The participating teachers indicated that creating tutorials and exploring apps, software and programs useful for online instrumental teaching would be valuable projects. They noted that practicing online teaching in small segments would be a useful pedagogy class project prior to the extended six-week online teaching practicum or internship. As noted earlier, the teachers had, in fact, engaged in such authentic-context projects in previous pedagogy classes. Although they wished they had more such experiences, it is not clear where these could be incorporated in the existing pedagogy curriculum.

Implications and Recommendations for Educational Training of Online Instrumental Teachers

Music educators should consider how to respond to students' current and future needs, particularly with respect to online instrumental teaching and learning. Based on the findings from the two studies in this chapter, implications and recommendations for teacher training are explored.

The purpose of music education and instrumental pedagogy programs is to prepare future educators to work with many types of learners in increasingly diverse settings. Although online courses are common at the tertiary level, most future music teachers are not trained to teach online. Nevertheless, it should be expected that more adults and parents of children will choose online music instruction for its convenience and accessibility to qualified instrumental teachers. In general, preservice teachers rarely develop skills that are necessary for teaching online (Muilenburg & Berge, 2015). Challenges facing teacher educators include lack of institutional support for online practica, rapidly changing technology, few examples of outstanding online instruction to serve as models and a steep learning curve for inexperienced teachers. However, ignoring the fact that future teachers will likely have to teach online should no longer be an option in music programs.

Teacher discomfort (including initial apprehensiveness, extra workload, embracing adaptive teaching practices and experiencing exhaustion) with the six-week teaching practicum reported in this chapter illustrates how challenging it is to teach instrumental lessons online, even with small projects (included throughout the pedagogy curriculum) that prepare for teaching success in this environment. Novice online teachers will likely experience a steep learning curve with prolonged forays in the new teaching medium. In general, young professional musicians and teachers experience anxiety when first teaching/performing and may lack appropriate coping strategies to deal with normal apprehension and concern of the unknown (Zhukov, 2019). Thus, instrumental pedagogues might consider specific strategies on how to prepare teaching interns for possible natural initial discomfort with online teaching and how to help teachers lean into and grow by using thoughtful reflective practice during situations that push them beyond their comfort level.

Case studies are not generalizable (Dillon & Greene, 2003), and as such these three teachers may have demonstrated a unique phenomenon when they didn't recognize the full value in the exposure to online teaching technology, tools and strategy development in previous pedagogy classes. However, since most research points to the value of distributed learning over time, educators might explore ways to make the authentic-context activities, which are distributed over time, more meaningful and recognizable. Reflective practices such as *Students as Partners* (Coutts, 2019) or transformative reflection and collaboration projects (Carey et al., 2016, 2018) may become important features of preparation activities prior to prolonged online instrumental teaching experiences and internships.

While teachers understand the rationale and uses for possible tools that create online learner engagement–from a declarative knowledge standpoint–the lived experience of teaching students online through a multi-week internship or teaching project develops procedural knowledge. These approaches may effectively support online teachers to discover the true importance of ongoing student engagement. The teachers studied in this chapter taught young adults in a music program with varying levels of motivation to study piano. These differences encouraged teachers to test and find verified ways of keeping the students engaged in their piano practice between synchronous lessons. It is likely they will use these skills with their future younger piano students as well.

The teachers in this study were exposed to apps and teaching technology in their pedagogy classes to prepare them for online teaching. Indeed, their prior classes involved the creation of asynchronous tutorials and exploration of teaching technology relevant for pianists. Budgetary constraints in the school of music and the pedagogy program precluded a broader survey of teaching technology, software and apps; however, these products change rapidly. More importantly, as new products are brought to market and teachers' online instructional needs evolve, teachers should be able to assess the value and viability of emerging products and learn to use them effectively due to their exposure to products and deeper experiences with several educational tools. Rather than using expensive pianos and technology available only in institutional settings, the purpose of this particular intensive online teaching practicum was to engage the teachers with a readily accessible video-conferencing platform, an open-source LMS, and piano students working under real-world circumstances. In this regard, the project was a success.

The online practicum described in this chapter was a capstone project. However, the teachers who had prior experience with online teaching (i.e., Candace) and online lessons (i.e., Ana) may have experienced benefits even greater than those reported, had the six-week teaching experience occurred closer to their previous encounters with online teaching and learning. Future educational researchers might explore timing of key online projects and experiences, within a broader pedagogy curriculum. The amount of energy and preparation time required, and potential fatigue experienced with teaching music online, needs to be acknowledged and teaching interns need to plan for such demands since online teaching opportunities are beneficial learning experiences. This extended online teaching practicum met several of the criteria of high-impact practices in online teaching and learning (Linder & Hayes, 2018): the teaching activity was an internship that included personal reflection and feedback from an expert supervisor and peers, it included collaborative learning experiences among peers and it was a capstone project for the teachers (Linder & Hayes, 2018; Pike, 2018). Indeed, the teachers in this study reported that the six-week online teaching experience was extremely valuable, and it increased their online teaching skills.

However, an administrative and curricular consideration emerged. While fitting this particular online practicum into the pedagogy curriculum was possible, it was extremely taxing on the teachers as it required more time, energy and effort than a similar F2F pedagogy practicum. Therefore, curriculum coordinators and administrators need to ensure that ample course credit is given for online internships, practica or service-learning projects. Instructors and supervisors of teacher educators should carefully consider the amount of time that teaching interns will need to devote to preparation, teaching, reflection and feedback and curtail other course activities or recommend lighter course loads during semesters when intensive online teacher training occurs.

Finally, peer learning and shared communities of practice surfaced as an important theme of this study. Research in online learning environments (Palloff & Pratt, 2005, 2007) and internships in other fields (Goldsmith & Martin, 2009; Low, 2008) support this finding. When there is not a suitable cohort of peers for learning support, instructors can engage in reflection on practice and reflection-in-action (Schön, 1987), transformative learning practices including student and teacher reflection (Carey et al., 2018) or create meaningful projects that will be explored together with an internship team (Pike, 2018) to help teaching interns improve and consolidate their online teaching practice. If the first online teaching experience occurs with experienced instrumental teachers within a community or school setting, support, mentoring and reflection from colleagues, peers and online teaching experts can increase online teaching competency (King et al., 2019a; Pike, 2020b).

Conclusion

Although research needs to continue, there is already a body of knowledge about the benefits of online music study, the best practices of excellent online instrumental teachers and a promising small body of research exploring how teachers can develop effective online teaching skills. With the ubiquity of online learning, an increased awareness of the need for greater accessibility to music lessons and a recognition that online music study can fill some of the existing gap, instrumental music teachers need to develop competency in teaching music online. Researchers have raised awareness of the similarities and differences between online and face-to-face music lessons and have demonstrated opportunities, benefits and drawbacks to online instrumental tuition. Now, tertiary music educators need to explore how teachers are trained for a future that is already here. Researchers and practitioners in the music community might share and explore how instrumental pedagogy curricula are being adapted to meet this need and how online teaching modules are implemented into undergraduate and graduate programs. Cases of successful online practica and internship experiences might be collected so that educators can develop a shared practice of effective teacher preparation for online instrumental music teaching.

References

Bennett, K. (2010). A case study of perceptions of students, teachers and administrators on distance learning and music education in Newfoundland and Labrador: A constructivist perspective. *Canadian Music Educator, 52*(2), 48–49.

Bernard, R. M., Abrami, P. C., Borokhovski, E., Wade, C. E., Tamim, R. M., Surkes, M. A., & Bethel, E. C. (2009). A meta-analysis of three types of interaction treatments in distance education. *Review of Educational Research, 79*(3), 1243–1289. https://doi.org/10.3102/0034654309333844

Carey, G., Coutts, L., Grant, C., Harrison, S., & Dwyer, R. (2018). Enhancing learning and teaching in the tertiary music studio through reflection and collaboration. *Music Education Research, 20*(4), 399–411. https://doi.org/10.1080/14613808.2017.1409204

Carey, G., Harrison, S., & Dwyer, R. (2016). Encouraging reflective practice in conservatoire students: A pathway to autonomous learning. *Music Education Research, 19*(1), 99–110. https://doi.org/10.1080/14613808.2016.1238060

Comeau, G., Lu, Y., & Swirp, M. (2019). On-site and distance piano teaching: An analysis of verbal and physical behaviours in a teacher, student and parent. *Journal of Music, Technology & Education, 12*(1), 49–77. https://doi.org/10.1386/jmte.12.1.49_1

Cornett, V. (2020). Mental and emotional well-being in the time of COVID-19. *Piano Magazine, 12*(2), 49–54.

Coutts, L. (2019). Exploring partnerships: A students as partners pedagogical approach for fostering student engagement within an academic music course. In P. D. Pike (Ed.), *The musician's career lifespan: Proceedings of the 22nd international seminar of the ISME commission on the education of the professional musician (CEPROM)* (pp. 121–140). ISME. https://www.isme.org/other-publications/proceedings-ismes-ceprom-commission-2018

Creswell, J. W. (2012). *Qualitative inquiry and research design: Choosing among the five approaches*. Sage.

Dammers, R. J. (2009). Utilizing internet-based videoconferencing for instrumental music lessons. *Update: Applications of Research in Music Education, 28*(1), 17–24. https://doi.org/10.1177/8755123309344159

Dell, C. A., Hobbs, S. F., & Miller, K. (2008). Effective online teacher preparation: Lessons learned. *MERLOT Journal of Online Learning and Teaching, 4*(4), 601–610. https://jolt.merlot.org/vol4no4/dell_1208.htm

Dillon, C., & Greene, B. (2003). Learner differences in distance learning: Finding differences that matter. In M. G. Moore & W. G. Anderson (Eds.), *Handbook of distance education* (pp. 235–244). Lawrence Erlbaum Associates, Publishers.

Duffy, S., & Healy, P. (2017). A new medium for remote music tuition. *Journal of Music, Technology & Education, 10*(1), 5–29. https://doi.org/10.1386/jmte.10.1.5_1

Dumluvwalla, D. (2020). Striving for excellence in online piano pedagogy: Characteristics of expert teachers using the video-conferencing format. *Piano Magazine, 12*(2), 15–18.

Dye, K. (2016). Students and instructor behaviors in online music lessons: An exploratory study. *International Journal of Music Education, 34*(2), 161–170.

Goldsmith, L., & Martin, G. E. (2009). Developing and implementing an effective online educational leadership internship. *International Journal of Leadership Preparation, 4*(1), 1–12. http://www.eric.ed.gov/contentdelivery/servlet/ERICServlet?accno=EJ1068484

Holden & Westfall. (2008). *ERIC*. https://files.eric.ed.gov/fulltext/ED501248.pdf

Irwin, P., & Coutts, R. (2020). Learning alone together: A qualitative investigation exploring virtual connectedness. *International Journal on Innovations in Online Education, 4*(4). https://doi.org/10.1615/IntJInnovOnlineEdu.2021036472

Johnson, C. (2017). Teaching music online: Changing pedagogical approach when moving to the online environment. *London Review of Education, 15*(3), 439–456. https://doi.org/10.18546/LRE.15.3.08

Johnson, C. (2022). *A framework for teaching music online in higher education*. Bloomsbury Publications. https://doi.org/10.5040/9781350201880

King, A., Prior, H., & Waddington-Jones, C. (2019a). Exploring teachers' and pupils' behavior in online and face-to-face instrumental lessons. *Music Education Research*, 21(2), 197–209. https://doi.org/10.1080/14613808.2019.1585791

King, A., Prior, H., & Waddington-Jones, C. (2019b). Connect resound: Using online technology to deliver music education to remote communities. *Journal of Music, Technology & Education*, 12(2), 201–217. https://doi.org/10.1386/jmte_00006_1

Kirk, S. (2020). The new normal of piano teaching. *Piano Magazine*, 12(2), 12–14.

Kolb, D. A. (2015). *Experiential learning: Experience as the source of learning and development.* Pearson Education, Inc.

Kruse, N. B., Harlos, S. C., Callahan, R. M., & Herrings, M. L. (2013). Skype music lessons in the academy: Intersections of music education, applied music and technology. *Journal of Music, Technology & Education*, 6(1), 43–60. https://doi.org/10.1386/jmte.6.1.43_1

Kruse, N. B., & Veblen, K. K. (2012). Music teaching and learning online: Considering YouTube instructional videos. *Journal of Music, Technology & Education*, 5(1), 77–87. https://doi.org/10.1386/jmte.5.1.77_1

Kuh, G. D. (1993). In their own words: What students learn outside the classroom. *American Educational Research Journal*, 30(2), 277–304. http://doi.org/10.2307/1163236

Larreamendy-Joerns, J., & Leinhardt, G. (2006). Going the distance with online education. *Review of Educational Research*, 76(4), 567–605.

Linder, K. E., & Hayes, C. M. (Eds.). (2018). *High impact practices in online education: Research and best practices.* Stylus Publishers.

Lock, J. (2020, May 16). *Traversing the online learning landscape: Embracing opportunity in designing robust learning* [Keynote conference presentation]. Teaching Music Online in Higher Education Conference. Melbourne Conservatorium of Music. www.teachingmusiconlineinhighered.com/programme

Low, S. (2008). Supporting student learning during physical therapist student internships using online technology. *Journal of Physical Therapy Education*, 22(1), 75–82.

Mercer, A. (2009). Social influences on learning in an online environment. *Canadian Music Educator*, 51(2), 54–55.

Merrick, B. (2020). Changing mindset, perceptions, learning, and tradition: An "adaptive teaching framework" for teaching music online. *International Journal on Innovations in Online Education*, 4(2), 1–17. https://doi.org/10.1615/IntJInnovOnlineEdu.2020035150

Moore, M. G., & Anderson, W. G. (Eds.). (2003). *Handbook of distance education.* Lawrence Erlbaum Associates, Publishers.

Muilenburg, L. Y., & Berge, Z. L. (2015). Revisiting teacher preparation: Responding to technology transience in the educational setting. *The Quarterly Review of Distance Education*, 16(2), 93–105.

NASMHandbook2019–20. (2020). https://nasm.arts-accredit.org/wp-content/uploads/sites/2/2020/01/M-2019-20-Handbook-02-13-2020.pdf

Orman, E. K., & Whitaker, J. A. (2010). Time usage during face-to-face and synchronous distance music lessons. *American Journal of Distance Education*, 24(2), 92–103. https://doi.org/10.1080/08923641003666854

Orto, C., & Karapetkov, S. (2011). Music performance and instruction over high-speed networks. *Polycom White Paper*. Retrieved July 30, 2020, from http://docs.polycom.com/global/documents/whitepapers/music_performance_and_instruction_over_highspeed_networks.pdf

Palloff, R. M., & Pratt, K. (2005). *Collaborating online: Learning together in community.* Jossey-Bass.

Palloff, R. M., & Pratt, K. (2007). *Building online learning communities.* Jossey-Bass.

Paul, S. J., Teachout, D. J., Sullivan, J. M., Kelly, S. N., Bauer, W. I., & Raiber, M. A. (2001). Authentic-context learning activities in instrumental music teacher education. *Journal of Research in Music Education*, 49(2), 136–147. https://doi.org/10.2307/3345865

Pauling, B. (2008). Engaging the digital natives. In T. Evans, M. Haughtey & D. Murphy (Eds.), *International handbook of distance education* (pp. 385–415). Emerald Group Publishing Limited.

Pike, P. D. (2015a). Using a synchronous online teaching internship to develop pedagogical skills and explore teacher identity: A case study. *Journal of Music, Technology & Education*, 8(3), 227–242. https://doi.org/10.1386/jmte.8.3.227_1

Pike, P. D. (2015b). Online piano lessons: A teacher's journey into an emerging 21st-century virtual teaching environment. *American Music Teachers*, 65(1), 12–16.

Pike, P. D. (2017a). Improving music teaching and learning through online service: A case study of a synchronous online teaching internship. *International Journal of Music Education, 35*(1), 107–117. https://doi.org/10.1177/0255761415613534

Pike, P. D. (2017b). *Dynamic group-piano teaching: Transforming group theory into teaching practice.* Routledge.

Pike, P. D. (2018). Internships. In K. E. Linder & C. M. Hayes (Eds.), *High impact practices in online education: Research and best practices*(pp. 147–163). Stylus Publishers.

Pike, P. D. (2020a). Teaching music online: Past, present and future opportunities. *Piano Magazine, 12*(2), 62–64.

Pike, P. D. (2020b). Synchronous online lessons: A gateway to learning for older adults. In H. Partti (Ed.), *Ethics and inclusion in the education of professional musicians: Proceedings of the 23rd international seminar of the ISME commission on the education of the professional musician (CEPROM).* ISME. https://www.isme.org/other-publications/isme-ceprom-commission-2020-pre-conference-seminar-virtual-proceedings

Pike, P. D. (2020c). Preparing an emerging professional to teach online: A case study. *International Journal on Innovations in Online Education.* https://doi.org/10.1615/IntJInnovOnlineEdu.2020034417

Pike, P. D., & Shoemaker, K. (2013). The effect of distance learning on acquisition of piano sight-reading skills. *Journal of Music, Technology & Education, 6*(2), 147–162. https://doi.org/10.1386/jmte.6.2.147_1

Ruippo, M. (2003). Music education online. *Sibelius Academy Papers, 2,* 1–8. Retrieved July 28, 2020, from https://www.academia.edu/638538/Music_Education_Online

Schön, D. A. (1987). *Educating the reflective practitioner.* Jossey-Bass.

Scott, C., & Medaugh, M. (2017). Axial coding. In *The international encyclopedia of communication research methods.* John Wiley & Sons, Inc. http://doi.org/10.1002/9781118901731.iecrm0012

Simonson, M., Zvacek, S., & Smaldino, S. (Eds.). (2019). *Teaching and learning at a distance: Foundations of distance education*(7th ed.). Information Age Publishing, Inc.

Stake, R. E. (2005). Qualitative case studies. In N. K. Denzin & Y. K. Lincoln (Eds.), *The Sage handbook of qualitative research* (3rd ed., pp. 443–466). Sage.

Stevens, R. S., McPherson, G. E., & Moore, G. A. (2019). Overcoming the "tyranny of distance" in instrumental music tuition in Australia: The iMCM project. *Journal of Music, Technology & Education, 12*(1), 25–47. https://doi.org/10.1386/jmte.12.1.25_1

Talent-Runnels, M. K., Thomas, J. A., Lan, W. Y., Cooper, S., Ahern, T. C., Shaw, S. M., & Liu, X. (2006). Teaching courses online: A review of the research. *Review of Educational Research, 76*(1), 93–135.

Vas, R., Weber, C., & Gkoumas, D. (2018). Implementing connectivism by semantic technologies for self-directed learning. *International Journal of Manpower, 39*(8), 1032–1046. https://doi.org/10.1108/IJM-10-2018-0330

Waldron, J. (2009). Exploring a virtual "community of practice": Informal music learning on the Internet. *Journal of Music, Technology & Education, 2*(2–3), 97–112. https://doi.org/10.1386/jmte.2.2-3.97_1

Waldron, J. (2012). Conceptual frameworks, theoretical models and the role of YouTube: Investigating informal music learning and teaching in online music community. *Journal of Music, Technology & Education, 4*(2–3), 189–200. https://doi.org/10.1386/jmte.4.2-3.189_1

Waldron, J., & Veblen, K. K. (2009). Lifelong learning in the Celtic community: An exploration of informal music learning and adult amateur musicians. *Bulletin of the Council for Research in Music Education, 180,* 59–74.

Waldron, J. L., & Veblen, K. K. (2008). The medium is the message: Cyberspace, community, and music learning in the Irish traditional music virtual community. *Journal of Music, Technology and Education, 1*(2–3), 99–111. https://doi.org/10.1386/jmte.1.2and3.99/1

Webster, P. R. (2012). Key research in music technology and music teaching and learning. *Journal of Music, Technology & Education, 4*(2&3), 115–130. https://doi.org/10.1386/jmte.4.2-3.115_1

Wlodkowski, R. J. (1999). *Enhancing adult motivation to learn: A comprehensive guide for teaching all adults* (Rev. ed.). Jossey-Bass.

Yamaha Corporation of America. (n.d.). *Disklavier brings remote learning and entertainment to a global audience.* Retrieved July 31, 2020, from http://yamahaden.com/news/spotlight-on-disklavier/item/243-disklavier-brings-remote-learning-and-entertainment-to-a-global-audience

Zhukov, K. (2019). Current approaches for management of music performance anxiety: An introductory overview. *Medical Problems of Performing Artists, 34*(1), 53–60.

6 Informed Teaching and Practice in Music Education

Exploring Music Technologies, Curriculum Design and Learning Environments in an Everchanging World

Brad Merrick

Introduction

For years, researchers and educators in music education and music technology have espoused the need to modify practice. There are many important factors highlighted throughout this chapter – all of which have relevance to the way that music education will emerge in the future. These include:

- The many varied and wide-ranging implementation processes and curriculum documents that continue to exist, creating inconsistent understanding of music technology and the value it affords learning in music,
- The many varied definitions of music technology and ICT in music learning, many of which are outdated and not fit for purpose,
- The current reliance on a system-based education that places an emphasis on external assessment and core subjects, which has heightened the challenge through the crowded curriculum impact across school settings, both in Australia and internationally,
- The diminished priority of music education within school-based learning as other subjects and priorities impact access to an ongoing music education, combined with the reduced level of teacher preparation in these discipline specific areas (with minimal preparation in the use of ICT and music technology),
- The rapidly increasing use of the internet and social media, which has enabled access to varied music technologies for use in combination with a diverse range of general ICT resources for many types of Android and Mac devices,
- The increased online activity and connection with learners and teachers (due to the COVID scenario) which has become more the normal mode of delivery in many locations, highlighting the functionality of technologies as enablers of learning in many ways,
- The wide-ranging evidence highlighting the diverse uses of music technology and ICT to assist learning and student engagement in various ways (i.e., podcasts, online, synchronous-asynchronous resources and teaching, ensemble recordings),
- An ever-increasing body of literature that both highlights and further evidences the capacity of these technologies to engage and connect users in diverse locations,
- The continued evolution and revision of new technologies, apps, software, online environments, and devices to enable creative and collaborative tasks,
- Increased connectivity and engagement with technologies for information, music creation, and social connection, enabling learners to work with others across time zones, regions, or status, creating increased learning equity and access.

DOI: 10.4324/9781003041474-9

Combined with other factors, these important points should be viewed as an indicator of the subsequent leverage that music technologies and ICT offer in learning environments and the ways they can enable teachers, students, and the music education community to increase purpose, enjoyment, and connectivity moving forward. As a result, the chapter explores the notion of how we need to consider music teaching through the context of purposefully embracing technologies to support student learning. Through a considered example of curriculum examination, the chapter is positioned to demonstrate the need for, and adoption of technology use in music teaching and learning. A short research study further highlights the need for a considered technology-in-teaching approach. Finally, the chapter concludes with the establishment of a teaching mindset framework (i.e., DTN) that promotes technology-enhanced music teaching through student-centred contexts.

Key issues related to modifying learning environments to facilitate the increased use of music technology and ICT amongst students as part of their music education are tabled, along with a range of suggestions to assist in the design of school-based or tertiary training, all of which will reinforce the need to connect and embed music technology within Australia and around the world. Here, a case is made to further clarify and provide a framework to support how school-based learning environments are created for students and teachers with relevance to their available technologies and access. Reference is made to the need for more relevant and purposeful teacher training in ICT and music technology, combined with students' increased use of and preference for multiple technologies as they learn music, whether engaged in listening, composition, or performance. The chapter concludes with a series of recommendations that facilitate increased relevance of technology-based learning, and clearer structure for integrating music technology in school-based music learning.

Definitions

In this chapter, the following definitions are given to provide clarity for the reader.

ICT (**Information Communication and Technology**) – is a general term that refers to the broad use of different types of technology that exist in society across a range of settings, scenarios, and combine business and educational contexts. The acronym ICT is not discipline-specific and is seen to include the multitude of technology-based provisions that facilitate the ongoing access to, and global communication within, the connected world in which we live.

Music Technology – for the purpose of this discussion, it is defined as "any existing or emerging digital device or tool, the use of hardware and/or software and/or web-based applications in any way to support learning about, the creation of, and the performance of music" (Merrick, 2017, p. 171).

Investigating Curriculum and Learning within Australia

The Balance Between Music Education and External Assessment

Access to Music Education and learning in Australia continues to face the challenge of mandatory external assessment and testing programs managed by government-affiliated bodies such as Australian Curriculum, Assessment and Reporting Authority (ACARA, 2021a). They have supported a predominant focus on core subject disciplines and the related literacy and mathematical skills of learners engaged in different stages of their schooling. Using a series of graded external assessment tasks administered in Year 3, 5, 7, and 9 for every school student, termed the National Assessment Programme – Literacy and Numeracy [NAPLAN], (National Assessment Programme, 2021), the Australian Federal Government seeks to better understand each child and their academic capacity through national and external international benchmarks, i.e., Programme for International Student Assessment (PISA, 2021).

In Australia, there is a constant tension amongst parents (Rogers et al., 2018) and teachers (Thompson, 2013) about the value of these assessments and the connected anxiety and stress created in children across the early years of schooling (Roberts et al., 2019). Furthermore, there is a significant amount of school time committed to these key core learning areas (Rogers et al., 2016). This focus on core learning and assessment is often seen to diminish student access to other key areas of school curriculum, including access to music learning, the arts, and humanities. A large body of research has emphasised the inherent value of learning music in three main areas: the contribution it affords students in other areas of their school-based education (Hallam, 2010), the evidence that highlights the importance of music learning in facilitating student wellbeing (Barrett & Bond, 2015; Bonneville-Roussy & Vallerand, 2020), and the overall value of artistic passion as musicians.

There is a tension that exists when trying to balance what is taught in schools. Commonly referred to as the *crowded curriculum*, it addresses four key areas:

1. **Curriculum expansion** refers to the tendency to include new content items in the curriculum in response to new societal demands without appropriately considering what items need to be removed.
2. **Content overload** refers to the actual dimension of curriculum overload, rather than as it is perceived or experienced (i.e., the excessive amount of content to be taught and learned in relation to the time available for instruction).
3. **Perceived overload** refers to the perceived or experienced dimension of overload, as reported by teachers and students.
4. **Curriculum imbalance** refers to disproportionate attention given to certain areas of the curriculum at the expense of others without appropriate adjustments in the low-priority areas (OECD, 2020).

Driven by the national assessment agenda (i.e., NAPLAN) and the public comparative measure-based systems such as Programme for International Student Assessment (PISA, 2021), these tenuous priorities dominate political discourse and agendas for school funding and teacher improvement. In Australia, students focus on their final Australian Tertiary Admission Rank score [ATAR] (Universities Admission Centre, 2021), as it serves as a student's relative position to all other students completing school that year as they seek to access further university study. Students who wish to further their study in music- or arts-based industries are often challenged by this form of learning environment, which is dominated by a very competitive focus on measurement and comparison of core skills between schools and students. While core tertiary academic disciplines are determined solely by the ATAR, many of the tertiary music performance and music education courses use an entry process that is formed through a composite of both the ATAR score and other audition-based submissions and tasks. Faced with early decisions between core and music subject electives, many aspirant music students who wish to enter the profession have also critically had to take up prior access to quality music learning.

Curriculum Design and Implementation in Australia

In recent years, Australian state- and territory-based education systems have been required to align their teaching, learning, and assessment structures to the Australian Curriculum. This curriculum was announced as an innovation in 2008 by the Minister for Education with the overarching focus being to draw together "the best programs from each State and Territory into a single curriculum to ensure every child has access to the highest quality learning programs to lift achievement and drive-up school retention rates" (Gillard, 2008).

The national initiative was overseen by The Australian Curriculum, Assessment and Reporting Authority (ACARA) and was later called the 'Australian Curriculum', rather than the 'National Curriculum' as first proposed. After broad consultation and the subsequent curriculum design from stakeholders around the country, the responsibility for implementation at a local level within school systems were absolved to the various states and territories by the Federal Government stating that

> State and territory curriculum and school authorities are responsible for the implementation of the Australian Curriculum in their schools, in line with system and jurisdictional policies and requirements. They make decisions about the extent and timing of take-up and translation of the intended Australian Curriculum into the curriculum that is experienced by students.
>
> (ACARA, 2021b)

With this curriculum adoption, there has been little support for teachers working in the discipline of music and the broader subject areas of the arts. Overall, the implementation of this national framework has been challenging for teachers, school administrators, and for the continuity of learning for students. The focus on external assessments and core subjects has impacted the implementation of music and subject areas of the curriculum that are not prioritised within the broader academic core learning focus.

Curriculum Connections with Technology Across Learning Environments (F-10)

All schools, teachers, and students between Foundation years and Grade 10 (F-10) are expected to engage with and use the Australian Curriculum (2021a) as the overarching learning framework to guide the teaching of music to all students across Australia. This is part of the subject organiser termed 'The Arts' (ACARA, 2021c), which includes the disciplines of Music, Drama, Visual Art, Media Arts, and Dance. The curriculum design uses a series of general capability descriptors wherein Information and Communication Technology (ICT) is categorised with the intention of guiding all teachers to connect digital technologies in their design and delivery of teaching (see Figure 6.1). Although the curriculum has been designed and written to connect and align learning across the country, the expectation for implementation itself creates challenges for equitable delivery of the core skills, content, knowledge, and related capacities.

Through this interconnection of curricula and learning capabilities, teachers are expected to engage learners through various technologies within the mandated Arts curriculum. While a statement exists for mandatory implementation of the Australian Curriculum for F-10 learning years, this leaves the final two years of secondary school study (Years 11–12) and the implementation of the subject of music (i.e., music skills, knowledge, and content) up to the individual systems to oversee and implement. As mentioned earlier, these are

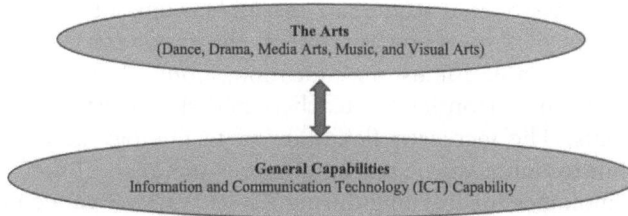

Figure 6.1 Current connection between the arts curriculum and general learning capabilities. (ACARA, 2021c)

pivotal years for attaining an ATAR and seeking entry into tertiary study or the workforce more broadly.

In Years 11–12 stages of learning, it is important to note that there is significant variance between state and territorial educational authorities (i.e., relative to subject structures, content, and assessment modes), as well as the integration and application of music technology across the learning stages. This inconsistency in the provision of specified music study (Years 11–12) across schools in Australia has a significant impact on how students complete their secondary education experience and learn about music. Subsequently, the years leading to possible entry into further tertiary study contain many varied teaching approaches towards the integration of technology and underscore notable differences in learning environment – including critical factors such as resources, teacher confidence, and teacher efficacy.

Interpreting Curriculum that Informs Technology Application in Music Environments

In a search for consensus, it is apparent that music technologies are often distinctly defined and referenced within established education systems. This continues to provide a constant challenge for even the most connected technology user. In Australia, this challenge is apparent in the state of Victoria's Victorian Music Study design, where "digital and audio technologies are (defined as) a means to manipulate sound through electronic devices with digital capabilities for the purpose of creating, enhancing, and exploring musical outcomes" (Victorian Curriculum and Assessment Authority, 2016, p. 13). Conversely, the Australian state of New South Wales's music curriculum for students in Years 7–10 references music technology by "encouraging (teachers) to use the full range of technologies available to them, in the classroom and in the wider school context", providing an outdated definition of music technology which states "ongoing developments in analogue and digital electronics have meant that musicians have access to a wide range of new instruments and sounds as well as the means to record and manipulate sounds" (New South Wales Education Standards Authority, 2003, p. 19).

In examining the various attempts to define music technology within music education practice, the ongoing challenge to find alignment is not uncommon; many note that it has been problematic for several years (Cain, 2004). Historically, music educators have continued to emphasise the need to "focus on what constitutes effective teaching and learning with music technology" (Savage, 2012, p. 493), rather than just technologies themselves. Research has continued to investigate teachers' application of different technologies and use within school curriculum for many years (Merrick, 1995; Eyles, 2018).

Whether it be in a classroom, a studio, an ensemble room, a technology lab, the community hall, or a room of a house or apartment, the exponential growth of new technologies and devices available for use in education, alongside increased access, creates both a challenge and a new frontier for teachers and students to embrace within their learning environments. The increased flexibility of technology access, positioned with the fundamental shift to online music teaching in previous years (Johnson, 2017) and the dependence on technologies for learning during the COVID-19 pandemic, has prompted further focus on ICT as a means of connection and wellbeing in all that we do (Baker et al., 2018; Merrick, 2020; Phillips & Killian Lund, 2019). Music technologies used to develop capacity amongst students who are learning music support accessibility, whether it be learning through podcasts (Bolden & Nahachewsky, 2015), listening via apps (Cho et al., 2019), the flipped classroom (Kazanidis et al., 2019), the online orchestra (Rofe et al., 2017), or through the ever-changing online-offline learning community (Waldron, 2013) that we experience daily.

Challenging the efficiency and effective implementation is an underlying issue for music educators – the inconsistency with which each curriculum defines, explains, and supports the integration of music technology within established learning frameworks. In many cases, policies are outdated, limited in detail, or they have yet to align the diverse and contextualised use of technologies in our lives in such a manner as to help future-proof its use in education for ongoing development within society (King et al., 2017).

Given the substantial variation and misalignment between many of these publicly available documents, it is little wonder that teachers and the institutions aiming to immerse future music students in the best music technology experiences that they can offer encounter challenges in their work and professional capacities. As systems, institutions, and governments look to effectively facilitate music learning and education more broadly, it is essential that we observe substantial factors that impact key policies: the substantial yearly growth in the global use of technology (Statista Research Department, 2021), as well as the proliferation of a category of learners who are more dependent on digital tools than any other generation in the history of mankind.

Emerging Technologies and the Implications for Music Educators

The Revisioning of Technologies, Definitions, and Related Pedagogy

The task of effectively integrating music technologies into classrooms by music educators is compounded by the varying degrees of specialist training offered to undergraduates in their teacher preparation – and the subsequent understanding of these technologies within education more broadly. For many, the preference to use acoustic instruments and older technologies that have been the mainstay of the profession and music industry for many years still exists. There are new and emerging technologies effectively supporting our connected world, and new resources are emerging faster than they can be adopted. For example, according to Business of Apps (2021), more than 60,000 new tracks are added to Spotify every day. This further suggests there is a need to ensure systems can rigorously support those working in school-based learning environments to implement music technologies effectively. Realistically, this also means the definitions used in and around music making and learning have a dualistic currency and utility attached to them whereby they acknowledge all technologies in their broadest sense. An updated definition is required. Therefore, it is suggested that the definition "any existing or emerging digital device or tools, the use of hardware and/or software and/or web-based applications (used) in any way to support learning about, the creation of, and the performance of music" (Merrick, 2017, p. 171) provides ample scope for a broad context and could be adapted for this scenario. Through continuous reference to earlier definitions, we are able to see how the domain has developed, connecting technology in music instruction and learning to the use of hardware and software resources to develop teaching about music and various music experiences (Webster, 2012).

Finally, there is a need to draw on more adaptive curriculum design and creative pedagogy to enable focused and purposeful use and application of these technology-based tools. Historically, with the notion of concept-based learning being critical, as opposed to content-based curriculum, previous attempts to define music technology have been connected with the importance of providing meaningful learning opportunities that involve activity, inquiry, and exploration on the part of the student (Kirkman, 2009). For many years, the relationship between the learner and technology has been a critical part of the process and continues to be an essential focus area (Reynolds, 2010). Therefore, increased clarity of the learning process and alignment with global developments are required to ensure music technology receives adequate time allocation and priority within the music curricula that are being developed in Australia and around the world.

Global Technology Access – the Data and Use of Social Media

The use of technology in music and learning continues to be both a motivator and connector for students and teachers in Australia and around the world more broadly. We are seeing an increase and surge in mobile device users, with use now surpassing more than 4 billion unique users around the world. Similarly, social media use continues to increase, with the first quarter of 2021 seeing more than 2.85 billion users of Facebook worldwide and more than 3.45 billion people engaging in the combined use of products such as WhatsApp, Instagram, and Messenger (Statista Research Department, 2021). Together, this highlights the way in which social networking technologies have become more accessible and more mainstream to users for similar applications within communities around the world.

As the largest music streaming service in the past year, Spotify had more than four million downloads in 2021 (Statista Research Department, 2021). With more than 345 million users worldwide, online music providers like Spotify are highly successful at disseminating music to mobile devices (Business of Apps, 2021). Such publicly available data supports evidence of the sustained adoption in the access and use of technology for music listening in conjunction with the impact of social media-based platforms, such as Facebook, Instagram, and Twitter, within society.

Therefore, considering this data, how we develop the sense of social agency through these virtual and real experiences needs continued consideration as we look to ensure that music technology is embedded purposefully within music learning across Australia and around the world.

Challenges for Teacher Preparation and Professional Learning

If students are to have the capacity to embrace new music technologies purposefully in their performance, composition, listening, and learning across all dimensions of their educational experience and beyond, they need to have supportive learning experiences with technology in their classroom learning. However, the inconsistent creation of curriculum frameworks, combined with their often-unsuccessful implementation and adoption, further challenge teachers and students in how to effectively implement technology in their teaching and learning. The data presented earlier highlights how teachers and students have increased access to use technologies more broadly in their learning. An increased focus on music-specific engagement and application is central to this argument to ensure music technology becomes a regularly used, purposeful learning resource, rather than an afterthought or an add-on to the curriculum.

There are many tertiary institutions seeking to prepare music teachers to enter the workforce in the best ways possible with increased subjects and courses focusing on aspects of music technology in teaching training programs. However, the variance in the documentation, support materials, definitions, and guidance for using technology as part of teaching music is a foreboding hurdle that requires management of appropriate resourcing and training to ensure consistent application.

Recent studies (see Waddell & Williamon, 2019) highlight that musicians have a positive attitude toward using technologies, and often use apps to replicate traditional technologies (i.e., a digital metronome or a tuner). However, it is apparent that music technology is still greatly underused and often impacted by limited availability and support (Gall, 2013). Further, implementation is often left to the capability of the individual instructors and teachers involved. Increased access, support, and advocacy needs to be actioned to ensure that music technology and the incorporation of more generic communication technologies (e.g., Zoom, Teams, and Google) are embedded in teacher training courses as well as combined with accessible and ongoing professional learning. There is a need to ensure that both existing and newly graduated teachers have the content knowledge, skill capacity, and resourcing to provide their students with a connected and purposeful journey with music technology throughout their educational experience.

Diverse Music Technology-based Applications Used to Develop Student Learning

An informed music curriculum that sees music technology embedded throughout all stage-learning levels in different contexts is paramount. This can be achieved by drawing on research that explores music teaching and the investigation of technology integration. There are diverse and critical areas to consider within the reshaping of music technology-based learning. The scope is extremely broad yet requires us to reconceptualise curriculum needs from its structural nuance for embracing technology use, rather than merely choosing something because of its alignment to traditional content or prescribed knowledge and skill view. This focus ensures an openness for future curriculum design.

There are multiple examples of research evidencing technology as a supportive teaching tool in music. Examples of different types of learning experiences that may be considered in more creative curricula could include: using mobile tablets for composition (Chen, 2020), enabling community connection with music technologies (Merrick, 2012), DAW (Digital Audio Workstations) as pedagogy (Walzer, 2020), using mobile phones for contemporary performance (Wallerstedt & Hillman, 2015), online networking to develop performance ensembles (Hanrahan et al., 2019), learning music through flipped classrooms (Zheng et al., 2020), enhancing geographical and regional connections (Stevens et al., 2019), or using Spotify to develop thinking (Almqvist, 2019). In this teaching posture, it is important to consider the importance of attitudes of learners towards using technology (Waddell & Williamon, 2019) as we acknowledge existing approaches employed by teachers in music education – whether it be the development of sound-based music teaching (Wolf & Younie, 2018) and teachers' approaches to developing composition with technology (Wise, 2016).

To this end, we look to create new and innovative ways to connect music learning to technology while embracing the known challenges (e.g., resourcing, training, and attitudinal) that exist within the apparent conservative approaches to music teaching that are still prevalent in many areas of music learning.

Connecting Music Technologies and ICT to Student Learning

Making the Shift – Future-Focused Learning Design

Many school-based curricula are fully online and continue to develop organically as the new content, skills, and assessment practices are updated regularly. The *Australian Curriculum* (ACARA, 2021a) is an example of an online environment that seeks to acknowledge the challenge of design and implementation in the 21st century. Through the examination of successful frameworks, the use of music technology can be reconceptualised and embedded purposefully within larger, music-specific curricula.

In seeking to realise the implementation of music technology as part of an informed and ever-changing online music curriculum, there are several factors to consider if we hope to integrate music technologies and ICT into all aspects of teaching and learning going forward. We need to ensure that any shift acknowledges and includes the provision of change fatigue (Dilkes et al., 2014) amongst teachers. In making the shift, we need to change our mindset and embrace the challenge of transitioning away from the more traditional underlying principles of design and implementation (Prideaux, 2003). Overarching all of these considerations are the final pieces of the learning puzzle, ensuring that users can successfully engage with and enact innovative mindset models and related system- and jurisdiction-based curriculum, to achieve a cohesive conceptualisation of student learning (Moss et al., 2019).

Here, the assumption is often made by the various education jurisdictions that the teacher will inherently look to existing documents, be upskilled, and have the confidence to implement updated and relevant curriculum in these constantly changing areas of music technology.

As noted earlier in the chapter, curriculum, and learning design to a point, can often be restricted as it forms a line in the sand at a given point of time, as publication that has a date of creation, a year of implementation that traditionally accompanies any new or revised learning document.

So, as we move to solve the issue that exists with music technology, our collective challenge will be positioned around several key aspects that will need to be constantly reviewed to ensure alignment. These include:

1. The currency and relevance of the included knowledge, technology, and learning experience,
2. The capacity of the teacher to interpret and implement new music technologies to enable learning in these contexts,
3. The willingness to accept that creative understanding will emerge, and that learning and assessment will continue to evolve, and
4. A willingness to embrace a cyclical and ongoing process of adaption and modification within teaching practice and student learning.

In adopting these principles, we will need to show diversity in the methods we employ to assess and measure new musical knowledge and artistic practice to validate learning and creativity. Most importantly, we need to be willing to enter and engage with learning environments that will not fit into or align with existing structures and hierarchies of music learning that have been in place for many years. It will be fascinating to see if we progress the opportunity that sits in front of us globally at this time, or if we find ourselves still contemplating a similar shift as we look to embed music technologies within the world's learning environments and curriculum structures ten years from now. That is the most critical piece of the puzzle, as music educators seek to reflect on and look to reimagine the classrooms, ensemble rooms, and music studios of the future. One thing can be guaranteed: music technology and ICT will not wait, and every day that we are left behind sees music as a subject possibly lose relevance and authenticity in a world that is ready for change if we are willing to stop, listen, and respond.

Research into School-based, Informal Learning Environments in Music Education

The following section focuses on an eight-year longitudinal study undertaken by the author. Segmented into consecutive two-year periods, adolescent music students (i.e., aged 14 to 17), were asked to share their approaches for using technologies and offer insights into the way they engaged in their music learning.

The study was completed at a secondary school in Australia as part of a larger study that examined how students were engaging with learning music and technologies. This data is reflective of a collective participation sample of students (N=137) over eight years with a two-year period between each collection point. Table 6.1 outlines the number of participating students each year.

Figure 6.2 visualizes a series of collective datasets that evidence an increased use of technologies for listening and viewing, along with the changes in approaches to learning regarding accessing information via technology. Students completed an 11-point scale indicating their level of agreement across various key areas of their learning. Mean scores are presented across the year groups.

The data underscores the extent to which music educators and administrators need to continue to reflect upon and reshape the learning environments that are used in music education – by incorporating music technology into the centre of the experiences. As we continue to reshape how we best enhance students' musical development in school settings, we can also ensure the connection of the experience to all students who are involved.

Three discussion points emerge from the data presented in Figure 6.1:

1. Students are predominantly working out the music that they perform by ear. This acknowledges an increased preference for using devices and technologies to access the music that they perform. Although there is not a gradual increase or decline, there is a notable – and sustained – high use of this approach in its connection to learning.

Table 6.1 Number of participants involved in the longitudinal study across years.

Year of study	Number of Student participants	Percentage of total sample N=137
2007	n=21	15.3%
2009	n=27	19.7%
2011	n=27	19.7%
2013	n=33	24.1%
2015	n=29	21.2%

Students' Approaches to Learning Music

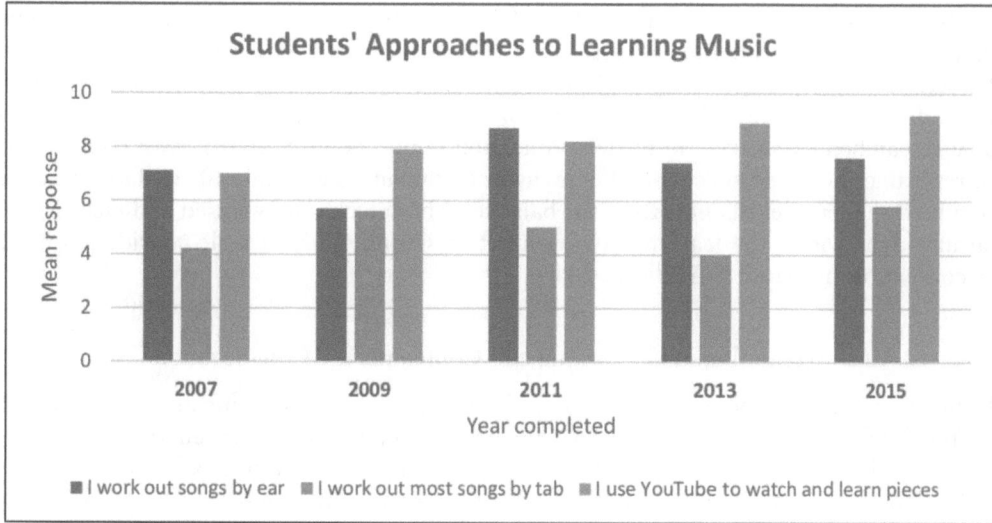

Figure 6.2 Students' approaches to learning music (2007–2015).

2. Many students are shifting towards informal approaches of interpreting popular music by referencing TABs for guitar chords via technologies online. This highlights the need to consider adopting a more eclectic approach to learning within the school environment and beyond.
3. Students have continued to progressively increase their reliance on YouTube as a technology to inform their own learning, whereby they can review and access songs and performances. This continues to be even more evident with the increased use of different platforms in the present day, combined with the increased use of devices globally.

Although the period of the research is limited to the years of 2007–2015, there is much that can be considered for curriculum and the context of music learning. Here it is important to reconsider the way in which we allow students to mediate their participation with music learning via technologies, rather than prescribing when and how they can access these resources and tools as part of a defined continuum of learning. One such change would be to adapt one's teaching to a more student-centred approach and aligning the technology purposefully to the learners' individual musical journey.

Student-centred learning supports autonomy of learner control. Much of the research and emerging data into music technologies and ICT highlight an increasing dependence on various tools that allow the individual to have control relative to their needs and interest at that point in time (see reference to Spotify and the use of listening apps earlier in this chapter). It is apparent that learners want to explore their learning through their choice of technologies rather than use specific technologies provided as part of their environment – be it a school, studio, or other type of learning institution.

There is no denying that music technologies are widely employed in many facets of our daily interactions around the world. We continue to see technologies explored throughout the past decade. Some of these innovative practices include areas such as: podcasts to increase student understanding (Bolden & Nahachewsky, 2015; On Tam, 2012), videoconferencing (Denis, 2016), and online lessons and remote instruction (Duffy & Healey, 2017;

Hurlbut, 2018; Johnson, 2017; King et al., 2017). Many of these innovations have become accepted forms of teaching, but this is not always the accepted practice. Similarly, we have also seen technologies used to heighten thinking and cognition (Giacumo & Savenye, 2020) across different learning settings. Furthermore, the use of blended learning has continued to be researched extensively in tertiary education (Smith & Hill, 2019), with students often reporting increased success and enjoyment (Dziuban & Moskal, 2011). However, the continued challenge exists in getting the balance of both technology-based and face-to-face learning right within the learning environment or setting, with suitable consideration for the context of the learning (Hilliard, 2015).

Increased Music Technologies in Learning and Contemporary Collaboration

During 2020 and into the present day, it has been apparent that teaching around the world, and much of the music making that has connected communities, has been almost fully dependent on both ICT-based technology (e.g., Zoom, MS Teams), web-based resources (e.g., Vimeo, YouTube, MOOCs), and a multitude of emergent software for Android and Apple devices. There are also a multitude of web-based collaborative music creation and storage solutions to enable students and teachers to record and share music (https://edu.soundtrap.com/soundtrap-spotlight-student-made-podcasts), with many also using video and audio through open-source software with technologies like JackTrip (https://www.jacktrip.org) to facilitate online live performance over the internet with reduced latency (i.e., delay in sound).

Given the rapid increase in technology use in music learning and ICT-based interactions more broadly over the past two years, it is unlikely we will revert to the pre-COVID levels of technology use in the years to come. The required shift to implement technology has been an unexpected catalyst that has forced change to occur with the realisation that many of the challenges incurred have allowed solutions to emerge – successful and accessible technology options for students are now available. Through the difficulties encountered, the creative and adaptive use of technology has enabled human connection and socialisation at a time when humans have needed support and connection more than at any time in history.

Redefining the Value and Purpose of Music Technology and ICT in Music Learning

As noted in the earlier sections of this chapter, we need to examine documentation and learning purpose within the existing jurisdictions in Australia and examine similar processes from an international perspective. A consistent delivery and structure for implementing music technology needs to accompany the updating of professional skill amongst existing teachers combined with the preparation of our future teachers. This can in turn ensure teachers in music education are skilled to fully utilise learning environments that allow students to access and engage with music technologies in more equitable and relevant ways.

Navigating to an effective solution means isolating the purpose. In this context, understanding the purpose of integrating music technology in music education is paramount. We need to think deeply about the *Why?* We need to ask ourselves and our students why we are using the technology. This response is to be determined by the learner and teacher in partnership. Merely offering a list of tasks, content, resources, and strategies that we feel every student would benefit from completing and mastering can disregard the importance of student autonomy. Teachers differentiate curriculum and learning to cater for student interest in other disciplines based on ability. Music, which we know is one of the arts-based subjects that fosters so much student creativity and individuality, is no different. It cannot be a one-size-fits-all model if we desire the learning to be authentic and centred in the real world (Herrington & Herrington, 2007; Lombardi, 2007).

Issues in Curriculum Design and Effective Implementation

Although there has been considerable research into the use of music technology in different settings for learners, there is much to gain from considering multiple frames of reference as we look to the future of music technology within diverse learning contexts. We need to continue to examine literature that considers the 21st-century music teacher (Wallerstedt & Hillman, 2015) and creative and innovative practice. It is essential for all institutions to view learning from beyond their borders. We cannot afford to be limited by research and knowledge within our discipline. Rather, we need to continue to adapt and collaborate beyond the boundaries that exist through so many of the hierarchical systems that are seen as the pillars of successful learning models.

As economics, sustainability, and global issues continue to impact learning and society, we need to consider learning environments that foster individual capabilities and harness global capacities (OECD, 2018). In music education, it is essential to draw on experiences from other diverse modes of learning and environments (tools, software, disciplines, and industries). There are commonalities that are accessible and adaptable within these frames of reference, which can be better utilised to ensure the ongoing currency of music technology and ICT across all learning in school settings.

Recommendations and Thoughts for Consideration

Substantial modification of school-based curriculum and teacher training course structures is now necessary to enable music education to flourish through the adoption and use of music technology. Here, the proposal is for music technology, in its many shapes and forms, to be seen as the connection or "glue" that allows learners and teachers to realise authentic, purposeful experiences that are both relevant and structured. Together, this can ensure there is a tangible and observable outcome that arises from the engagement process itself.

It is time for students to be enabled to have agency over their learning, utilising their capacity and interests to engage with music technology and other ICT-based tools to appropriately promote learning that impacts thinking, action, and change. Wherever students have the devices or access to software and hardware to enable learning through technology-based interaction and creative exploration, music educators and institutions should embrace these opportunities more broadly. Bypassing opportunities to impact possible technology use is due to a lack of perceived usability and technology-based efficacy amongst teachers (Holden & Rada, 2011) and results from challenges in using it for assessment in the learning process (Hartell et al., 2015). Yet these issues are teacher-facing.

When considering a way forward, a proposed learning structure (plugin) should enable users to rapidly move through an action plan: 1) Do, 2) Through, and 3) New. In Phase One, students can identify a desired action or purpose, problem, or issue within the learning context (i.e., what is the learner wishing to Do?). In Phase Two, the students connect with the most accessible and functional form of music technology (i.e., the Through). In the final Phase Three, we engage the student so that it leads to enhanced (i.e., the New) understanding and facilitates a solution, output, or new application of knowledge.

A simple structure whereby teachers can enable relevant and accessible music technologies is a clear approach that can underpin a more developed and complex pedagogy as it evolves. In essence, we seek to understand *Why?* the technology is important in the learning process.

The diagram here (see Figure 6.3) has been designed to allow teachers and students to think deeply about the technology they have available to use, and more importantly, the way in which it will allow them to develop, create, and explore new skills, knowledge, and understanding. Pivotal to this process is that each student immerses themselves in each of the stages presented: firstly, the action of conceptualising what they wish to explore and activate in their own learning; secondly, considering the most suitable technology through which to explore the learning; and thirdly, creating new or different knowledge that enhances student understanding and engagement as a learner. For teachers, it is recommended they reflect on these questions to guide their integration of technology within their classroom settings.

- Do you know the why, what, and how for each of these processes?
- Can you guide the student to understand, modify, expand, or derive new knowledge using music technology?

If we are to enable a more connected approach to the use of music technology (i.e., within the teaching profession and amongst musicians, technology experts, and leaders), we need to create an environment that provides a pathway to allow students and teachers to draw upon relevant research and literature regarding the use of the technology. Importantly, a simple structure like the DTN is needed to ensure the action of the learner at any given point of time. It acknowledges and enables the appropriate music technology (whatever it may be) so that a solution or possible new understanding (skill or knowledge) can be facilitated in a meaningful way. In other words, the curriculum may need to work alongside a living – almost organic – environment which is not published *per se*. It continues to be redefined and emerges contextually for the student and/or teacher as they explore and become immersed in opportunities to learn in their own environment.

In essence, the combined music task, focus of learning, and related music technology provide connectivity and relevance to the participant so that new understandings and applications of knowledge appear – and most importantly, have authenticity. Historically, much of the learning we see develop is derived from a prescribed or finite knowledge source

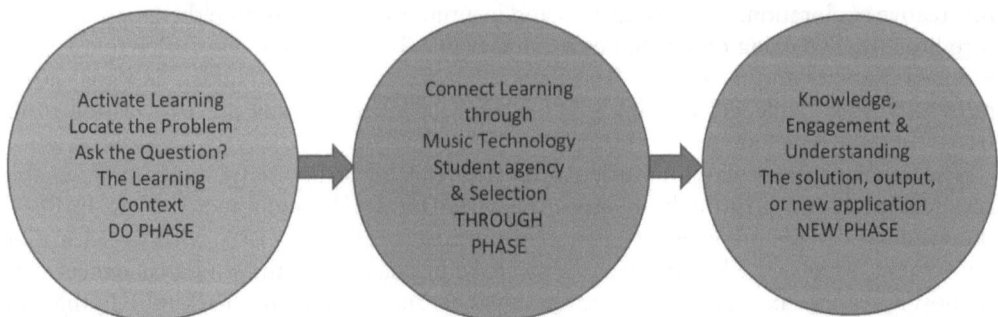

Figure 6.3 The DTN music technology learning environment plugin: DO – THROUGH – NEW.

that has been annotated and developed over time. In contrast, the nature of technology as a means of engagement requires an acceptance that the palette available to the learner can and does regularly change.

Most importantly, this shift is positioned by employing the simple learning structure (see Figure 6.3) to guide the learning experience and offer relevance to each learner at a single point in time. Like an online interaction that continues to grow in a personalised way, the repositioning of curriculum as a structure allows music technology to be relevant while affording maximum purpose to the student, regardless of their age, location, experience, or prior understanding.

Conclusion: Towards the Future of Music Education

As we reflect, we can see the exponential increase in social interaction, access to devices, and internet usage have had a critical influence on student learning. The global increase and ongoing reliance on online tools and the diverse range of music technologies readily available to enable student-teacher interaction suggests there is a need to reflect and recalibrate our modes and design of learning, harnessing the potential that exists. The intention is to ensure the provision of relevant guidelines, structures, and resources that enable teachers to offer effective integration of music technology into music education in a much more contextualised and meaningful way – and across diverse settings, learning levels, environments, and opportunities. Musicians and music educators continue to look for effective ways to embed existing learning theory and research into technology-based learning (Johnson, 2017; Merrick, 2020; Montgomery et al., 2019). Together, we can see this area receives considerable focus and development within the music learning community. Yet, a more unified and connected approach is required to sufficiently support the necessary curriculum shift is adequately positioned for the future.

It is understood that new modes of teaching and learning will continue to emerge. Technology advancement will continue to move forward. As such, educational systems, leaders, and technology providers will need to collaborate more purposefully to consider the impact and patterns of use with technology – particularly with reference to the many different locations and settings.

Further, it is apparent that a significant change is needed within music education, as outlined in this chapter. Both within Australia and around the world, research into the areas of curriculum design, accessibility for students and teachers, and the currency of working definitions are needed to ensure that learning is connected through the purposeful use of music technology, with the aim being to enable learning via technology for all students, regardless of their age, background, or musical experience. Coupled with the significant growth in both the access and availability that exists around the world, these topics in research are anything but fortuitous.

If we are to advance this charge so that music technology use is standard within all student learning, then there is a need to create considered learning environments and structures – not just curriculum documents. Concerted efforts to support students and teachers will become drivers to meaningful engagement with music technologies in creative, individualised, and collaborative ways, depending on the setting circumstance and mode of interaction (i.e., synchronous, asynchronous, or face-to-face interaction). This notion of enhancing practice with technology has been raised before (Himonides, 2012), and the question continues to be centred around the collection of evidence to validate this usage as part of our identity as musicians, teachers, and learners more broadly. It could result in a return to the premise of engaging in effective teaching and learning practice by means of purposeful and authentic approaches for student engagement in a 21st-century context.

References

ACARA. (2021a). *The Australian curriculum*. https://www.australiancurriculum.edu.au/

ACARA. (2021b). https://www.australiancurriculum.edu.au/f-10-curriculum/implementation-of-the-australian-curriculum/

ACARA. (2021c). *The arts curriculum*. https://www.australiancurriculum.edu.au/f-10-curriculum/general-capabilities/

Almqvist, C. F. (2019). Thinking, being, teaching and learning with Spotify: Aspects of existential and essential musical *building* through listening in the classroom. *Journal of Music, Technology and Education, 12*(3), 279–296. https://doi.org/10.1386/jmte_00011_1

Baker, F. A., Jeanneret, N., & Clarkson, A. (2018). Contextual factors and wellbeing outcomes: Ethnographic analysis of an artist-led group songwriting program with young people. *Psychology of Music, 46*(2), 266–280. https://doi.org/10.1177/0305735617709520

Barrett, M. S., & Bond, N. (2015). Connecting through music: The contribution of a music programme to fostering positive youth development. *Research Studies in Music Education, 37*(1), 37–54. https://doi.org/10.1177/1321103X14560320

Bolden, B., & Nahachewsky, J. (2015). Podcast creation as transformative music engagement. *Music Education Research, 17*(1), 17–33. https://doi.org/10.1080/14613808.2014.969219

Bonneville-Roussy, A., & Vallerand, R. J. (2020). Passion at the heart of musicians' well-being. *Psychology of Music, 48*(2), 266–282. https://doi.org/10.1177/0305735618797180

Business of Apps. (2021). *Key Spotify user statistics*. https://www.businessofapps.com/data/spotify-statistics/#1

Cain, T. (2004). Theory, technology, and the music curriculum. *British Journal of Music Education, 21*(2), 215–221. https://doi.org/10.1017/S0265051704005650

Chen, J. C. W. (2020). Mobile composing: Professional practices and impact on students' motivation in popular music. *International Journal of Music Education, 38*(1), 147–158. https://doi.org/10.1177/0255761419855820

Cho, S., Baek, Y., & Choe, E. J. (2019). A strategic approach to music listening with a mobile app for high school students. *International Journal of Music Education, 37*(1), 132–141. https://doi.org/10.1177/0255761418819016

Denis, J. (2016). Band students' perceptions of instruction via videoconferencing. *Journal of Music, Technology and Education, 9*(3), 241–254. https://doi.org/10.1386/jmte.9.3.241_1

Dilkes, J., Cunningham, C., & Gray, J. (2014). The new Australian curriculum, teachers and change fatigue. *Australian Journal of Teacher Education, 39*(11). https://doi.org/10.14221/ajte.2014v39n11.4

Duffy, S., & Healey, P. (2017). A new medium for remote music tuition. *Journal of Music, Technology and Education, 10*(1), 5–29. https://doi.org/10.1386/jmte.10.1.5_1

Dziuban, C., & Moskal, P. (2011). A course is a course is a course: Factor invariance in student evaluation of online, blended, and face-to-face learning environments. *The Internet and Higher Education, 14*(4), 236–241. https://doi.org/10.1016/j.iheduc.2011.05.003

Eyles, A. (2018). Teachers' perspectives about implementing ICT in music education. *Australian Journal of Teacher Education, 43*, Article 8. https://doi.org/10.14221/ajte.2018v43n5.8

Gall, M. (2013). Trainee teachers' perceptions: Factors that constrain the use of music technology in teaching placements. *Journal of Music, Technology and Education, 6*(1), 5–27. https://doi.org/10.1386/jmte.6.1.5_1

Giacumo, L. A., & Savenye, W. (2020). Asynchronous discussion forum design to support cognition: Effects of rubrics and instructor prompts on learner's critical thinking, achievement, and satisfaction. *Educational Technology Research and Development, 68*(1), 37–66. https://doi.org/10.1007/s11423-019-09664-5

Gillard, J. (Minister for Education). (2008). Delivering Australia's first national curriculum. *Media Release*. Parliament House, ACT. https://ministers.dese.gov.au/gillard/delivering-australias-first-national-curriculum

Hallam, S. (2010). The power of music: Its impact on the intellectual, social, and personal development of children and young people. *International Journal of Music Education, 28*(3), 269–289. https://doi.org/10.1177/0255761410370658

Hanrahan, F., Hughes, E., Banerjee, R., Eldridge, A., & Kiefer, C. (2019). Psychological benefits of networking technologies in children's experience of ensemble music making. *International Journal of Music Education*, 37(1), 59–77. https://doi.org/10.1177/0255761418796864

Hartell, E., Gumaelius, L., & Svärdh, J. (2015). Investigating technology teachers' self-efficacy on assessment. *International Journal of Technology and Design Education*, 25(3), 321–337. https://doi.org/10.1007/s10798-014-9285-9

Herrington, A. & Herrington, J. (2007). Authentic mobile learning in higher education. In *AARE 2007. International educational research conference*, 28 November 2007, Fremantle, Western Australia. http://researchrepository.murdoch.edu.au/5413

Hilliard, A. T. (2015). Global blended learning practices for teaching and learning, leadership, and professional development. *Journal of International Education Research (JIER)*, 11(3), 179–188. https://doi.org/10.19030/jier.v11i3.9369

Himonides, E. (2012). Commentary: Music learning and teaching through technology. In G. E. McPherson & G. F. Welch (Eds.), *The Oxford handbook of music education* (Vol. 2, pp. 428–432). Oxford University Press. https://doi.org/10.1093/oxfordhb/9780199928019.013.0028

Holden, H., & Rada, R. (2011). Understanding the influence of perceived usability and technology self-efficacy on teachers' technology acceptance. *Journal of Research on Technology in Education*, 43(4), 343–367. https://doi.org/10.1080/15391523.2011.10782576

Hurlbut, A. R. (2018). Online vs. traditional learning in teacher education: A comparison of student progress. *American Journal of Distance Education*, 32(4), 248–266. https://doi.org/10.1080/08923647.2018.1509265

Johnson, C. (2017). Teaching music online: Changing pedagogical approach when moving to the online environment. *London Review of Education*, 15(3), 439–456. https://doi.org/10.18546/LRE.15.3.08

Kazanidis, I., Pellas, N., Fotaris, P., & Tsinakos, A. (2019). Can the flipped classroom model improve students' academic performance and training satisfaction in Higher Education instructional media design courses? *British Journal of Educational Technology*, 50(4), 2014–2027. https://doi.org/10.1111/bjet.12694

King, A., Himonides, E., & Ruthmann, A. (Eds.). (2017). *The Routledge companion to music, technology, and education*. Routledge, Taylor & Francis Group.

Kirkman, P. (2009). *Embedding digital technologies in the music classroom: An approach for the new music national curriculum*. (p. 35). www.kirki.co.uk/main/ (Accessed 15 October 2012).

Lombardi, M. M. (2007). Authentic learning for the 21st century: An overview. *Educause learning initiative, ELI paper no.1* (p. 13). https://library.educause.edu/-/media/files/library/2007/1/eli3009-pdf.pdf

Merrick, B. (1995). The use of music technology in the N.S.W. High School teacher perspective's and curriculum direction. In H. Lee & M. Barrett (Eds.), *Honing the craft: Improving the quality of music education, conference proceedings of the Australian Society for Music Education* (pp. 192–197). Artemis Publishing.

Merrick, B. (2012). Embracing new digital technologies: Now and into the future. In G. E. McPherson & G. F. Welch (Eds.), *The Oxford handbook of music education* (Vol. 2, pp. 670–673). Oxford University Press. https://doi.org/10.1093/oxfordhb/9780199928019.013.0056

Merrick, B. (2017). Popular music and technology in the secondary school. In A. King, E. Himonides & A. S. Ruthmann (Eds.), *The Routledge companion to music, technology, and education* (pp. 171–180). Routledge.

Merrick, B. (2020). Changing mindset, perceptions, learning and tradition. An adaptive teaching framework for teaching music online. *International Journal on Innovations in Online Education*. https://doi.org/10.1615/IntJInnovOnlineEdu.2020035150

Montgomery, A. P., Mousavi, A., Carbonaro, M., Hayward, D. V., & Dunn, W. (2019). Using learning analytics to explore self-regulated learning in flipped blended learning music teacher education: Learning analytics and teacher education. *British Journal of Educational Technology*, 50(1), 114–127. https://doi.org/10.1111/bjet.12590

Moss, J., Godinho, S., & Chao, E. (2019). Enacting the Australian curriculum: Primary and secondary teachers' approaches to integrating the curriculum. *Australian Journal of Teacher Education*, 44(3), 24–41. https://search.informit.org/doi/10.3316/aeipt.222919

National Assessment Program. (2021). https://www.nap.edu.au/

New South Wales Education Standards Authority. (2003). *Music 7–10 syllabus*. https://educationstandards.nsw.edu.au/wps/portal/nesa/k-10/learning-areas/creative-arts/music-7-10

OECD. (2018). *The future we want.* OECD. http://www.oecd.org/education/2030-project/about/documents/

OECD. (2020). *Curriculum overload: A way forward.* OECD Publishing. https://doi.org/10.1787/3081ceca-en.

On Tam, C. (2012). The effectiveness of educational podcasts for teaching music and visual arts in higher education. *Research in Learning Technology, 20.* https://doi.org/10.3402/rlt.v20i0/14919

Phillips, N. C., & Killian Lund, V. (2019). Sustaining affective resonance: Co-constructing care in a school-based digital design studio. *British Journal of Educational Technology, 50*(4), 1532–1543. https://doi.org/10.1111/bjet.12799

PISA. (2021). *Programme for international student assessment.* https://www.oecd.org/pisa/

Prideaux, D. (2003). ABC of learning and teaching in medicine: Curriculum design. *BMJ, 326*(7383), 268–270. https://doi.org/10.1136/bmj.326.7383.268

Reynolds, N. (2010). Technology and computers in music and music education. In N. Reynolds & M. Turcsányi-Szabó (Eds.), *Key competencies in the knowledge society* (Vol. 324, pp. 333–343). Springer Berlin Heidelberg. https://doi.org/10.1007/978-3-642-15378-5_32

Roberts, P., Barblett, L., & Robinson, K. (2019). Early years teachers' perspectives on the effects of NAPLAN on stakeholder wellbeing and the impact on early years pedagogy and curriculum. *Australasian Journal of Early Childhood, 44*(3), 309–320. https://doi.org/10.1177/1836939119855562

Rofe, M., Murray, S., & Parker, W. (2017). Online Orchestra: Connecting remote communities through music. *Journal of Music, Technology and Education, 10*(2), 147–165. https://doi.org/10.1386/jmte.10.2-3.147_1

Rogers, S. L., Barblett, L., & Robinson, K. (2016). Investigating the impact of NAPLAN on student, parent, and teacher emotional distress in independent schools. *The Australian Educational Researcher, 43*(3), 327–343. https://doi.org/10.1007/s13384-016-0203-x

Rogers, S. L., Barblett, L., & Robinson, K. (2018). Parent and teacher perceptions of NAPLAN in a sample of Independent schools in Western Australia. *The Australian Educational Researcher, 45*(4), 493–513. https://doi.org/10.1007/s13384-018-0270-2

Savage, J. (2012). Driving forward technology's imprint on music education. In G. E. McPherson & G. F. Welch (Eds.), *The Oxford handbook of music education* (Vol. 2, pp. 491–512). Oxford University Press. https://doi.org/10.1093/oxfordhb/9780199928019.013.0032

Smith, K., & Hill, J. (2019). Defining the nature of blended learning through its depiction in current research. *Higher Education Research & Development, 38*(2), 383–397. https://doi.org/10.1080/07294360.2018.1517732

Statista Research Department. (2021). Mobile internet and apps. *Mobile internet usage worldwide – Statistics & facts.* https://www.statista.com/topics/779/mobile-internet/

Stevens, R. S., McPherson, G. E., & Moore, G. A. (2019). Overcoming the "tyranny of distance" in instrumental music tuition in Australia: The iMCM project. *Journal of Music, Technology and Education, 12*(1), 25–47. https://doi.org/10.1386/jmte.12.1.25_1

Thompson, G. (2013). *The International Education Journal: Comparative Perspectives, 12*(2), 62–84. ISSN 1443-1475 © 2013 www.iejcomparative.org

Universities Admissions Centre. (2021). https://www.uac.edu.au/

Victorian Curriculum and Assessment Authority. (2016). *Victorian certificate of education music study design 2017–2022.* https://www.vcaa.vic.edu.au/Documents/vce/music/2017MusicSD.pdf

Waddell, G., & Williamon, A. (2019). Technology use and attitudes in music learning. *Frontiers in ICT, 6*, 11. https://doi.org/10.3389/fict.2019.00011

Waldron, J. (2013). YouTube, fanvids, forums, vlogs, and blogs: Informal music learning in a convergent on- and offline music community. *International Journal of Music Education, 31*(1), 91–105. https://doi.org/10.1177/0255761411434861

Wallerstedt, C., & Hillman, T. (2015). "Is it okay to use the mobile phone?" Student use of information technology in pop-band rehearsals in Swedish music education. *Journal of Music, Technology and Education, 8*(1), 71–93. https://doi.org/10.1386/jmte.8.1.71_1

Walzer, D. (2020). Blurred lines: Practical and theoretical implications of a DAW-based pedagogy. *Journal of Music Technology & Education, 13*(1), 79–94. https://doi.org/10.1386/jmte_00017_1

Webster, P. R. (2012). Technology in music instruction and learning. In N. M. Seel (Ed.), *Encyclopedia of the sciences of learning* (pp. 3285–3287). Springer US. https://doi.org/10.1007/978-1-4419-1428-6_1710

Wise, S. (2016). Secondary school teachers' approaches to teaching composition using digital technology. *British Journal of Music Education, 33*(3), 283–295. https://doi.org/10.1017/S026505 1716000309

Wolf, M., & Younie, S. (2018). Overcoming barriers: Towards a framework for continuing professional development to foster teaching sound-based music. *Journal of Music, Technology and Education, 11*(1), 83–101. https://doi.org/10.1386/jmte.11.1.83_1

Zheng, X., Kim, H., Lai, W., & Hwang, G. (2020). Cognitive regulations in ICT-supported flipped classroom interactions: An activity theory perspective. *British Journal of Educational Technology, 51*(1), 103–130. https://doi.org/10.1111/bjet.12763

7   Music, Play, Games and Education

Tim Summers

Introduction

A recently developed body of scholarship has sought to emphasize the playfulness of music. Many of these discussions have occurred with reference to music in digital games. Scholars claim that video games are a particularly obvious site for revealing the connection between music and play, and that engaging with music has game-like and playful qualities even outside video games. Music, the argument goes, has long been a 'ludic' medium. What, then, are the implications of this play-emphasizing perspective for music educators?

This chapter is not primarily concerned with teaching video game music and need not necessarily apply to education involving digital technologies. Rather, the interest is in how an awareness of music and play, particularly informed by the findings from the context of video games, might affect teaching. Suggestions herein should not be taken as prescriptions or strident evangelizing of one approach over another. Instead, this chapter means to provide another set of tools or perspectives for teachers to consider when planning and delivering lessons.

This chapter considers three dimensions of music, video games and play: i) the role of interfaces in scaffolding musical creative processes, ii) interactivity and musical-dialogic teaching and iii) participatory culture as a type of informal learning that provides musical specialization and technical expertise. An epilogue suggests just some of the ways that these ideas might be implemented in a school curriculum. First, it is worth considering precisely what is meant by 'play' in this context.

Play

As one might imagine, there are a huge number of ways that ideas of play have been conceptualized. As scholars define and redefine play, they reflect the preoccupations and priorities of their research. Not least among such discussions are educational theorists who have long recognized the educational value of play (Bateson & Martin, 2013; Patte & Brown, 2013; Sutton-Smith, 1997). Conceptions of play, irrespective of the disciplinary incarnation, typically involve three dimensions – 1) the suggestion of some rules, frame or boundary for play, 2) creativity and dialogue within those frames/rules/spaces and 3) the notion of some aesthetic or attitude of fun. Within these general principles of play, playfulness may have many incarnations. One of the most influential attempts to map the different flavours of play was conducted by Roger Caillois. He proposed many different modes of play and identified overarching constituents of play: ludus and paidia (2001 [1961], pp. 27–36). Ludus refers to the rule-based aspects of play, such as the way we accept the rules of the game

DOI: 10.4324/9781003041474-10

and gain pleasure from playing within those game mechanics. Paidia, linguistically referring to childhood, respects the kinds of play with free improvisation, unstructured exuberance and its joy as we 'play about'. Ludus and paidia are compatible and both typically found in play, though the extent to which one or the other is emphasized, depends on the kind of play at hand. This perspective, which binds together both systems of rules and aesthetic experiences, has been fruitfully applied to music. It is perhaps a glib observation, but the 'playing' of games and 'playing' of music are not as distant as we might initially imagine.

Interfaces and Scaffolding

Music Interfaces and Play

Two recent scholarly discourses have emerged simultaneously regarding music, play and instrumental interfaces. On the one hand, discussions about music and video games have examined how games afford modes of interacting with music – i.e., how video games serve as musical interfaces. On the other hand, examinations of musical instruments as interfaces have used video games as a useful site for investigating the relationship between music, play and instruments.

As long as scholars have been discussing game music, they have described ways in which the mechanics of games offer degrees of musical control. How much agency are players given over the musical output of a game? Are they given the opportunity to create new musical materials, or may they only choose from a set number of pre-determined musical outputs? How constrained are options for changing audiovisual synchronization, rhythms, melodies, tempi, timbres and so on? Simply because a game depicts musical activity does not necessarily mean that it provides a great degree of player control over the music. Games that are specifically themed around music (such as *Guitar Hero*) highlight this issue of player agency (Liebe, 2013), but games which are not ostensibly about music making can include a significant degree of player-determined musical output, especially when reactive musical systems are used. It is for this reason that music analyst Steven Reale provocatively asks whether the noir mystery action game *L.A. Noire* is a 'music game' (2014).

Musicologist Michael Austin draws comparisons between affordances of video game interfaces and those of instruments. He describes both in terms of the potential sonic outputs players can produce, and the players' control over these outputs. He explains that "Sound in video games and musical instrument playing are [both] driven by interaction" (Austin, 2016a, p. 11). He outlines how the interactive possibilities of games determine the forms of music-making that each particular game affords (Austin, 2016b, p. 109; D'Errico, 2016). The components of both games and instruments "determine what the user can or cannot do with the artifact, and whether or not the player uses them for their intended purposes. These affordances are the game's (or instrument's) dynamics" (Austin, 2016b, pp. 111–112). Austin draws on the work of Robin Hunicke, Mark LeBlanc and Robert Zubeck, who proposed an influential way of conceptualizing a game system. Under their 'MDA Model', the consumption of games is a process of 'Rules→System→ "Fun"', which is mapped to the design components of 'Mechanics→Dynamics→Aesthetics' (Hunicke et al., 2004). We can easily map a musical instrument to this same system, and paying attention to the 'mechanics' of the instrumental interface can reveal how this aspect affects the aesthetic outcome (see Figure 7.1).

By looking at the structural parameters of the instrumental interfaces, we can become better aware of the musical potentials they provide, and the ways in which players and

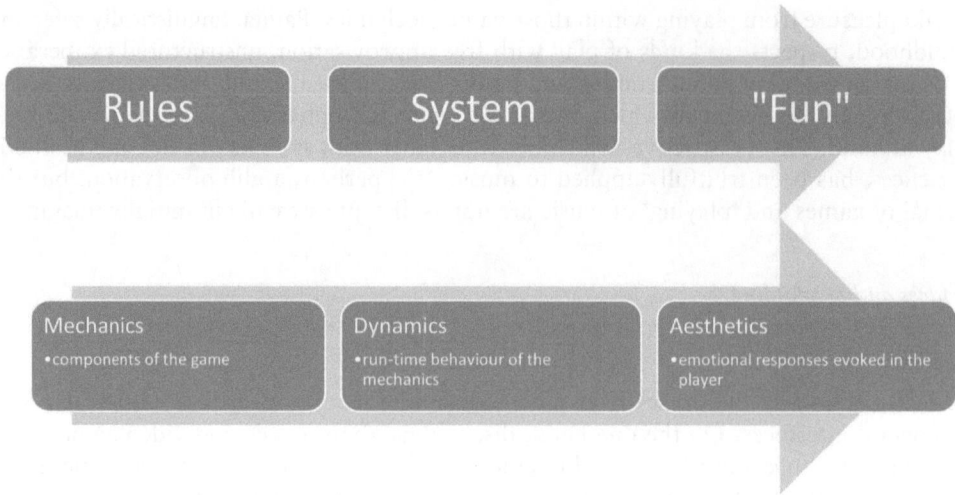

Figure 7.1 MDA framework, after Hunicke et al. (2004).

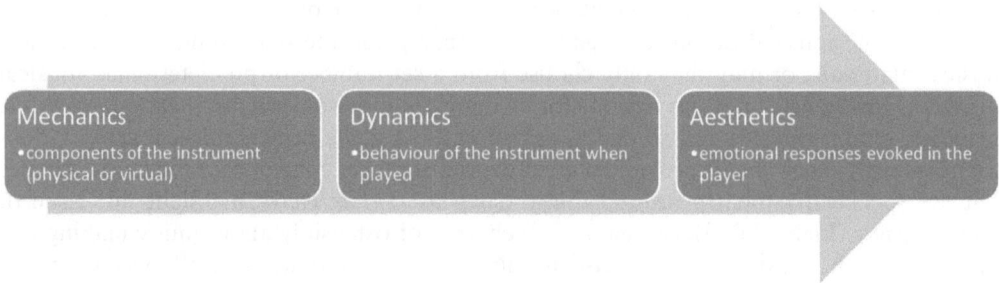

Figure 7.2 MDA framework for instruments.

musicians are encouraged to use them. Roger Moseley, for example, asks us to think "of such [instrumental] interfaces not merely in terms of the work accomplished, or the information transmitted thereby, but as facilitators of play" (2016, p. 59).

Moseley's work is part of a recent trend of critical organology. Along with scholars like Emily Dolan (2012), this entails considering musical instruments as interfaces. Moseley is particularly concerned with the keyboard as musical interface, both in a mechanical and a cultural sense. He writes:

> The interface of the keyboard can be approached as a zone where the digital and the analog come together under the rubric of play. . . . This entails approaching keyboards not merely as data buses or digital/analog converters, but as interfaces at which information is transmitted, knowledge conferred, selfhood (per)formed, and agency (re)distributed via the digital making of differences. . . . [A]n interface does not simply act as a conduit by which a musical thought is realized; it also . . . trains its players by establishing its affordances and mapping them onto a delimited range of sonic outcomes.
>
> (Moseley, 2016, pp. 70, 90)

Moseley describes how the keyboard "provides a platform on which musical motives, gestures, propositions, and ripostes can be put into play" (2016, p. 67). He describes how the keyboard serves as a complex site for playful engagement.

As a field of play, the keyboard offers access to a wide range of ludomusical experiences, whether performed as recreations of prior events, conceived as simulative praxis under a particular set of cultural conditions, or configured in the infinitely finite terms of an emergent improvisatory process. . . . While the rules governing how such processes play out might be hard-coded, the manner of their representation and the scope of the motion they afford and constrain can vary widely . . . Via both ludus and paideia, recreative dynamics cast reciprocal and complementary roles for humans and machines, mediated via the interfaces that couple them.

(2016, pp. 117, 267)

In other words, keyboards are sites for playful musical processes, and these interfaces train their uses as much as users are trained to use them. Alexander Rehding puts it this way:

As interfaces, keyboards are the connectors between the performer's fingers and the instrument, transforming haptic input into musical output, transducing kinetic energy into mechanical sound waves. In this, they function as a gateway from one world to another. But, crucially, they can only convert certain kinds of energy, they allow only certain kinds of data to pass. Interfaces thus impose order and exert control; they set the rules and police the exchange flow. This is why it is useful to think of interfaces as bandwidth filters that allow or enhance certain kinds of engagements, while inhibiting others.

(2019, p. 218)

Both of these academic perspectives (i.e., Austin and Moseley/Rehding) highlight the importance of musical interfaces and how they facilitate, inhibit and encourage particular ways of playing with music, depending on the parameters of the interface in question. Both describe the playful, creative activity that occurs with these interfaces.

Interfaces in the Classroom

For the classroom, interfaces are a critical dimension to how educational objectives are obtained and how creative work is enabled. One useful perspective may stem from research on creative processes in music.

Several studies of the compositional process characterize the creative act in terms similar to problem solving. Composers manage the mechanics of composing by moving from general or conceptual ideas to the specific musical materials and choices. Then they iterate on proposed solutions and forms of that material, editing and revising the music until an optimum solution is found (Collins & Dunn, 2011; Donin, 2012; McAdams, 2004; Pohjannoro, 2016). Psychologists and theorists often describe that process of moving from the general to the specific as one of defining a problem space; composers turn conceptual or abstract ideas into challenges or problems to which they can then propose solutions or responses (Impett, 2016, pp. 653–656). David Collins, for example, characterizes composition in terms of a "generative process of problem proliferation and successive solution implementation, occurring not only in a linear manner but also recursively" (2005, p. 193). It is no great leap to see how this process of setting up rule systems or criteria and finding innovative solutions to those problems can be understood as playful, especially when multiple different possibilities are considered and tested.

Scaffolding has been a foundational aspect of teaching design for decades. Teachers create frameworks to support and enable students' learning through engagement with a task without the need for students to work from first principles. As Wood, Bruner & Ross describe in their seminal article on the topic,

> 'scaffolding' [is a] process that enables a child or novice to solve a problem, carry out a task or achieve a goal which would be beyond his unassisted efforts. This scaffolding consists essentially of the adult 'controlling' those elements of the task that are initially beyond the learner's capacity, thus permitting him to concentrate upon and complete only those elements that are within his range of competence. The task thus proceeds to a successful conclusion. . . . It may result, eventually, in development of task competence by the learner at a pace that would far outstrip his unassisted efforts.
>
> (1976, p. 90)

When teachers create scaffolds for learning tasks, 'controlling' task elements, they are creating interfaces for students to use in order to access the task for learning.

What then do these ideas of interfaces, creativity and play potentially imply for music educators? We are prompted to be aware of how interfaces (instruments or other technologies) scaffold learning for students, irrespective of whether the instrumental/technological interfaces are explicitly part of the learning topic. These interfaces present and serve as creative spaces for play and learning. Ideally, these interfaces need to be aligned to learning outcomes and recognized for the education that the interfaces themselves provide.

When, for instance, students are presented with software like Garageband (a straightforward digital audio workstation), the online drum machine Groove Pizza or the synthesizers of the Learning Synths website, each interface affords different possibilities and inhibits others. The same is true of physical instruments, of course – a diatonic Orff xylophone restricts harmonic experimentation and encourages work with in a timbrally-specific problem space, emphasizing diatonic melodic creativity and staccato rhythmic invention.

Interfaces are themselves types of, and agents of, musical knowledge. Interfaces teach students particular dimensions of musical creativity, even ideas of musical success and failure (just as games inhibit and permit certain parameters of musical agency). An interface defines musicality and what it means to be, or to do music. They present and stage musical expertise and ability – in particular, what types of musicality are reinforced, encouraged, criticized, rewarded and so on. This has particular importance where issues of ability and access are involved. Students with pre-existing musical proficiency with particular technologies or instruments may easily be presented as 'more musical' when a particular interface comes to stand for musicality. Similarly, interfaces can easily discriminate against disabilities (e.g. demanding fine motor skills) unintentionally conflating interface proficiency with musical ability. The interfaces we use inevitably train our students and form their understanding of music, because they establish the spaces of possibility within which the musical play occurs. They are not value-free, and come to define different types and aspects of music, often implicitly teaching what 'correct', 'good' musical results sound like. One solution would be to use a variety of interfaces, and, where possible, use flexible or adaptable interfaces. In practice, there is little that many teachers will be able to do to alter software interfaces, for example, but they are able to take steps to frame those interfaces and design tasks that mesh with the possibilities and ways of working embedded in interfaces of any kind, including instruments and software.

Scaffolding Play in Music Education

Recalling from earlier, interfaces support the user to connect with the act of play through active interactions. More ambitiously, interfaces can help with defining the problem space for creative work, scaffolding creative acts. This need not require software engineering or instrumental adaptation, but structuring tasks that facilitate and encourage creative play of both paidia and ludus within the parameters provided by the interface. Depending on the interfaces available, teachers may scaffold elements of the task to concentrate space for creative play on the aspects most important for the learning outcomes. Tasks that are too open-ended or too restrictive are not likely to facilitate playful creativity effectively. Additionally, rather than treating technologies or instruments as neutral tools, we can recognize the creative learning that occurs when students learn how to experiment with technological interfaces. Interfaces may also be used and deployed to help with the iterative process of creation.

To support the incorporation of using interfaces while planning lessons, teachers might like to reflect on the following questions:

- How might experimentation *with* the interfaces be recognized in assessment criteria?
- What experiences with the interface might students have prior to the lesson (whether from the curriculum or elsewhere), and how might differentiation reflect those varying experiences?
- To what extent does the task mesh with the intended ways of working with the interface? How might the situation be mitigated if a technology or instrument is being used 'against the grain'?
- Does the interface create or help define spaces for play that match the learning outcomes? If learning priorities, for example, concern melodic development, how might the technologies be best adapted to focus on this as a problem space for creative play?
- Are the technological parameters (both those inherent in the technology, and any limits or scaffolds set by the teacher) balanced between restriction and freedom to provide scope for creative play? This might be differentiated through the class. How might concerns of accessibility, especially the embodied modes of interaction, affect this degree of scaffolding?
- Is there a way for the interface (alone or in tandem with another technology) to encourage the self-reflexion inherent in the creative process? For example, if an instrument does not provide for recording, could students use the audio recorded on a smartphone to facilitate that process?
- Can students become aware (implicitly or otherwise) of how interfaces affect the outcomes and possibilities of their music? This might be as explicit as 'choosing the right tool for the job' or thinking critically about the technologies they use, and how those technologies delimit the possibility space of creation.

Fundamentally, then, we can deploy and frame musical interfaces in the classroom to facilitate creative play, directing and structuring tasks and interfaces to make playful exploration useful and satisfying. We can ensure interfaces allow students to crystalize challenges and problems, as well as giving them the means to solve them.

Music, Interactivity and Dialogues

When video games react to their players, to a greater or lesser extent, a connection is formed between game and gamer. This connection can be understood as a dialogic relationship since the player and game respond to each other, prompting and inviting response from the other party (Holquist, 2002, p. 39).

It has long been understood that dialogic relationships are important aspects of the interaction between student and educator, part of the mechanic of education that involves a teacher or knowledgeable 'other' (Bruner, 1996; Vygotsky, 1978, p. 86). One advocate for paying more attention to the nature of this dialogic relationship is Robin Alexander, who suggests that we "construct meaning" partly "from interaction with others" (2008, p. 11). Games serve as one such 'other' as part of a dialogic relationship.

Alexander, along with most commentators on dialogues, considers the topic primarily (or exclusively) in a verbal sense, rather than musical.[1] Drawing upon development theory and types of talk described by Mercer (2000), McHardy Sinclair and Coulthard (1992), and Dillon (1990), Alexander concludes that discussion and scaffolded dialogue are most effective during moments when the dialogue is:

collective: teachers and children address learning tasks together;
reciprocal: teachers and children listen to each other, share ideas and consider alternative viewpoints;
supportive: children articulate their ideas freely, without fear of embarrassment over 'wrong' answers; and they help each other to reach common understandings;
cumulative: teachers and children build on their own and each other's ideas and chain them into coherent lines of thinking and enquiry;
purposeful: teachers plan and facilitate dialogic teaching with particular educational goals in view.

(Alexander, 2008, p. 28)

Learning from games, and the large body of scholarship that suggests the importance of play to learning, we might add further categories here – that dialogues in a music classroom should be playful and musical.

This dialogic interactivity is one of the ways games provide (intentionally and/or otherwise) musical educations. Musical interactivity might be as simple as starting the music when the game begins (likely prompted by the player), or it might involve more complicated dynamic systems that respond to events in the game round (such progression towards an in-game location). Furthermore, as KC Collins points out, "the stakes for players' involvement, interpretation and therefore attention are much higher in games [than film], so they listen more actively" (2013, p. 22). The result is that players are prompted to attend to the music and relate it to the game content. They interpret the musical materials depending on the specifics of the game at hand. For instance, through game play, I learn how the music changes when zombies are nearby in *Resident Evil 4*, I interpret the musical indications of the game state in *Tom Clancy's Splinter Cell*, use music to help me detect crime scene clues in *L.A. Noire*, rely on music to help with navigation across the ocean in *The Legend of Zelda: The Wind Waker* and so on.

In the case of so-called music games, where the relationship between music and gameplay is central to the conceit of the game, it is particularly obvious that we seek to relate the gameplay and music to each other. Indeed, this is how games are able to teach specific musical skills, as has been documented in classroom studies (Cassidy & Paisley, 2013; Jenson et al., 2016; Lesser, 2020; Roesner et al., 2016). In one study, using *Guitar Hero*, it was found by researchers that the:

> accumulation of wider musical skills, such as rhythm, pitch, dexterity, hand-eye coordination . . . and subsequent acknowledgement of the relationship between aural and notated musical representation, engendered a deeper appreciation of wider musical participation. Additionally, recognition of the incremental mastery of these skills appeared to precipitate concordant levels of self-esteem, motivation and intrinsic value of the activity, which, crucially were not solely attributed to that of the music game context, but rather to the experience of performing, appreciating, and creating music in a much more general sense.
>
> (Roesner et al., 2016, p. 210)

Musical interactions between player and game, however, do not need to necessarily have specific ludic outcomes in terms of 'winning' and 'losing'. Witness, for example, the paidia of players who experiment with playing the instruments in *Legend of Zelda: Majora's Mask* far beyond anything strictly functional in terms of the game. Many a game's musical interactivity provides a spark of joy for players outside any functional purpose. In *Animal Crossing: New Horizons*, for instance, players manage an island of colourful anthropomorphic animals, and gamers can input an 'island tune' which serves as a short motif sung by the island inhabitants during interactions. Despite serving no practical function in the game, players avidly share their compositions and tune choices in the game's online community.

Games, through their interactivity, create dialogic relationships with their players. They also prompt players to listen closely to and interact with music.

Playing games, playing music and engaging in dialogues are performative, physical acts. Melanie Fritsch has examined in detail the conceptual performative nature of games and music (2018). She notes how both games and music involve two aspects of what it means to perform. They involve performance both in the sense of a singular aesthetic 'performed' event and in the sense of skilful display whose meaning is understood through an external frame of reference, model or set of cultural rules and criteria (Fritsch, 2018, pp. 18–35). She suggests that this commonality of performance across games and music is part of the significance of game music, and tied directly to how players gain musical and game competencies through play. In games then, we are dealing with performative dialogues that involve music. It is partly for this reason that Fritsch emphasizes how players "desire not just to play the games, but also to play *with* them" (2016, p. 92).

It is all too easy to understand a performance as the end point of a musical-creative process – a moment when the creative work is 'presented' to a receptive but passive audience. Certainly, the Western Art Music tradition has long presented and perpetuated this kind of image (Small, 2001, p. 342). Even as we come to better understand that such a concept of performance is reductive at best, misleading at worst, still the opportunity for performative dialogue is rare. Yet it is widespread in games, where musical materials invite a performative response (à la Alexander).

Games already emulate musical dialogic teaching. In games, we engage in performance, and an interactive, dynamic performance at that. When we play 'with' the game system, it is not unidirectional, and we enter a performative relationship with the interactive medium. In games, performances (including musical performances and soundings) explicitly invite a response – it is for this reason that games work so well as educational experiences. We might create similarly musical-dialogic relationships in our classrooms. Many games provide dialogues that involve music, but few games (notable exceptions aside) provide the opportunity for music-medium responses. Here, classrooms can do better and adopt the interactivity and performativity of games with the qualities of dialogism outlined by Alexander to create musical-transactional dialogues.[2] Learning from both games and Alexander's discussions of dialogues, we should perhaps seek dialogic interactions that are performative, playful and musical:

performative: teachers and children emphasize the enactment of music as a communicative act, one that prompts interpretation and response in kind;

playful: teachers provide frames, structures or rules within which creative activity can take place, and that responses and exchanges within those frames are encouraged; opportunities to 'fail safely' are provided; and

musical: exchanges and responses between learners and teachers occur in the sonic medium, perhaps through specific musical development of musical materials, but also more generally through musical reaction and response.

Games teach listening and analysis through interactivity and dialogic relationships, because the interactivity of the medium prompts gamers to attend closely to the music. These dialogues are also performative through the embodied responses of players and performed sounding of the music. This is especially the case when players respond to the music in such a way that then prompts a further musical change. Games, as performative entities with their interactive relationships with player and implicit and explicit musical educations, illustrate the educational possibilities of performative dialogues.

Tasks in music classrooms can be structured to facilitate and encourage music-medium exchange and verbal dialogues about music (as will be illustrated). Such dialogues can occur as peer learning between students, between teachers and students and even between pre-existing music and student compositions. These musical exchanges might occur in a specific sense of borrowed or emulated musical materials and techniques between partners and participants, or in a broader sense of musical responses and inspirations.

Collective, reciprocal, supportive, cumulative and purposeful dialogues can be created in musical projects that encourage exchange, communal effort and engagement in sonic materials. Class projects with input from all students and an emphasis on revising, adapting and developing musical materials in response to others, and as dynamic musical exchange, seem particularly well-suited to playful, musical dialogic encounters. At its core, musical dialogism blends listening and practice, and encourages learners to use their agency to engage in a personal relationship with the musical materials to further the learning objectives. The emphasis on communal effort with individual voices is an important part of another context of video game music.

Participatory Cultures and Game Music

One does not need to spend very long exploring the cultural domain of video game music before becoming keenly aware of the huge amount of fan musical labour that occurs related to game music. Fans undertake labour when they spend tremendous efforts performing, remixing/rearranging, transcribing, documenting and preserving video game music (amongst many other activities).

This fan labour takes a wide variety of forms. We noted earlier that gamers both play and play *with* games, but this is not bounded by the limits of the game text. Perhaps the most common and widespread practices are those where musicians create cover versions of music from games and/or stage musical performances of their arrangements (whether for live in-person audiences or for presentation on sites like YouTube) (Diaz-Gasca, 2018; O'Leary & Tobias, 2017; Stedman, 2012). Game music culture also involves traditions of using and adapting game technology to make new music. These activities include a variety of creative remixing practices and the chiptune subculture (Driscoll & Diaz, 2009; Paul, 2014).

From a music educator's perspective, the extent to which these fan activities closely resemble (in form if not content) tasks set as mainstays of music curricula is striking. This encompasses both rather more traditional images of musical educational exercises, such as transcription and analytical listening, as well as more recent pedagogical approaches. Indeed, the now-common practice of 'informal learning' in secondary school music curricula (often found, at least in the UK, under the branding 'Musical Futures') seems especially similar to the fan activities of creating and performing arrangements of music from games.

I have elsewhere suggested that there are particular reasons why game music might be such an especially rich site for the practice of musical covers (Summers, 2021, pp. 274–287). Between the interactive nature of the music in games, which responds to player actions, and the frequently non-realistic timbres of much game music, it is challenging for one particular version of a piece of game music to stand as being universally definitive. As soon as a musician chooses to create a cover of a piece of game music, they are forced to make creative choices – 'How many repetitions should a looping cue have?' 'What variations should a cue with dynamic content use?' 'How should unrealistic timbres be adapted to performance?' The result is that game music immediately opens out a variety of interpretive possibilities. Small wonder that the same pieces of game music are so often covered repeatedly.

Fan musical practices range from the relatively conventional to the rather more unexpected. Take, for example, fan-made interpretations of the main 'overworld' theme that recurs throughout the *Legend of Zelda* franchise. Versions on YouTube include those for:

- Solo piano (BachScholar, 2015),
- A trio of performers on marimba (Mart0zz, 2011),
- Multi-tracked a capella voices (McGroove, 2013),
- Jazz ensemble (The Consouls, 2015),
- Tesla coil (Kurdoghlian, 2009),
- Sampled and tuned dog sounds (Sbassbear, 2018),
- Note blocks in *Minecraft* (Amosdoll Music, 2019),
- The mechanical sounds of computer hardware (Zadrożniak, 2017),
- Commodore 64 SID chip (Vytah, 2017),
- *Mario Paint Composer* (Adolfobaez, 2007).

These last two examples are part of broader traditions of fan activity. Programming music for the Commodore 64 SID chip is an example of chiptune music-making. Chiptune or chip-music is a musical style that uses, or emulates, the sound technology of older video game consoles where sound was generated by particular chips, rather than by playback of pre-recorded sound (McAlpine, 2018). For example, present-day artists might write music for the 2A03 chip used in the Nintendo Entertainment System console, or, as mentioned, the Commodore 64's SID chip. Some composers might choose to write music for these chips directly (see, for example, Rich "Tufty" Hollins's 2018 album *Spectronica*), while others may instead use the distinctive timbres as important elements of the compositions (much of Anamanaguchi's output falls into this category). Chipmusic is counterintuitive to much accepted wisdom about music and technology, rejecting assumed values of technological progress in favour of using older technology with limited abilities and idiosyncratic qualities.

Mario Paint Composer is another example of musicians and fans choosing to work with a drastically limited set of tools. *Mario Paint Composer*, an adaptation of the game *Mario Paint*, is a music sequencer with severe limits on timbres, polyphony and rhythms. Yet, as Dana Plank has investigated, a sizable subculture has developed around creating music and covers using *Mario Paint* (2016).

What motivates amateurs (often young people) to undertake these kinds of musical activities outside the classroom? Even though there is a great variety of manifestations of game music fan practice (from our piano covers to chiptunes and *Mario Paint Composer*), one uniting thread is that these exist as part of a participatory culture.

Henry Jenkins et al. define a 'participatory culture' as one with:

1. relatively low barriers to artistic expression and civic engagement,
2. strong support for creating and sharing one's creations with others,
3. some type of informal mentorship whereby what is known by the most experienced is passed along to novices,
4. members who believe that their contributions matter, and
5. members who feel some degree of social connection with one another (at the least, they care what other people think about what they have created).

Not every member must contribute, but all must believe they are free to contribute when ready and that what they contribute will be appropriately valued.

(2009, pp. 5–6)

These qualities of the participatory culture motivate and sustain fans' musical engagements.

Low barriers to artistic expression can be understood in both practical terms (i.e. access to instruments and technologies) and in terms of aesthetics. Tools for chiptune music can be found online for free, as is *Mario Paint Composer*. As noted earlier, fans making covers must immediately make musical decisions concerning foundational elements of the cover (timbral, stylistic and structural decisions cannot be avoided). From the outset, fan musicians are putting their own creative stamp on a cover.

All these creative practices exist as part of online communities (serving Jenkins et al.'s qualities 2–5). Some are very specific, as in chiptune communities surrounding particular chips and styles, or the *Mario Paint Composer* forums. Chiptune communities share compositional techniques and programming materials,[3] while in the case of *Mario Paint Composer*, a forum for innovative ways to use the software "serves as a repository for this fan knowledge, as the users continue to refine their virtuosic command of the program, critique each other's work, and mentor new users" (Plank, 2016, p. 51). There are also sites and communities like OverClocked ReMix, where user-submitted remixes of game music are evaluated and published online (O'Leary, 2018). Even more generally, though, because of the thriving online culture of game music, musicians who create and self-publish a performance of game music online have (or at least feel as though they will have) a ready audience to listen to, evaluate, and respond to their music.

Melanie Fritsch points out that as fans engage with game music in these ways, they are using and developing a variety of cultural and technical literacies. She writes:

When people play with the sound and music, or create their own music videos using musical and other material from the games, they not only remix the music, but also mingle musical and other cultural practices. They use their knowledge of (and competences regarding) several contexts in order to create meaning themselves.

(Fritsch, 2016, p. 93)

Not least among these competencies are musical literacies – the development of which is facilitated by the participatory cultural context.

The participatory cultures surrounding game music may prompt valuable ways to consider dynamics of interaction in the music classroom, with a view to engaging and motivating learners. Of course, an emphasis on student-student relationships (especially for peer learning and peer assessment) is nothing new in educational practice, but game music participatory cultures emphasize the degree to which musical materials and techniques serve as the basis for these dynamics to be created, rather than simply being created on an organizational/structural level in terms of task and assessment design.

One of the attractions for fans engaging in game music labour is the emphasis on re-contextualization and adaptation of game music to new ensembles, genres and styles. This is part of the way that musicians gain ownership of their interpretation of the pieces, understanding them not as a second-degree derivate 'lesser than' the original, but as a distinctive aesthetic statement in its own right. An increased emphasis on this approach that de-emphasized the authority of an original would be useful and open up more creative possibilities, as well as providing a greater sense of musician agency.

It is perhaps understandable that classroom engagements with informal learning have often been specifically connected to non-notated music and popular musics (partly stemming from Lucy Green's extraordinarily influential volume *How Popular Musicians Learn*, 2001). Informal learning practices have often been hesitant to engage with specifics of notation and intricate technical detail. Such a perspective risks reinforcing false binaries of popular/classical musics, and notated/non-notated music. Game music fan activity operates across these divisions, both in terms of style and musical literacies. It also provides alternative modes of musical literacies beyond European Classical Notation (such as the tracker software used for chiptune music). Technical challenge and notated musical literacies are entirely compatible with informal learning and participatory cultures: many of these pieces of music and software systems are difficult to master. Participatory cultures, for all their 'amateur' associations are still sites of high levels of performance skill and technical knowledge, even if these take a form different to formal musical traditions.

Games and their surrounding cultures encourage a playful attitude to sonic materials and technologies through the qualities of a participatory culture, which encourages sharing of music and knowledge, developing participants' musical literacies and skills. Though the 'low culture' subject and playful attitude may imply it is insubstantial, video game fan culture illustrates how effectively complex technical expertise and the performance of challenging musical materials can be motivated and enabled by participatory cultures. Similar dynamics may be cultivated in the classroom for similar ends.

Musical sharing and peer (student-student) interaction/mentorship can relatively easily be facilitated in a classroom setting. The sense of reciprocal value (that 'contributions matter' and they 'care what other people think about what they have created') can be further enhanced by avoiding too much segregation between groups of learners in small group tasks. Greater interactivity between learner subsets, including the exchange of techniques, information and even musical materials (in the vein of the earlier discussions of 'musical dialogues') can further help to create participatory musical cultures in classrooms.

We might also seek to better involve students in our classes who already engage in these kinds of musical activities (remixing game music, chiptune, and so on), and provide opportunities for them to show their expertise in these technologies and their literacy in these domains in our classrooms. This seems especially valuable when geek culture has so often been derided by musical and educational orthodoxies.

At its core, the fan communities of game music show the value of participatory cultures for music education. Game music is continually adapted and re-adapted repeatedly for performance and technologies re-purposed, and all the while musicians develop, utilize and refine their musical abilities. Those who engage with these practices evince and develop skills across many musical domains – analytical skills, aural skills, technological mastery, performance skills, notational skills (of varying kinds), musical-cultural literacy, stylistic (re)contextualization, even entrepreneurship as they create and promote their work. Music classrooms might at least be open to integrating some of these dynamics and materials into pedagogic practices.

Conclusion and Epilogue

This chapter has only considered three specific areas in which music teachers might find ideas of games and play fruitful. By considering the fundamental aspects of play – the interfaces, the components of rules, creativity and fun aesthetics, fusing ludus and paidia – we not only recognize elements that motivate and reward engaging with music generally, but we can turn some of these qualities to educational ends. I would argue that it is worthwhile making music education consciously playful, and being aware of how spaces and frames of play shape musical education. This chapter has suggested just some ways in which fruitful play can be encouraged, in part, by mirroring aspects of playful music in games and game culture.

Much of the preceding discussion has been rather abstract. This is perhaps an inevitable consequence of an argument that aims for broad applicability to a variety of teaching contexts and musical materials. To compensate for that abstraction and to illustrate in a (slightly more) concrete fashion how some of these ideas might be put into practice, what follows is a broad-strokes framework for how these ideas might be embedded into a module of high school classroom music teaching. Some of the organizational aspects in terms of the assessments and differentiation could easily become more playful by following Meghan Naxer's suggestions of how progress and attainment can model RPG progression and reward systems (2020, pp. 146–158). Readers, I hope, will forgive that this is still some way from a set of ready-to-deploy lesson plans (not least with respect to assessment), but at least it may serve to suggest how these conceptual considerations might be integrated into lesson design.

Overall project: Students will create music for a role-playing game, depicting characters, environments and events musically. Individually or in groups, students will learn to write music for particular functions in a Japanese Role-Playing Game (JRPG), then create adaptive music and evaluate the success when the music is implemented into a game environment. Finally, students will present interpretations of another group or individual's work.

Key objectives:

- Students will gain introductory media and musical literacy while developing skills in analysis and composition.
- Students will learn the fundamentals of musical implementation and interactivity in games.

Table 7.1 Module: video game music.

Project Stages (each stage may constitute multiple lessons)	Learning Objectives	Tasks	Interfaces	Dialogues	Participatory Culture
Introductory lessons (analytical listening and media-music literacy skills)	Understand that music is used to depict characters, locations and events. Understand musical signs (semiotics) and styles are used by musicians to communicate with listeners. Understand how music and gameplay can interact in games.	Listen and explore examples of video game music, either teacher-selected choices or student-proposed examples. Guided listening tasks to help identify musical communication and relationship with gameplay. Develop vocabulary for discussing musical and media features.	Consider, in the examples discussed, the degree and nature of musical control afforded the player (i.e. what musical agency the player has, and how they exert that power).	Illustrate dialogic nature of musical interaction in games. Exchange and discussion about musical materials. Cover versions of materials also encouraged to be discussed and shared.	Students, together with teacher, asked to suggest examples of music in games that they liked, and to explain why. These can be collected as a shared listening list.

(Continued)

Table 7.1 (Continued)

Project Stages (each stage may constitute multiple lessons)	Learning Objectives	Tasks	Interfaces	Dialogues	Participatory Culture
Composing Music for the (J)RPG (compositional skills)	Identify how composers have musically invoked characters, locations and events in music. Explain the connection between musical features and the game content. Understand how music communicates in games. Show awareness of how music is deployed in games, and the functions it serves. Explain connections between musical content and the functions of music in games. Compose a piece of music to serve a particular communicative function in a game.	Listen to examples of music from Japanese Role-Playing Games (JRPGs), especially following the so-called 'eight melodies' template – i.e. the central eight cues of a JRPG: castle, town, field (overworld), dungeon, battle, title/opening, end, boss/villain. See also music for winning/losing and other hero characters. Use guided listening to identify musical elements and how the music functions in the game. Students, in groups or individually, write music for one of these functions in the game, using some of the features identified in the antecedent examples.	Mirroring the previous stage, discuss how players will interact with music in this game, and how that will affect the music. Depending on available technologies, teachers scaffold templates and tasks to provide specific problem-spaces for composing short looping cues. This might include model DAW sessions, pre-set accompaniments, or defined structures. More advanced students may explore additional interface features, expanding the problem space.	Illustrate how many JRPG games use similar musical materials and topoi for the same kind of music, showing how games take inspiration from each other. Students write their music as a response to the music that they have been shown/found. Students can identify how their music follows, adapts or reacts against the examples they have heard, understanding the process as a musical dialogue.	Throughout the compositional stages, provide moments for students to share questions, problems, ideas, solutions and so on. This way, a sense of a whole group endeavour can be created, rather than just as individual agents, by continually referring to models of music from other games (amateur and professional).

(Continued)

Table 7.1 (Continued)

Project Stages (each stage may constitute multiple lessons)	Learning Objectives	Tasks	Interfaces	Dialogues	Participatory Culture
Composing Adaptive Music (advanced compositional skills and understanding of game programming)	Understand how game music is different from linear media music. Understand how dynamic music is made and programmed in games. Use dynamic music techniques in a new composition.	Listen to examples of adaptive music in games (esp. layering and sequencing of modules). Identify musical features that make adaptive music successful and the conditions under which musical changes occur. Either adapt an existing cue (from the previous stage) into an adaptive piece, or write a new battle theme with dynamic stages. For example, write a looping segment, and then create layers which can be faded in/out.	As in the previous stage, but now with respect to dynamic music, discuss how players will interact with music in this game, and how that will affect the music. Again, as in the previous stage, depending on the interfaces at hand, provide templates and models to concentrate space for creative play on adaptive music processes. More advanced students may explore additional interface features, expanding the problem space.	Adaptive musical techniques are identified, borrowed, adapted and redeployed from originating work in the students' own compositions. Students also iterate on their own work.	Create a class notebook of effective techniques of dynamic music and 'problem solving'. Students are encouraged to post questions to, and draw ideas from, this notebook. Real-world participatory cultures, such as support forums may also be used as resources, depending on class and level.

(Continued)

Table 7.1 (Continued)

Project Stages (each stage may constitute multiple lessons)	Learning Objectives	Tasks	Interfaces	Dialogues	Participatory Culture
Response to other compositions (evaluation skills; performance skills)	Evaluate the qualities of the student's own composition and those of others. Be able to receive and act on constructive criticism. Develop creative output in response to the work of others.	Listen to the cues created by others, and provide peer feedback. Students should consider how to revise their music to better fit with the other music that will also be in the game. Instrumentation, themes and other musical materials can be shared and adapted across groups. For example, a character theme can be integrated into a 'title' or 'end' theme, alternative variations can be created and so on. Peer and teacher criticism is used to revise the music.	Students asked to reflect how the technological interfaces have affected aspects of their music (whether positively or negatively), and if there are opportunities to revise the work or adapt the technology in response.	Explicit musical dialogues created when student composers are asked to draw on and develop materials created by others. Observations from earlier sessions about the dialogism of interactive music also emphasized.	The sense of a communal effort, supportive environment and a receptive audience is created as part of the peer-feedback process.

(Continued)

Table 7.1 (Continued)

Project Stages (each stage may constitute multiple lessons)	Learning Objectives	Tasks	Interfaces	Dialogues	Participatory Culture
Implementation, Testing and Evaluation (critical listening skills)	Understand how computational processes manipulate music. Understand how musical features can be affected by computational processes.	Either students may implement the music themselves into a template game (using RPG Maker or a mod), or the teacher does this for them. Students play the game and use guided listening and reflection to evaluate the music. The difference between the engine's manipulation of the music and the students' expectations can be discussed. If time allows, they may revise the music in light of implementation.	Students encouraged to understand how game interface manipulates their music, both as they expected and otherwise. Pupils encouraged to revise work to better adapt to interfaces.	Musical materials in dialogue with each other and gameplay in game engine. Manipulation of material by engine and player. Iteration possible if time allows.	Students hear their work in context of the group-created outcome – they have contributed to something together.

(Continued)

Table 7.1 (Continued)

Project Stages (each stage may constitute multiple lessons)	Learning Objectives	Tasks	Interfaces	Dialogues	Participatory Culture
Covers Task (critical listening, interpretation and performance skills)	Be able to devise and create an interpretation of another piece. Use musical processes and interpersonal relationships to develop a new musical interpretation. Understand the creative challenges and opportunities of producing a cover version.	Students produce a cover version (acoustically performed or otherwise) of a piece from *another* group or composer in the class. They are encouraged to radically rework the music and can discuss the piece with the original creators to find out more about the composition being covered, including process of construction and other musical details.	Students and teachers work together to match available technologies to the ambitions of covers. Students can understand the creative possibilities represented by the instruments, and work with, or against, conventions of those interfaces. This task may also encourage translation of musical material across instrumentation, and result in adaptation. For example, music for one instrument may need to be adapted when it is translated to another, or may simply be made more effective/idiomatic on another instrument, illustrating how interfaces determine musical outcomes.	Dialogue of musical content through adaptation and creation of cover version. Verbal dialogue in interaction with other groups. Teacher may also create variations on students' work.	Collaboration and consultation between groups cultivated as materials varied and developed. Support between groups as work developed, including sense of drawing on and contributing to wider project, as musical materials adapt.

- Students will learn how music can communicate narrative and ludic qualities.
- Students will understand how dynamic music functions, and be able to identify key musical qualities of these systems.
- Students will be able to critically interpret musical material and compose music to a specific brief.
- Students will be able to use music to communicate non-verbally, applying musical techniques with the knowledge of precedents and musical conventions, procedures and devices.
- Students will be able to explain and justify their musical decisions based on the aims of communication.
- Students will develop creative musical and critical skills.

Notes

1. Curiously, even writing about music and classroom dialogues has very often focused on talking about music (e.g. Major, 2008; Major & Cottle, 2010). For the few exceptions, see Morgan et al., 2000; O'Neill, 2011; Miell & MacDonald, 2000; MacDonald & Miell, 2000).
2. The idea of musical 'transactions' is here borrowed from Keith Swanwick (1999, p. 44).
3. See, for example, the community-evolved techniques of 1-bit music reported in Troise (2020, pp. 44–74).

References

Adolfobaez. (2007, September 24). Mario paint – The legend of Zelda overworld theme [Video]. *YouTube*. https://www.youtube.com/watch?v=tYVoC_9UMpY

Alexander, R. (2008). *Towards dialogic teaching: Rethinking classroom talk* (4th ed.). Dialogos.

Amosdoll Music. (2019, June 19). I made the Zelda Theme using Minecraft note blocks [Video]. *YouTube*. https://www.youtube.com/watch?v=NwerxZE8GPc

Austin, M. (2016a). Introduction – Taking note of music games. In M. Austin (Ed.), *Music video games: Performance, politics, and play* (pp. 1–22). Bloomsbury.

Austin, M. (2016b). Sample, cycle, sync: The music sequencer and its influence on music video games. In M. Austin (Ed.), *Music video games: Performance, politics, and play* (pp. 107–123). Bloomsbury.

BachScholar. (2015, March 19). The legend of Zelda | title theme & main theme | Cory Hall, piano [Video]. *YouTube*. https://www.youtube.com/watch?v=wndYa18AIn0

Bateson, P., & Martin, P. (2013). *Play, playfulness, creativity and innovation*. Cambridge University Press.

Bruner, J. S. (1996). *The culture of education*. Harvard University Press.

Caillois, R. (2001). *Man, play and games*(M. Barash, Trans.). University of Illinois Press (Original work published 1961).

Cassidy, G., & Paisley, A. (2013). Music-games: A case study of their impact. *Research Studies in Music Education*, 35(1), 119–138.

Collins, D. (2005). A synthesis process model of creative thinking in music composition. *Psychology of Music*, 33(2), 193–216.

Collins, D., & Dunn, M. (2011). Problem-solving strategies and processes in musical composition: Observations in real time. *Journal of Music, Technology and Education*, 4(1), 47–76.

Collins, K. (2013). *Playing with sound*. The MIT Press.

The Consouls. (2015, October 7). The legend of Zelda (main theme) Fusion Jazz cover – the consouls [Video]. *YouTube*. https://www.youtube.com/watch?v=XFRX9A9V64Y

D'Errico, M. (2016). *Interface aesthetics: Sound, software, and theecology of digital audio production* [Doctoral thesis, University of California, Los Angeles].

Diaz-Gasca, S. (2018). Super smash covers!: Performance and audience engagement in Australian videogame music cover bands. *Perfect Beat*, 19(1), 51–67.

Dillon, J. T. (1990). *The practice of questioning*. Routledge.

Dolan, E. (2012). Toward a musicology of interfaces. *Keyboard Perspectives*, 5, 1–12.

Donin, N. (2012). Empirical and historical musicologies of compositional processes: Towards a cross-fertilization. In D. Collins (Ed.), *The act of musical composition: Studies in the creative process* (pp. 1–26). Ashgate.

Driscoll, K., & Diaz, J. (2009). Endless loop: A brief history of chiptunes. *Transformative Works and Cultures*, 2. https://doi.org/10.3983/twc.2009.096

Fritsch, M. (2016). "It's a-me, Mario!" Playing with video game music. In M. Kamp, T. Summers & M. Sweeney (Eds.), *Ludomusicology: Approaches to video game music* (pp. 92–115). Equinox.

Fritsch, M. (2018). *Performing bytes: Musikperformances der Computerspielkultur*. Königshausen und Neuman.

Green, L. (2001). *How popular musicians learn*. Aldershot.

Holquist, M. (2002). *Dialogism* (2nd ed.). Routledge.

Hunicke, R., LeBlanc, M., & Zubeck, R. (2004). MDA: A formal approach to game design and game research. In *Proceedings of the AAAI workshop on challenges in games AI*. AAAI Press.

Impett, J. (2016). Making a mark: The psychology of composition. In S. Hallam, I. Cross & M. Thaut (Eds.), *The Oxford handbook of music psychology* (2nd ed., pp. 651–666). Oxford University Press.

Jenkins, H., with Purushotma, R., Weigel, M., Clinton, K., & Robison, A. J. (2009). *Confronting the challenges of participatory culture* (Updated ed.). MIT Press.

Jenson, J., De Castell, S., Muehrer, R., & Droumeva, M. (2016). So you think you can play: An exploratory study of music video games. *Journal of Music, Technology and Education*, 9(3), 273–288.

Kurdoghlian, D. (2009, September 18). Legend of Zelda Theme on two singing Tesla Coils [HD] [Video]. *YouTube*. https://www.youtube.com/watch?v=jsuRlYZV6zY

Lesser, A. J. (2020). An investigation of digital game-based learning software in the elementary general music classroom. *Journal of Sound and Music in Games*, 1(2), 1–24.

Liebe, M. (2013). Interactivity and music in computer games. In P. Moormann (Ed.), *Music and game: Perspectives on a popular alliance* (pp. 41–62). Springer.

MacDonald, R., & Miell, D. (2000). Musical conversations: Collaborating with a friend on creative tasks. In R. Joiner, K. Littleton, D. Faulkner & D. Miell (Eds.), *Rethinking collaborative learning* (pp. 65–78). Free Association.

Major, A. (2008). Appraising composing in secondary-school music lessons. *Music Education Research*, 10(2), 307–319.

Major, A., & Cottle, M. (2010). Learning and teaching through talk: Music composing in the classroom with children aged six to seven years. *British Journal of Music Education*, 27, 289–304.

Mart0zz. (2011, July 24). Legend of Zelda – Main theme on marimba [Video]. *YouTube*. https://www.youtube.com/watch?v=qYtrnr4chfU

McAdams, S. (2004). Problem-solving strategies in music composition: A case study. *Music Perception*, 21(3), 391–429.

McAlpine, K. (2018). *Bits and pieces. A history of chiptunes*. Oxford University Press.

McGroove, S. (2013, November 22). Zelda a link to the past – overworld theme acapella [Video]. *YouTube*. https://www.youtube.com/watch?v=CgAEMZBRGI0

McHardy Sinclair, J., & Coulthard, M. (1992). Towards an analysis of discourse. In M. Coulthard (Ed.), *Advances in spoken discourse analysis* (pp. 1–24). Routledge.

Mercer, N. (2000). *Words and minds: How we use language to think together*. Routledge.

Miell, M., & MacDonald, R. (2000). Children's creative collaborations: The importance of friendship when working together on a musical composition. *Social Development*, 9, 348–369.

Morgan, L., Hargreaves, D., & Joiner, R. (2000). Children's collaborative music composition: Communication through music. In R. Joiner, K. Littleton, D. Faulkner & D. Miell (Eds.), *Rethinking collaborative learning* (pp. 52–64). Free Association.

Moseley, R. (2016). *Keys to play: Music as a ludic medium from Apollo to Nintendo*. University of California Press.

Naxer, M. (2020). A hidden harmony: Music theory pedagogy and role-playing games. In W. Gibbons & S. Reale (Eds.), *Music in the role-playing game: Heroes and harmonies* (pp. 146–158). Routledge.

O'Leary, J. (2018). *A corpus-assisted discourse analysis of music-related practices discussed within chipmusic.org* [Doctoral thesis, Arizona State University].

O'Leary, J., & Tobias, E. (2017). Sonic participatory cultures within, through, and around video games. In R. Mantie & G. D. Smith (Eds.), *The Oxford handbook of music making and leisure* (pp. 543–566). Oxford University Press.

O'Neill, S. (2011). Learning in and through music performance: Understanding cultural diversity via inquiry and dialogue. In M. Barrett (Ed.), *A cultural psychology of music education* (pp. 179–200). Oxford University Press.

Patte, M., & Brown, F. (2013). *Rethinking children's play*. Bloomsbury.

Paul, L. J. (2014). For the love of chiptune. In K. Collins, B. Kapralos & H. Tessler (Eds.), *The Oxford handbook of interactive audio* (pp. 507–530). Oxford University Press.

Plank, D. (2016). Mario paint composer and musical (re)play on YouTube. In M. Austin (Ed.), *Music video games: Performance, politics, and play* (pp. 43–82). Bloomsbury.

Pohjannoro, U. (2016). Capitalising on Intuition and Reflection: Making Sense of a Composer's Creative Process. *Musicae Scientiae, 20*(2), 207–234.

Reale, S. B. (2014). Transcribing musical worlds; or, is L. A. Noire a music game? In K. J. Donnelly, W. Gibbons & N. Lerner (Eds.), *Music in video games: Studying play* (pp. 77–103). Routledge.

Rehding, A. (2019). Opening the music box. *Journal of the Royal Musical Association, 144*(1), 205–221.

Roesner, D., Paisley, A., & Cassidy, G. (2016). Guitar heroes in the classroom: The creative potential of music games. In M. Austin (Ed.), *Music video games: Performance, politics and play* (pp. 197–228). Bloomsbury.

Sbassbear. (2018, September 14). Legend of Zelda theme song but with dog sounds (Legend of Zeldog) [Video]. *YouTube*. https://www.youtube.com/watch?v=gx-eTnkO8aQ

Small, C. (2001). Why doesn't the whole world love chamber music? *American Music 19*(3), 340–359.

Stedman, K. (2012). Remix Literacy and Fan Compositions. *Computers and Composition 29*(2), 107–123.

Summers, T. (2021). *The legend of Zelda: Ocarina of time – A game music companion*. Intellect.

Sutton-Smith, B. (1997). *The ambiguity of play*. Harvard University Press.

Swanwick, K. (1999). *Teaching music musically*. Routledge.

Troise, B. (2020). The 1-bit instrument. The fundamentals of 1-bit synthesis, their implementational implications, and instrumental possibilities. *Journal of Sound and Music in Games, 1*(1), 44–74.

Vygotsky, L. S. (1978). *Mind in society: The development of higher psychological processes* (M. Cole, V. Jolm-Steiner, S. Scribner & E. Souberman, Eds.). Harvard University Press.

Vytah. (2017, October 31). [C64] Zelda theme (SID cover by Linus) – oscilloscope view [Video]. *YouTube*. https://www.youtube.com/watch?v=l7q3X5iT_fs

Wood, D., Bruner, J., & Ross, G. (1976). The role of tutoring in problem solving. *The Journal of Child Psychology and Psychiatry, 17*(2), 89–100.

Zadrożniak, P. (2017, January 7). The Floppotron: The legend of Zelda [Video]. *YouTube*. Retrieved July 9, 2020, from https://www.youtube.com/watch?v=ZGlVt3x-QWI

8 Music Representation and Modelling

A Signal Processing Perspective

Augusto Sarti, Fabio Antonacci and Alberto Bernardini

Introduction and Aerial View

Music plays a prominent and pervasive role in the life of people of any culture or age. It has the ability to evoke powerful emotional responses; alter or regulate the mood; enhance desirable emotional states (or diminish undesirable ones); elicit a sense of togetherness through entrainment; and much more. To more sophisticated listeners, in fact, it can offer complex and articulated emotional narrations with no need of a semantic context. Music makers have always relied on their experience and on the "tools of their trade" to produce this impact on their listeners – but in the past few decades they have grown to increasingly rely on science and technology as well.

Originally (before the electronic era), the "technical" focus was on the development of acoustic musical instruments of better timbral properties, acoustic projection, and constructive quality; improved range and dynamics; enhanced responsivity and ergonomic personalisation. With the arrival of the first phonograph, near the end of the 19th century, the focus shifted to analog recording and reproduction technologies. It did so in a nearly exclusive fashion for over eight decades, bringing music to an ever-growing audience. Things changed quite dramatically in the mid-1960s, when the early computers made their first appearance. A world of new possibilities opened up for music makers:

- early digital sound synthesis techniques (Hiller & Ruiz, 1971) began expanding the timbral space that was accessible to musicians until then;
- the introduction of digital reverberation (Välimäki et al., 2012) made us all less dependent on the environment of fruition;
- digital audio effects (Zölzer, 2011) and digital audio recording and production technologies (Fine, 2008) broadened the horizons of music production;
- novel human-machine interaction solutions (Tzanetakis et al., 2013) gave performers enhanced expressivity power;
- novel audio compression and encoding algorithms (Brandenburg, 1999) enabled an unprecedented expansion in music access modalities.

The next big technological revolution in the music market came when the first Internet music repositories began to appear in the 1990s. The Internet Underground Music Archive (IUMA) was the first one of this sort in existence (1993), even before the era of the World Wide Web (it originally existed as FTP and Gopher sites). IUMA's purpose was to help independent artists distribute their music to fans while bypassing traditional distribution models and record labels. IUMA was acquired by eMusic in 1998, which immediately began

DOI: 10.4324/9781003041474-11

offering online access to music through Internet radio, live streaming feeds, or downloads. The idea of universal and ubiquitous access to large repositories of music was beginning to take shape. It became a reality with the arrival of the first large-scale audio streaming services, such as Last.fm (2002) and iTunes (2003), followed by Pandora Internet Radio (2005), Spotify (2008) and Apple Music (2015). These services suddenly revolutionised the music industry and reversed the negative trend in revenues that had been experienced until then, and they deeply changed our music consumption habits. With millions of songs at our reach and the disappearance of "physical" music stores, the need of learning how to navigate in a sea of musical content grew more and more urgent.

Research on Music Information Retrieval (MIR) (Downie, 2003) played a crucial role in this revolution. It helped by developing algorithms for automatically enriching musical content with metadata (tags or descriptors) of all sorts, thus enabling a divide-and-conquer approach to content management which offered more powerful search tools for the users. Tagging Music, in fact, was a rather straightforward business when it concerned author, title, year of production, etc. However, when it came to classifying music based on genre, mood, and other high-level descriptors, classification errors and subjective evaluations would get in the way. A wide range of solutions were therefore proposed for automatic music tagging, based on advanced audio-driven classification/clustering techniques as well as machine intelligence algorithms (Celma, 2010). It soon became clear, however, that music discovery could not be based just on traditional search mechanisms (a.k.a. "pull" solutions). In fact, when it comes to music, we seldom know exactly what we are searching for; and when we do know, we usually don't know how to describe it. It is also very difficult for us to predict what music would be "right" at any given time, or what would pleasantly surprise us; and it is even harder for us to predict whether we would better appreciate a musical piece if we took the time to listen to it again. This is why music recommendation (i.e., that concerned with "push" solutions) became such a popular area of research within MIR. One of the first algorithms to be popularised was developed for Last.fm, which progressively built a profile of the listener based on frequently played tracks. Pandora improved on this idea of music recommendation to offer even more personalised musical streams. Today's streaming services offer all sorts of personalised radio channels and playlists, as well as music discovery channels. These are all examples of research trends within MIR, such as playlist generation, personalisation of audio streams, and music discovery (Celma, 2010; Chiarandini et al., 2011; Irene et al., 2019).

But the breadth and span of MIR is inherently much wider than that, and its venues of exploration seem to grow by the day. MIR, in fact, covers a wide range of other applications including: evaluating similarities between melodic lines or even polyphonic progressions; developing advanced music representation and indexing solutions; recognising musical pieces from raw audio; detecting plagiarism; recognising music covers or bootlegs; transcribing music or extracting musical descriptors (chords, beat, tempo, rhythmic signature, tonality, etc.) from raw audio; segmenting an audio file based on its musical structure (e.g. intro, verse, refrain, etc.); recognising musical instruments, singers, performers, authors, or even performative styles, again from raw audio; modelling improvisational styles; and more. Scientific advancements in the MIR area are progressing at a staggering pace, and sometimes it is difficult to identify a common trend or understand where research should be heading. It is quite clear, however, that research is progressively moving up in its level of abstraction and is becoming more and more "human-centric". In fact, in the past few decades, it has shifted its focus from physics and computational acoustics to the perception of audio and acoustic phenomena, and is currently focusing more and more on brain sciences and even psychological aspects of listening. So, if we are to embark into a quest aimed at understanding where research is heading or should be heading, we might as well begin with addressing perception in growing order of level of abstraction.

Role of Perception of Sounds and Soundfields

Let us begin with sound and sound-field perception. The past century has seen a flourishing of research activities focused on studying human perception of sound and acoustic stimuli in general (Gelfand, 2004). These activities, which were initially aimed at improving our understanding of hearing loss (Pickles, 1982) and help develop countermeasures, later proved useful for advancements in musicological studies as well as applications of audio and acoustic signal processing.

Perception of loudness was first studied by Fletcher and Munson (1933) in a series of experiments that led to the derivation of the celebrated equal-loudness curves, which explain how we need to change the sound pressure level of a pure tone as its frequency changes, in order to perceive it at constant loudness. This proved extremely useful for orchestration and music production purposes, as it helped us understand how to balance the orchestral rendering of musical pieces – but it also enabled the development of several technological solutions for audio rendering (e.g., loudness compensation). A wide range of perceptual experiments followed over the decades concerning auditory masking effects, more specifically frequency and temporal masking (Moore, 2004), which constituted the starting point for the development of perceptual audio compression techniques (Brandenburg, 1999), such as MP3 and AAC. Other interesting studies were conducted within the perception of pitch (Houtsma, 1995), and how it changes as a function of tonal frequency and sound pressure level. This shed light on a wide range of problems related to the tuning of musical instruments, or the perceptual "de-tuning" phenomena in live performances in specific acoustic conditions. The very same studies helped develop perceptual descriptors that are used today for a careful design of digital audio analysis and processing systems.

A great deal of work has also been devoted to understanding how the environment affects the sound that we perceive, and how much spatial information we are able to extract and use from an acoustic scene. The interest in sound reverberation was originally motivated by the pressure of music broadcasting and recording industries. Studio environments, in fact, were known to produce too "dry" a sound for any form of consumption, while concert halls with the desired ideal reverberation were not suitable for recording purposes. The earliest artificial reverberation experiments date back to nearly a century ago, using echo chambers built for the purpose (Rettinger, 1957). After that came electro-mechanical devices (typically plates and springs) and tape delays (Välimäki et al., 2012). The arrival of the digital era (late-1960s) brought a plethora of new computational solutions. Back then, computational power was hard to come by, therefore a brute-force direct implementation of the Room Impulse Response (RIR) filter was out of the question. This is why perceptual reverberation (Gardner, 2013) was the only option. Such solutions, in fact, were not aimed at reproducing the response of an actual room, but only focused on the features of reverberation that would improve the perception of quality and make the recording more aesthetically pleasing. Over time, computational power became less expensive, and algorithms of higher computational complexity could finally be adopted as a viable solution. We went from perceptual reverberation structures (Moorer, 1979; Schroeder & Logan, 1961), to networks of delay lines (Välimäki et al., 2012), and then to the now-affordable brute-force direct implementation of recorded/estimated RIR filters.

All the families of reverberation solutions described here are aimed at making the sound more pleasant and plausible – but they are not suitable for capturing the true role of spatial acoustics in listening experiences. Through spatial sound we constantly make sense of our surroundings: we place ourselves and others in the acoustic scene; we single out speakers in a crowd, recognise them, and keep track of their emotional state; and last but not least, we sense the "mood of the room". We do so dynamically: by moving around and exploring our acoustic surroundings. Gaining spatial control of sound is also an art form and a source of expressivity for music makers. And it is a wonderful immersive experience for the listeners, as it can help them regain the focus on music that is so hard to attain in an era of information overload.

Surprisingly enough, early studies of spatial audio perception began over a century ago by Lord Rayleigh (1907), receiving renewed attention in the past few decades (Blauert, 1996; Conetta et al., 2015) with the development of the first 3D audio rendering solutions. Today, we identify two wide families of spatial audio systems:

- Soundfield rendering: based on spatial distributions of loudspeakers, including ambisonics (Gerzon, 1985), higher-order loudspeakers (Samarasinghe et al., 2013), wavefield synthesis (Boone et al., 1995), and plenacoustic rendering (Bianchi et al., 2016; Canclini et al., 2014).
- Binaural rendering: based on headphones or two loudspeakers with cross-channel interference suppression).

While the former family of solutions aims at reproducing the correct soundfield around us, the latter aims at reproducing the correct signals in our ear canals, effectively bypassing our body's response to the soundfield. Binaural solutions, therefore, need to inherently account for the acoustic response of our body (i.e., outer ear, head and torso).

The acoustic response of our body plays a crucial role in our spatial perception of sound. The so-called Head-Related Transfer Function (HRTF), also sometimes referred to as the anatomical transfer function, describes the frequency response of our body to an acoustic stimulus coming from a specific location in space (Blauert, 1996). The HRTF, in fact, compactly accounts for: the density, size, and morphology of our head; the shape of our ears and ear canal, and the geometry and structure of our nasal and oral cavities. It does so by describing in great detail how some frequencies are boosted while others are attenuated depending on the direction of arrival of an acoustic source (W. Zhang et al., 2010). Knowing the HRTF allows us to develop solutions for 3D audio rendering that use a simple pair of headphones to "inject" into our ear canals signals that already incorporate our own body response (binaural rendering). However, since our body is unique, each person's HRTFs is significantly different from another. This is why we talk about "personalized" HRTF. Understanding how far the "personalization" needs to be pushed is a crucial aspect in the feasibility of binaural rendering techniques (Jin et al., 2018). Similar considerations apply to immersive audio rendering based on spatial distributions of loudspeakers. Understanding the limits of perception in relation to the limits of spatial audio rendering systems is, in fact, crucial for successfully developing 3D audio rendering systems based on loudspeaker arrangements (Bianchi et al., 2012).

Role of Music Perception and Cognition

So far, we have discussed perception of sounds and soundfields, or we often term it "early hearing", due to the focus on phenomena at a low level of abstraction. When it comes to developing tools and technologies that help with making music as well as listening to music, the perceptual aspects that we need to focus on (and develop a sense for) are at a higher level of abstraction – they need to be concerned with how we perceive and understand the many musical layers: timbral, tonal, rhythmic, contrapuntal, harmonic, structural, expressive, etc. (Deutsch, 1999).

In the past three decades or so, research in neuroscience and cognitive science (Chanda & Levitin, 2013; Koelsch & Siebel, 2005) have shed new light on how we perceive and make sense of music. This new understanding has had a deep impact on how we approach research within the various disciplines of Signal Processing, particularly in MIR. One aspect with which neuroscience has helped us a great deal, for example, concerns how we develop music cognition models starting from "raw" auditory stimuli. Our brain, in fact, appears to follow a bottom-up approach, based on a process of feature extraction, followed by one of feature integration. It begins with extracting "early" musical features using dedicated and specialised neural networks, which capture very specific low-level information about music, such as pitch, timbre, spatial location, loudness, reverberation, tone durations, onset times, etc. Feature extraction is carried out in parallel by neural circuits that reside in different areas of the brain and therefore can operate independently of one another. One such bottom-up processing paradigm also explains why these musical attributes can be successfully treated as "separable". This low-level processing takes place in the peripheral and evolutionarily "older" regions of our brain (i.e., cochlea, auditory cortex, brain stem, and cerebellum), and its output forms the basic building blocks that higher-level processing can work with in the feature integration phase, which takes place in our "centers for higher thought", mostly in the frontal cortex of our brain. This higher-level processing is constantly hard at work to predict what comes next in music. In order to do that, it relies on the models that we build, on familiarity with the piece and/or with the musical genre, and on whatever prior information we have on what we are listening to. As we will discuss in the next section on Music Representations and Models, this hierarchical bottom-up approach is adopted in MIR research in exactly the same fashion.

Another aspect that research in neuroscience and cognitive science have begun to find answers about is how music is able to steer emotions and move us (Juslin & Sloboda, 2001; Levitin, 2006). The most interesting findings date back only a couple of decades ago, when new links were found between neurochemistry and cognition, which made it possible to shed some light onto the mechanisms behind musical emotions (Blood & Zatorre, 2003; Blood et al., 1999; Panksepp, 2003). These emotions, in fact, were found to be associated to specific regions of the brain that are known to be involved in reward, motivation, and arousal (Huron, 2006). These results turned out to be a milestone in brain studies, as they triggered numerous explorations in the minds of music lovers. One extremely intriguing aspect of this exploration was that pleasure in music listening does not just come when our expectations are fulfilled, but also when expectancy for some of the musical parameters are violated to a certain degree (Shany et al., 2019). It is exactly this balance between fulfilment of expectation and surprise that gives us pleasure in listening. This is an aspect of music perception that is certainly worth exploring further, as it could help us develop a wide range of applications in support of musicians and listeners. See potential applications later in this chapter.

Music Representations and Models

As mentioned in the previous section, Music Information Retrieval (MIR) adopts a paradigm inspired by the bottom-up processing that takes place in our brain while we try to "take in" and make sense of musical stimuli. Algorithms of MIR, in fact, usually operate in a feature-based bottom-up fashion, and the related features tend to be hierarchically organised, according to their level of abstraction:

- Low-Level Features (LLF) (Mitrovíc et al., 2010) are highly specialised descriptors of well-defined signal characteristics. Temporal descriptors, for example, capture signal features that evolve over time, such as the Zero-Crossing Rate, its amplitude or its power, etc.; frequency descriptors summarise the spectral behaviour of the signal (e.g. spectral tilt and spectral flux); perceptual features describe signal properties that are useful for low-level perceptual modelling, such as masked perceptual loudness, partial loudness of the emotional difference, and perceptual bandwidth (Sezgin et al., 2012).
- Mid-Level Features (MLF) are descriptors that capture more complex aspects of the musical excerpt according to precise musicological definitions. They process LLFs to extract descriptors of rhythmic, harmonic, tonal, and structural knowledge, such as tempo, beat, chords, etc. (Dittmar et al., 2007)
- High-Level Features (HLF) tend to carry an abstract meaning that is easily grasped by humans but is hard to frame in a precise definition. They are usually derived from MLFs (though they sometimes also use LLFs), and they are usually employed for modelling timbral modulation, song dynamics, rhythmic qualities, melodic properties, and mood descriptors of a musical piece in a semantic context (Zanoni et al., 2012). Examples of HLFs are gloominess, etherealness, or tenderness.

This hierarchical way to organise descriptors and algorithms has proven effective for a wide range of applications. It includes musical genre classification (McKay & Fujinaga, 2004) to timbral characterisation in musical instruments (Antonacci et al., 2015), to chord tracking (Di Giorgi et al., 2017), and is particularly useful when it is important to maintain control over the various levels of abstractions. For example, if we are interested in an HLF that gauges the "sadness" of a musical excerpt, it is likely that MLF estimators such as chord trackers, tonality, and tempo extractors will play a relevant role. At the same time, these same MLF estimators, would prove useful for other applications or for enriching the content with additional metadata.

HLFs, however, are not usually derived from MLFs (and perhaps LLFs) in a rule-based fashion, as they are not precisely defined. It is in fact much easier for us to describe them through examples. This is why HLFs are usually implemented as machine learning algorithms based on Artificial Neural Networks (ANNs) with representation learning (Jain et al., 1996). ANNs are computational structures of biological inspiration based on a network of "artificial neurons" (i.e., simple mathematical functions that perform an elementary operation consisting of feeding the weighted sum of inputs to a nonlinear "activation" function). Though the biological similarity is very faint (i.e., ANNs are not analog in nature, and do not exhibit any form of plasticity), such systems are able to learn representations by processing examples. Learning can be supervised, semi-supervised, or unsupervised. We talk about supervised learning when the training examples are already fully labelled for the purpose. Semi-supervised learning, instead, uses a combination of labelled and unlabelled data, with a prevalence of the latter. Unsupervised learning, on the other hand, needs no labelling for the training, and only a certain degree of human supervision is required. This latter learning strategy is often referred to as self-organising and is frequently based on statistical analysis (e.g., principal component analysis or clustering).

ANNs are inherently organised in a layered fashion, where each layer processes the output of the previous one. Signals are fed to the lowest layer (input layer) and travel up to the highest layer (the output layer), possibly passing through layers more than once. The input layer could be LLFs and/or MLFs; otherwise, layers can extend all the way down to the "raw audio signal" level and bypass hand-crafted features altogether. Whatever the choice, layers in these "deep learning" algorithms are "self-organised" by growing level of abstraction. Therefore, they closely adhere to the bottom-up processing model, widely accepted in brain sciences. In such models, however, the representations that emerge in intermediate layers are hardly decipherable, therefore they cannot be harvested as meaningful or interpretable features for other applications. This lack of interpretability of intermediate levels, however, is partly compensated by an improved feature optimisation, which leads to algorithms that largely outperform those based on ANNs processing "explicit" MLFs and LLFs. When modelling music representations, we generally adopt an explicit hierarchical model when it is clear what descriptors are needed to extract the high-level descriptors that we are interested in. When things are less clear, it is recommendable to adopt layered ANNs that extend to the lowest levels of abstraction using a deep learning approach.

In general, applications based on deep learning are strictly task-oriented, and are often highly sensitive to how we collect and organise training data. We need the training dataset to be representative and unbiased, which is usually extremely difficult to attain. Only a handful of companies have access to "big data", and their asset is indeed in the massive amount of data that they collect on a daily basis, as well as in how they manage it. Such companies, whose business is in search engines, social media, etc., put a great deal of effort into developing rich and unbiased datasets, unencumbered by models, untainted by proclivities. Such data, in fact, is particularly useful for capturing elements such as: collective behaviour and general trends; for understanding and modelling the average impact of specific stimuli; for content classification purposes; for predicting general statistical descriptors; for generating plausible synthesised data; etc. The same lack of data modelling, however, is also the reason why this approach with "big data" cannot be readily applied to very specific situations.

One example that we focus on in our labs is computational acoustics applied to virtual environments and extended realities. If the goal is to generate a reverberation that is plausible for a specific environment, then AI-driven computational acoustics can do wonders. But our perception of spatial audio is not just a matter of æsthetics. We use spatial audio to place ourselves in the acoustic scene, to balance, to navigate and to make sense of the environment. For these purposes, we use the early echoes of the Room Impulse Response (RIR), which change a great deal as we move around from one ear to the other, and even if we rotate our head ever so slightly. The use of machine learning algorithms is not suitable for this specific application context due to the sheer variety of acoustic environments (i.e., geometry, materials, etc.). No dataset would ever be enough for data-driven acoustic prediction algorithms of this sort.

Another area of application that we focus on, where machine learning is useful but only for a limited range of situations, is the study of vibrational and timbral properties of historical violins. The data required for training machine learning algorithms, in this case, is so hard to come by as to render any purely data-driven AI algorithms utterly ineffective. In fact, we use machine intelligence only for instrument and timbral classification purposes (Buccoli et al., 2015; Setragno et al., 2017a, 2017b, 2017c), though some data-driven applications of prediction of vibrational behaviour are possible in controlled conditions (Campagnoli et al., 2020).

When it comes to music representations and models, similar considerations apply, though for different reasons. We know that music enjoyment is the result of a fine balance between fulfilment of expectation and surprise (Pachet, 1999), as long as it takes place at a specific threshold of music complexity, which depends on our ear training level and other psychological factors (Huron, 2006). Such threshold shifts over time through attentive exposure to music. This explains why music is in constant need of evolving, which makes it particularly difficult for music modelling algorithms to keep up (whether based on explicit modelling or on deep learning). When they do succeed, they only take care of one aspect of music enjoyment, which is that associated with the fulfilment of expectations. Modelling musical "surprise" is still an ephemeral aspect of music that escapes definition; therefore, it is best left in the hands of musicians and in the ingenuity of composers.

Research in audio and musical signal processing can empower music makers with powerful tools, which can help them automate some of the tedious aspects of music composition, arrangement, orchestration, or even performative drilling, though research is still in the early phase of methodological development, and not due to a lack of effort. Music makers and researchers have many things in common: they are constantly pushing boundaries, trying new things, while building a cumulative expertise, but their approach differs in the way they communicate their own methodologies. Researchers tend to rely on formal definitions, and their communication is based on a scientific language that is universally understood and shared, while musicians often resort to using examples. "Enaptic" learning (learning by doing) works wonders in music training, especially when concerning ephemeral aspects of music theory, composition, and performance, but it limits or even hinders cross-communication between fields of expertise (particularly between music practice and music engineering). Researchers and technology designers, in fact, will only limit their reach to what they know and are able to understand in their own terms. We can only hope for a stronger symbiosis between musicians and researchers, based on more intense cross-pollination efforts.

Rhythmic Modelling

Rhythmic structures can be extremely complex and layered, and are prone to very interesting mathematical modelling. The metric structure of a musical piece, in fact, exhibits a rich inherent hierarchy of components ranging from the tatum to the tactus (beat), and multiples thereof (covering measures and groups of measures). Metric subdivisions are often limited by the notation, which is inherently based on fractions that progress in a geometric fashion. In fact, a rhythmic signature is always a fraction whose denominator is a power of two (e.g., 3/4, 4/4, 6/8, 15/16, etc.). While this is universally accepted, it becomes a limit when it comes to modelling, for example, systemic polyrhythms (i.e., competing rhythms whose periodicity matches the measure), which require a rather creative use of n-tuples, with the result of making the reading more complicated and needing one of the multiple rhythmic components to dominate over the others, at least from the notational standpoint. Interesting notations were proposed in order to overcome these limitations. One, for example, was proposed by Brian Ferneyhough (Duncan, 2010) for polymetric rhythmic structures, based the juxtaposition of multiple rhythmic signatures, though it didn't remove the constraints of having denominators that are powers of two. Very seldom, however, do such notations and representations account for the way performers perceive and construct complex rhythms. A drummer that plays a systemic polyrhythm of "4 against 7", for example, will never imagine a measure lasting 28 tatums and counting the two rhythmic components as "4 beats lasting 7 tatums each" and "7 beats lasting 4 tatums each". Instead, he/she will memorise the patterns that the two competing rhythms will generate along the timeline. The type of mind model that the musician will naturally build will therefore be best helped by a representation (e.g., hence a visual notation) that emphasises the presence and the "rotating structure" of such patterns.

Another perceptual aspect of rhythmic structures resides in hierarchical structuring of rhythms. Israeli drummer and educator Yogev Gabay once proposed to the students of my "Computer Music Representations and Models" course an interesting example of layered rhythm, based on a subdivision of the complete 4/4 signature into two groups of three 1/8 beats and a group of two 1/8 beats. The result was a rhythm that is loosely perceived as a triple of "long-long-short" rhythmic "blobs". Then he replaced the two triplets forming the first two "long" groups with two quadruples of notes (without changing the total length of each group), and replaced the pair of notes forming the "short" group with a triplet (whose note kept the same tempo as the quadruple). The resulting rhythm was a new complex pattern that fit a signature of 11/8. In a live session with an audience of nearly 100 students, he kept switching between the two different patterns in a seamless fashion. The listeners kept perceiving the same "long-long-short" arrangement in both cases, only with slightly more "texturing" in the latter.

Taking perception into account in music representations and modelling can be extremely useful to performers as well as listeners. Performers can learn how to "play the impossible" in a much shorter time, while being aware of what the listeners will be able to perceive. At the same time, music visualizations that take perception into account can help listeners hear things that otherwise would "go over their head", with the result of increasing music enjoyment.

Unfortunately, rhythmic analysis tools are still limited to the analysis of the periodicity of specific musical features such as the energy onset, tonal features, and chroma-grams (Mitrovíc et al., 2010). The applications of such algorithms, in fact, are usually limited to capturing the metric structure of music, with a specific focus on tempo and beat estimation (Tomic, 2008). It is important to stress that applications devoted to tempo extraction and beat tracking are, in fact, already quite challenging to develop, particularly when dealing with musical excerpts of high rhythmic complexity (Di Giorgi et al., 2016). The literature, however, is rich with mathematical tools that are aimed at studying the cyclo-stationariety of signals in general. Such tools can be extremely useful in the musical signal processing realm. For example, phase autocorrelation (Eck, 2007) is a powerful tool for visualising multiple periodicities along with starting points of each one of the periodic components (phase). Such tools can therefore become particularly useful for extracting metric or poly-metric information on the rhythmic structure. Multi-resolution methods inherited from the field of Pattern Analysis and Machine Intelligence can enable us to develop the perceptual models described earlier.

Harmonic Modelling

Just like rhythmic analysis, harmonic analysis is also in its infancy within MIR, as it is limited to chord estimation, tonality estimation, and similar extractors of harmonic musical descriptors (Mauch & Dixon, 2010). Such descriptors are not easy to extract, especially when working with audio signals that contain a complex mix of many musical instruments. In order to deal with such problems, probabilistic methods combined with robust estimation solutions need to be developed (Di Giorgi et al., 2013). In Di Giorgi et al. (2017), a comparison between several approaches based on state-space machines and machine intelligence algorithms was proposed, and numerous interesting conclusions were drawn. One fascinating comparison concerns what an algorithm is able to learn in an autonomous fashion simply by analyzing excerpts of harmonic progressions. Using a state-space machine of controllable "acumen" (represented by its number of states), we could ascertain that with only two states, one such machine would be able to learn and classify harmonic progressions into "major" and "minor" ones. As the number of states grows, the machine learns about the existence of dominant resolutions, etc. We do the same by simply listening to music. Another aspect that was shown in Di Giorgi et al. (2017) was the existence of a "window of sensitivity" to harmonic subtleties controlled by harmonic complexity, sort of an inverted "U", as hypothesised in Pachet (1999).

There is still a great deal of research that needs to be done in the area of harmonic analysis. Harmony is subject to interesting mathematical modelling that promises to deliver interesting applications for musicians and for music listeners. For example, the duality between modal scale representation and chord representations (chord tones plus tensions) suggests the existence of some sort of algebraic structure that could be fruitfully exploited for modelling, for example, harmonizers, and for developing systems that assist in orchestration. It is also interesting to consider how a whole harmonic structure can be generated by a scale. We are all accustomed to Western harmony, which is generated by the Ionian scale. In order to generate this harmonic structure, we look to the dominant scales (only one in this case, the mixolydian mode) and construct our harmonic resolutions based on that structure. This, as musicians know very well, is not the only option. Other scales can generate entirely different harmonies. For example, the melodic minor scale can generate a whole new harmony that has a much richer structure of colours and tension, as it exhibits two different dominant scales (second- and seventh-degree modes of the melodic minor scale) and new and exotic dominant resolutions associated with them. Even an exatonal scale could be used for the purpose of generating harmony with an even greater variety of resolutions since all modes of the exatonal scale can be interpreted as dominant. Of course, this discussion is here limited to a very specific type of harmonic analysis, related to tonal music. Different models need to be developed and studied for other styles of progressions, e.g. modal, atonal, or mixes thereof. Understanding such aspects for an engineer is, of course, not an easy feat; therefore, communication with musicians becomes absolutely crucial. However, this communication could benefit musicians as well, as it would force them to come to an explicit description of such aspects of music modelling, no longer based on examples, thus leading to a deeper understanding of the mechanisms involved.

Structural Modelling

The structure of a musical piece is a long-term representation that captures the prosody of the narration, and it is responsible for emotional surprises and the building of tension and relief in the listener. At the level of the whole musical piece, it describes its subdivision into musical sections, such as intro, chorus, and verse in popular music. A review of early methods for music structure analysis is given in the book chapter by Dannenberg and Goto (2008). This structure is often referred to as "musical form", and it carries a great deal of information. American physician Arthur Benner Lintgen, for example, is known for his infallible ability to recognise classical phonograph records with the naked eye. This ability of his was even experimentally verified in the early '80s and was described as a process of visual pattern recognition, which inspired Foote (2000) to develop a MIR system based on structural similarity. Modern methods aimed at studying the musical structure of a piece are feature-based (Paulus et al., 2010). Such methods, in fact, turn the music signal into a sizeable feature vector, and then compare each entry of this vector with all other entries. The resulting Self-Similarity Matrix (SSM) turns out to exhibit a collection of visual patterns, each identifying a different section of the piece, similarly to what Arthur Lintgen does for structural recognition of musical records. Various methods have been developed, based on the SSM, some based on incorporating invariance to time shifts (Marwan et al., 2007), tempo contractions/expansion (Müller & Kurth, 2007), and transposition invariance (similarity between chromagram and all cyclically-shifted versions of itself) (Goto, 2003).

All such solutions are very effective for the structural segmentation of a musical piece, but we are still far from developing a structural model that can capture and predict the emotional impact that long-term structural organisations can have in listeners. Similarly, it would be important to model structural predictability and expectation to understand how to create pleasant structural surprises (widely used in all musical genres). Finally, it would also be critical to model the relations that exist between various sections and model structural tension and complexity to understand, capture, and predict the emotional impact of specific structural choices.

Modelling Melodic Lines and Improvisation

The melodic line is a central aspect of the musical piece. It is what stays with you when the musical piece is over, what you hum and remember. We have no mathematical model that is able to capture what we love of a melody and what makes our heart beat faster. All we have are simple rules and recipes coming from the traditional notion of "Cantus Firmus". Such rules unfortunately fail to capture the elusive musical aspects that make a melody memorable. What makes modelling so hard is also the fact that melody appreciation is not rooted in musical rules, but is within the domain of behavioural psychology, as our memories traces and character traits play a profound role in characterising it.

Counterintuitively, we do a great deal better when it comes to modelling jazz improvisation. This should not surprise us too much. Jazz improvisation is often erroneously believed to be the result of fast processing that allows the performer to decide each individual note on the fly. Yet this is not what happens. Jazz improvisation is, in fact, the result of musical model building at progressively higher levels of abstraction. A pianist practices scales in all keys in order to create extensive "muscle memory" that will free the brain from the burden of having to worry about low-level muscular control in pattern generation. Similarly, a pianist undergoes extensive drilling for chord "comping" in order to automate harmonic progressions and voicings, to let the brain focus on melodic improvisation. The improvisational line is in turn made of patterns and excerpts that are combined through a combined process of pattern transformation, fusion, and juxtaposition. Transformations are needed to adapt a melody to a specific harmonic progression and a given rhythmic signature. This process can be reasonably well framed in a rule-based fashion. Pattern fusion and juxtaposition are also the subject of musicological study, but are yet to be used in specific applications.

A simple and effective framework for modelling jazz improvisation based on this idea of probabilistic pattern juxtaposition through harmonic transformations was proposed by Gillick et al. (2010) and Keller and Morrison (2007), and includes the construction of grammars of patterns and licks that characterise the style of a given performer. Ingrained in this representation is the notion of "abstract melody", which describes a melody not in terms of its absolute notes, but in terms of intervals of tonal uncertainty, which creates sufficient "wiggle room" for harmonic and rhythmic adaptation.

Modelling the Emotional Impact of Music

Understanding emotions in music is a subject of study that has fascinated researchers for the longest time. The literature is rich with solutions for inferring the emotions that are expressed by the composer and/or the performer (emotional "potential"), and some methods have recently emerged for assessing the emotions that are induced in the listener (emotional impact), using physiological signals.

State-of-the-art methods for assessing the emotional "potential" of music are part of a field of study known as "Music Emotion Recognition" (MER). Such solutions rely on strong simplifications, as they employ generic categorical or dimensional models for representing emotions (Juslin & Laukka, 2004). Categorical approaches use a finite set of emotional descriptors for tagging pieces of music, while in dimensional approaches musical pieces are located in a continuous multi-dimensional space (e.g. the Valence-Arousal space). Recent works have focused on the extraction of cognitive features such as music complexity (Di Giorgi et al., 2017) and tension (Farbood, 2012), with the purpose of understanding their role in music perception.

As far as induced emotions are concerned, the collection of physiological signals aimed at sensing the physical and emotional status of a person is becoming more pervasive and effective. The sensors that are more widely used for assessing the emotional state can be divided in two categories. The former infers the emotional state from facial expression (Y. Zhang et al., 2016), speech, body posture, gestures, and gait (Noroozi et al., 2021) by using cameras or microphones. Data collection in this case is simple, but the uncertainty of the outcome is quite relevant. The latter concerns signals that are directly linked to the activity of the Central Nervous System (CNS) or the Peripherical Nervous System (PNS). CNS activity can be measured with an ElectreEncephaloGram (EEG), which offers high temporal resolution at the cost of a low spatial resolution, or functional Magnetic Resonance Imaging (fMRI), which offers much higher spatial resolution with slower response times. Such systems are usually rather invasive and quite expensive, though we are beginning to see low-cost EEG systems of relatively low invasiveness. Sensing PNS activity is far less invasive, as it involves collecting physiological signals such as galvanic skin response, heart rate (Yoo et al., 2005), respiration patterns, skin temperature (Bernardi et al., 2006), blood volume pressure, temperature, etc. Sensors of this sort are becoming increasingly inexpensive and pervasive. Today they can be found in smart watches, bracelets or rings, or even in clothing articles. The physiological signals that they collect can be indicative of the emotional status of a person, though they have yet to be conclusively connected to more specific emotional reactions, such as those elicited by music.

Understanding how the emotional potential controlled by the composer/musician succeeds in having a specific emotional impact on the listener, cannot be done by focusing on music models or on physiological reactions. We need to study their interplay, which happens through the "human filter". In other words, we need to learn as much as we can from brain sciences, music cognition, and behavioural psychology of how to develop a workable model of our music perception. We believe that one promising way to do so is to exploit our own inherent layered music cognition models to devise an effective "divide-and-conquer" strategy. We can think of our perception of music as articulated in several layers: timbral, rhythmic, harmonic, tonal, and structural, to name the most relevant ones. Each one of these layers plays a distinct role in the musical piece and in music cognition; and tends to involve different areas of the brain. Such layers, however, interact together through various mechanisms of reinforcement, masking, etc. We can envision working with such descriptors first in an "intra-layer" fashion, and then in an "inter-layer" fashion. Within each layer, it would be important to focus on two categories of descriptors of emotional potential: "tensive" descriptors and "textural" descriptors. The former is associated with our ability to predict how music is going to evolve; therefore, it controls our sense of pleasure associated with mechanisms of expectation and reward. The latter captures the complexity and richness of the stimulus and is therefore responsible for other forms of pleasure associated with "being surprised" by unexpected turns. Within the harmonic layer, for example, harmonic tension captures the sense of "resolution" that we perceive in a progression of chords or voicings. Music theory teaches us how to steer harmonic tension into a "prosodic rollercoaster" that tickles our need to predict resolutions and being rewarded when such predictions are fulfilled. Harmonic tension, however, is only a descriptor of the "potential" (stimulus). In order to predict its emotional impact (perceived tension), we need to assess the individual tendency to "resonate" in response to such a stimulus. It is therefore important to resort to a second class of descriptors that capture the "complexity" of the stimulus in each layer. In fact, the emotional impact of harmonic progressions is weighted by our own ability to predict how it will evolve. A harmonic progression that is too simple will be perceived as boring, while one that is too complex will "go over our head" and not score much of an emotional response. There is, however, a "golden zone" in harmonic complexity that makes us maximally sensitive to harmonic progressions (Pachet, 1999). This "window of sensitivity" depends on the textural complexity of the stimulus, which weighs the impact of descriptors of harmonic potential (such as tension). This sort of an "inverted U" masking curve was proven to be in place through recent studies (Di Giorgi et al., 2017). It is reasonable to expect that similar considerations apply to other musical layers, and we are currently focusing on the rhythmic layer. Modelling the "window of sensitivity", particularly its peak (i.e., threshold of complexity), corresponds to "modelling the human filter". In fact, the individual threshold of complexity depends on the listener's musical/ear training, tastes, and listening habits. It also depends on specific psychological traits such as extroversion and sociability, curiosity, or being prone to step outside of one's "comfort zone". We therefore believe that one of the goals of future research should be to understand how to estimate it with the minimal amount of information possible, e.g., physiological signals, listening logs, questionnaires, etc.

Even more interesting is the issue of how complexity and tension interact across musical layers. Musicians, especially jazz performers, are very much aware of how rhythmic, harmonic, and melodic layers can interact in a constructive fashion by boosting each other up; just as they know that one layer can easily mask another by steering the listener's attention away from some aspects of the performance (that's how musicians sometimes hide their performative shortcomings). Understanding how musical layers join forces to elicit an emotional reaction in the listener is therefore crucial for developing predictive models of the emotional impact of music, and for learning how to compactly convey articulated emotional cues in a generative fashion. Again, such masking phenomena depend on the listener, and can only be understood, modelled, and personalised through the analysis of physiological signals, listening logs, and questionnaires. The availability of such models would pave the way to the development of a wide range of applications that would help both music makers and listeners, and create the conditions for better emotional communication between them, with the result of filling the widening gap that has emerged in the past few decades. These models, in fact, could help a composer make music with multi-layered depth, so that a wider range of listeners would always find something emotional somewhere among the layers. The same tools could be used to learn more about the audience and offer them a better (i.e., more stratified) listening experience.

As for listeners, new visualization tools could be developed for helping the audience learn more about what they are listening to in order to enter a path of musical evolution and growth.

Conclusions

There is no doubt that the impact of technology on music in the past few decades has been deeply transformative. It has "empowered" musicians with a wide range of tools for composition, orchestration, arrangement, production, performance, and even distribution and management. This did wonders in a way, as it visibly accelerated their artistic growth. We all expected, a bit naively perhaps, that this would offer music makers more opportunities to emerge and be noticed out of sheer talent and innovative ideas. This "democratisation" process, however, has created more pressure and more competition, with the result of significantly "raising the bar" for music makers. It has tremendously accelerated music evolution by reducing the "time to market" of any new paradigms in music composition and performance. At the same time, technological advancements have empowered listeners by giving them unprecedented access to recorded music and livestreams. This came, however, at a significant price, because our ability to absorb changes in music has remained the same, if it hasn't diminished.

Music education, in fact, still has little room in today's school system, and learning through focused listening is becoming more difficult due to information flooding and overload. We therefore have two music communities that advance at increasingly different paces: that of music makers, whose pace is mounting; and that of music listeners, whose evolution appears to be stalling, if not regressing. The gap between such communities is therefore widening, and the consequences of this are already beginning to show. For example, as shown in Nielsen's yearly reports on music, audiences of jazz and classical music do not seem to have benefited at all from the transformational changes brought by technology. If anything, in the past 5 years they seem to have slightly declined, occupying in 2019 less than 1% of the market segment in the US (in 2015 they occupied 1.3% of the market share) each.

We believe that technology should focus on filling this gap. This can only be done by beginning to focus on listeners, on how to make their perception and understanding of music evolve over time. This requires a deeper understanding of how music generates emotions and how better musical knowledge and awareness helps improve listening experiences and enjoyment.

References

Antonacci, F., Canclini, A., Corradi, R., Liberatore, A., Miccoli, S., Sarti, A., & Zanoni, M. (2015, June). A multidisciplinary approach to the characterization of bowed string instruments: The musical acoustics lab in Cremona. In 22nd *international congress on sound and vibration*. International Institute of Acoustics and Vibration (IIAV).

Bernardi, L., Porta, C., & Sleight, P. (2006). Cardiovascular, cerebrovascular, and respiratory changes induced by different types of music in musicians and non-musicians: The importance of silence. *Heart*, 92(4), 445–452. British Cardiovascular Societi. https://doi.org/10.1136/hrt.2005.064600.

Bianchi, L., Antonacci, F., Canclini, A., Sarti, A., & Tubaro, S. (2012, September). A psychoacoustic-based analysis of the impact of pre-echoes and post-echoes in soundfield rendering. In *International workshop on acoustic signal enhancement (IWAENC)*. IEEE.

Bianchi, L., Antonacci, F., Sarti, A., & Tubaro, S. (2016). Model-based acoustic rendering based on plane wave decomposition. *Applied Acoustics*, 104, 127–134. Elsevier.

Blauert, J. (1996). *The psychophysics of human sound localization*. MIT Press.

Blood, A., & Zatorre, R. (2003). Intensely pleasurable responses to music correlate with activity in brain regions implicated in reward and emotion. *Proceedings of the Natural Academy of Sciences (NAS)*, 98, 11818–11823.

Blood, A., Zatorre, R., Bermudez, P., & Evans, A. (1999, April). Emotional responses to pleasant and unpleasant music correlate with activity in paralimbic regions. *Nature Neuroscience*, 2(4), 382–387.

Boone, M., Verheijen, E., & Van Tol, P. (1995). Spatial sound-field reproduction by wave-field synthesis. *Journal of the Audio Engineering Society*, 43(12), 1003–1012. AES.

Brandenburg, K. (1999). MP3 and AAC explained. In *AES – audio engineering society, international conference on high-quality audio coding*. AES.

Buccoli, M., Zanoni, M., Setragno, F., Antonacci, F., & Sarti, A. (2015). An unsupervised approach to the semantic description of the sound quality of violins. In *EURASIP European signal processing conference (EUSIPCO)*. EURASIP.

Campagnoli, C., Pezzoli, M., Antonacci, F., & Sarti, A. (2020, August). Vibrational modal shape interpolation through convolutional autoencoder. In *Proceedings of the 49th inter-noise conference*. International Institute of Noise Control Engineering (I-INCE).

Canclini, A., Markovic, D., Bianchi, L., Antonacci, F., Sarti, A., & Tubaro, S. (2014). A robust geometric approach to room compensation for sound field rendering. *IEICE Transactions Fundamentals of Electronics, Communications and Computer Sciences*, 97(9), 1884–1892. IEICE. https://doi.org/10.1587/transfun.E97.A.1884

Celma, O. (2010). *Music recommendation and discovery – the long tail, long fail, and long play in the digital music space*. Elsevier: Springer.

Chanda, M., & Levitin, D. (2013, April). The neurochemistry of music. *Trends in Cognitive Sciences*, 17(4), 179–193.

Chiarandini, L., Zanoni, M., & Sarti, A. (2011, October). A system for dynamic playlist generation driven by multimodal control signals and descriptors. In *IEEE International Workshop on Multimedia Signal Processing (MMSP)* (pp. 1–6). IEEE.

Conetta, R., Brookes, T., Rumsey, F., Zielinski, S., Dewhirst, M., Jackson, P., Jackson, P., Bech, S., Meares, D., & George, S. (2015, December). Spatial audio quality perception (part 1): Impact of commonly encountered processes. *Journal of the Audio Engineering Society*, 62(12), 831–846. AES.

Dannenberg, R., & Goto, M. (2008). Music structure analysis from acoustic signals. In D. Havelock, S. Kuwano & M. Vorlander (Eds.), *Handbook of signal processing in acoustics* (Vol. 1, pp. 305–331). Springer.

Deutsch, D. (1999). *The psychology of music* (2nd ed.). Academic Press.

Di Giorgi, B., Dixon, S., & Sarti, A. (2017, November). A data-driven model of complexity for tonal chord sequences. *IEEE/AES Transactions on Audio,Speech and Language Processing*, 25(11), 2237–2250. IEEE/AES. https://doi.org/10.1109/TASLP.2017.2756443

Di Giorgi, B., Zanoni, M., Böck, S., & Sarti, A. (2016). Multipath beat tracking. *Journal of the Audio Engineering Society*, 64(7/8), 493–502. AES. https://doi.org/10.17743/jaes.2016.0025

Di Giorgi, B., Zanoni, M., Sarti, A., & Tubaro, S. (2013, September). Automatic chord recognition based on the probabilistic modeling of diatonic modal harmony. In *Eight international workshop on multidimensional systems (nDS)*. VDE Verlag.

Dittmar, C., Bastuck, C., & Gruhne, M. (2007, December). Novel mid-level audio features for music similarity. In *International conference on music communication science (ICOMCS)*. ARC Research Network in Human Communication Science (HCSNet). HCSNet.

Downie, J. (2003). Music information retrieval. *Annual Review of Information Science and Technology*, 37, 295–340.

Duncan, S. (2010). Re-complexifying the function(s) of notation in the music of Brian Ferneyhough and the "new complexity". *Perspectives of New Music*, 48(1), 136–172. JSTOR.

Eck, D. (2007). Beat tracking using an autocorrelation phase matrix. In *IEEE international conference on acoustic speech and signal processing (ICASSP)* (vol. IV, pp. 1313–1316). IEEE.

Farbood, M. (2012). *A parametric, temporal model of musical tension*. Music Perception.

Fine, T. (2008). The dawn of commercial digital recording. *ARSC Journal*, 39(1), 1–18.

Fletcher, H., & Munson, W. (1933). Loudness, its definition, measurement and calculation. *Journal of the Acoustical Society of America (JASA)*, 5, 82–108. ASA.

Foote, J. (2000). ARTHUR: Retrieving orchestral music by long-term structure. In *Proceedings of the international society of music information retrieval (ISMIR)*. ISMIR.

Gardner, W. (2013). Reverberation algorithms. In M. Karls & K. Brandenburg (Eds.), *Applications of digital signal processing to audio and acoustics* (2nd ed., Ch. 3). Springer.

Gelfand, S. (2004). *Hearing an introduction to psychological and physiological acoustics* (4th ed.). Marcel Dekker.

Gerzon, M. (1985). Ambisonics in multichannel broadcasting and video. *Journal of the Audio Engineering Society, 33*(11), 859–871. AES.

Gillick, J., Tang, K., & Keller, R. (2010). Machine learning of jazz grammars. *Computer Music Journal, 34*(3), 56–66. MIT Press.

Goto, M. (2003, October). A chorus-section detecting method for musical audio signals. In *IEEE workshop on applications of signal processing to audio and acoustics (WASPAA'03)*. IEEE.

Hiller, L., & Ruiz, P. (1971). Synthesizing musical sounds by solving the wave equation for vibrating objects: Part 1. *Journal of the Audio Engineering Society, 19*(6), 462–470. AES.

Houtsma, A. J. (1995). Chapter 8 – pitch perception. In B. C. Moore (Ed.), *Hearing* (pp. 267–295). Academic Press.

Huron, D. (2006). *Sweet anticipation: Music and the psychology of expectation*. MIT Press.

Irene, R., Borrelli, C., Zanoni, M., Buccoli, M., & Sarti, A. (2019, September). Automatic playlist generation using convolutional neural networks and recurrent neural networks. In *EURASIP European signal processing conference (EUSIPCO)*. EURASIP.

Jain, A., Mao, J., & Mohiuddin, K. (1996). Artificial neural networks: A tutorial. *Computer, 29*(3), 31–44. IEEE. https://doi.org/10.1109/2.485891

Jin, C., Zolfaghari, R., Long, X., Sebastian, A., Hossain, S., Glaunes, A., Tew, A., Shahnawaz, M., & Sarti, A. (2018, April). Considerations regarding individualization of head-related transfer functions. In *IEEE international conference on acoustics, speech and signal processing (ICASSP)*. IEEE.

Juslin, P., & Laukka, P. (2004). Expression, perception, and induction of musical emotions: A review and a questionnaire study of everyday listening. *Journal of New Music Research, 33*(3), 217–238. Taylor & Francis. https://doi.org/10.1080/0929821042000317813

Juslin, P., & Sloboda, J. (2001). *Music and emotion: Theory and research*. Oxford University Press.

Keller, R., & Morrison, D. (2007). A grammatical approach to automatic improvisation. In *4th sound and music computing conference (SMC)*. National and Kapodistrian University of Athens.

Koelsch, S., & Siebel, W. (2005, December). Towards a neural basis of music perception. *Trends in Cognitive Sciences, 9*(12), 578–584. Science Direct. https://doi.org/10.1016/j.tics.2005.10.001

Levitin, D. (2006). *This is your brain on music – the science of a human obsession*. Dutton.

Marwan, N., Romano, M., Thiel, M., & Kurths, J. (2007). Recurrence plots for the analysis of complex systems. *Physics Reports, 438*(5–6), 237–329. Science Direct.

Mauch, M., & Dixon, S. (2010, August). Simultaneous estimation of chords and musical context from audio. *IEEE Transactions on Audio, Speech and Language Processing, 18*(6), 1280–1289. IEEE. https://doi.org/10.1109/TASL.2009.2032947

McKay, C., & Fujinaga, I. (2004, October). Automatic genre classification using large high-level musical feature sets. In *Conference of the international society of music information retrieval (ISMIR)* (vol. 2004, pp. 525–530). ISMIR.

Mitrović, D., Zeppelzauer, M., & Breiteneder, C. (2010). Features for content-based audio retrieval. *ELSEVIER Advances in Computers, 78*, 71–150. Elsevier.

Moore, B. (2004). *An introduction to the psychology of hearing* (5th ed.). Elsevier Academic Press.

Moorer, J. (1979). About this reverberation business. *Computer Music Journal, 3*(2), 605–639. MIT Press. http://doi.org/10.2307/3680280

Müller, M., & Kurth, F. (2007). Towards structural analysis of audio recordings in the presence of musical variations. *EURASIP Journal on Advances in Signal Processing, 2007*(1). EURASIP. https://doi.org/10.1155/2007/89686

Noroozi, F., Corneanu, C. A., Kamińska, D., Sapiński, T., Escalera, S., & Anbarjafari, G. (2021). Survey on emotional body gesture recognition. *IEEE Transactions on Affective Computing, 12*(2), 505–523. IEEE. https://doi.org/10.1109/TAFFC.2018.2874986

Pachet, F. (1999, February). Surprising harmonies. *International Journal of Computing Anticipatory Systems, 4*, 139–161. CHAOS.

Panksepp, J. (2003). At the interface of the affective, behavioural and cognitive neurosciences: Decoding the emotional feelings of the brain. *Brain and Cognition, 52*(1), 4–14. Elsevier. https://doi.org/10.1016/s0278-2626(03)00003-4.

Paulus, J., Müller, M., & Klapuri, A. (2010). Audio-based music structure analysis. In *Proceedings of the conference for the international society of music information retrieval (ISMIR)* (pp. 625–636). ISMIR.

Pickles, J. (1982). *An introduction to the physiology of hearing*. Academic Press.

Rayleigh, J. (1907). On our perception of sound direction. *Philosophical Magazine, 13*, 214–232.

Rettinger, M. (1957, January). Reverberation chambers for broadcasting and recording studios. *Journal of the Audio Engineering Society, 5*(1), 18–22. AES.

Samarasinghe, P., Poletti, M., Salehin, S., Abhayapala, T., & Fazi, F. (2013). 3D soundfield reproduction using higher order loudspeakers. In *2013 IEEE international conference on acoustics, speech and signal processing (ICASSP)* (pp. 306–310). IEEE.

Schroeder, M., & Logan, B. (1961). Colorless artificial reverberation. *Journal of the Audio Engineering Society, 9*(3), 192–197. AES.

Setragno, F., Zanoni, M., Antonacci, F., & Sarti, A. (2017a). Feature-based timbral characterization of ancient and modern violins. In *International symposium on musical acoustics (ISMA)*. The Schulich School of Music, McGill University.

Setragno, F., Zanoni, M., Antonacci, F., Sarti, A., Malagodi, M., Rovetta, T., & Invernizzi, C. (2017b). Feature-based analysis of the impact of ground coat and varnish on violin tone qualities. *Acta Acustica United with Acustica, 103*(1), 80–93. EDP Sciences.

Setragno, F., Zanoni, M., Sarti, A., & Antonacci, F. (2017c). Feature-based characterization of violin timbre. In *EURASIP European signal processing conference (EUSIPCO)*. EURASIP.

Sezgin, M., Gunsel, B., & Kurt, G. (2012). Perceptual audio features for emotion detection. *EURASIP Journal on Audio, Speech, and Music Processing, 16*(1). EURASIP. https://doi.org/10.1186/1687-4722-2012-16

Shany, O., Singer, N., Gold, B., Jacoby, N., Tarrasch, R., Hendler, T., & Granot, R. (2019, April). Surprise-related activation in the nucleus accumbens interacts with music-induced pleasantness. *Social Cognitive and Affective Neuroscience, 14*(4), 459–470. OUP. https://doi.org/10.1093/scan/nsz019.

Tomic, S. T., & Janata, P. (2008). Beyond the beat: Modeling metric structure in music and performance. *Journal of the Acoustical Society of America, 124*(6), 4024–4041. ASA Acoustical Society of America. https://doi.org/10.1121/1.3006382

Tzanetakis, G., Fels, S., & Lyons, M. (2013). Blending the physical and the virtual in music technology: From interface design to multi-modal signal processing. In *21st ACM international conference on multimedia* (pp. 1119–1120). ACM (Association of Computing Machinery).

Välimäki, V., Parker, J., Savioja, L., Smith, J., & Abel, J. (2012). Fifty years of artificial reverberation. *IEEE Transactions on Audio, Speech, and Language Processing, 20*(5), 1421–1448. IEEE.

Yoo, S. K., Lee, C. K., Park, Y. J., Kim, N. H., Lee, B. C., & Jeong, K. S. (2005, August). Neural network based emotion estimation using heart rate variability and skin resistance. In *International conference on natural computation* (pp. 818–824). Springer.

Zanoni, M., Ciminieri, D., Sarti, A., & Tubaro, S. (2012, August). Searching for dominant high-level features for music information retrieval. In *EURASIP European signal processing conference (EUSIPCO)*. EURASIP.

Zhang, W., Abhayapala, T., Kennedy, R., & Duraiswami, R. (2010, April). Insights into head-related transfer function: Spatial dimensionality and continuous representation. *Journal of the Acoustical Society of America (JASA), 127*(4), 2347–2357. ASA Acoustical Society of America. https://doi.org/10.1121/1.3336399

Zhang, Y. D., Yang, Z. J., Lu, H. M., Zhou, X. X., Phillips, P., Liu, Q. M., & Wang, S. H. (2016). Facial emotion recognition based on biorthogonal wavelet entropy, fuzzy support vector machine, and stratified cross validation. *IEEE Access, 4*, 8375–8385. IEEE. https://doi.org/10.1109/ACCESS.2016.2628407

Zölzer, U. (2011). *DAFX: Digital audio effects*. John Wiley & Sons, Ltd.

9 State and Practice of Music Education Software Design

Matthias Nowakowski and Aristotelis Hadjakos

Historical Perspectives

In his extensive overview of the history of music technology, Peter Webster (2002) addresses and explores how music technology is closely connected to his contemporaries of technological change. Using references that date back to the 1600s, Webster highlights both technology and digital technology. Important to the timeline of music education, Webster suggests the advent of computer music and digital forms of music education can be traced back to the 1960s. He supports this timeline by identifying Wolfgang Kuhn and Reynold Alivin's (Stanford University, USA) development of intonation tuning (i.e., pitch extraction through frequency processing) in 1967. Additional music education technological explorations during the 1960s included the first experiments with ear training (see Ned Deihl).

The opportunities for further independence and automation became realised as technology continued to progress. One of the first examples of a system to provide Computer Aided Instruction (CAI) was the PLATO (Programmed Logic for Automatic Teaching Operations) system. PLATO was first used in music teaching in 1973. At this point, it becomes apparent that technological pioneers in this field began to shift into companies that developed music software, such as Digital Audio Workstations (DAW).

Webster's (2002) general prediction of music education, its continued development and exploration of technology, such as the importance of mobile (music) devices and the relevance of the internet in music teaching, have proven true as of today. Current technology uptake in music education is built upon the general digital audio software and the unforgettable influence of the "MPE3" file format, which afford and mobilise music worldwide.

As we continue to explore the historical and existing educational applications and their future potential, it would be futile to aim at listing all music education software. Further, there is a coupled obsolescence of such an endeavour, given the short development and life cycles of web and mobile application engineering. Therefore, to reflect the current state of use in music education software, Table 9.1 provides the reader with seminal papers that address the key topics in music education software found in research. Discussing current software becomes our starting point to the next level of abstraction.

Software Design

The implications associated with technology used in music education suggest there is a prevailing discourse that pedagogy influences educational technology. In the 1970s, basic research was more relevant, such as implementing the evaluation of textual tasks and how to combine them with sound input. Today we see a more significant focus on distribution and

DOI: 10.4324/9781003041474-12

mobility. Regarding Human Computer Interaction (HCI), we can align certain software development and design trends with current pedagogical ideas. These three "waves" of HCI differ in concepts about humans, computers and their relations (Bannon, 1995; Bødker, 2006; Duarte & Baranauskas, 2016):

1. The first wave, roughly positioned around the advent of the first commercially available graphical user interfaces (early 1980s), was primarily concerned with ergonomics in computer interaction. The main question focused on was whether or not someone could accomplish a task more efficiently. This view is purely based on engineering and asserts a true reality that fits this wave's experimental and objective (positivist) approaches.
2. The second wave (1990s to 2000s) is more situated in cognitive science. It focuses on mental processes (e.g., attention, memory, problem solving, creativity, etc.) rather than mental models and ergonomics. Humans can operate more freely and are immersed in this virtual reality, so more qualitative research is required and applied.
3. The third wave (2000s to present) is based on understanding subjective realities, which are products of social, political, cultural, economic, ethnic, etc. influences. One objective reality is replaced with a plethora of realities which are under construction, also while interacting with the software. In earlier waves, interaction was only associated with work- or task-related contexts. This wave also focuses on private and everyday contexts, which is enabled by availability of digital technologies and the rise of the Internet of Things (IoT). Therefore, research is highly dependent on personal interaction between the researcher and the user.

The third wave is associated with the term "constructivist-interpretivist" (Duarte & Baranauskas, 2016). It is especially relevant in the context of pedagogy (Bandura, 1993) and music pedagogy (Johnson, 2020), wherein "constructivism" refers to learning based on personal experiences by which meaning, and interpretation, is created by the learner itself. This approach changes the scope from a purely single user perspective (i.e., one human interacts with one computer) to a multi-user perspective (i.e., multiple humans interact with multiple humans and/through multiple computers), which opens the way for digital researching collaboration. Focus on this is also usually subsumed under the term "social constructivism".

In music, these waves of HCI can be retraced along with the development of computer music (Tanaka, 2019). The experiments in sound synthesis in the 1970s and 1980s meet the positivist view, where the physical world is emulated and enhanced by the computer. In this mindset, we can see PLATO as a good example of first-wave HCI; tasks were transmitted to the computer without reflecting mental processes that could arise from the interaction. The second wave addresses increasing real-time signal processing and interaction with it in stage performances (e.g., the development of Max/MSP). The third wave might reflect music as an everyday commodity by which social interaction is possible (e.g., by sharing favorite songs in Spotify via Facebook) and expresses social affiliation, or perhaps in turn affects song recommendations songs in Spotify, if one clicks on it.

Contextualizing software design from this historical perspective, the potential arises for discussing it in terms of adequate interaction by learners and how software could benefit from these research methods. For this, we will first discuss current types of software used in music education (Section 2). Due to strong diversification, this does not include a comprehensive list of software products but a categorization by which we can identify problems and opportunities. Next, we will state and discuss the challenges and requirements for a solution of educational software design. Designing methods for learners, especially in music, is the focus of the next section, where we will discuss HCI design strategies through the lens of LCD. Then we will present an ongoing software development project at our university, where these strategies are exemplified on an interface for interactive music notation (Section 4). At last, the conclusion (Section 5) will sum up our reflections and open some perspectives of further research and application areas.

Software in Music Education

Categories

In a more recent contribution, Webster (2016) gives a detailed overview of software used in music education. It is noticeable that a large part of the software mentioned lacks an exclusively educational purpose, with some exceptions like SmartMusic, Practica Musica and MusicTheory.net. This incongruity of purpose and use-case seems to be a more common observation (Cheng & Leong, 2017).

The purpose of these tools is to create music (i.e., using DAWs, score editors), measure features such as pitch and keeping time or be explorative tools which utilize user input creatively. Webster's study shows a low number of pedagogy-specific software with a measurable output in music, which also correlates with the results of studies about teachers' active use of tools in music education (Eyles, 2018; Upitis et al., 2016). A recent qualitative survey at our university on teaching under the circumstances of the COVID-19 pandemic supports these findings (Personal communication, E. Nolte, July 1, 2021):

- Online platforms are virtual spaces in which students and teachers can interact. They are commonly used to share audio/video recordings and other educational content. Both commercial platforms, such as the social video platform YouTube, and educational platforms (i.e., the university's LMS and tools) are used in practice.
- Content creation tools range from DAWs, recording/editing software, musical notation programs to text processors and office productivity software. The teachers use these tools to create educational content, the students to complete their tasks or they can be used to share musical performances and facilitate communication between students and teachers.
- Communication and Organization: Tools such as chats and e-mail are used for asynchronous communication. Video conferencing systems are used to teach online seminars and to provide one-to-one tuition. Online calendars and tools like Slack, Trello and Doodle are commonly used for organizational purposes. Some of these programs are mostly standalone applications and have to be purchased through separate licenses.

In principle, online platforms can reduce the need for the teacher to be present, because content can be retrieved asynchronously, allowing students maximum time flexibility. For this, a lot of high-quality educational content is already available online. Some of these are also implemented in learning management systems (LMS) and have been used successfully in various academic disciplines and educational settings. Common LMS platforms support a variety of educational approaches like blended learning, flipped classrooms and MOOCs. However, the most commonly used LMS, such as Moodle, have very limited support for learning musical content, especially regarding music notation and adequate audio processing.

Content creation tools include DAWs like GarageBand, Audacity or Cubase, and score editors like MuseScore, Finale, Sibelius, etc. This software is primarily non-educational, with the exception of GarageBand. Garage Band has functions to incorporate and download digitally supervised learning content, and its tools are mostly used in professional areas to provide many functions for mixing and editing. Furthermore, music notation programs make it possible to realize any kind of score. Experiments in different music-learning contexts show that replaying a score is highly valued (Todea, 2015; Kang & Yoohop, 2021).

Challenges and Requirements

Research in e-learning and online education consists primarily of describing case studies, tool developments and best practices. Conceptual frameworks like TPACK (technological, pedagogical and content knowledge) could provide valuable direction. Taking technology into account allows us to model courses for digital means (Bowman, 2014). With technology in mind, we would like to raise the following challenges and requirements for educational software in music.

- **Individuality of Education:** Music education (in any context) differs from other education subjects. STEM courses are often based on larger groups in which discrete and verifiable knowledge is conveyed. For reviewing, grading and distributing of such courses, the LMS has the advantage of being easily scalable to large numbers of students. In contrast, music education relies heavily on development of personal musical skills such as playing an instrument, music theory and creativity. For this, we should find a way to use LMS and other digital learning opportunities to "scale down" in these learning contexts to achieve relevant learning experiences and outcomes.
- **Adaptation of Learning Content and Assessment:** Adapting music education courses to another medium also means adapting teaching methods for it. Learning with software discharges teachers from being present, which increases transactional distance, meaning that dialogue as an important learning action is omitted (Moore, 1993). Learning

Table 9.1 Overview of papers listing music education software.
N.B. Most of the software mentioned in these papers is still functional.

Paper	Description
Dittmar et al. (2012)	Software and web resources based on music information retrieval technology, games
Webster (2016)	Overview of software, web resources and mobile applications. Categorization for early, middle and higher education as well as creating, responding and performing.
Gilbert (2016)	Suggested technologies for use within selected ISTE "Essential Conditions". Categorized for different levels of musical expertise.
Nart (2016)	Listing of software for tutorials, games, drill and practice, notation, sequencing and recording
Gorgoretti (2019)	Non-music-related software in music education
Apaydinli (2020)	Discussion of current tutoring systems
Pierce et al. (2020)	Mobile music games based on their respective revenue model
Erickson (2021)	Mobile applications for singing

content, practical music education and music theory and its assessment have to be translated meaningfully and media-appropriately into the digital realm.

- **Digital Literacy:** Knowing how to operate digital tools, in general, is one of the basic skills which must be developed. This will not only help handle the applications at hand but will also help to access new software faster. This includes knowledge about the expected outputs of music software (i.e., waveforms, spectrograms, etc.) and setting up a recording environment for the adequate transmission of performances. In the long term, building a certain skill set, which could be expected as standard, would be desirable.
- **Quality of Sound:** Transmitting sound in collaborative settings or synchronous learning sessions is partially achieved by programs such as Jamulus. Decent sound quality is mainly assured when the video is omitted or the quality is at least reduced. Integrating this for distant learning with other server applications is a challenge for balanced server loads and adequate transmission bandwidths.

Who Are the Learners in Music?

Analyzing challenges also needs to consider the user in mind, what they need and who they are. Here we will give a first outline of the domain model based on the Learner Centered Design definition of "learners", who are the counterpart to the "user" in general User Centered Design (Quintana et al., 2000). For simplicity and consistency, we will illustrate the definitions in the context of our music theory learning interface, which is based on an LMS integrated music score notation interface (see Section 4):

1. *Learners gain new information about an activity while actively using the tool to get it done.* In general, new information is achieved via tasks and exercises. Therefore, the designers should aim to reduce complexity and present content in chunks where possible. For example: When solving an ear training exercise, there should only be options for rhythm notation if rhythm is a part of the ear training task.
2. *Learners lack domain expertise.* Specific terminology and the knowledge of typical actions cannot be presupposed at an early learning stage. If a particular concept is not yet required or known by the learner, these options should be omitted. The buttons or menu items should use pictures of the concept, making them more self-explanatory. MuseScore, for example, has an understandable pictorial language for the main options in the initial window.
3. *Learners might not be intrinsically motivated.* With a lack of motivation, the learner should not be required to discover the software. All relevant menu items, buttons and tasks should be readily available or at least be easy to find.
4. *Learners' understanding grows as they grow into the domain.* As a course goes on and the learners gain experience, our interface should resemble a full-fledged music notation program. This could be bound to exercise progression (and so giving the learner opportunities to "unlock" functions). This also prepares the learners to use their knowledge of music theory and music notation programs outside of a restricted learning context.

Design Methods for Music Education Software

Our goal is to enrich e-learning with human-centered software design principles. Design aims to implement effective and efficient ways to achieve a certain goal, whereas e-learning design is concerned primarily with translating curricular requirements, keeping students motivated and conveying instruction in a manner that's adequate for distance learning (Horton, 2011; Johnson, 2020; Keller & Suzuki, 2004). Bridging the gap between the triad of learning, instructional design and software design, Learner Centered Design is a promising field of research and development which emerged in the last few years. Focusing on general HCI challenges, Learner Centered Design creates a direct link between usability and learning success; e.g., interface design flaws most often lead to users resorting to complicated auxiliary constructs which can be detrimental to accessing instructions and learning content (Schmidt et al., 2020). In addition to explaining the use of Learner Centered Design in music, we will open the perspective to other methods.

Removing as many of these usability barriers as possible is a goal of HCI research. This is achieved by analyzing the users' abilities and needs to ensure that the design matches the needs and capabilities of the people for whom it is intended (Norman, 2013). When talking about music software, score editors for example may show clearly how to place a note or how to replay the music written. Still, more extended actions like placing tempi and binding them to the right measure, setting harmonic annotations, replaying specific voices or copying, pasting and moving multi-system measures to the right or left might involve deep knowledge about the data model provided by the software, where sub menus might be hidden and what interaction modes (e.g., mouse, keyboard, midi device) are supported. This might lead to a higher cognitive load for a certain task than usually required, which in turn may affect the learning outcome negatively. These problems with score editor interface design are also true for DAWs. Typical for this kind of software is a lack of learnability due to a professional or at least regularly involved target group, which means there is a lack of *visible* guides on how to interact with the software. Everyone who reads these lines has probably had problems setting up midi devices for a DAW and couldn't find the proper configurations to record inputs or make a sound. In some instances, they may have wished for an interactive assistant, similar to Microsoft's "Clippy".

Taking the path of Learner Centered Design requires adjusting HCI principles to this particular kind of user since the goal is to acquire expertise in a domain, but not to improve or support someone's handling of a program and constantly interpreting in terms of one's goal. To pass the "gulf of expertise", the Learner Centered Design proposes a constructivist theory. Inspired by the "gulf of execution and evaluation", it differs by being a one-way road from non-expertise to expertise instead of a cycle of reacting to and perceiving the world. Gaining expertise, therefore, can be established by actions like learning by doing and actively working in a domain's culture (Quintana et al., 2000).

Contextual design (Holtzblatt, 2001) recognizes that the user's interaction with an interface is usually embedded in a larger system of tasks and workflows. Therefore, it advocates for continued immersion in the user's work environment to inform the design team. To understand the user's need in this system, the designers conduct contextual inquiries in the user's work settings. Contextual design structures the design process into different steps, including work modeling, consolidation, work redesign, user environment design and prototyping. In participatory design (Muller & Druin 2012), the end-users and other stakeholders are systematically integrated into the design process. The goal is that the design takes place in the "third space" (Muller & Druin, 2012) and to blur the distinction between the user and the designer (Titlestad et al., 2009). In the third space, ideas come together, assumptions are checked, and new creativity is fostered. For music LMS, participatory design could involve students, teachers, the school's or university's administration and the social context (parents, friends, etc.). In participatory design, there are a large number of practices to design the third space: specialized workshop formats, storytelling with text and photos, the co-creation of prototypes and many more (Muller & Druin, 2012).

Usability testing is a systematic way to evaluate the quality of a user interface. An overview of evaluation methods is provided by Dix et al. (2003). The evaluation can measure aspects of usability, such as effectiveness, efficiency and learnability, or the focus on aspects of user experience, such as satisfaction, enjoyment and pleasure. In quantitative evaluation, variables such as error/success rates, time to completion, or user satisfaction are measured. User satisfaction is commonly measured with standardized questionnaires like the System Usability Scale (Lewis, 2018) or the AttrakDiff questionnaire (Hassenzahl et al., 2003). While quantitative evaluation is often used in the summative evaluation, qualitative methods are perhaps most useful in formative evaluation, informing the ongoing design of a software system. This can be done with semi-structured interviews, focus group discussions, observation and video analysis of system usage, etc. Another common testing method that can inform the design is expert-based analytical evaluation, which is often informed by heuristics or guidelines. Ardito et al. (2004) developed guidelines for the expert evaluation of e-learning applications.

As the Society for Learning Analytics and Research (SoLAR) states, Learning Analytics

is the measurement, collection, analysis, and reporting of data about learners and their contexts, for purposes of understanding and optimizing learning and the environments in which it occurs. . . Learning Analytics sits at the convergence of Learning (e.g. educational research, learning and assessment sciences, educational technology), Analytics (e.g. statistics, visualization, computer/data sciences, artificial intelligence), and Human-Centered Design (e.g. usability, participatory design, sociotechnical systems thinking).[1]

Designing a tool in an LMS, for example, lets us potentially access all interactions a student has with it and gathers all this information, which can be then used in learning or software design. Therefore, it is a viable tool for HCI methods and evaluation (Gašević et al., 2017; Mangaroska et al., 2019 Viberg et al., 2018). Since every student can be analyzed individually, it bears the potential to focus on personalized learning, which then can be used by automatic or instructor support, or automatic exercise creation tailored to the student's needs. Since music is still underrepresented in Learning Analytics,[2] one goal should be to further systematize the collected data for the domain and inform theory and design (Mangaroska et al., 2019).

The Point of Departure for Music LMS

As a practical example, we would like to bring up a current project which we are working on; it is part of a cooperation of five music universities. The goal is to make music theory classes digitally widely accessible and shareable. For this we needed to develop a music notation interface that is integrated with an LMS.[3] Existing music notation programs inspire the interactions.

As implied by the directions provided by Learner Centered Design, we achieve a reduction of complexity by showing the user the most relevant domain information first: the score, buttons to change note and rest durations and one options menu. This sets the focus on possible relevant interactions: changing the content of a given score. The menu button changes between certain input modes, such as keyboard or mouse or choosing annotation layers, such as general annotation or harmonic annotation (see Figure 9.1). Depending on the chosen option, the menu bar might be reduced or extended, e.g., to display a button to extend notes into a chord that omits knowledge of a key combination and replaces it with visible interaction information (see Figure 9.2). For global settings or less common options, we use a collapsible sidebar.

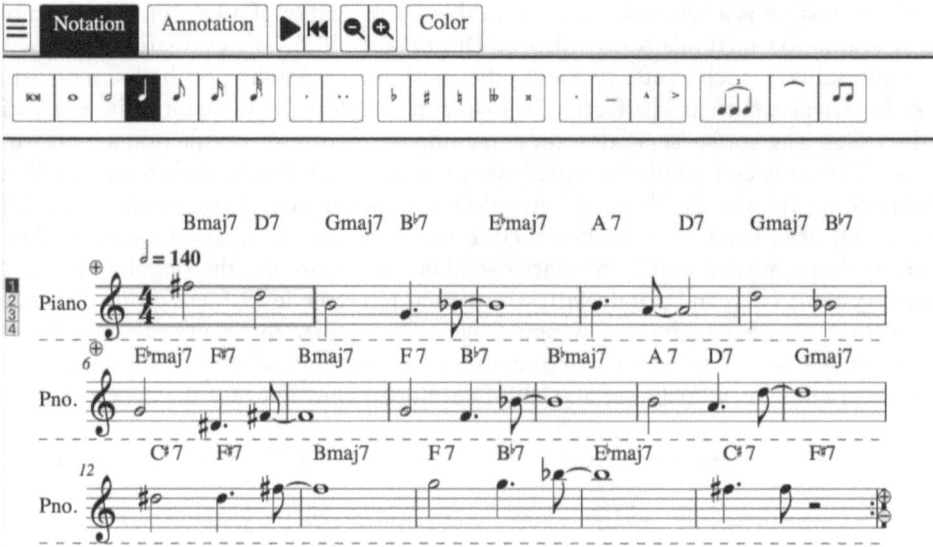

Figure 9.1 Initial notation user interface in the H5P container with score already loaded.

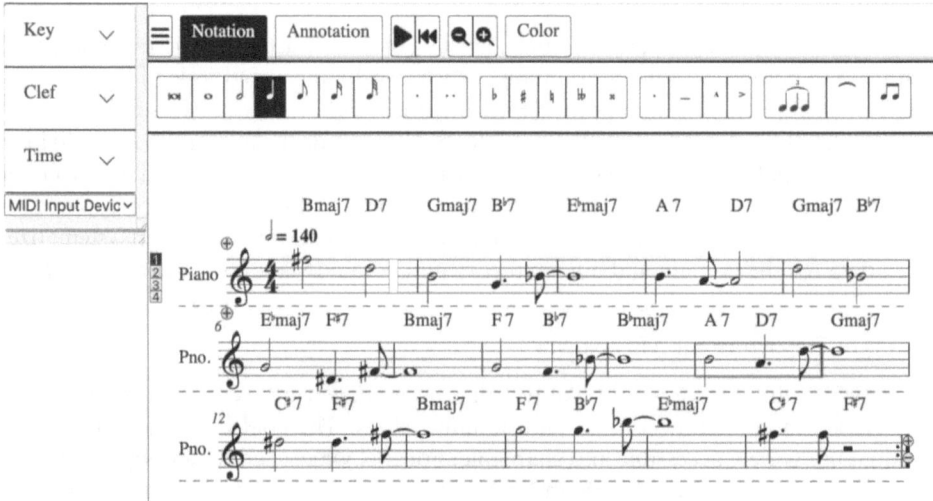

Figure 9.2 Extended toolbar for optional keyboard manipulations.

We are applying contextual and participatory design strategies. For this purpose, we are cooperating with five music theory professors, who serve as co-designers of our systems. We get their input at regular meetings conducted online with the participants in their usual environment. Formative qualitative evaluations are conducted through focus group discussions with a working prototype operated by the developer. At a later stage, when the interface is used by third parties, we plan to conduct user studies to get qualitative feedback together with ratings of user satisfaction measured by the System Usability Scale.

By using the LMS for testing and evaluating learning usability and learning success, it is a low-threshold environment to implement learning requirements:

- Socially relevant tools (chats, forums, personal messages, etc.) are already available in most LMS.
- They provide multiple ways of implementing new tools (if there are no already downloadable plugins).
- All interactions are potentially trackable and thereby usable for Learning Analytics.

The last two points are of interest when applying research methods for developing applications for learners. For most LMS platforms, new plugins can be programmed in the PHP programming language. The most significant detriment of this is that it is highly version-dependent and LMS-specific (e.g., transferring it from Moodle to Canvas would require developing it from the ground up). Another way would be to develop an application via the H5P plugin, which allows for the use of more common Javascript programming language; the programming interface is especially geared toward interaction in task handling and course creation. This also bears the advantage that many common programming libraries are available and can be integrated into one's own project. In our case, the Verovio notation engraving library presents an already available solution for rendering scores as SVG data. And despite running in its container, LMS communication is maintained via the xAPI interface. It is also sharable, since every application can be packed and installed in another LMS without reprogramming it. As another option, there is the Learning Tools Interoperability (LTI) specification, which allows for connecting courses with external resources but also transfers relevant information to the LMS for task completion This is realized in a gallery discussion tool in Quintana et al. (2021).

For course creation, it is important to give the instructors a way to configure interaction possibilities adequate for a certain task (e.g., only allowing basso continuo annotations or disabling audio feedback). This is an implementation for actively customizing the educational mode as stated by the Learner Centered Design definition. Here an educational expert (who might also be a domain expert) decides on the complexity of the system image for a learner.

As of now we see the following added values of this project:

- **Contemporaneity:** Through the development of the notation engraving library Verovio and its integration via H5P into the LMS used at the universities, students will now have a tool available that meets today's requirements for notation and annotation options, which eliminates the need for costly purchases. At the same time, the same tool can be used in all courses, eliminating the need for cumbersome familiarization with new systems.
- **Compatibility:** Teachers can continue to use their previous notations with Sibelius, Finale or Dorico through the included file import types MusicXML, HumDrum, MEI and ABC and now prepare them interactively for teaching.
- **Availability:** Integrating the H5P framework into the LMS immediately makes its functionalities available to all institutions. A high degree of sustainability can be assumed, as H5P is growing worldwide, adapting to new operating systems and browsers at regular intervals and is optimized for mobile devices.

- **Expandability:** H5P applications can be developed in the future with significantly less effort. For an application of form analysis, an exercise tool based on algorithmic specifications can be made, which could be used in other applications for controlling instrumental playing and notation input via pen.

Conclusion and Future Perspectives

Beginning with the consideration that educational software is part of historical and technological changes, we argue that the current use of software in music education does not reflect the required technological design despite a constructivist consensus in pedagogy. The design should be based on understanding the social and cultural context of learning as exemplified by Learner Centered Design. It is a pedagogical take on User Centered Design. We see it as a promising way to raise attention in music education, develop new applications, and further develop theory building from a technological perspective. We propose LMS and related technologies as viable solutions for initiating research in this field.

Introducing a person into a new domain benefits from a reduced interface, of which the instructor may have complete control. This is realizable with developing applications for LMS in which we have several possibilities to implement such tasks (native, H5P or LTI). Still, tools like Jupyter or other streaming-based editors (Dannenberg et al., 2015; Seifert et al., 2020) give many configuration options with which the student can interact. Taking this as a model, our previously outlined domain "music" may be even complemented by the domain of "informatics".

As we implied earlier, our current solution will at first cover one dimension of a constructivist learning model through interactive activities, as teachers and students will not interact with each other directly. This does also mean that any collaboration between students has to be reflected and implemented in the future. To overcome this one-sidedness, some solutions would be worth thinking about:

- Unsorted (not graded) and anonymous displays of solutions for more complex composition and harmony tasks, as well as commenting, could be a way to enable some interaction between students and the teacher.
- Exploring the subject through wikis or videos by teachers or students integrated into the LMS.
- In a field which is heavily dependent on explicit memory, a certain number of teacher-provided tasks would not be enough to explore the subject by the student in a self-managed way. It would be sufficient to create logic to generate and evaluate tasks automatically, where for example machine learning approaches could be employed to generate such sequences. In a creative environment, this also raises the question of how much of an error margin we can program to label a solution as "right" or "acceptable".
- Students might collect musical examples from other pieces or earlier exercises in a digital notebook to reflect their knowledge of music theoretical concepts.
- Graphical input for touch interfaces, like smartphones and tablet computers, can be a more dynamic interaction method for users who switch from paper to digital means (Forsberg et al., 1998; Miyao & Maruyama, 2004; Lee et al., 2016).

Together, these ideas suggest potential explorations for further implementation and research in the field.

Notes

1. https://www.solaresearch.org/about/what-is-learning-analytics/
2. As of today, we could only find the following publications on music and learning analytics: Guillot et al. (2016), Kumar et al. (2018), Montgomery et al. (2019).
3. The VIBE interface and associated LMS applications can be found at: https://github.com/H5P-MusicNotation

References

Apaydinli, K. (2020). Intelligent tutoring systems in music education. In A. Akin (Ed.), *Current studies in social science* (pp. 3–32). IKSAD Publications.

Ardito, C., De Marsico, M., Lanzilotti, R., Levialdi, S., Roselli, T., Rossano, V., & Tersigni, M. (2004). Usability of e-learning tools. *Proceedings of the working conference on advanced visual interfaces* (pp. 80–84). ACM Digital Library.

Bandura, A. (1993). Perceived self-efficacy in cognitive development and functioning. *Educational Psychologist, 28*(2), 117–148.

Bannon, L. J. (1995). From human factors to human actors: The role of psychology and human-computer interaction studies in system design. In R. M. Baecker, J. Grudin, W. A. S. Buxtin & S. Greenberg (Eds.), *Readings in human–computer interaction* (pp. 205–214). Morgan Kaufmann.

Bødker, S. (2006). When second wave HCI meets third wave challenges. In *Proceedings of the 4th nordic conference on human-computer interaction: Changing roles, NordiCHI '06. Association for computing machinery* (pp. 1–8). https://doi.org/10.1145/1182475.1182476

Bowman, J. (2014). *Online learning in music: Foundations, frameworks, and practices.* Oxford University Press.

Cheng, L., & Leong, S. (2017). Educational affordances and learning design in music software development. *Technology, Pedagogy and Education, 26*(4), 395–407.

Dannenberg, R., Stiles, J., Li, Y., & Zhang, Q. (2015). An online interactive course on computer music. *International computer music conference 2015, ICMA, CEMI* (pp. 28–33). University of North Texas.

Dittmar, C., Cano, E., Abeßer, J., & Grollmisch, S. (2012). Music information retrieval meets music education. In M. Müller, M. Goto & M. Schedl (Eds.), *Multimodal music processing* (Vol. 3, pp. 95–120).

Duarte, E. F., & Baranauskas, M. C. C. (2016). Revisiting the three HCI waves: A preliminary discussion on philosophy of science and research paradigms. In *Proceedings of the 15th Brazilian symposium on human factors in computing systems, IHC '16. Association for computing machinery* (pp. 1–4). https://doi.org/10.1145/3033701.3033740

Erickson, H. M. (2021). Mobile apps and biofeedback in voice pedagogy. *Journal of Singing, 77*(4), 485–500.

Eyles, A.-M. (2018). Teachers' perspectives about implementing ICT in music education. *Australian Journal of Teacher Education, 43*(5). https://doi.org/10.14221/ajte.2018v43n5.8

Forsberg, A., Dieterich, M., & Zeleznik, R. (1998, November). The music notepad. In *Proceedings of the 11th annual ACM symposium on user interface software and technology* (pp. 203–210).

Gašević, D., Kovanović, V., & Joksimović, S. (2017). Piecing the learning analytics puzzle: A consolidated model of a field of research and practice. *LEARNING, 3*(1), 63–78.

Gilbert, D. (2016). Revitalizing music teacher preparation with selected "essential conditions". *Journal of Music, Technology and Education, 9*(2), 161–173. https://doi.org/10.1386/jmte.9.2.161_1

Gorgoretti, B. (2019). The use of technology in music education in North Cyprus according to student music teachers. *South African Journal of Education, 39*(1). https://doi.org/10.15700/saje.v39n1a1436

Guillot, C., Guillot, R., & Kumar, V. (2016). MUSIX: Learning analytics in music teaching. In Y. Li, M. Chang, M. Kravcik, E. Popescu, R. Huang, Kinshuk & N.-S. Chen (Eds.), *State-of-the-art and future directions of smart learning* (pp. 269–273). Springer.

Hassenzahl, M., Burmester, M., & Koller, F. (2003). AttrakDiff: Ein Fragebogen zur Messung wahrgenommener hedonischer und pragmatischer Qualität. In G. Szwillus & J. Ziegler (Eds.), *Mensch & computer 2003* (pp. 187–196). Vieweg + Teubner Verlag.

Holtzblatt, K. (2001). Contextual design: Experience in real life. In H. Oberquelle, R. Oppermann & J. Krause (Eds.), *Mensch & computer 2001* (pp. 19–22). Vieweg + Teubner Verlag.

Horton, W. (2011). *E-learning by design*. John Wiley & Sons.

Johnson, C. (2020), A conceptual model for teaching music online. *International Journal on Innovations in Online Education*, 4(2). https://doi.org/10.1615/intjinnovonlineedu.2020035128

Kang, S., & Yoo, H., (2021). Elementary students' music compositions with notation-based software and handwritten notation assisted by classroom instruments. *Bulletin of the Council for Research in Music Education*, 227, 29–44. https://doi.org/10.5406/bulcouresmusedu.227.0029

Keller, J., & Suzuki, K. (2004). Learner motivation and e-learning design: A multinationally validated process. *Journal of Educational Media*, 29(3), 229–239. https://doi.org/10.1080/1358165042000 283084

Kumar, K., & Vivekanandan, V. (2018). Advancing learning through smart learning analytics: A review of case studies. *Asian Association of Open Universities Journal*, 13(1), 1–12. https://doi.org/10.1108/AAOUJ-12-2017-0039

Lee, H. L., Gong, S. J., & Chen, L. H. (2016). An online handwritten recognition system of music score. In *2016 international conference on machine learning and cybernetics (ICMLC)* (pp. 552–557).

Lewis, J. R. (2018), The system usability scale: Past, present, and future. *International Journal of Human–Computer Interaction*, 34(7), 577–590.

Mangaroska, K., & Giannakos, M. (2019). Learning analytics for learning design: A systematic literature review of analytics-driven design to enhance learning. *IEEE Transactions on Learning Technologies*, 12(4), 516–534. https://doi.org/10.1109/TLT.2018.2868673

Miyao, H., & Maruyama, M. (2004). An online handwritten music score recognition system. In *Proceedings of the 17th international conference on pattern recognition, ICPR 2004* (pp. 461–464).

Montgomery, A. P., Mousavi, A., Carbonaro, M., Hayward, D. V., & Dunn, W. (2019). Using learning analytics to explore self-regulated learning in flipped blended learning music teacher education. *British Journal of Educational Technology*, 50(1), 114–127. https://doi.org/10.1111/bjet.12590

Moore, M. G. (1993). Theory of transactional distance. In D. Keegan (Ed.), *Theoretical principles of distance education* (pp. 22–38). Routledge.

Muller, M. J., & Druin, A. (2012). Participatory design: The third space in human-computer interaction. In J. A. Jacko (Ed.), *The human-computer interaction handbook: Fundamentals, evolving technologies, and emerging applications* (3rd ed., pp. 1125–1154). Taylor & Francis.

Nart, S. (2016). Music software in the technology integrated music education. *Turkish Online Journal of Educational Technology-TOJET*, 15(2), 78–84.

Norman, D. (2013). *The design of everyday things: Revised and expanded edition*. Basic Books.

Pierce, C., Woodward, C. J., & Bartel, A. (2020). MeWare for sale: Developer's approaches to serious mobile music games. In *DiGRA'20 – Proceedings of the 2020 DiGRA international conference: Play everywhere,Tampere,Finland*.

Portowitz, A., Peppler, K. A., & Downton, M. (2014). In Harmony: A technology-based music education model to enhance musical understanding and general learning skills. *International Journal of Music Education*, 32(2), 242–260.

Quintana, C., Krajcik, J., & Soloway, E. (2000). Exploring a structured definition for learner-centered design. *Fourth international conference of the learning sciences* (pp. 256–263). Erlbaum.

Quintana, R. M., Haley, S. R., Magyar, N., & Tan, Y. (2021). Integrating learner and user experience design: A bidirectional approach. In M. Schmidt, A. A. Tawfik, I. Jahnke & Y. Earnshaw (Eds.), *Learner and user experience research: An introduction for the field of learning design & technology* (pp. 235–251). EdTech Books.

Repenning, A., Zurmühle, J., Lamprou, A., & Hug, D. (2020). Computational music thinking patterns: Connecting music education with computer science education through the design of interactive notations. In *CSEDU 2020–12th international conference on computer supported education*. https://doi.org/10.5220/0009817506410652

Schmidt, M., Tawfik, A. A., Jahnke, I., & Earnshaw, Y. (2020). *Learner and user experience research: An introduction for the field of learning design & technology*. EdTechBooks.

Seifert, U., Klaßmann, S., Varelmann, T., & Dahmen, N. (2020). Computational thinking in der musikwissenschaft: Jupyter notebook als Umgebung für Lehre und Forschung. In *Freie Beiträge zur Jahrestagung der Gesellschaft für Musikforschung 2019* (pp. 309–319). Paderborn, Detmold, Germany.

Tanaka, A. (2019). Embodied musical interaction. In S. Holland, T. Mudd, K. Wilkie-McKenna, A. McPherson & M. Wanderley (Eds.). *New directions in music and human-computer interaction* (pp. 135–154). Springer.

Titlestad, O. H., Staring, K., & Braa, J. (2009). Distributed development to enable user participation: Multilevel design in the HISP network. *Scandinavian Journal of Information Systems, 21*(1), 3.

Todea, D. (2015). The use of the MuseScore software in musical e-learning. *The 10th international conference on virtual learning* (pp. 88–94). Bucharest, Bulgaria.

Upitis, R., Abrami, P. C., & Boese, K. (2016). The use of digital tools by independent music teachers, international association for development of the information society. In *International conference on mobile learning* (pp. 108–112). Algarve, Portugal.

Viberg, O., Hatakka, M., Bälter, O., & Mavroudi, A. (2018). The current landscape of learning analytics in higher education. *Computers in Human Behavior, 89*, 98–110. https://doi.org/10.1016/j.chb.2018.07.027

Webster, P. (2002). Historical perspectives on technology and music. *Music Educators Journal, 89*(1), 38–43.

Webster, P. (2016). Computer-based technology. In G. E. McPherson (Ed.), *The child as musician. A handbook of musical development* (2nd ed., pp. 500–519). Oxford University Press.

10 Audio Education

Perspectives from Industry

Andrew King

Introduction

This chapter considers the perspectives of industry professionals with a breadth of experience and focusses upon current practice in the audio industry. It builds upon previous research (King & Himonides, 2016) by capturing the lived experience of these experts and their perspectives of working in the music business. It examines the current working environment, process and design, and the human aspects of working in music production. It achieves this by considering: the location where activities take place; insights into professional projects; how technology influences the way they work; the tools they use in the creation of audio projects; specific online ways of working; collaboration with artists; considerations for the curriculum and advice for students; and the current and potential use of Artificial Intelligence (AI) in music production. It is anticipated that these insights will provide useful considerations for music technology educators when considering the current nature of audio education and the employability of the students they teach.

An earlier study King (2016) tried to develop an understanding of the transition from analogue to digital technologies and what the key perspectives were for producers that could potentially relate to music production in the digital age. Digital recording in some music studios began in the 1970s before moving into the mainstream with the ability for consumers to purchase music on compact disc in the early 1980s (Patmore, 2009) and their associated *Red Book*[1] standards. Early use of digital recording was largely confined to the commercial studio using devices such as the PCM-1, which used video tape as a storage medium. *Digital signatures* (2016) by Brovig-Hanssen and Danielson discusses digital technology in music production from the perspective of several commercial case-studies all framed within the context of popular music. This volume gives an insight into works by artists such as *Kate Bush* and *Prince*, and the experimentation that took place as enabled by the development of digital technology at that time. The authors argue that digital technology has created a new palette for music; a form of *Schizophonia* exists now that music can be either live or recorded and addresses the argument of *human versus machine*. From a music production perspective, there are certainly advances in terms of creative use, however, these are often digital versions of analogue technology. For example, a reverb plug-in used to be a plate on the wall and an echo used to come from a chamber, not a software app. However, the speed of operation and availability of software in the digital world has meant professional standards are possible outside the commercial facilities. The argument concerning human versus machine is particularly pertinent at present given the developments of AI and music – in particular, the new affordances these technologies will give music production and how this could affect agency in relation to some of the (human) roles involved.

DOI: 10.4324/9781003041474-13

The Dawn of the DAW (Bell, 2018) or Digital Audio Workstation (DAW) demonstrates how music creation has been revolutionised in the sense that the affordability of the technology has meant access to music production tools is now possible for many musicians. Some authors have referred to this as a *democratisation* of music production through technology, although this term does not come without its challenges. Taylor (2001) illuminates this discussion in terms of accessibility and ideas around *cultural democracy* and debates this terminology. What is evident is that learners and educators have access to tools that allow the creation of music by digital means that were not possible a few decades earlier. The ability to compose, record, edit, and distribute music via digital means (for example, see King, 2012) has long been possible for students and teachers without the need to access industry facilities that can often be expensive. Although it should be stated that for certain types of music capture facilities for the initial recording stage are often still carried out in large-scale facilities (such as AIR or Abbey Road Studios) and require expensive microphones and mixing consoles. However, the process to then analyse, arrange, edit, overdub parts, and ultimately master[2] the tracks can be completed using a DAW. The evolution of the music studio, and production more generally, has led to profound changes both in terms of industry practice and education opportunities. This chapter begins by considering what is meant by agency and affordances, the music studio, and technology in the music curriculum.

Agency and Affordances and Sound Recording

In his work *Strange Sounds*, Taylor (2001*)* sets out two contrasting positions in thinking about technology and agency: technological determinism and voluntarism.[3] The main differences are described as: 'technological determinism as a kind of top-down model and voluntarism its polar opposite' (Taylor, 2001, p. 25). The difference in position would appear to be that from a technological determinist standpoint, the theory attributes agency to technology and therefore has the power to change the lives of human beings. Voluntarism begins with the precept that the technology is neutral and is only good or bad depending upon its use. As suggested by Taylor, there are several shades of grey between this dichotomy within social theory, but it is not possible to fully engage in a debate of this nature in this chapter.

What is meant in terms of affordances in this chapter is based upon the work of Gibson (1979) and the subsequent debate and study in ecological psychology presented through the lens of computing by Norman (1998). For this research, this is interpreted as the actions or possibilities within an environment (i.e., the recording studio) and the user. Whilst in early sound recording the possibilities were limited by both the capabilities of the technology from early mono recordings through stereo to early multi-track capture methods for up to 48-track recording, the availability of outboard technology expanded so that it was possible to process and add effects to audio tracks both in isolation and across an entire song. Early recording devices, such as microphones, mixers, and the disc or magnetic tape used to capture recordings, all added noise or hiss to a recording; engineers had to carefully consider what equipment to employ because of these limitations. Fast forward to the 21st century: digitally recorded productions have largely overcome issues over track count, processing, and noise – which has greatly expanded the number of affordances or actions possible in the studio.

The ability to capture multiple takes of the same performance by an instrumentalist in isolation and making the decision later can be perceived in both a positive and a negative light. Increasing the number of options available does allow a form of non-destructive editing (for example, see Huber & Runstein; 2017, p. 211) and a large collection of takes can be stored for later use. However, the locus of control would seem to pass from the performer to the engineer who is now able to select the performance to be used, or piece together different performances for the final mix – albeit often in consultation with the musicians. This needs to be considered alongside the increased ability to edit tracks quite precisely using a range of tools during the post-production stage that could alter and elongate the process. The range of affordances has enriched the tools at the disposal of the studio team with the possible side effect that it could potentially make the process more time-consuming: problematic when considering the commercial pressures.

The Music Studio: Art, Technique, and the Curriculum

The earlier texts relating to music production often focused upon the technology and techniques necessary for audio engineering. Borwick's (1994) *Sound Recording Practice* was an early example of such a comprehensive handbook. More recent works, such as *Sound and Recording* (Rumsey & McCormick, 2009) and *Modern Recording Techniques* (Huber & Runstein; 2017), provide similar depth, insight, and reference to the field. What is meant by a studio and the roles of those working in the industry is something that has changed over the decades. Moorefield (2005) examines this through the perspective of *The Producer as Composer*, describing how the role of producer came about, the changing nature of how a studio was perceived as a musical instrument, and details of key artists and genres such as *hip-hop* that contributed to these technological changes. The shift towards the consideration of the artistic merits of music production are probably best epitomised by *The Art of Record Production* (Frith & Zagorski-Thomas, 2012), with further insights in the second edition focussed on creative practice (Zagorski-Thomas et al., 2019). Both editions mark a move away from the description of technology and technique towards an understanding of the roles within the studio and the creative practice. Bennett (2019), in *Modern Records, Maverick Methods*, notes that of the other contributions to our understanding that do exist from an insider or industry perspective many are 'social and experiential accounts of working with well-known artists' (p. 12). Bennett also goes on to state that 'all are male and the vast majority worked with rock musicians' (ibid). This volume is also framed within an exhaustive study across multiple musical genres that maps out the technology and process in popular music production from 1978–2000. The point about representation is also well made, since this is an issue both in terms of the literature and careers within the industry. This is despite some high-profile female producers working in the industry, such as Sylvia Massy, Suzanne Ciani, and Sonia Pottinger. Armstrong (2016) highlights this as an issue within educational practice with technology and the gendering of music education, and the challenges it presents.

Music technology has existed for several years throughout the music curriculum from school-age children all the way to higher education. Gall (2017) discusses this from an autobiographical perspective, drawing upon experiences of training teachers and official government reports in England, whilst also informed by large-scale studies that highlight a European perspective. Creativity seems to be at the core of the agenda when using technology with a vast array of technologies and systems now available. Some of this creativity has focused upon new approaches and sonic exploration, whilst some has developed traditional musical skills such as training the ear. Gall goes on to highlight issues such as a lack of pre- or in-service training and a lack of available investment in equipment: the National

Plan for Music Education[4] will attempt to address the former issue concerning training. Boehm et al. (2018) revisited a previous article (Boehm, 2007) which provides a comprehensive oversight of music technology at the higher level in UK universities. Within this research, they highlighted the shift towards music production style courses over the previous decade and the view of music technology as either arts, science, technology, or production. Many HE music programmes teach audio engineering as part of a music technology or music production offering. These programmes offer relevant engineering skills around audio capture, mixing, and mastering using both large-format mixing consoles and Digital Audio Workstations (DAW). There is therefore a need to not only teach the relevant skills but also to understand the perspectives of industry practitioners beyond the technology and to share insights around practice and the artistic elements. King (2017) focusses on this at the tertiary level, drawing insights from a key industry and education accreditation lead. Drawing upon the needs of industry bodies and examining the curricula and employability, such themes as skills, roles, attitudes, tools, teaching, spaces, the freelance nature of the industry, and how students are equipped to survive emerged. These insights, in part, informed the questions for the interviewees in this study.

The Art of Record Production journal and conference provides a new platform to consider the technology as well as these artistic elements. This valuable resource highlights discussions on areas such as intellectual property (May, 2007), roles within the studio (Ojanen, 2012, examining the technological divide (Bennett, 2009), and ecological approaches to mixing audio (Bourbon & Zagorski-Thomas, 2017) that also examine agency and audio staging.[5] This examination of technology and its use informs this present study. Rather than attempt to explain the technical design or the operation of recording studio technology, it focuses upon expert views concerning *how* and *why* studio practice may take place. Bates (2012) attempts to describe *What Studios Do* from the social and musical performances that take place from within. Six key elements are isolated concerning: the affect/effect on sound; isolation from outside; focus attention and sight upon objects; constrain paths of audibility; cultivate practice and social activity; and become pilgrimage sites. Certain studios are revered for their acoustic properties, often isolated from outside distractions and noises, use of monitoring systems and talkback communication methods, and can be a hive of activity in terms of practice and social interactions. The latter point about pilgrimage can be viewed in many guises, one of the most famous being the connection between Abbey Road Studios and the Beatles.

Perspectives from Industry

The research design for this study was qualitative in nature and involved in-depth interviews with record producers currently working in the music industry. Interpretative Phenomenological Analysis (IPA; Smith et al., 2013) was the approach used for the study and the subsequent analysis and presentation of the findings. IPA uses an idiographic approach and the understanding of the phenomena from each participant's perspective and a summary is developed. Through analysis of the coded data, the researcher focusses upon meaning and then identifies important themes for the interviewee. What follows is integrative analysis to compare the responses of all the participants. The main aim of the research was to:

- Explore the practice of audio and music production from a professional perspective
  With the following sub-aims:

  - How practitioners work in the music industry; and
  - What the potential future technological developments are.

This investigation differs from a previous study (King, 2016) that examined the transition from analogue to digital technologies and attempted to preserve the viewpoints of industry experts for future generations in terms of the lived experience. It was anticipated that these expert opinions may be valid in terms of considering approaches to studio practice and curriculum design in the academy. This present study focusses on the people, environment, process, and design within pedagogical recording studio practice, and therefore aligns to the ideas explored in this volume. The environment section was to more fully understand where practice took place and the sorts of technology now commonly used. Both process and design give in-depth insights into recent projects in terms of stages involved, how digital technology is used, the use of the Digital Audio Workstation (DAW) and outboard equipment, and tools used to collaborate in online environments for both the creation and sharing of music production artefacts. The people section builds upon this to understand whether online collaboration influences workflow, the core elements for music production from a pedagogical perspective, and viewpoints for working in the industry. The final part of this study also addresses how AI is being used and potential future directions for music production.

The framework for the study was initially drawn from a previous study (see King, 2016) as shown in Figure 10.1. This suggested framework, which had drawn together the industry perspectives in the study, was a result of the analysis of the producer perspectives. It brought together potential avenues of exploration for studio practice and considerations for educators and practitioners of music production. It was anticipated that by understanding both the human perspective and the knowledge and skills, it may help to aid current practice or at the very least preserve the perspectives of renowned industry experts.

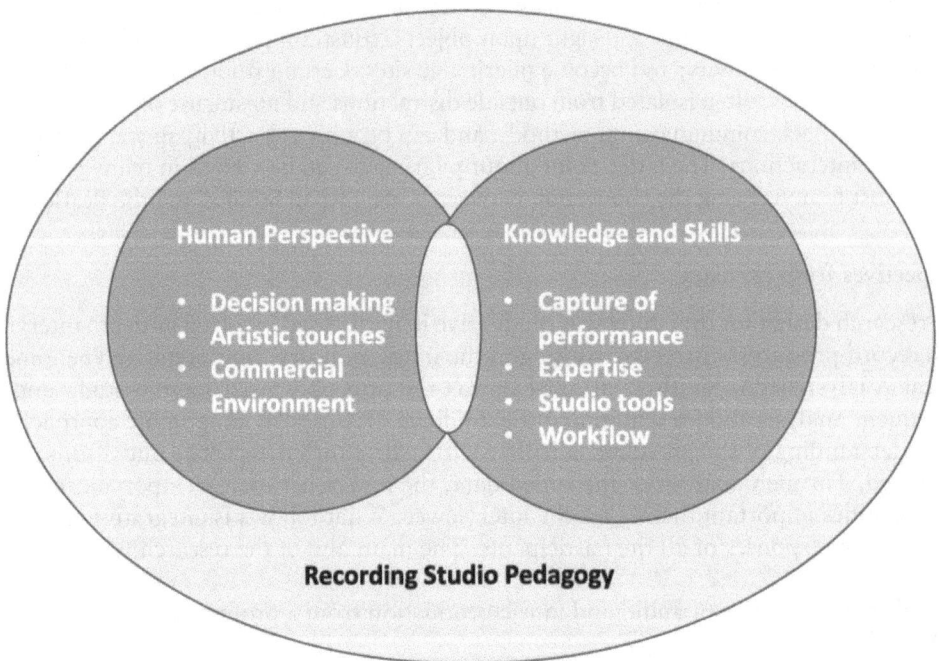

Figure 10.1 Potential considerations of recording studio pedagogy.

The three producers approached to be involved in this study were all currently working in the industry and had worked across different genres of contemporary music:

- Phil Bodger (PB), who has worked with artists including Maxi Priest; The Housemartins; D Mob; The Lighthouse Family; The Proclaimers; Imogen Heap; Bryan Ferry; Tina Turner; Stevie Wonder; and the Brand New Heavies.
- Dr Gary Bromham (GB), co-chair of the Joint Audio Media Education Service (JAMES: an industry accreditation organisation), who has worked with artists including Bjork; George Michael; Sheryl Crow; Delta Goodrem; and the Maccabees.
- Robin Reumers (RR), Director of Education (Abbey Road Institute), who has worked with artists including Alejandro Sanz; Alessia Cara; Paula Arenas; Pablo Alborán; Bryan May; Fonseca; Lola Astanova; Hardwell; Oliver Heldens; and Ela Taube.

The sampling strategy for the study was based upon the principles set out by Kemper et al. (2003) in that: the producers approached were considered within the context of the main research question in terms of expertise; they would be able to produce insights into audio production from a lived-experience perspective; the sample size fits within IPA guidelines (see Smith et al., 2013, p. 51), has followed ethical protocols; appropriate data can be drawn from the study; and uses an efficient approach to a sampling scheme All have considerable experience across many years of practice and across various genres/approaches to music production that include rock, classical, and electronic music practice in the UK, Europe, and the United States. In addition, all are still working in the industry and have experience of teaching within HE, and in some cases programme leadership. IPA requires an idiographic focus that requires understanding the data from the viewpoint of each participant, rather than an overarching set of laws that are more generally applicable (Prior & Leech-Wilkinson, 2014). The researcher initially produces a summary for each participant. This is followed by phenomenological coding focusing on the data and to attempt to block out external influences and observe patterns and contradictions. Themes that emerge from the data are then identified and reviewed. Finally, an integrative analysis of themes that have emerged from each interview takes place, and a subsequent narrative is constructed. From an ethical standpoint, all participants were sent an information sheet about the project prior to interview, ethical clearance for the project was obtained from the relevant university ethics committee prior to the study commencing, and consent was provided by participants. The participants are also from different ethnic backgrounds and therefore represent different cultural viewpoints/perspectives. It was not possible during the timescale to obtain a viewpoint of a producer from a different gender; this is the result of the lack of female engineers and producers, which is problematic throughout the industry.

Analysis and Discussion

What follows is an analysis and discussion of each of the core areas relating to the structure of the edited volume: environment; process; design; and people based upon the summary themes and an integrative analysis. Care has been taken to not give a preference in terms of the order in which the producers views' are presented, to avoid giving the appearance of a rank. Instead, from the summary themes and coded data key statements are provided to illuminate discussion. These statements sometimes offer complementary or differing viewpoints, and each is given equal treatment in terms of the following narrative. The first stage of the analysis was to explore the different themes arising from each participant. Table 10.1

Table 10.1 Superordinate themes and sub-themes from the producer interviews.

Super-ordinate themes	Subsidiary Themes
Knowledge and Skills	• Capture of performance
	• Expertise
	• Studio tools
	• Workflow
Approaches & Perspectives	• Decision making
	• Artistic touches
	• Environment
	• Commercial

includes the super-ordinate and subsidiary themes that were coded at this point of the analysis. This coding of themes is based on the analysis of the dataset from King (2016). However, the term *Human Perspective* has been replaced by *Approaches and Perspectives* to better represent the subsidiary themes in this study.

The next sections represent the integrative analysis of these themes from the three music producers. The following section highlights examples from the cross-cutting areas identified: environment (both physical and online); process and design; people; and artificial intelligence.

Physical Environment

The first area of analysis is drawn from the environment identified in the previous study but now with a consideration of location as well. All interviews took place in 2022. Since this was after a global pandemic, clarity over the approach used before, and after, was sought from participants. Robin Reumers noted that:

RR: Working with artists has not changed that much, since my focus is on mixing and mastering [a track or album]. These [sessions] are for the most part unattended, although the artist may come in to check the mix. . . . for one recent session that was recording and written with Christina Aguilera, [it included] fifteen writers plus team, so twenty people in total . . . people feel for the creative process it is important to connect with each other.

RR highlights here that mixing and mastering parts of their industry work (for an example of production processes, see King, 2012, p. 484) tend to happen with the engineer/producer working alone in the studio with some input from the artist at various points to listen to work to obtain feedback. However, the writing and recording parts tend to be *attended*, suggesting the pre-production and initial capture of recorded tracks (vocals, instrument parts) take place as an activity in the studio. PB has a slightly different work environment:

PB: I am now working in a second bedroom in my house. I used to have a small studio in Brighton with a *ProTools* system which I rented . . . I wasn't using a console because I was mainly mixing; if I needed to record, I would go off and work in a proper studio. Over the last year, I have got[ten] into podcast . . . after someone asked me to do a tape sync[6] for an interview.

PB had worked in several large studios and had become more freelance later in their career after a brief hiatus away from the industry (2014–2017). Although they did still record film music in the larger studio environments, a lot of the activity either took place on location (live recordings such as podcasts) or from home. GB shared a similar narrative about their work environment:

GB: It's an attic studio . . . it's [acoustically] treated, it's a couple of pair of speakers . . . I work on headphones a lot more than I used to because a lot of music is now listened to on headphones, so it is remiss of you to at least not check your mixes . . . so it is very much an in-the-box system based around universal audio . . . I guess I am embracing the paradigm of an analogue studio.

GB's work environment tended to be more in the commercial studio sector at the start of their career and had changed to a home studio. They use Universal Audio digital software plugins which emulate (and from a visual perspective often simulate) analogue technology. What is also revealing is that production takes place entirely within the box (or within the DAW), which for many educators may be common in terms of how students have produced music for the last 10–20 years, but was not always the case for industry professionals.

Process and Design

The interviewees were first asked to describe a recent project and the stages involved from this perspective. Here, PB discusses a recent project in 2021 with John Owen Williams (record producer):

PB: He [John] had a track he had recorded and sent it to me and asked can I help with this . . . basically he sent me a logic session . . . there were 20 guitar tracks . . . the lead vocal was spread over three or four tracks . . . the drums were all programmed from a variety of different places . . . the work involved some rebalancing of the song but not the arrangement . . . moved the timing of some parts and reprogrammed the drums . . . this involved EQ the snare drum . . . change the hi-hat pattern . . . and a fair bit of time editing the guitars.

Anecdotal evidence from the record production community suggests this type of work is not uncommon in the music industry. An artist or producer may send session files to another expert for support after the initial pre-production and recording stages. What comes across strongly is the need to bring a sense of order to the session that probably may not have been the case had they followed their own ideas around workflow from the start of the project. A follow-up question around communication between artist/producer and engineer revealed:

PB: I was just sending him mixes . . . he wasn't particularly interested in the specifics of what I had done . . . he would just listen to them and say, "yeah, that sounds better" or "that doesn't sound better"; he might say, "there was a guitar in the bridge and I can't quite hear it, can you turn it up" and these were the types of conversation.

GB describes a recent project that shares similarities with PB's experience:

GB: Grice [Peters] approach[ed] me to mix an EP . . . and he sent me, as is very common these days, 160 tracks . . . and it's usually because they can't make decisions about what they want and it falls upon me as the mix engineer to make a lot of those decisions . . . and I do a rough mix and send to the artist, and they give me feedback . . . they didn't like the initial mix . . . so I take out the one bit of analogue workflow which is a compressor and EQ and do it all in the box . . . and they say "yeah, that's what I want", so it kind of felt like the death of the analogue workflow to me.

The rest of the EP was mixed on a laptop and a pair of headphones whilst GB travelled across Europe. GB corresponded with the artist sending various mixes for approval, and this is how the work was completed. This change of work environment and approach was very different for GB but has started to become common practice. Slater (2016) discusses this from the viewpoint of processes of learning in the project studio that have become increasingly common for freelance audio professionals.

For RR, the breadth of activity suggests that they need to be agile in terms of how they approach recording projects:

RR: Every project is so different . . . one Mexican artist was creating an album of legends . . . each a legendary song working with a different artist some from maybe 20–30 years ago . . . each song a duet . . . at our studio we worked on three songs out of the 11 on the album . . . the artist met with the producer ahead of the recording to discuss what they wanted to do . . . what parts of the old song they wanted to keep . . . the tempo in piano original was way out in terms of timing, maybe 15 bpm, so we decided to do that to the grid . . . then we started recording, there was also an orchestra in Prague that was recorded remotely . . . that would take three to four weeks, then the artist would come into the studio and record the vocals . . . a rough mix would be sent to the A&R manager . . . once everyone was happy we started mixing the track . . . there were two or three revisions . . . it was then sent for mastering in LA [Los Angeles] . . . that bit would have been challenging since so many studios and places were involved and they had to make it sound like an album . . . [to] sound cohesive.

For RR, this was a common way of working. Similar to some albums produced in the latter part of the 20th century different studios could be used and the work pieced together, sometimes even with a time lapse of several years between some of the album's content and additional tracks recorded and produced later:

RR: When I started it was the early days of digital . . . I still learnt partly on tape machines . . . I think we have lost some things . . . not in terms of sound quality . . . for me the discussion should not now be whether digital is as good as analogue . . . artists know it is all digital now and we can manipulate anything, change the pitch, change the timing . . . artists will ask to do things [in different] takes, whereas in analogue it had to be rehearsed and ready, so people were really well prepared to come into the studio and do the song.

They went on to discuss music distribution from a digital perspective:

RR: It is so easy to release music nowadays and things happen way more quickly . . . before, you would work on one album for 12 months and now it's working on single [song] after single, then working on this EP . . . it is a lot more chaotic but not necessarily bad chaotic.

GB goes on to describe the production process they often use now and how this has changed over time:

GB: Recording and mixing where they merged into one have now become two very separate entities for me. I go to a studio for the recording of a band . . . capture a lot of the quality, the space or sound of the outboard . . . mixing for me is very different to even ten years ago.

GB was discussing their move away from the analogue paradigm and how the mixing process was for them now away from the recording studio. They went on to state:

GB: Recallability, that's a big deal now; you don't work on one song now, you work on several different songs . . . when I was talking to Andrew Scheps,[7] he gets bored working on one song now and wants to switch between four or five songs . . . and that's a real luxury now, it used to be such grief doing recalls . . . and you would not dare to take [the song] off the desk until you felt like you got it right.

GB went on to discuss the number of affordances now possible with digital technology:

GB: One of the criticisms [of digital technology] is that we have an infinite number of options . . . when I work in the box it has the potential to never ever be finished . . . we have to be in a place to say enough is enough, it is not going to get any better.

When discussing digital technology and how they approach working, PB stated the following:

PB: I don't think it has really changed the way I work . . . I am much less precious about the equipment . . . I try to get less concerned about the tools and the equipment . . . I can work in any environment and the tools are in my head . . . it is all about the music and the content . . . I am relying upon my ears more than anything to make those judgements.

PB goes on to talk about whether they work exclusively within the DAW or not:

PB: I have always used analogue signal flow into a DAW in terms of recording . . . if I am at home I work exclusively in the DAW . . . I will use outboard if it's available, but I am not wedded to any of it.

This pattern of increasing working in the DAW for the mixing and mastering stages seems to be a common approach. GB shared a similar view in terms of using analogue at the recording stage, although sometimes other studio processes were relevant:

GB: I re-amp . . . to send stuff out through a guitar pedal and re-track it . . . distortion for me is a bigger thing than, say, EQ. I will try a plug-in [to emulate this] but sometimes I just don't get the same thing in digital domain, sometimes I need something that is crunchy or distorted . . . and it has some personality. The problem with some plug-ins is they do things in a very predictable way.

RR discussed the tactile nature of some technology in their response:

RR: I love using analogue and outboard during the recording with a console . . . mostly for the psychological effect; when you are working with an artist, it is super difficult to seem interested when you are working behind a screen . . . if you are working on a console and twisting knobs you can make it seem like you are enjoying it . . . mostly for the experience, for the people to feel you are part of what they are doing.

But for the mixing stage of their workflow, RR reinforced the points of GB and PB:

RR: For mixing I do not use outboard gear [occasionally]. I have some creative effects not available as plug-ins that I use . . . for the pace [at] which we work now, it is impossible for me to use outboard.

RR was discussing the differences of working 20 years ago in which doing a recall of a song meant setting up the mixing console and all the outboards again and the artist was often given less critical feedback. For modern mixes, RR felt there is far more detailed feedback for changes required for a mix that would make this challenging for the speed at which they have to work without the ease of digital recall. Therefore, the affordances of the technology and a greater understanding of what was possible from an artist's perspective meant a greater degree of feedback and agency in terms of the sound of the finished work.

Online Environment

Online tools have developed considerably over the last decade and are being used more often in the music industry. Considering this from a music producer's perspective, GB stated:

GB: The sessions exist in the cloud . . . the person I am collaborating with always has access to the same version of the song . . . we can collaborate in real time. I use a programme called ChronoSync[8] . . . I am using Audiomovers[9] . . . the latency can always be a problem . . . although I can do some tracking over the internet.

GB is describing how they use cloud-based services to store session and audio files and then other tools such as Audiomovers to collaborate online to stream and record parts remotely. RR uses a similar approach and also uses Audiomovers for online collaboration for clients to listen to mixes and give feedback remotely; however, this was for about 10 percent of the sessions they managed. RR also went on to make the point that mixing tended to happen in isolation so the producer could get objective feedback from the artist or record company with a fresh perspective. In addition to the tools described earlier, PB also uses SquadCast, which is a cloud-based recording studio which they have used extensively for podcast work. When discussing workflow using online tools and differences from face-to-face production, PB stated:

PB: [this difference] is not so much for me . . . I always did mixing on my own . . . in a studio . . . and I would just send the mix off at the end of the day . . . someone would send a bunch of notes . . . and I would send another mix back.

The method for over the last 10 years for PB has been to upload the files to a secure online storage device. Prior to this, it would have been a physical fixed format which would need to be transported. GB similarly works this way, but prefers people in the room if possible:

GB: I just think some of the meaning gets lost on a Zoom call . . . there is this sense you have to wait for someone to respond . . . and it probably wouldn't be like that in the room.

RR discusses collaborative workflow from a songwriting and production perspective in online environments:

RR: It can be really cool, you have an idea and you want to bounce it off someone who can't be in the room . . . for production I can be in Miami and need an orchestral recording and it makes sense to be in Prague, and it doesn't make sense to fly out there . . . you need to give feedback [from a distance] and we use things like Source-Connect[10] to listen in real-time and give feedback.

RR also went on to state they only do this when necessary, since the process of listening and working online feels more exhausting than working in the studio. However, the fact that digital technology afforded this type of working practice meant production could continue remotely with the added benefit of not adding to the carbon footprint of the project.

People

All the industry experts had experience in delivering workshops at HE level; for GB, this meant significant experience as a programme leader, and for RR, Director of the Abbey Road Institute in Miami. When reflecting upon the core elements necessary for a music production curriculum, RR commented:

RR: Nowadays, if you focus on production, it's like you no longer have just one role . . . as a modern producer, you need to be involved in contracts with different people . . . you have to engineer stuff . . . you have to know about royalties, deals with publishers, with labels.

RR is making a similar point to Thompson and Harding (2019, 2023) about the music industry being viewed as a service industry and the breadth of skills required to work in the field. In addition, the changing nature of the studio in the internet age was described by Théberge (2012) regarding the different roles in the studio and the related diminishing number of opportunities for professional apprenticeships in larger-scale studio facilities. RR went on to state the importance of technical knowledge about microphones and plug-ins, but shared this insight about creativity:

RR: Students new to recording get hung up on the technical aspects . . . later on in their career they realise they matter less than they do . . . always put the song first and work out the emotion of the song . . . all of the rest is important, but it is secondary.

PB had views relating to creativity that focussed upon critical listening:

PB: Get the students to listen . . . need to understand how to use your ears . . . analyse recordings, listen to the bass, listen to the strings, what's the trumpet doing?

PB went on to talk about the importance of workflow to the audio professional:

PB: being disciplined in your workflow is really important . . . focus on one thing at a time . . . and decision making . . . that's massively important and especially now since it is so easy not to make decisions . . . pre-production planning is very important . . . and understand what the artist wants, what is their vision.

The question of agency and affordances in terms of decision making was something discussed in King (2016) in terms of recording studio practice. It was perhaps easier because of digital technology to move the decision making to a later stage (discussed with production processes earlier). GB stated the importance of considering creative artforms beyond the relevant skills necessary for the role:

GB: You need to stress the importance that this is an interdisciplinary field . . . if someone asks me for a punchy or airy sound, I need to be able to map technical parameters to aesthetic spaces . . . we need students to see it's multi-dimensional . . . it's about communication, creativity, but it's also about technical knowledge . . . it's about experimentation; there isn't one way to do something.

GB's point regarding experimentation contradicts RR, who stated the commercial nature of studio projects meant this was not possible. The interdisciplinary nature of some artistic practice is an important point for educators to consider. It is unlikely students entering into a career in the industry will work in isolation all the time. Therefore, it is important to develop other skills relating to communication and creativity during studies. RR commented about working in the music industry:

RR: The most important thing is loving what you do . . . figure out what makes you unique . . . the beauty today is there are so many fields in audio, not just music production; there is audio for games, audio for films . . . figure out what you are good at and create your own niche.

Creativity was also an important factor for PB:

PB: You have got to be creative . . . you've got to be personally creative . . . if you can write and compose, do that . . . be creative in terms of projects and clients . . . there is that word *networking*, of course . . . come up with ideas, and go and talk to people about them.

PB was speaking here of the extensive podcasting work they have done and how some of that work was generated by approaching potential clients and selling them their ideas about why their company needs to do this. PB felt podcasting was a good way in because of the ease of getting the technology and the potential for paid work.

GB talked about the opportunities in related disciplines in the audio world:

GB: They [students] need to be broad-minded; there is film, live sound . . . they need to embrace the idea they will need to be a jack of all trades and embrace multiple roles . . . they must be savvy with intelligent production tools.

Artificial Intelligence (AI)

The final exploration with the industry experts led to the cutting edge of audio production and the evolution of Artificial Intelligence (AI). GB, newly graduated doctor from Queen Mary School of AI in music, commented:

GB: There is an ethical issue here; you have all these people jumping up and down and thinking they are going to be replaced . . . actually, it happened in the 1980s with drum machines . . . until people understand the meaning of the technology, it will seem like some sort of threat . . . artificial intelligence needs to be seen as an assistive tool as a way to augment creativity and not replace it . . . I think it will allow more time for creativity, not less.

PB focused on how much is curated from a digital perspective when considering AI:

PB: I think about playlists when you go on Spotify . . . you listen to a track, and it suggests a whole bunch of other stuff . . . there are plug-ins that will mix your track for you . . . other things like a plug-in that write the music for some TV programme or other I am sure will be happening soon.

RR had similar views and hopes for AI in terms of assisting the production process:

RR: Here is what I will hope it will do . . . for me, the best way AI can help is helping the creative process and not replac[ing] it . . . helping to analyse recordings when things don't quite sound right . . . having AI to help assist with that process . . . I think it could help the whole industry in general because there are now more people making music than ever before . . . what I hope doesn't happen is for it to make things sound more the same, which has happened in certain genres.

Thomas and King (2019) studied the impact of digital technology on the production process in heavy metal music and the sonic signatures that are created, as well as the challenges posed by using new technologies. There are also considerations for audio students on how digital tools are used to assist in music production. RR went on to mention some of the key tools they use in practice:

RR: Izotope from the production side [is] doing stuff on the production side for de-noising or detecting certain things . . . or isolating certain parts where you have, say, a guitar and a vocal and you just want to isolate the vocal . . . Izotope has a plug-in called *Neutron*, which makes suggestions about the track.

The software plug-in *Neutron* can be used on either an individual instrument track (such as a piano) or the whole song. There is an *assistant* button that, when deployed, listens to the audio recording and makes alterations to the tone, dynamics, sound characteristics, and stereo imaging. The AI makes the suggested changes, and the producer can then make further alterations to the sound based upon those same controls. This is one example of AI as an assistive tool currently being used in music production.

Conclusion and Implications for Teaching

Since those interviews took place in 2022, the pace of development of AI in music production has increased. On 2 November 2023, a new Beatles song, *Now and Then*, was created from a demo tape John Lennon produced in 1977. Paul McCartney stated in a recent interview that they tried to do something with the track around the same time that *Free as a Bird* was released in 1995 but the balance of the piano against the vocal made it hard to distinguish John Lennon's vocal, so the project was abandoned. McCartney claimed AI was used to isolate the voice and make the completion of the track possible; audio restoration via machine assisted learning (MAL) was key to the success of being able to isolate and treat the piano and vocal separately to increase the amplitude of the latter. It is clear that without the development of digital technology this *last* Beatles release would not have been possible. These developments offer opportunities to learn the necessary skills required to approach music production in new and exciting ways.

AI and Music Production Tools

The nature of audio production has undoubtedly changed in the last 20 years. The agency and affordances of technology discussed earlier in the chapter have come into sharp focus especially when considering the change roles in the studio, how much the technology can potentially influence the process and change the outcome. It raises questions not only how the production is undertaken but the influence of the technology on the creative process. Preparing students for a career in the industry not only requires a thorough technical understanding but also the necessary business and entrepreneurial skills to succeed (see Thompson & Harding, 2019, 2023). Add to this the development of AI-based tools, and the digital audio world will again see roles adapt and change with the technological evolution. Moffat and Sandler (2019) describe approaches in Intelligent Music Production (IMP) and how these can analyse, interact, and modify audio. What is emphasised alongside the different nature of these tools is the need for people to be able to interact with these tools. Avedeeff (2019) highlights the first album from a human-AI collaboration perspective that utilises Sony's Flow Machines Technologies: *Hello World*. The world of audio production is changing, and professionals and educators will need to keep up.

Whilst for some industry experts in this study the capture of performance for certain genres does still take place within a more typical studio environment, the mixing and mastering elements seem to be entirely (or at least largely) in the box (DAW) for their working practice. The tools used are mostly digital or often digital versions of previous analogue technologies. Therefore, the principles of signal modifiers such as compression and noise gates alongside signal generators such as reverb and chorus still need to be taught; in fact, it has become more critical that this is understood to avoid the use of default settings within the software plug-ins. Using tools to make artistic touches was an important consideration for the producers; this aligned with a previous study (see King, 2016), and AI has a role in supporting this process. There was a strong sense that digital technology had enabled an increased speed of production and how they responded to feedback in terms of how quickly things need to be delivered; this is contrary to the increase of affordances and the anecdotal views of some producers. The freelance nature of the industry is also emphasised with only one of the three producers working in a dedicated facility, whilst the other two worked largely from home; this demonstrated the changing nature of the environment.

Environment

The physical environment can mean different things to the modern-day audio professional, with the need to be agile and swap between studio, home, and on-location to carry out the tasks associated with audio production. Online environments and collaborative work have become second nature now with so many tools available not only for the sharing of files but also the real possibility of synchronous methods of working practice; some of these tools are not prohibitively expensive. A DAW is essential alongside high-quality monitoring in terms of loudspeakers and headphones. The online environment has also become critical, going beyond cloud storage methods and genuine online collaboration tools for the creation of audio work. Tools now exist to achieve real-time creative collaborations and the possibility to reduce the carbon footprint of music production by limiting the need to be in the same physical space, which is important in a global industry.

Workflow

Workflow in the studio can be considered from both macro- and micro-levels, and both are important to the trainee producer. On a macro-level the entire project – whether this is an album, EP, single track, podcast – needs to be carefully managed. The stages involved in a project, such as pre-production, production, and post-production (see Table 10.2), are a useful way to consider planning for a studio project. Workflow appears to have changed for certain projects, as well as the producer's/engineer's own role within the creative process: lack of involvement before the mixing stage of an audio production has meant engineers/producers adapting their role to give a sense of workflow and critique of the recorded artefact. This suggests the agency has shifted from an engineer merely capturing and modifying an audio signal to more of a curation of recorded tracks and helping to select the best approaches and giving critical feedback.

The stages could be considered alongside agile working methodologies used in business to plan and execute projects. The initial project or client idea needs to have a clear understanding of the resources required depending upon the nature of the project. This could be anything from a podcast for a client for their business to a recording of a small ensemble or larger projects such as a full orchestral recording. Once this is set out, the scheduling of the various stages of when tasks will be completed and responsibilities assigned to teams or

Table 10.2 Suggested music production and workflow on a macro level.

Stage	Workflow
Pre-production (planning/review)	• Project idea • Resources required (physical and human) • Project design/stages • Contracts & Fees
Production (Design/manage)	• Project capture • Mixing/editing • Feedback
Post-production (Delivery)	• Mastering • Feedback • Project delivery

individuals need to be understood. The contracts and fees need to be agreed by all parties, which has become more critical given PB's comments around the engineer's role encompassing both technical and creative aspects of music production. There are challenges around commercial pressures that impact workflow, which is something highlighted by RR, that aligns with results from a previous study (see King, 2016).

The micro-level of music production workflow is often the part that causes the most confusion between industry and those interested in learning about audio production. At this level, workflow can mean:

- How is the recorded artefact captured: recording of a live ensemble/artist, multi-track in which parts are recorded separately, or a blend of the two?
- What audio processes are deployed upon capture: are any tools such as compression or equalisation applied?
- When mixing the captured audio tracks do you start mixing and editing from the bottom up (lowest frequency sound, such as a kick drum) or from the top down (the vocal or instrument melody line), or does this depend upon the project?
- Are the recorded parts mixed into audio stems – for example, eight channels of drum microphones mixed to a stereo sub-mix?
- In what order are processes such as equalisation, compression, limiters, and signal generators applied in the mastering of an audio track?

These are just some of the considerations, and the way this is achieved will differ between audio professionals. When students talk about workflow, this is often what is meant – how do you go about recording, mixing/editing, and mastering, and what techniques and tools do producers use? This may be out of a desire to *sound* like a particular song or, on an instrumental level, asking how was that kick drum recorded, and what techniques were used to make it sound that way? Or were sampled drums used with a real human player, or were these drum sounds programmed? There are other considerations as well, such as arrangement of the song or the placement with the stereo-field (see Dockwray & Moore, 2010), as well as dynamic levels within the track. These are often the types of knowledge students want from music producers during masterclasses at a university – how do you go about producing *music* is the key question, rather than the management of the stages of production. The answer of course is that it depends upon what the client wants, the genre of music, and the commercial pressures that experts must consider, as highlighted by Phil Harding in Part 3's Industry Perspective.

Final Thoughts

The study is limited by the size of the sample, such as the demands of the in-depth approach of IPA. A large-scale study of multiple producers' perspectives would be welcome but challenging, given the demands on their time and access to such industry professionals is largely through networks that are not as accessible and apparent as other professions. Thompson (2019) covers some of these aspects in *Creativity in the Recording Studio* whilst Massey (2009) *Behind the Glass* covers a range of insights from commercial record producers. Brovig-Hanssen and Danielson (2016), as discussed earlier, also approach this from the perspective of industry case studies. More in-depth texts exist of producers, such as *Rick Rubin: In the studio* (2013) or *Little Symphonies*, which deals with the life and work of Phil Spector.

The perspective of producers who identify as a different gender is also problematic. The industry-driven record production website is an exhaustive source of studio tours and video interviews with leading industry engineers and producers; the fact that of the 224 in-depth interviews, only six are from female professionals is reflective of the representation within the industry. This is something Burgess (2013) considers from both industry and educational settings. Organisations such as the *Yorkshire Sound Women Network* (YSWN) are trying to address both gender and racial inequality in the industry and through regional surveys, estimating that only 10% of studio roles are held by women, which is similar to the number of student enrolments for degree programmes highlighted by Burgess between 2004 and 2010 in the UK. It is important for all music production programmes at HE level to champion this work and shine a light on these challenges.

AI and music production are also moving at such a pace that even at the time of publication of this volume things will have likely changed again. The study of AI in music education more generally, and the opportunities and challenges it presents, requires further in-depth study.

Acknowledgements

I wish to acknowledge the contributions of the three audio professionals in this study for the time they gave to the project and their unique insights: Phil Bodger; Gary Bromham; and Robin Reumers.

Notes

1 This was a technical specification of standards set out for CD that relates to tracks, sectors, block layout, coding, and sampling.
2 The mastering of a track or album is the final tweaks to the completed format (whether this is stereo or some form of surround or immersive form) typically involving multi-band compression, EQ, and dynamic processing within a specific linear order. It is worth noting that some recorded music in fixed formats (such as vinyl or CD) still requires specific expertise and equipment such as that found at Air Mastering.
3 Endnote text is missing
4 2022 National Plan for Music Education in England: The power of music to change lives (accessed September 2022)
5 In its most basic form, audio staging is positioning instruments within a stereo or other immersive field for playback to create an image of the performance. For more detailed information and some descriptions of staging see Moore (1993), or Dockwray and Moore (2010).
6 A tape sync is a process in which an interview takes place either on telephone or online and a sound engineer at each location captures the recording in situ, which is sent to a mix engineer to piece together. The advantage of this process is to try and make the audio recording sound like it is in the same location or at the very least achieve a high standard of fidelity.
7 Andrew Scheps is an American engineer and producer and label owner who has won awards for their work with the Red Hot Chili Peppers, Adele, Metallica, and Jay-Z.
8 This relatively inexpensive toolkit for MacOS can back up the data at two locations and keeps the files in sync.
9 AudioMovers allows users to stream, record, and collaborate using uncompressed files over a remote network
10 Source-connect has the same function as AudioMovers.

References

Armstrong, V. (2016). *Technology and the gendering of music education*. Routledge.
Avedeeff, M. (2019). Approaches in intelligent music production. *Music and the Machine: Issues in Contemporary Music Practice*, 8(4), 130–133
Bates, E. (2012). What studios do. *The Art of Record Production*, 7, 1–25.
Bell, A. P. (2018). *Dawn of the daw: The studio as musical instrument*. Oxford University Press.

Bennett, S. (2009). Revolution sacrilege! Examining the technological divide among record producers in the late 1980s. *The Art of Record Production, 4*.

Bennett, S. (2019). *Modern records, maverick methods: Technology and process in popular music record production 1978–2000*. Bloomsbury.

Boehm, C. (2007). The discipline that never was: Current developments in music technology in higher education in Britain. *The Journal of Music, Technology, and Education, 1*(1), 7–21.

Boehm, C., Hepworth-Sawyer, R., Hughes, N., & Ziemba, D. (2018). The discipline that became: Developments in Music Technology in British higher education between 2007 and 2018. *The Journal of Music, Technology, and Education, 11*(3), 251–267.

Borwick, J. (1994). *Sound recording practice*. Oxford University Press.

Bourbon, A., & Zagorski-Thomas, S. (2017). The ecological approaches to mixing audio: Agency, activity, and environment in the process of audio staging. *Journal of the Art of Record Production, 7*.

Brovig-Hanssen, R., & Danielson, A. (2016). *Digital signatures: The impact of digitization on popular music sound*. MIT Press.

Burgess, R. J. (2013). *The art of record production: The theory and practice*. Oxford University Press.

Dockwray, R., & Moore, A. F. (2010). Configuring the sound-box 1965–1972. *Popular Music, 29*(2), 181–197. https://doi.org/10.1017/S0261143010000024

Frith, S., & Zagorski-Thomas, S. (2012). *The art of record production: An introductory reader*. Ashgate.

Gall, M. R. Y. (2017). Technology in music education in England and across Europe. In S. A. Ruthmann & R. Mantie (Eds.), *The Oxford handbook of technology and music education*. Oxford University Press. https://doi.org/10.1093/oxfordhb/9780199372133.013.2

Gibson, J. J. (1979). *The ecological approach to visual perception*. Lawrence Erlbaum Associates.

Huber, D. M., & Runstein, R. E. (2017). *Modern recording techniques*. Focal Press.

Kemper, E. A., Stringfield, S., & Teddlie, C. (2003). Mixed-methods sampling strategy in Social Science Research. In A. Tashakkori & C. Teddlie (Eds.), *The handbook of mixed-methods research in social and behavioural research* (pp. 273–296). Sage.

King, A. (2012). The student prince: Music-making with technology. In G. McPherson & G. Welch (Eds.), *The Oxford handbook of music education*. Oxford University Press.

King, A. (2016). Studio pedagogy: Perspectives from producers. In *Music, technology, education: Critical perspectives*. Routledge.

King, A. (2017). Music production: Education and industry. In King, A., Himonides, E., & Ruthmann, S. A. (Eds.), *The Routledge companion to music, technology, and education*. Routledge.

King, A., & Himonides, E. (2016). *Music, technology, education: Critical perspectives*. Routledge.

Massey, H. (2009). *Behind the glass volume 2:Top producers tell how they craft the hits*. Backbeat Books.

May, C. (2007). A multi-tiered music industry? Intellectual and property rights, open access and the audience for music. *The Art of Record Production, 2*.

Moffat, D., & Sandler, M. B. (2019). Approaches in intelligent music production. *Music and the Machine: Issues in Contemporary Music Practice, 8*(4), 2–14.

Moorefield, V. (2005). *The producer as composer*. MIT Press.

Norman, D. (1998). Affordance, conventions and design. *Interactions, 6*(3), 38–43.

Ojanen, M. (2012). The role of the audio engineer in the mastering process. *The Art of Record Production, 10*.

Patmore, D. (2009). Selling sounds: Recordings and the record business. In N. Cook (Ed.), *The Cambridge companion to recorded music* (1st ed., pp. 120–139). Cambridge University Press.

Prior, H., & Leech-Wilkinson, D. (2014). Heuristics for expressive performance. In R. Timmers, D. Fabian & E. Schubert (Eds.), *Expressiveness in musical performance: Empirical approaches across styles and cultures* (pp. 34–57). Oxford University Press.

Rumsey, F., & McCormick, T. (2009). *Sound and recording*. Focal Press.

Schmidt Horning, S. (2013). *Chasing sound: Technology, culture & the art of studio recording from Edison to the LP*. John Hopkins University Press.

Slater, M. (2016). Processes of learning in the project studio. In A. King & E. Himonides (Eds.), *Music, Technology, Education: Critical Perspectives*. Routledge.

Smith, J. A., Flowers, P., & Larkin, M. (2013). *Interpretative phenomenological analysis*. Sage.

Taylor, T. D. (2001). *Strange sounds*. Routledge.

Théberge, P. (2012). The end of the world as we know it: The changing role of the studio in the age of the internet. In S. Frith & S. Zagorski-Thomas (Eds.), *The Art of Record Production*. Ashgate.

Thomas, N., & King, A. (2019). Production perspectives of heavy metal record producers. *Popular Music, 38*(3), 498–517.

Thompson, P. (2019). *Creativity in the Recording Studio: Alternative Takes*. Palgrave Macmillan.

Thompson, P., & Harding, P. (2019). Collective creativity – A service model of commercial pop music production at PWL in the 1980s. In R. Hepworth Sawyer, J. Hodgson, J. Paterson & R. Toulson (Eds.), *Innovation in music: Performance, production, technology, and business* (pp.143–159). Routledge.

Thompson, P., & Harding, P. (2023). Creativity and education: The "service model" of pop music songwriting and production in action. *IASPM Journal, 3*(1). 157–181. ISSN 2079–3871. https://doi.org/10.5429/2079-3871(2023)v13i1

Zagorski-Thomas, S., Isakoff, K., Lacasse, S., & Stévance, S. (2019). *The art of record production: Creative practice in the studio*. Routledge.

11 Strategies for Teaching Audio Production Online

Jason Torrens and Paul Doornbusch

Introduction

Education in many professions often requires practical training that authentically replicates the environment and tasks needed to successfully carry out the work. Practical training is non-negotiable for those entering a professional career upon graduation (e.g., accounting, surgery, dentistry). Audio production is also a sector wherein students must acquire skills to be proficient operators and designers of complex audio systems (see glossary). Audio students are generally taught how to operate a recording studio or large live sound system through an immersive learning environment. This authentic approach has been successful in practice-based, face-to-face education where students learn in professional-standard facilities as part of an educational institution.

The COVID-19 pandemic of 2020–21 caused much disruption to education – including higher education and practical training. While some education was deemed essential to continue in-person (e.g., medicine), the majority of learning was deemed non-essential and consequently forced into remote, and online, teaching and learning. This pivot proved a challenge for institutions and faculties reliant on intensely practical education and training.

Traditionally, it has been more logical to teach this discipline face-to-face. There are many practical activities which would be difficult to learn in an online environment. Until 2020, there lacked the technical ability, and the need, to deliver most of these practical concepts online. The COVID-19 pandemic has introduced this need and resulted in many creative solutions to what was not previously a problem.

Using an autoethnographical approach, the following chapter examines the challenges and opportunities faced by the audio production teaching staff at the *Australian College of the Arts* (Collarts) in Melbourne, Australia, during the COVID-19 pandemic of 2020–21. Solutions resulting from the three main practical streams in the Audio Production Degree at Collarts (i.e., recording techniques, live sound techniques, and post-production)[1] are explored to surface the opportunities, such as remote control of campus computers where possible, and the unique demands required for each stream in terms of low-latency, high-quality, internet audio transmissions (e.g., surround-sound monitoring while mixing a film remotely). Emerging questions for teaching audio and music production online are explored and effective remote teaching and learning strategies, techniques, and tools are suggested. It is important to note that even though we have solutions for many of the previously unattainable online delivery methods for audio production, some concepts are still impossible to experience online, and these are discussed in the following sections. What is still missing from online delivery will be briefly examined at the end of each discipline section.

DOI: 10.4324/9781003041474-14

Teaching Audio Production Online

The literature on teaching audio production *online* is limited and requires further investigation. Ancillary fields, such as online music lessons, or even more recently, Networked Music Performance (NMP), are themselves nascent. The availability of literature on teaching audio production in general is unfledged when compared to those fields outside of music and the arts. Providing "An Expert panel's view of the future of audio education to 2019", Tough (2010) states: Formal research specifically on AET curricula is nonexistent, with the exception of that of Lightner (1993), Sanders (1994), and Walsh (1996), whose research and contributions pioneered the field. (p. 3)

Since 2010, there have been further papers and books published on the topic of education in audio production. Examining approaches for reviewing curricula for audio education programs, Ryan and Hunter (2021) highlight eight publications "on the quest to define and implement a more-perfect audio curriculum" (p. 2). The literature referred to in these nine sources range from 2013–2016 (seven are papers), with the exception of David Tough's industry review in 2010 and a 1978 Audio Engineering Society audio education trends symposium (see Geoffrey et al., 1978). Practical elements of the industry have moved so rapidly that information becomes obsolete quickly.

However, this literature does not address teaching audio production *online*. Hence, when the 2020/21 COVID-19 pandemic forced audio education programs globally to go online, a range of new technologies and innovative ideas were developed and implemented in a short period of time. In examining the practical and pedagogical aspects of teaching audio production online, it is apparent that it is still in its infancy and thus is not well documented yet. Therefore, we will attempt to look at this amongst the practical solutions section of this chapter.

Determining Online Curriculum for Audio Production

Before examining *how* one should teach audio production online, it is relevant to first examine *what* is normally taught face-to-face in this type of curriculum to determine whether the online methods are meeting the needs of students and the Intended Learning Outcomes (ILOs)of the degree. As expected, some elements of the curriculum will be easier to deliver online than others.

From audio production curriculum literature, it is evident, and agreed upon by the authors of this chapter, that the following primary practical concepts occur regularly. According to Tough (2010), the following elements are ranked highest by the industry and are considered most sought after:

- knowledge of effects including EQ, reverbs, delays, gates, limiters
- audio signal flow in the recording studio
- backup and organize session data
- recording session procedures for tracking, overdubbing, and mixing sessions
- competency in the use of studio microphone techniques
- ability to interface and integrate various audio formats into practical working systems
- knowledge of acoustics
- associate the relationship of similar component functions between various consoles and software programs
- understand the . . . function of electronic components and their relationship to each other

- demonstrate knowledge of the Pro Tools program
- demonstrate . . . knowledge of live sound system setup
- demonstrate . . . working knowledge of sound engineering for commercials
- know different types and functions of virtual instruments

Research further suggests the developmental sequence of how to teach the essentials. For example, Leonard's (2020) "A Survey of Current Music Technology & Recording Arts Curriculum Order" (2020) highlights that by 2020, there was more consensus on the main topics pertinent to audio production education than in previous years. These included: Audio Editing, Live Sound, Studio Recording, Electronic/Computer music, Mastering, Game Audio, Mixing, and Audio for Video/Film. However, as Leonard proposes, there needs to be more research done in this area to provide consensus on their developmental sequence. It indicates consensus around the topics which are to be taught.

Ready to Keep Pace

Like many technology-based industries, audio production and engineering are changing rapidly and education should keep pace. Students, teachers, and administrators need to be abreast of the changes required.

When discussing what the industry deems necessary to include in the curriculum, it is often a challenge to get this across to the administrators in the institution. Most administrators in these areas have no specialized background or familiarity with the audio engineering discipline or the music industry in which it operates. A handful of administrators may have been music industry professionals at one time; however, they may not currently be abreast of the constant changes within the audio engineering field (Tough, 2010, p. 2).

The adaptive transition to online audio education due to COVID-19 put yet more demands on the ever-developing audio industry for how to teach practical components online. However, tools used to deliver this education online can themselves provide exciting new opportunities for teacher and student learning and growth. COVID-19 has impacted the world such that the whole audio industry is now having to embrace these new teaching tools or risk being left behind. Having forced many colleges to immediately adapt in a very practical way, the cost and administrative burden has challenged some institutions. Scheirman (2013) points out, "It is difficult enough for education programs to make investments in state-of-the-art equipment for hands-on learning about sound reinforcement or music production" (p. 4). In order for teachers and students alike to learn together, Scheirman (2020) suggests "an experiential learning model using such resources can be a highly effective way to engage students and hold their interest" (p. 3).

This statement became the authors' reality in March 2020 as we began to work out how to engage students online in a practice-based discipline. Proportionately, students and teachers found new ways to solve problems and move forward with their learning. Our Collarts administration team viewed the move to online as necessary, which subsequently ensured teaching and creativity were not interrupted. We found unforeseen benefits of working with our students to find innovative solutions. They were invested in the outcome; they felt like part of the process; and the learning outcomes were very effective. When aiming to stay abreast of industry trends, Scheirman (2013) proposes that it can be a challenging, albeit effective, approach to get students and educators working together with new tools. Together they can be part of the workflow process developments in the industry.

In many ways, upon reflection, the challenges of being forced to teach audio production online resulted in a beneficial situation. This supports the similar research of Ryan and Hunter (2021), who stated, "Educational systems need to change over time to maintain relevance" (p. 9). The challenges of COVID-19 forced institutions like Collarts to update their relevance in online streaming and engage in high-quality resources resembling those in the production industry.

As audio production educators aim to ensure relevance for the main industries we teach, there are many approaches to doing so. For example, Collarts runs annual CAC (Course Advisory Committee) meetings each year for every course. These meetings help us update the education and resources we provide our students. Australia's Tertiary Education Quality and Standards Agency (TEQSA), the governing body on higher education, requires these meetings specifically for the purpose of staying current.

Keeping pace also requires the constant development of new curriculum materials and content topics. Changes to industry standards in technology tools, signal processes, and new digital solutions result in the need for education to incorporate similar tools and practices. As we transition to an online teaching mode, ensuring students have substantial practical application of essential audio education, like signal flow, becomes paramount.

A Case for Online Audio Production

Collarts operates on trimesters and offers a Diploma of Audio Production in two trimesters, or a Bachelor of Arts – Audio Production Degree over six trimesters, which is possible to complete in two years. Transitioning to teaching this online was dramatic, as students enrolled when the COVID-19 pandemic hit had expected their education to be delivered face-to-face. Initially, students were impressed with the adapted online delivery. Some students reveled in the experience, succeeding more than they previously had. Others accepted the online delivery at first and then deferred some subjects, waiting for lockdowns to end. All students agreed the learning they experienced from the online delivery and its unique components was highly valuable and an experience they otherwise would not have had.

The success of the students and the rates of retention could be indicators of how successfully our new online education was implemented, especially when such large changes are made to what was originally a purely practical face-to-face delivery. The following tables show the student retention and student success results from 2019 and 2020 from the Collarts Bachelor of Audio Production degree. These figures are further explored in the paper "Teaching a Practical Audio Degree in a Pandemic" (Doornbusch & Torrens, 2021) as they evidence how "students responded very positively to the experience" (Doornbusch & Torrens, 2021)

Table 11.1 Audio production program retention rates (2019 and 2020).

Period	2019 Student Retention Rate	2020 Student Retention Rate
Trimester 1	80%	93%
Trimester 2	75%	94%
Trimester 3	80%	94%

Table 11.2 Success rates for students passing enrolled units (2019 and 2020).

Period	Percentage of Success Rates 2019	Percentage of Success Rates 2020
Trimester 1	80%	93%
Trimester 2	75%	94%
Trimester 3	75%	94%

Table 11.2 suggests that students had more success learning during their 2020 school year. This success rating prompted our further examination of the issues, challenges, and strategies encountered when teaching audio production online.

Practical Strategies and Tools for Teaching Audio Online

The following list of tools, strategies, and facilities were implemented in a variety of ways to assist students in working from home. Remote controlling campus computers and equipment and the ability to send high quality audio to and from the learners was paramount. Having limited staff onsite to manage equipment and perform was also necessary at times.

Based on our four main degree streams, the following section addresses key approaches used for teaching: 1) Online Recording Studio Techniques, 2) Online Live Production, 3) Online Post-Production, and 4) Online Audio Theory.

1.   *Online Recording Studio Techniques*

1.1   *For Mixing*

Learning how to mix online can simply involve video conferencing. By augmenting these simple tools, it is possible to lift the quality of the learning experience. The following section provides considerations for supporting effective teaching approaches.

Sharing of screens with both student and teacher: Students benefit from seeing the teacher's screen, which is common practice. What is more effective is when the student can show their work by sharing their screen with the teacher. This is also a common tool for most video conferencing software and became a staple of online classes.

Control of student computers: If instructors can take control and demonstrate exactly what needs to be done on the student computer, the stress and time of problem solving is reduced. The student must allow this control and can revoke it at any time.

High-quality audio: For critical listening to be effective in a production environment, reciprocal users must have audio that is of higher quality than what most video conferencing tools allow. For this, many institutions worldwide started using a separate tool which ran parallel to the video conference and passed the audio from their Digital Audio Workstation (DAW) or alternate software from teacher to student, and in many circumstances from student to teacher. There are a variety of tools that can be used to accomplish this; for example, Audio Movers™ can stream the audio directly to a browser window on the receiving computer. The quality of audio and the latency can be adjusted to allow different internet bandwidths on the student end. If student bandwidth allows, this could be raised right up to 24bit, 48kHz PCM audio if required.

Video conference recording quality: As the COVID-19 pandemic caused significantly increased demand for video conferencing, the quality of audio often became a concern. This was improved by companies like Zoom™ who implemented the feature *Original Sound*, allowing stereo instead of what was previously only mono and increasing the audio quality to 192kbps. This is almost usable for some critical listening situations, though the recording from Zoom™ gets reduced back to mono and is a lower bit rate. Therefore, students wanting to rewatch a lecture or experience this class asynchronously would not get the full audio quality experience.

Improving lecture recording quality: Collarts uses a Content Management System (CMS) that takes the video conference recordings of lectures and classes, e.g., Zoom™ meetings, and automatically stores them conveniently in the Learning Management System (LMS). The system we use, ECHO360™, also increased the quality of their recordings during 2020 to allow for stereo 256kbps audio quality. Along with the improvements in audio quality, ECHO360™ also increased the video quality available for captures to 1080p, which enabled many of the more detailed software demonstrations to be viewed successfully.

Recording the extra audio stream: This proved to be a challenge, as when you separate the high-quality audio feed from the conference or meeting it does not appear in the recording of that meeting. Therefore, creating a combined, separate audio feed that includes the conference audio with conversation from teachers and students along with the high-quality feed is required. Other audio routing software can be used here to feed high-quality audio to a separate virtual device for recording. Products such as Rogue Ameoba's Loopback™, the freeware Soundflower™ product, or for Windows users, products like VB-Audio *Virtual Cable*™ were suitable solutions. Evidently, it is futile to use these tools if the recording is being reduced to an unacceptable quality. Therefore, a separate screen, video, and audio recording should be used, leaving the conference tool just for communication.

Bringing it all together: The final component to be implemented was the standalone screen capture software ECHO360™ provides, Personal Capture™. This was a perfect solution to record the conferencing audio, high-quality audio feed, and the screen capture. This solution also uploads straight to the LMS when complete. A final feature Personal Capture™ provides is for a dual-video component to be recorded for either screen and video separately, two cameras, or two screens, whichever is required for that particular class.

This collection of tools requires intense computer system resources of the computer, resulting in the need for a high-powered device. Audio professionals likely have the systems required, or they will need to upgrade. Note that in the years ahead when network bandwidth improves, we expect that video conferencing software will include high-quality, multi-channel audio capture and storage as standard.

1.2. Recording Studio Classes

Demonstrating recording from home: For teachers to work effectively from home, they needed interfaces, microphones, instruments, and the ability to play and record these instruments. Some instructors used extra cameras to obtain greater focus for demonstrations. Many utilized smartphone cameras that could feed directly into the conferencing software. As soon as an instrument like drums had to be demonstrated, more complex solutions were needed.

Demonstrating recording from Collarts: This scenario was used for classes that needed to demonstrate the recording of a full drum kit, piano, or other large recording environments not possible at home. This was also useful for demonstrating large-format console workflows.

This scenario also became the preferred method once lockdown restrictions were relaxed and we could combine students on campus with students online. This is a prime example of a hybrid class workflow, which we now use whenever possible. Combining and modifying some of the solutions in the previous Mixing section were also required.

The sharing of screens was mostly one-directional, from the studio or instructor computer to the students at home. Control of studio computers was often provided to the students. This was done via Jump Desktop™ or the video conferencing software, depending on the student's need for responsive control. Usually, this was when students were involved in remote recording sessions.

High-quality audio was sent from the studio computer to the students (see Figure 11.1) at home to hear the nuances of the microphone setups and instruments in the space. Recording of these classes continued to be executed using ECHO360™ as the studio camera feed, and the studio screens could be recorded simultaneously. This dual camera feed wasn't possible to send to those students online; therefore, we needed extra solutions for these more complex situations. Software video switchers needed to be deployed for many reasons, mainly for ease of use. Instructors could then easily switch from a high-resolution camera to demonstrating elements from the studio computer showing the DAW.

Figure 11.1 Collarts studio computer with video switchers.

To demonstrate the detail of this practical activity required a reliable, easily controlled, and very high-quality camera facility. This would give online students the best experience possible. Pan Tilt Zoom (PTZ) cameras were mounted on the ceiling in between the control room and the live/recording space. Remote control of these cameras allowed quick zoom and focus of almost any area of the studio space. Presets were programmed for quick movement between these scenarios so the instructor could press *Console* to focus on the mixing console, or *Drums* to focus on the drums. Finite movements were then possible with joystick-like buttons that allowed smaller movements to other positions.

Considering that the teacher or operator in this scenario was constantly moving around the space, we needed to deploy a portable microphone, and a wireless lavalier microphone was the logical solution to this. We used high-quality RF lavalier microphones and transmitters; the receivers were plugged into the audio interface to feed to the conference online.

When in hybrid mode,[2] it is advantageous for the online attendees to hear what is being said by more than just the teacher with their lavalier microphone. What is essentially a reverse talkback in studio situations, often referred to as a "Listen Mic", was then deployed to the second input on the interface. This room microphone solution has proved to be a valuable tool in all hybrid class situations to help the online and face-to-face students participate in discussions.

To hear the online students' audio, it was not practical to feed the conference audio from students online straight to the *very expensive* studio speakers. A simple solution was a foldback speaker fed from the instructor's audio interface teaching space. This allowed two-way conversations between the students in the classroom and the students online.

These functions, video switching, and other controls needed to be easily managed – we needed a solution to control them all from one place or device. Pulling from the gaming and streaming industry, we found the Elgato Stream Deck™ to be the perfect solution. This device allowed the teacher or operator complete access to the video switching, camera control, and any other necessary features of the live class or recording session. Teachers then found that having to return to this Stream Deck™ in a fixed location resulted in a lot of back and forth whilst trying to teach. Therefore, implementing the Elgato™ iOS application linked to the Stream Deck™ on an iPad allowed the teacher to move around the room freely. They could then control the necessary cameras, video switching, and audio features from any location in the space. Another benefit of using a portable tablet was being able to split the screen and display the conference chat on the iPad as well. This allowed flexibility in movement, control of the environment, and improved communication with online students. A simple computer hub could incorporate the camera input, Stream Deck™ connection, audio interface for microphones, and output to foldback wedge, and an extra display output for monitoring was deployed when necessary. Managing all of this is not a simple procedure, though it is possible, as it was executed successfully by many of our teachers.

1.3 Remote Recording Studio Sessions for Students

The facilities and solutions described in the previous section are largely applicable to students wishing to do larger studio recordings remotely for their assessments. Many students have equipment at home or borrow equipment from the college to complete simpler, smaller recordings. Though when it comes to recording instruments that they do not play or have at home like drums, piano, and so on, these remote recording studio sessions provided a solution for them.

Collarts employs expert staff that can operate the previously mentioned equipment and be the musician and performer in the studio. This could easily be expanded to include one or two people operating the equipment, with others performing on the chosen instrument. Students should prepare, plan, and execute as many of their recording sessions as possible. The preparation of the DAW session with demo elements, click tracks, and specifications of the microphones is all completed by the student before the session is booked. Once this is arranged, the following is possible.

Students produce the session remotely receiving vision of the studio cameras, screens, plus the high-quality audio feed. Students can act like they are in the studio engineering, producing, and advising on the adjustments of any necessary components. It is possible to control the studio computer to record tracks, create new playlists, and any other necessary functions usually done by the person operating the studio.

Once the recording session is complete, the multitrack files are uploaded to an online storage solution and shared with the student. They can then continue editing, mixing, and finishing their assessment from home.

1.4 Challenges

In these larger recording sessions, students do not physically control the studio console or patch in the cables. These tools must be demonstrated with other means, like online simulators and digital examples, LMS quizzes, descriptive elements, and anything else applicable to that stage of the course.

The feeling and energy of being in the studio space is only partially replicated with these online solutions, though it is far more engaging than simply writing about it. The authors feel that as virtual reality becomes more common, like Audio Fusion's VirtualStudio3D™ (see Fisher, 2021), there will be greater improvements in this area in future decades.

2. Online Live Production

Aspects of the solutions we used for live sound production were already in use for the delivery of our courses. We commonly routed multitrack audio from live performances into a mixing console so students could practice. This was achieved by sending the individual outputs from a DAW, e.g., Pro Tools™ session, to either an analogue or digital mixing console. Added to this, we captured live video of the performances for students to see what is happening on stage. This emulates what they would normally see from the Front of House (FOH) console. Sound checks that are usually conducted in live performances were also captured so students could work on each signal one at a time.

2.1 Digital Consoles

The challenge of how to do this in an online environment so students could operate a mixing console remotely was not entirely as hard as first imagined. Many of the digital mixing consoles (see Figure 11.2) can be controlled by a connected computer instead of the console itself. We allow students remote access to that computer, using the highly responsive Jump Desktop™. This meant the students could control the mixing console in real time from home. Seeing faders on a console move around while being controlled by students at home, often in other countries, is an exciting experience both for the students and the staff. This same computer was loaded with the DAW session including the multitrack recording

Figure 11.2 Collarts digital mixing console.

of audio fed to the digital console, where the video can be displayed alongside the mixer. By combining this with a conferencing tool and a high-quality stereo mix from the digital console, we had a solution for mixing live remotely.

2.2 Analogue Consoles

For the first stage of our live sound stream, we focus on analogue mixing consoles and workflows. This required a different set of solutions: 1.) Instructional material in the LMS, 2.) A software mixer that emulates live sounds console, e.g., Harrison MixBus™, and 3.) Implementation of Audio Fusion's SoundCheckPro™. Fisher (2021) documents this new innovative tool in his Audio Education Society paper "Signal Flow Training with Virtual Simulations as a Co-Curricular Tool" (2021). This tool allows us to simulate live and studio environments for students to learn signal flow, patching, and processing without the need for students to physically be in a space.

Like the recording studio solutions, these analogue and digital live sound solutions allow 24-hour unsupervised access, a large improvement in accessibility for students.

2.3 Other Live Sound Solutions

We asked ourselves the question, "Why stop at audio?" As described here, all the solutions are aimed at mixing audio. Once remote control of consoles, computers, and networks (discussed in the Audio Systems unit) at Collarts were obtained, students and staff continued to ask, "what is next?" Could we control other live broadcast technology, such as lighting, AV, DMX, timecode, OSC, and vision control? It all incorporates signal flow and can expand student exposure of other entertainment industry roles closely aligned with theirs. This also exposes students to areas they often find attractive for employment.

The first example of a completely integrated execution of this was during a transitional phase of lockdown where state restrictions allowed a small number of staff on campus but no students. Our audio staff team went to campus where we performed a set of music. Students then operated the following live performance remotely from their homes in a variety of locations around the state of Victoria (Australia). They managed the workflows learned in this Live Sound unit, combined with knowledge obtained in the Audio Systems unit.

1. Route dozens of channels of high-quality multitrack digital audio from the Auditorium stage to our digital mixing console
2. Digitally send this multitrack audio from our Auditorium space to our Theatrette
3. Remote control a digital worksurface in the Theatrette, controlling the audio from the Auditorium (students with their own control surface at home were able to do this in real time with tactile control)
4. Feed a high-quality stereo broadcast mix to them at home, and also to an online stream
5. Control the lighting console and lights remotely from home, including moving lights using MIDI and DMX
6. Control multiple PTZ (Pan Tilt Zoom) cameras from home with presets using show control software like *Q LabTM*
7. Control software video switchers feeding the livestream
8. Control the monitor or foldback console, in this case a different console, such as Behringer X32™, including IEM (In Ear Monitor) feeds
9. Running an entire live event remotely, streamed to the internet, is a valid and useful skill for their careers going forward. Since these tools have been incorporated into the unit, students now volunteer to run full livestream events for the college. Some even obtained work outside the college running livestream events using the knowledge learned in these units.

2.4   Challenges for Live Sound

Tactile control is often considered a necessary part of the "hands-on" nature of the audio industry. Yet concurrently, live sound engineers are now using tablets and other remote devices to control their systems, even with the choice of tactile control. The versatility and portability of these mobile devices allow engineers to adjust parameters from anywhere in a venue, making life easier in live production situations. The industry in general is trending to digital management, routing, and control, resulting in less need for physical and tactile control. Many of the online live production solutions provided here are aligned with this trend.

Dual control, the use of two hands or moving two faders at the same time, is another physical concept that is removed when only one mouse is available for controlling parameters. Two thoughts arise from this. The first is to consider anyone with a physical disability that cannot use both hands, where a single mouse education is more inclusive. To assess students on using both hands is limiting and less inclusive. Secondly, those students who wish to have tactile or dual control can use a control surface to operate devices remotely. This solution could provide control of campus facilities in a much lower price range, potentially using a modern smartphone or tablet as a touch surface to manipulate multiple controls simultaneously.

3. Online Post-Production

Online Post-Production is a fully online subject (i.e., semester-long class) that explores the fundamentals of post-production audio.

3.1 Post-Production Fundamentals

The fundamentals of Post-Production are easier to manage in an online environment. Students require the use of a computer, DAW (specifically Pro Tools™ in this case), and the use of a microphone to record the various elements of sound for film. Specific equipment, like shotgun microphones and field recorders, are used at various times throughout the early study units. These items were borrowed from the college, used onsite when possible, or at times even mailed to students for short time periods. Alternatives were also proposed and allowed (i.e., instead of a shotgun microphone, student owned a large diaphragm condenser microphone which could produce the same outcome for many circumstances).

Since stereo is the only delivery requirement for the first few units, extra software was not needed to manage surround sound requirements until the more advanced units. This reduced the number of students needing access to facilities provided in later units (i.e., advanced facilities were only needed in the second half of the Post-Production stream).

3.2 Advanced Post-Production Requirements

Post-Production requires some of the most advanced and expensive software of all the streams. Being able to access industry-standard restoration software (e.g., iZotope RX Advanced™) is necessary for a thorough Post-Production education. Collarts managed to be creative with our normal arrangement of using this software. Yearly subscriptions or timed licenses were purchased, instead of permanent licenses that are locked to computers on campus. This meant each student could have access to this array of advanced software tools for the latter part of their degree and work on this at home with a simple re-allocation of budget and temporary license assignments.

System resource demands also need to be addressed. Post-Production sessions can require hundreds of audio tracks, video playback, and plugins loaded into the session that feed a Dolby Renderer. As such, this puts significant demands on computer resources. Many student computers struggled to cope with this heavy load. In this scenario, students could remotely access Collarts computers to finish their assignments.

3.3 Dolby ATMOS at Home

One of the biggest challenges for this stream was how to teach surround sound and the current industry-standard platform of Dolby Atmos™. The concepts and principles of operating our comprehensive Dolby Atmos™ Theatrette and equipment are mostly software-based, which left us with the final challenge of getting our 20-speaker (13.1.6) surround environment over the Internet and into remote student headphones.

Binaural audio processes sound down into a stereo feed that can be experienced on head-phones as surround sound. Fortunately, the Dolby Atmos Renderer allows you to simply turn on this binaural feed. The outcome is that only two channels need to be sent across the Internet to our students. Considering we already solved how to send high-fidelity ste-reo audio to students, this simple solution allowed us to teach Dolby Atmos mixing to the students. What we expected to be a subpar experience for the students turned out to be one of joy, success, and increased passion for the students as they could manage it from home without needing to book a specific physical space.

3.4   Challenges

Like all of these practical solutions, the experience of physically being in the room, operat-ing the AVID S6™ console, hearing the 20 speakers in full with a huge cinema screen in front of you, is a visceral experience and difficult to replace. The ability to have students learn the tools for operating and executing the required components is still possible online. With some of our student work made during the heaviest of our lockdowns being featured on the Dolby™ website, we feel this is a quality outcome.

4.   Online Audio Theory

Once many of the aforementioned solutions were discovered for practical units, staff and students continued to think more critically for other engaging ways to improve learning. Some learning outcomes were broad enough to allow creative solutions in completing as-sessments at home. Additionally, small changes were made to learning outcomes and assess-ments via our Learning and Teaching committee meetings. These meetings also proved to be a useful forum for all disciplines at Collarts to share solutions they had discovered for their related discipline. This resulted in finding additional engaging solutions for the theoretical subjects – many of which have now become permanent fixtures in our units.

4.1   Acoustic Theory

During our third Audio Theory Unit, Acoustics, we asked students to use their own home spaces for the assessments. Students found room modes of their mixing spaces, bedrooms, or whatever space they were studying in. A simple measuring tape and a speaker could ensure students experienced the acoustical phenomenon of standing waves, room modes, and in some cases, what treatment could do in improving a room's acoustics. Seeing stu-dents with mattresses and blankets against a wall behind them was not uncommon in some of these classes. Before moving online, students would be encouraged to do this, but as it was usually demonstrated on campus, students rarely completed this themselves at home. Lockdowns enforced creativity, improved understanding of the spaces they mix in, and the importance of room acoustics.

Another topic covered in this unit is convolution. Often, we completed this on campus by finding interesting or desirable spaces students would like to sample and deriving the impulse response to use in convolution reverb plugins. Instead, together we found a new creative approach to this task. Students recorded sine sweeps in rooms of their house, or samples of their kitchen taps, garage doors, dog barks, and other creative sounds to use as impulses. These could then be used creatively in production by convolving drums with taps, or guitars with dog barks, while still gleaning a deeper understanding of the principles of convolution. Students could benefit from using high-quality reference microphones for this and any other acoustic experiments, though understanding the linearity, or lack of linearity, of the equipment they had at their disposal was also a valuable learning experience. For students wishing to undertake more serious room measurement and analysis, we purchased extra entry-level reference/instrumentation microphones that students could borrow or have mailed to them for completing their assignments.

4.2   Audio Electronics

Our Audio Electronics subject teaches students to solder, make an XLR cable, and then build a guitar pedal of their choosing from a kit. This is usually done on campus. A solution for remote students involved borrowing an electronics pack, consisting of a case with soldering iron and all other necessary materials to complete the project. Considering students all have some sort of camera and access to the learning material, students could demonstrate their soldering via video conference.

4.3   Audio Systems

This unit resulted in surprising benefits for students learning at home. In this unit, students learn about audio networks, distribution, data, and the current industry trends towards Audio over Internet Protocol (AoIP) and Audio over Ethernet (AoE). A large number of the new products entering the industry are using this facility to send audio via ethernet cables on Local Area Networks (LANs). This trend demands some knowledge from the IT industry, where learning about concepts like IP addresses, packets, network bandwidth, network stacks, digital audio protocols, and latency are all necessary. Creating simple tasks for students at home, like accessing their home router, finding their MAC and IP addresses, then learning about DHCP, DNS and many other IT-based concepts was enlightening for the students. This provided students with practical knowledge and tools, as well as a personal, deeper understanding of the topics we need to address in this unit.

Further to this, our Audio Systems unit is used to examine the most current industry tools, methods, and practices in networked audio. Dante™ is one of the world leaders in networked audio products. Developed by the Australian company Audinate, their online certification program is quickly becoming a valuable asset to students, and often a requirement for employment opportunities coming in from industry. Using Audinate's™ online training tools in this unit is not just an up-to-date and authentic industry qualification for the students; it is an example of the tools and facilities we actually use to provide their education. We were able to augment their learning of the protocol by giving them supervised control of the college infrastructure to route audio around the college. When students combined this audio theory unit with the same stage/concurrent live sound unit, a world of possibilities was opened to them.

Recommendations

All of this is only possible when the procedures and requirements for departments like ours have strong institutional support from the college leadership. The willingness of the college leadership to do everything possible for students cannot be overstated. Booking systems to provide remote access to our computer systems were an integral solution to many of our challenges. Our Student Services and frontline staff amended the existing room booking system to include 24-hour access, as well as instructions on how to access the facilities remotely.

Opportunities of flexibility to modify and redirect budget allocations to purchase the online tools were essential; without this, our solutions would not have been possible. Having agile instructors who could learn the new technological tools mentioned throughout this chapter is necessary, and it is not easy for the beginner instructor or the beginner technologist. Experts are needed to manage and implement all these solutions. Audio engineers and producers will have a head start, and hopefully some integration and future literature will allow this to become standard practice, with an easier pathway to success for those new to the area.

How the pedagogy might be considered, managed, and implemented for the solutions provided in this chapter would be a worthy area of future research. Investigating and considering asynchronous education, engagement, retrieval, and self-directed learning are all possible areas of investigation. Though even simply considering how students learn this technology face-to-face, "the pedagogy of how students will actually become proficient in using this technology remains somewhat murky" (Keyes, 2013).

Aspects to be developed in the future include: Lower latency will increase the ability to use more products remotely; 360-degree camera control will allow the user the ability to scan the room and see what they would like to see; More analogue emulation and ability to experience some of the more physical and challenging parts of the curriculum are very much areas for improvement and investigation; and Virtual reality and augmented reality developments, along with sensor developments and haptics, will allow for more physical and tactile experiences remotely. AudioFusion™ are developing their VirtualStudio360™, which shows an exciting future.

Conclusion

Implementing the solutions described here illustrates that it is now possible to successfully provide a practical online education in audio production that was not previously possible. Recent technological developments are key elements of these solutions, providing students with a very high-quality experience. Teachers in audio production at Collarts have developed and refined these solutions to the point they can be relied upon. They will continue to be further developed for improvements and a wider variety of contexts as new technology and pedagogy allows.

We have noted that there are limitations and challenges, such as tactile control, immersive experiences, and the haptics of many practical elements, e.g., physically plugging in the cables. Unforeseen benefits from online delivery were also discovered, combined with an unexpected increase in industry relevance.

As these tools become more commonplace, we can expect that new tools, hybrid products, and new ways of implementing them will all foster better education and more inclusivity, allowing a richer experience for future students.

Acknowledgments

The authors of this chapter are greatly indebted to *The Australian College of the Arts*, and the following Audio Production staff who contributed to the discovery and creation of the solutions implemented during this period. Without their input, creativity, knowledge, and determination, many of these solutions would not have been possible: Dylan Mitrovich, Steeve Body, Daniel Murtagh, Luke Cincotta, Nick Rakers.

Glossary of Terms and Acronyms

AoE	Audio over Ethernet. The use of an Ethernet-based network to distribute real-time digital audio.
AoIP	Audio over Internet Protocol. The distribution of digital audio across an IP network such as the Internet.
Audio Production Audio Engineer Audio Engineering	In this chapter we use the term Audio Production and Audio Producer to describe the function of the person who operates the equipment that makes a sound recording, or mixes the recording, or mixes live sound, or edits and mixes the sound for a film or visual medium. Sometimes these people are called Audio Engineers, and while exceedingly few of them have an Engineering Degree (as it is unnecessary), it is not an incorrect term because one legitimate use of the term "engineer" is to denote a person who operates equipment, such as a train engineer. The Macquarie Dictionary defines "engineer" as: 1. a person professionally qualified in the design, construction, and use of engines or machines, or in any of the various branches of engineering: a mechanical engineer; an electrical engineer; a civil engineer. 2. someone who manages a ship's engines. 3. a member of the armed forces trained in engineering work. 4. a skilful manager. 5. US: an engine-driver. The education of people for this role can take several routes. Very occasionally, this can be a technical education in mostly electronic engineering, but usually it is a more creative education where students learn to operate the equipment and learn enough technical skills for that purpose, which is why we name the course Audio Production.
AV	Audio Visual
Binaural	Recording or playback to create or simulate a 3D stereo sound sensation for the listener on headphones.
DAW	Digital Audio Workstation
DMX	DMX is an acronym for Digital Multiplex, a standard digital communication protocol used to remotely control intelligent lighting fixtures.
Foley	The reproduction of everyday sound effects that are added to films, videos, and other media in post-production to enhance the audio. Named after sound-effects artist Jack Foley.
LMS	Learning Management System
MIDI	Musical Instrument Digital Interface
OSC	Open Sound Control. A protocol for networking multimedia devices and computers
PCM	Pulse Code Modulation, the most common uncompressed digital audio coding format.
SFX	A common abbreviation of Sound Effects for Post-Production

Notes

1. Post-production is the development and manipulation of audio for image and radio, for example, TV commercials and films. It has unique and significantly different requirements to recording studio work for music or live sound.
2. Hybrid mode is what we call the teaching mode where there are some students on campus face-to-face and some students online synchronously in the *same* class. This mode of delivery may become more common with some students being uncomfortable coming onto campus after lockdowns ends, or remaining online until they have been vaccinated.

References

Doornbusch, P., & Torrens, J. (2021, May 24). *Teaching a practical audio degree during a pandemic.* www.aes.org; Audio Engineering Society. http://www.aes.org/e-lib/browse.cfm?elib=21061

Fisher, S. (2021, July 22). *Signal flow training with virtual simulations as a co-curricular tool.* www.aes.org; Audio Engineering Society. http://www.aes.org/e-lib/browse.cfm?elib=21228

Geoffrey, L. W., Kenneth, W. J., Tom, L., Thomas, M. Y., Raghu, G., & Dale, C. M. (1978, May 1). 'Trends in audio education' a symposium. *Audio Engineering Society.* AES Convention, 60. https://secure.aes.org/forum/pubs/conventions/?elib=10254

Keyes, C. J. (2013, May 4). *Alternate software and pedagogical strategies for teaching audio technology to classically trained music students.* www.aes.org; Audio Engineering Society. http://www.aes.org/e-lib/browse.cfm?elib=16710

Leonard, B. (2020, October 22). *A survey of current music technology & recording arts curriculum order.* www.aes.org; Audio Engineering Society. http://www.aes.org/e-lib/browse.cfm?elib=20914

Lightner, J. W. (1993). *A survey of the professional audio industry in an eight state region to assess employers' perceived value of formal audio education and their perceived training needs for entry-level employees* [Master's thesis]. https://eric.ed.gov/?id=ED359404

Ryan, T., & Hunter, C. (2021, July 22). *A method for program-level academic review and revision in audio education – Part1.* www.aes.org; Audio Engineering Society. http://www.aes.org/e-lib/browse.cfm?elib=21213

Sanders, D. H. (1993). *The professional preparation of the audio engineer: A survey of studio personnel and recommendations for school curricula design* [Dissertation]. https://ezproxy.uow.edu.au/login?url=https://www.proquest.com/dissertations-theses/professional-preparation-audio-engineer-survey/docview/304049089/se-2?accountid=15112

Scheirman, D. (2013, July 25). *Are audio education programs keeping pace with new developments in industry?* www.aes.org; Audio Engineering Society. http://www.aes.org/e-lib/browse.cfm?elib=16865

Tough, D. (2010). Shaping future audio engineering curricula: An expert panel's view. *Journal of the Music and Entertainment Industry Educators Association, 10*(1), 149–171. https://doi.org/10.25101/10.8

Walsh, E. J. Jr. (1996). *Important occupational skills and knowledge needed in the preparation of the recording engineer: A survey of faculty perceptions* [Dissertation]. https://ezproxy.uow.edu.au/login?url=https://www.proquest.com/dissertations-theses/important-occupational-skills-knowledge-needed/docview/304349536/se-2?accountid=15112

Part 3

Current Issues

Industry Perspective

Phil Harding and Andrew King

Collaborating in the Studio

As an industry person, regardless of the importance of what happens in the studio, if you have a process that has gone well, the next part of the process (see Thompson & Harding, 2019, 2023) is what is the reaction of the main client? Whether your main client is the band or with the record company, you are judged by how well you did 'in the charts'. One cannot help but look at the commercial aspects and then reflect on the creative and technical highlights that happen in the studio.

Throughout my career as a recording/mix engineer and producer, *You Spin Me 'Round* (Dead or Alive, 1984) was the longest mix of my life (this is Phil writing). It was a difficult session working alongside Stock, Aitken, and Waterman and the differences of opinion amongst the team. This was one of four tracks being recorded in one day – and this was the last track of a long day. The producers decided the mix would follow straight after the recording – with the record company expecting delivery the next day. Pete Waterman turned up later in the evening and, feeling the tension in the room between the band members and technical team, cleared the room, leaving just the mix engineer (Phil) and Pete to mix the track that evening; the whole session lasted 36 consecutive hours in total.

The 12-inch version (preferred by DJs) was created first. Being a former DJ, Pete preferred this approach. Then, a club mix was created to get the build of a record going, despite the already-recorded 3-minute radio version. We spent the whole night with a 48-track analogue mixer going to a ½-inch tape machine to make the club mix. We mixed it down in 8- or 12-bar sections. The next day, the band returned, took a listen, and loved the track we had created. The band's management was eager to hear the track – and in the 1980s and 1990s, it was best to get them to visit the studio. After an initial release in 1984, the club mix went number one in 1985. It was a great achievement given the difficult creative process and work environment. The worldwide success and legacy of the track made it all worthwhile.

The British band East 17's song *Stay Another Day* (Steam, 1994) was the Christmas Number 1 in 1994. This recording was not as challenging from a creative perspective, although the lead singer Brian Harvey had concerns over the commercial direction of the track. The vocal tutor – who was also part of the backing for the track – was instrumental in guiding the lead vocalists to the completion of the track. Having been involved with the entire production and the mentoring that needed to take place to make the record number one for Christmas (a difficult thing to do in 1994) meant this was another career highlight. I have some really special moments from working in the recording industry – one of those was leaving Marquee Studios (London, UK) and going to work for PWL Studios (London, UK). Although it was financially a backwards step in terms of career hierarchy, it really accelerated what I was doing.

DOI: 10.4324/9781003041474-15

Teamwork is an important ability, and it includes understanding what your skills are and how you put these into a team environment. Maybe you do not have the business skills or are not good with the top line (or lyrics/vocals), and you need to put a team together to work in the industry. A look at the production credits on work often shows that a huge team of people have been involved. A good example of which is Ed Sheeran, who works with a team to create his music.

Technological Developments

Across the two decades where I did most of my work as an engineer or producer, we had a major technical leap when the LinnDrum machine was released in the 1980s. It was welcomed by a lot of producers and engineers in the pop and dance world. To an engineer, these devices meant the dynamics of the drum could be precisely controlled – which was often a challenge with a live drummer and led to technical issues such as distortion when recording. Apart from an orchestra, drums are one of the most difficult instruments to record because of the dynamics and the necessary multi-microphone technique. And, in the 1970s and 1980s, as engineers we were judged on our ability to record drums. This influenced clients who would either return to the studio for further recordings or draw in new clients who had heard a particular drum sound on a track. The drum machine made the process faster – and despite initial fears at the time, it was not the end of human drummers.

By the 1990s, some engineers wanted a MIDI (i.e., Musical Instrument Digital Interface) sequencer and audio recording package because recording to tape with a lot of outboard hardware being driven live through MIDI was a challenge, especially in the pop world. Working with Apple and the company now known as AVID, German company Steinburg created software called *Cubase*, which delivered a 4-track audio computer-based recorder. That was a revelation at the time. Ian Curlow (a record producer who worked alongside Phil) was a tester for the early *Cubase* development. It was at this time that the first system in a European studio was installed. The advantage of the software was demonstrated on a commercial project: taking a 48-track song with a tempo of 108 BPM, and by request of the management, changing the song's style and increasing its tempo to 120 BPM. The project was achieved, although the designer had to take the equipment away on several occasions to solve technical issues for the team to obtain the results the band management desired. It was a good example from my career of dealing with new technology and making it work for me.

Other software, such as *Protools* and *Logic*, have become critical tools in the music production process – although having a good pair of speakers is perhaps one of the most important tools. When working in studios, such as *Strongroom Studio* (London, UK) and at home, access to a quality pair of monitors becomes necessary when you take your work to a mastering engineer. The preference for the type of monitors may change during one's career, but the real judgment of the sound created is at that final stage when another audio professional hears your work. There are bad habits to avoid, such as relying solely on headphones. Although headphones are critical with modern listening habits to test the sound, there are still a lot of environments in public and home spaces that use speakers, whether that is in a cinema, live event, the radio, or watching a film at home.

Commercial Aspects and Environment

In terms of the technology that is used, the commercial aspects of recording dictate a lot of what happens in the industry. For someone starting out as a creative technician, songwriter, or producer, you need to be as flexible as possible – and the laptop is your most valuable tool. This allows us the flexibility to come to the client with the work, and it takes us out of the studio environment. Flexibility applies to the use of *Logic, Protools,* or other software as a live engineer, too. The roles have changed from being either a studio or a live engineer. Now you need to be both to survive in the industry. The role of live sound engineer can be one of the most challenging engineer roles, but a live session could later turn into a studio session or vice-versa. For example, a studio session that turned into a live gig for me happened with the artist Matt Bianco at the Montserrat Jazz festival. From those gigs, I learned that the live sound engineer aspects were as important as what was created on stage. The difference between having a successful gig or not is whether the live sound engineer is able to deliver to the audience what the artist on stage is trying to get across. There are audience expectations around how the music will sound, and this is often derived from commercial studio recordings.

From a creative perspective, large-format analogue mixing desks can have certain equalizers that may not work for every production. The use of digital plug-ins can help when working with different clients. To help the session with the client go more smoothly, it is important to have within your virtual tool kit a set of plug-ins that you can operate without the need for much experimentation. I am still using digital versions of analogue technologies from the 1970s because of their ease of use and the results that can be obtained. And the ability to have multiple versions and to not be restricted by the availability of hardware is a key consideration for digital technology.

Our musical environment and process are critical aspects for an audio professional working with an artist, such as a vocalist. And process is a difficult thing to teach. It is something that comes from experience and getting the mood right. Both are important for a good session. The vocalist is the most important session for pop and dance music production. It's about the performance you can get from them. They need to leave the session thinking the best possible performance was achieved in the recording. This feeds into the commercial aspects, as the vocalist or band will feed back to the manager about whether the session was a success or not.

Finally, the technical operation of the audio equipment must not get in the way of the sound of the recording. Sometimes working alongside another audio professional helps us achieve this. The recording session leads into the editing session, which can sometimes be two or three times longer than the recording session; working as part of the team helps facilitate both the technical and creative aspects. While the decision-making process takes longer now because there is so much more technology at our fingertips, this is the modern way of producing. It is important, however, to focus on what you are trying to achieve – there is a need to commit to decisions from a commercial perspective.

References

Thompson, P. & Harding, P. (2019). A 'service' model of creativity in commercial pop music at P&E studios in the 1990s. In J. O. Gullö, S. Rambarran & K. Isakoff (Eds.), *Proceedings of the 12th art of record production conference mono: Stereo: Multi* (pp. 287–302). Royal College of Music (KMH) & Art of Record Production.

Thompson, P. & Harding, P. (2023). Creativity and education: The 'service model' of pop music songwriting and production in action. *IASPM Journal, 3*(1), 157–181. ISSN 2079-3871. https://doi.org/10.5429/2079-3871(2023)v13i1

12 Ethics

Nicolas Gold and Ross Purves

Introduction

In recent years, the decreasing cost of electronic music technology and computing has enabled much wider access (offering increased opportunities for music creation, education, learning, and careers) to an ever-broader range of people with varied musical experience and abilities. Recent innovations in areas such as artificial intelligence (AI), cloud computing, social media, and streaming have changed the ways in which educators teach, students learn, and musicians create, collaborate, and perform. Technology mediates a great deal of music-making and music education in a variety of ways, placing it between music educators and their learners as well as mediating learners' interaction with music itself. Understanding, selecting, and appropriately using such technology is therefore challenging, and comes with inherent ethical considerations.

The shifting technological landscape and society's changing views on acceptability make ethical choices challenging: new concerns arise and old concerns appear in new guises. For instance, Angliss (2016) notes that trade unionists' alarm at the introduction of the first analogue electronic drum machines in the 1960s should be seen in the context of musicians' earlier fears over lost income due to the introduction of cinema sound and of sound recording itself. All three developments can in turn be situated within general historical trends towards mechanisation and automation with their origins in the Industrial Revolution some two centuries earlier. Yet the 1960s also witnessed new concerns regarding the ethical implications of increasing musical mechanisation and automation which, for the first time, went beyond anxieties over the impact on musicians' livelihoods. These emerged during the rise of mainframe computer-powered university electronic music studios and subsequently become more regularly and forcefully articulated in the 1980s with the introduction of the Musical Instrument Digital Interface (MIDI) and the proliferation of lower-cost digital audio equipment such as drum machines, digital synthesisers, and – most notably – samplers. Consequently, and as the following examples demonstrate, the 1960s through the early 1990s represented the first historical epoch in which musicians were required to confront ethical challenges presented by new technology on anything approaching a large scale.

Even at the early point of 1970, Strang (1970) argued that the use of computers in music would quickly become adopted as mainstream practice, citing parallels with patterns of "shock" followed by acceptance that met new instruments such as the saxophone, electric organ, and vibraphone, and the works of Schoenberg, Stravinsky, and Bartok. Strang appeared to brush aside concerns regarding the perceived infiltration of mathematical methods into musical composition and artistic interpretation. He was also less concerned about reduced employment opportunities for musicians. Significantly, however, he argued that

DOI: 10.4324/9781003041474-16

composers must carefully and actively reflect on which creative decisions should be delegated to the computer. Whilst computers, Strang predicted, had the potential to 'revolutionise music as no previous technological device [had] done' by the end of the century, this would in his view do little to alter 'the human responsibility for ethical and aesthetic judgements' (1970, p. 41).

By the 1980s, the development of personal computing and associated MIDI interface peripherals had put the integration and synchronisation of all emerging, mass-produced music technologies within the grasp of ever more musicians. On one hand, this democratisation was important in the development of new musical forms and practices, e.g., the influence of the Roland TR-808 and TR-909 drum machines on electronic dance music (Butler, 2006). On the other hand, it served to expose and even exacerbate ethical fault lines. For instance, whilst some percussionists were increasingly regarding drum machines as new and creative tools in their gig bags, others fought persistent fears of redundancy with attempted boycotts and bans (Frith, 1986; Brett, 2016). By the close of the decade, concerns had been raised regarding audience deception through lip-syncing, sampling and its reshaping of sound ownership, digital piracy, manipulation, and the ineffectiveness of contemporary copyright laws to regulate these situations (Van Tuyl, 1991; Porcello, 1991). These challenges were regarded as likely to strengthen, rather than disrupt, the traditional power structures within the music industry, with rank-and-file studio musicians and engineers more likely to lose out than the superstar artists, tour promoters, and record company executives of the time.

Tomatz (1989) observed that many designers and proponents of 1980s music technology had failed to consider the economic and cultural implications of their work. Unlike Strang, he, Van Tuyl (1991), and Porcello (1991) all took seriously the prospect of synthesizers, samplers, and drum machines displacing human instrumentalists. Tomatz encouraged educators to think carefully about how to advise students wishing to enter the rapidly changing worlds of commercial music and session recording. Notwithstanding this caution, however, he still felt that technology had the power to replace much 'rote work' within music education, freeing learners to focus on reaching 'much higher levels of achievement and expertise in a much shorter time' (1989, p. 69). Like Strang, Tomatz's view was that technophobia missed the point. Instead, there was a need to ensure that technology served to extend creative possibilities, rather than to render existing practices obsolete. Strang, Tomatz, Van Tuyl, and Porcello all took pragmatic, unalarmist views of developments, reflexively acknowledging their perspectives to be rooted in moments in time, whereas technology would march on undaunted. However, their shared insistence that the ethical implications of this march required active and dynamic consideration remains wholly relevant today.

It is our contention that this first historic epoch has given way to a second epoch – one that we continue to inhabit, which necessitates fresh, and indeed urgent, engagement on the part of musicians and educators. This second epoch is framed by more recent technological innovations relating to the rise of the Internet (particularly cloud computing and streaming technologies), as well as those related to AI, big data, new forms of human-computer interface, and various open source/design approaches. Nevertheless, this second epoch has emerged through evolution, not revolution, and many of the issues which characterised earlier debate remain salient.

Warren (2014, p. 1) argues that ethical responsibilities arise from the fact that musical activity involves "encounters with others". This position is reflected in the work of Elliott (2020) and Elliott and Silverman (2015, p. 20) who characterise ethics as "reflective, practical, and social", owing to human interaction being shared through experience, language, and situation. Bowman (2020) places ethics at the heart of music and of music education itself. He argues that these activities are inherently ethical (like Warren, in the sense of having an ethical nature rather than being essentially moral) in their very nature as practices. Bowman's contention is that practices are ways in which we learn the meaning of ethically responsible and responsive living. Roberts (2009) also notes the prevalence of ethical issues in music education, identifying longstanding tensions in balancing equality of access and opportunity with high musical standards and elite achievement. He also highlights ethical dilemmas regarding socio-economic and curricular impediments, multiculturalism, religious connotations, and realistic career development progression routes. He concludes that there is a need for dialogue, discussion, and research to inform the choices educators make in their task of sharing music. Allsup and Westerlund (2012) note that teachers make their choices in complex situations and under close scrutiny of their outcomes.

Andean's tripartite framework (2014) for considering the culturally-sensitive use of sound contains three key concepts: being informed, being sensitive, being responsible. These concepts apply equally well to the educational domain when considering technological innovations. In the remainder of this chapter, we therefore set out a range of ethical issues (providing information), discuss key points connected with them (identifying sensitivities), and discuss their implications for educators and education (identifying responsibilities). We structure our discussion based partly on the areas identified in the New Interfaces for Musical Expression (2020) conference ethics code, and under four themes:

- Accessibility, inclusion, and cultural considerations
- Ownership, consent, appropriation, and deception
- Sustainability, socio-economic fairness, and access
- Data, privacy, safety, and care

Accessibility, Inclusion, and Cultural Considerations

Technology has been proposed as a means of ameliorating barriers to access and inclusion in music-making and learning in various ways. Concurrently, effective coverage within education has also been seen as essential to the future development of more inclusive forms of music technology (Kosteletos & Georgaki, 2014). As the following examples from the literature demonstrate, a key ethical consideration for educators relates to the potential for unintended consequences of curricular, pedagogical, and technological choices. There is plenty of evidence to suggest that injudicious technological integration risks exacerbating as many barriers as may be reduced – see Armstrong (2011) for a pertinent example relating to gender. These risks need to be acknowledged and where possible minimised to open education to the widest possible range of learners.

Inclusivity in the context of disability is often addressed through the adaptation of instruments to reduce barriers to access. This can raise issues of equity. For example, by applying sports ethics, Stras (2015) highlights blurred boundaries between those technologies intended to enable participation by disabled musicians on equal grounds and others – such as pitch correction – that are seen to confer unfair musical advantages on others. With regards to the former type, Stras laments that the majority of music listeners are not yet ready to appreciate such performances for their implicit aesthetic merit, continuing instead to focus on so-called 'heroic narratives' of overcoming adversity through technological assistance. Curzi (2020) identifies exclusionary barriers and practices embedded in Western classical music and draws on examples to show how these might be challenged through responsive technology.

bell et al. (2020) highlight the two common models of disability, *medical* and *social*, and identify music education literature that addresses disability from both perspectives. Oliver (2009), describing the social model, emphasises the shift of focus from individual impairment towards 'disabling environments, barriers, and cultures' (p. 45), not considering problems in isolation, but equally not dismissing individually oriented interventions in disabled people's lives since the interventions may be of value. Music technology and music education thus have roles to play under both models: technological innovation in developing specific interventions, and, following Elliott's (2020) claim of the range of differences that ethical music education can make to students and adults (including social, cultural, and political aspects), the formation of empowered learners who are alert to environmental, cultural, practical, and societal barriers, and who are unafraid to challenge and change the professional culture into which they emerge.

Cultural inclusivity may also be an issue. Despite calls for music technology to fully embrace musics from beyond the West (Holzapfel et al., 2018), much software and hardware continues to reflect the forms and aesthetics of Western popular and classical music: not all cultures adapt as easily to quantisation (Kosteletos & Georgaki, 2014). As Holzapfel et al. (2018) argue, the implications of a lack of cultural sensitivity are potentially serious. They posit, for instance, that digital audio workstations (DAWs) with rhythm processing tools calibrated to quadruple meter might perform less satisfactorily for musicians working with additive meters. Over time, these musicians may shift their practices to align with what the DAW appears to do best. Allami (2019) notes that, while microtonal capabilities have long been implemented in software and hardware, they lack guidance on use and are mapped across a 12-tone keyboard irrespective of the way in which they are supposed to be used. Allami describes this as tokenistic, counter-intuitive, and detrimentally 'othering'. Whilst musical cultures are always in transition and diversity in influence is generally regarded as healthy, there is nonetheless a risk in such cases that key foundations of a musical culture might be unintentionally weakened through the expedient adoption of less culturally respectful tools. In a further example drawn from streaming music platforms, Holzapfel et al. (2018) point out that users' likelihood of receiving listening suggestions of non-Western musicians might be reduced if recommendation algorithms have been trained only on subsets of Western pop, potentially reducing these musicians' exposure and royalty income. Limited opportunities for non-Western musicians to engage with music technology development is part of the problem, according to Kosteletos and Georgaki (2014), who call for the adoption of inclusive design principles in the sector. They argue that designers should collaborate with ethnomusicologists and non-Western musicians on the development of new products. Linked to this area are broader issues of musical diversity and the exposure of learners to contemporary and emerging forms of music such as sound-based music (an engagement challenge tackled by Landy et al. (2013), for example).

We see music technology education at all levels as a fertile environment in which this awareness of, and openness towards, the aesthetics, practices, and values of other musical cultures can be nurtured and explored. Good-Perkins (2021, see Ch. 11 in particular) provides useful practical guidance for educators to reflexively recognise their own assumptions and interrogate what might otherwise inadvertently be seen as incontestable.

Ownership, Consent, Appropriation, and Deception

Part of the educator's ethical responsibility to their learners is to alert them to the value of their own and others' work, not just in artistic and aesthetic terms but also through an understanding of ownership, appropriate use, consent, and deception. In other words, encouraging and facilitating respect and responsibility whilst continuing to enable both learning and long-term creativity. Perhaps the most obvious example in this space is sampling but matters of music, software, and other forms of digital piracy are of course also relevant, and sources such as Voss (2013), Wu and Yang (2013), Sinclair and Green (2016), and Woolley (2015) provide useful case studies for educators wishing to explore various ethical debates and unintended consequences associated with this activity with students.

It has been common practice for many years for musicians to sample others' work and remix it into new music. Indeed, we may have now entered the 'post sampling' era, where this technique has become integral to the habitus of many practitioners and ingrained in music production (Behr et al., 2017). The debates in this space are not new (Porcello, 1991; Hesmondhalgh, 2006; Blake, 2010; Angliss, 2016; Behr et al., 2017), and we will not rehash them at length. There are considerations of intellectual property and associated law, sonic ownership, cultural appropriation, consent for sampling and use (including sound recorded in public places), licensing, theories of sampling practice (see Holm-Hudson, 1997), and so forth. From an educational standpoint, perhaps the challenge is to ensure that where musical material is reused, it is accompanied by teaching on the ethical issues involved in reusing and re-appropriating others' content (including more contentious approaches such as plunderphonics (Oswald, 1985 (later revised, 2004); Holm-Hudson, 1997) and considering the impact of context. Research has suggested that modern technology-based musicians tend to take a pragmatic approach to realising their musical options, using whatever is to hand and paying attention to creative impulses foremost, leading to a need for better alignment between social and legal contexts to support creativity (Behr et al., 2017). One key skill that should be taught and encouraged is awareness of the differences between, but interconnectedness of, flow-states and 'compliance monitoring'. In other words, decisions made in the moment of music creation need to be reflected upon in the light of ethical implications and the management of materials owned by others. The key, then, is for educators not to treat choices about music creation as distinct from their ethical issues, and sampling is perhaps the area in which this is most clearly seen. As Behr et al. (2017, p. 227) note, the legal complexities associated with copyright clearance have had a 'chilling effect' on musicians apt to sample in their work. Conversely, then, more ethically informed introductions to this practice may result in still more creative uses of sampling because practitioners are able to concentrate on music-making, confident that their use of the technique is not only legal but also ethical. A practical way forward is offered by Thibeault (2012), who argues for music education to move away from teaching *compliance*-based models of copyright emphasising illegality and infringement to a *creative rights* approach emphasising innovation, recognition, and informed reuse through licensing models such as Creative Commons.

Questions should be asked about how those being sampled might be appropriately traced, accredited, and remunerated (Hesmondhalgh, 2006) and whether sonic materials are being reused and juxtaposed in culturally-sensitive ways representative of their originating context (Andean, 2014; McCartney, 2016). These issues can be fraught and have ramifications beyond the immediate world of creative music technology, for instance within ethnomusicology and audio restoration/archiving (D'Agostino, 2020; Gilman & Fenn, 2019; Wallaszkovits, 2018). On one hand, there is an instinctive and strong ethical pull towards conservation when faced with the disappearance of minority or indigenous musical cultures. Similarly, great efforts are expended to preserve old and increasingly fragile sound recording media. Yet care must be taken to ensure that conservation is undertaken in ways that respect the original performers, their cultures, and the agreements under which recordings were made. Bennett (2017) usefully illustrates how these types of challenge can be fruitfully addressed within the educational context.

There is, we assert, still more to teaching the ethics of sampling. As a musical practice, sampling is now well over half a century old (if one acknowledges the application of pioneering analogue equipment such as the Chamberlin and Mellotron (Angliss, 2016)). Over this time, it has acquired a culture of its own, aspects of which have emerged via confrontation and efforts towards social emancipation, for instance as a means of subverting dominant power relations in the music industry (Porcello, 1991) or of signifying transcendence from earthly bonds in the case of Afrofuturism (Angliss, 2016). The richness of this culture should be acknowledged and understood, particularly as its creative and technical origins, not to mention the electronic hardware which first made it possible, recede further into history. A musician taught to sample without an awareness of the musical cultures that brought this practice into being might encounter similar ethical difficulties as a musician who samples sounds without acknowledging or understanding the culture that produced them. Both are potentially forms of cultural appropriation – the latter in terms of musical material but the former in terms of practice. Teaching sampling as a cultural – even historical – practice may also serve to remind student music technologists that they are heirs to distinct musical cultures no less significant than those bequeathed to young instrumentalists at conservatoires.

Yet appropriation of others' work goes beyond the appropriation of sonic resources. Teboul (2017) argues that, whilst there is much literature dealing with the design, use, and even misuse of music technologies and interfaces, there has been far less dealing with the origins of their electronic construction. Many programmes of music technology education now embrace makerspace practices in prototyping, hacking, circuit bending, and 'dirty electronics'. Therefore, educators might help learners understand that their creative innovations are only possible thanks to the labours of many others at different times and in different places. In turn, emphasis is also placed on potentially more equitable manufacturing practices such as open-source design and ethical/sustainable sourcing (Curzi, 2020).

Educators must also be concerned with the deceptive nature of music technology, of which there are two major aspects: (1) the promise of easier, better music, and (2) listener deception.

The proponents of music technology often promise that it can help to make 'better' music more 'easily' for those learning with it. Whether or not the music is 'better' or authentic is a discussion we shall leave unaddressed, since that is highly subjective. The ethical issues are found mainly within the *promise* of 'betterness' less than in its realisation. Should the short-term motivating achievement of creating 'good' (enough) music outweigh the loss of learning that would otherwise be required to create that music (i.e. that which is now embodied within a technological tool)? Would the failure to gain that knowledge adequately prepare a learner for their future career in music, for example? Would they have the skills and knowledge needed to interact with those who have learned music without the technology? The scope of musical knowledge conveyed, particularly in terms of what can be manipulated in the music domain is potentially limited to what is exposed on the surface of the tool. Benedict and O'Leary (2019) indicate that such pre-set parameters constrain creativity and suggest that educators consider, explore, and challenge their students' acceptance of the technological determinism that can be embodied in perceived-immutable designs (for example, by encouraging students to modify and create their own music technologies). Ideally, tools would permit a gradual reduction in the amount of scaffold support they offer, maintaining the appropriate balance of challenge and motivation at all points on a learner's trajectory.

Concerns over listener deception and manipulation have been raised in many areas of music technology, including live performance (Van Tuyl, 1991) and electroacoustic sound-scape composition. With regard to the latter, as McCartney (2016) notes, all work with soundscape-style audio material brings questions about the relationship between the work's intentions, the places where recordings have been made, and their inhabitants. Murray (2013) poses four questions as a starting point for an ethical framework of non-fiction film sound producers, and it strikes us that these questions also have wide applicability in any area of music technology education where promotion of verisimilitude is a priority. Murray's questions encourage us to consider the impacts of sound usage on the audience (potential to mislead), on participants (potential to misrepresent), on accuracy (potential to over-simplify or misrepresent), and on its becoming an archive (likelihood of being taken uncritically as historically accurate).

Sustainability, Socio-economic Fairness, and Access

Whilst the cost of music technology has dramatically decreased in the past thirty to forty years, it is still substantially out of reach for many. Educators' decisions (and how they prioritise cost) must therefore be influenced by what development possibilities they are trying to enable in their learners and the extent to which those learners have the financial resources to access and participate.

Bound up with all technology are issues of ephemerality, rapid technical evolution, and obsolescence (of both resources and skills). Technological changes are driven by new needs, which themselves drive new opportunities in cyclic fashion. They may also happen (as Kirn (2021) notes) because the business case (rather than the use case) ceases to be viable for the developer.

Therefore, the music technology educator must also consider the ephemerality and sustainability of the devices, software, and associated techniques that will support their curriculum. Life cycle assessments are powerful educational tools in this regard. For instance, Bates' (2020) source tracing of the precious minerals used in the construction of a studio preamplifier and Dunmade's (2013) environmental analysis of the manufacture and disposal of a plastic tambourine illustrate how finite, rare, and toxic raw materials are continuously mined, processed, and distributed to make the (often rapidly cast aside) equipment used by musicians every day. As Bates observes, the increased computer processing power required for the trend towards virtualisation draws ever more energy, leading to unsustainability of a different kind. As Curzi (2020) makes clear, there are no easy solutions here, but encouraging the next generation of musicians to adopt creative aesthetics drawing on the principles of 'less is more' and 'small is beautiful' appears to us to be an important responsibility for educators. In turn, educators may benefit in pedagogical terms from adopting a similar ethos in their teaching (Purves, 2018). More generally, musicians have a powerful platform on which to promote greater sustainability and there are prominent examples of concerts powered by solar and wind energy, 'eco-friendly' tour buses, and artist-led campaigns and efforts to divest profits from fossil fuels on which to draw (Green et al., 2016). Similarly, music festivals are now expected to limit their environmental impact through recycling, locally sourced catering, and sustainable merchandise.

Kosteletos and Georgaki (2014) note that barriers to engagement with music technology are not only financial but also knowledge-based. To some extent, the significant developments in and impact of the open source software and hardware communities (see Grzegorzewska, 2020) act as mitigation to this kind of knowledge barrier since the potential exists for devices and software to outlast and exist beyond their originators. Open approaches have potential to enhance participation through direct access to a wider public than those using academic software (Kosteletos & Georgaki, 2014). Such advantages are perhaps most pronounced in situations where potential users have the ability to create or rebuild devices or code for themselves.

One potential mitigation for these collective issues is to continuously evolve the curriculum in response to changes in the technological landscape, thereby aligning technological change with educational change at a fine-grained level. Small, incremental technology changes potentially offer a relatively low-risk means for educators to develop their practice over time (Purves, 2018). In a sense, these 'tweaks' also present lower ethical risks, since potential negative impacts on learners' experiences, educational progress, and future prospects due to a technological misstep may also be small. However, this implies that there is a need for educators to periodically 'audit' the combined ethical implications of a series of incremental changes to not miss more serious or larger risks that may have accrued.

A broader aspect to consider is the passing of knowledge and sharing of resources between educators. Burkart (2010) addresses the lack of physical 'objects' in digitally acquired music collections, arguing that the growing inability to possess recorded media (and associated artwork and documentation) may be psychologically ameliorated to some extent by the ability to seek out, curate, and share even larger digital collections, and to discuss these collections via independent online forums. However, these newer forms of cultural sharing have in some cases been actively discouraged by models of digital rights management, licenses which regard music as a service rather than as a product, and streamed distribution where all one really acquires is an obscured hyperlink to a cloud-based file.

Thus a teacher can curate digital music resources to support their teaching over many years but because streamed resources are not actually 'owned' by them even if entirely legally acquired, there are implications for how they can be used or passed on to another colleague, e.g. at the point of retirement or moving on. A practical example relates to technical and legal barriers encountered when attempting to embed streamed (as opposed to locally stored) musical examples within classroom presentation slides (Hampton-Sosa, 2017).

Studies such as Beaven and Laws (2007) and Green et al. (2016) illustrate the many ways that musicians and music businesses are now expected to be 'ethical' in commercial practices, social, environmental, and philanthropic areas. Fans, note Green et al., 'demand more from musicians than "just" music' (p. 231). Social media has made it easier than ever for consumers to scrutinise, critique, and reach out to individual artists and companies. To this end, educators may find a useful role for case studies of musicians who have adopted strict ethical codes in their work. A prominent example here is British musician and producer Matthew Herbert (2011), whose 'Personal Contract for the Composition of Music' places very specific prescription on, amongst other things, the use of synthesizer and effects processing presets, the sampling of previous work or sounds made by others, the replacement of acoustic instruments with synthetic alternatives, and full disclosure to listeners of all sounds and technologies used. Tasking learners to try producing music in line with a manifesto like this could encourage deep critical reflection and lead to valuable educational debate. Educators can also help learners to navigate future opportunities more critically. For instance, internships may appear to provide valuable access routes into professional careers. However, if these internships are unpaid, as can sometimes be the case in the music industry, then only learners with the necessary economic capital to support themselves will be able to reap the benefits and existing inequalities might ultimately be worsened (Mager, 2015).

Another issue is the extent to which learners can overcome geographical barriers to access opportunities. Whilst Bates (2014) was concerned with implications of remote practice for music therapy, we identify significant common ground with music education. Internet-mediated provision can reduce spatial isolation and time lost to commuting. Moreover, its importance as a form of infection control became all too obvious during the Coronavirus pandemic. However, there are significant ethical risks for educators to consider, including musical frustration and disjointed communication due to poor or latent Internet connections and technical failure. In both therapy and education contexts, musical communication cannot be replicated in hastily substituted text-based chat or email. Participant safeguarding and pastoral support must also be considered when working remotely, along with the issues surrounding data protection and privacy to which we turn next.

Data, Privacy, Safety, and Care

Developments in social media and online music streaming over the past decade have led to ethical concerns regarding privacy and the perceived exploitation of users' personal data. In the case of streaming services, the analysis of this data has become embedded in the business models of both platform providers and licensors of digital music (Randall, 2016; Drott, 2018). Listening histories are routinely harvested, something still not appreciated by many users (Singleton, 2019). Such techniques have been argued to be incompatible with individuals' rights to private musical and emotional identities as represented by this data (Randall, 2016). Drott argues that their use reconstitutes music as a tracking device across various spaces, turning a technology of self to one of surveillance (Drott, 2018).

For Holzapfel et al. (2018), such concerns stem from the increasingly blurred boundaries between technology (involved in creation, distribution, and listening) and music. Music has now become 'informationally enriched' (p. 47), with that information extending to far more than the digital sound itself. Failure to manage databases and algorithms ethically may therefore have economic, cultural, and individual impacts.

For music and music technology educators, these issues present ethical dilemmas of various kinds. Those responsible for educating individuals who might one day work professionally in these areas have an important role to help learners understand the value chain between research and development and the end user. Taking a lead from Holzapfel et al. (2018), educators might usefully draw on Huff's (2003) model of interactions between technology and society, which explicitly connects lower-level concerns relating to 'system design issues, trade-offs in design and performance' (Holzapfel et al., 2018, p. 46) with higher-level interactions involving 'other technologies and systems' (ibid.), and – ultimately – to larger impacts on societies in terms of privacy, property, power, and equity. Yet music educators also face implications in terms of their everyday pedagogical and resourcing choices. Those wishing to employ these kinds of tools in their teaching practice are advised to check carefully how learners' data might be harvested for profit by providers in the ways outlined. As Albert (2015) notes, settings to enhance online privacy are not always obvious to end users (sometimes by design) and those working with minors have particular ethical responsibilities in this area. Similarly, Albert points to the need to assess the potential for harm (e.g. cyberbullying and trolling) in situations where personal data, particularly in the form of recorded musical performances or collaborative creative activities, is exposed to peers or the wider Internet. The continuing inability of some learners to engage with these tools due to a lack of suitable equipment or connections is a further concern, something thrown into sharp relief by remote school and university working during the COVID-19 pandemic.

Educators must also be aware of the legal and contractual constraints that may apply to their use of online services, particularly where they are handling others' data. Cayari (2020) identifies a range of issues linked to terms-of-service agreements for online services (including surveillance and privacy), and notes that educators must consider the privacy of their students and the potential need for students' and parents/guardians' consent. Cayari advises that educators should adhere to applicable institutional, local, and national government policies (identifying measures such as the EU General Data Protection Regulation).

Sound itself has ethical implications through its physical properties (Andean, 2014). The deliberate application of extremes of loudness or frequency has been termed 'acoustic violence', and here it is instructive to recall Emmanuel Lévinas' argument that 'ethical philosophy begins with the simple understanding that the human begins in the responsibility for the other' (Labelle, 2010, p. 80). Very loud sound, such as that experienced at live concerts or entertainment venues, can of course result in hearing damage for performers, venue staff, and ticketholders. Brixen (2014) makes the point that it is human nature to push limits, and that sound engineers are as susceptible as anyone else, citing the 'loudness war' as an example. It has been similarly noted that by pursuing more powerful designs, audio equipment manufacturers are complicit in a desire for ever-louder sound levels (Labelle, 2010). Such arguments suggest that it is incumbent on educators to go further than simply alerting learners to legal sound limits. Brixen (2014) gives a good example of how the way that such limits are measured can lead to undesirable outcomes, e.g., over-emphasised low frequencies and poor sound quality despite maintaining legal compliance. Educators can usefully institute ethical discussions of these instincts and the potential implications for others. In addition, recent decades have witnessed the use of loud or endlessly looped music as forms of torture and the juxtaposition of music with on-screen violence (Andean, 2014; Cheng, 2014). These examples all suggest that the professional contexts in which a music technology or sound engineering student's skillset might one day be applied are not only diverse and potentially unforeseeable but also ethically complex, to say the least. As one of us has argued elsewhere (Purves & Himonides, 2021), music educators of all kinds must now increasingly support their students to develop so-called 'T-skills' or 'fusion skills', i.e. threshold expertise within a very broad range of interdisciplinary areas through which they can support and operationalise core musical activities. It seems to us that 'ethical literacy' should be preeminent amongst these skills, ready to help learners navigate unforeseen challenges in their future careers.

Conclusions

We began this chapter by considering Strang's (1970) identification of the potentially transformative power of the computer in music and his prediction that the responsibility for ethical judgement would not be (and we contend, has not been) modified by the transformation. This is perhaps unsurprising given that many authors describe ethics (in education particularly) as being fundamentally about the relational responsibilities we have towards each other (e.g. Warren, 2014; Bowman, 2020). Despite the massive technological innovation and mediative possibilities that have occurred since Strang's writing, the ethical aspects are largely unchanged: music education (with or without technology) remains fundamentally an activity concerned with relational interaction between people, replete with creative opportunities in musical and educational practice.

We have looked at a wide range of issues that impact contemporary educational curricula and practice with a view to helping educators (after Andean, 2014) identify what is important, be sensitive to the issues involved, and act responsibly as a result. Despite the essentially static nature of many of the deep issues, educators also need to engage in 'horizon-scanning', keeping a watching brief on new innovations, even if these feel too advanced to impact immediately. Technological impacts can happen rapidly: not so long ago, cloud-based music software was considered a 'young' technology (Thorgersen, 2012) but is now close to mainstream in many settings. There are many such innovations (and we acknowledge that the examples cited here are just recent instances of technologies in development for many years): for example, holographic performances by deceased musicians (Donoughue, 2018), brain-computer interfaces for emotion detection (Langroudi et al., 2020), artificial intelligence as a musical partner (Frisk, 2020) and as a composer (with attendant issues for copyright and other aspects (Sturm et al., 2019)), to highlight but a few.

Andean (2014), writing about the creative act, speaks of the impossibility of addressing all ethical matters in all possible ways, as well as of the goal needing to be one of engagement with open eyes. Engaged educators will no doubt continue to reflect, interrogate, and challenge all these new developments, seeking with open eyes to understand their potential and their limits, their implications and their biases, and with a continuing deep concern to seek the best for the formation of their learners.

References

Albert, D. J. (2015). Social media in music education: Extending learning to where students "live". *Music Educators Journal, 102*(2), 31–38. https://doi.org/10.1177/0027432115606976

Allami, K. (2019). Microtonality and the struggle for fretlessness in the digital age. *CTM 2019 Persistence Magazine*, 52–59.

Allsup, R. E., & Westerlund, H. (2012). Methods and situational ethics in music education. *Action, Criticism & Theory for Music Education, 11*(1), 124–148. http://act.maydaygroup.org/articles/AllsupWesterlund11_1.pdf

Andean, J. (2014). Towards an ethics of creative sound. *Organised Sound, 19*(2), 173–181. https://doi.org/10.1017/S1355771814000119

Angliss, S. (2016). Mimics, menaces, or new musical horizons? Musicians' attitudes toward the first commercial drum machines and samplers. In F. Weium & T. Boon (Eds.), *Material culture and electronic sound*(pp. 95–130). Smithsonian.

Armstrong, V. (2011). *Technology and the gendering of music education*. Routledge.

Bates, D. (2014). Music therapy ethics "2.0": Preventing user error in technology. *Music Therapy Perspectives, 32*(2), 136–141. https://doi.org/10.1093/mtp/miu030

Bates, E. (2020). Resource ecologies, political economies and the ethics of audio technologies in the Anthropocene. *Popular Music, 39*(1), 66–87. https://doi.org/10.1017/S0261143019000564

Beaven, Z., & Laws, C. (2007). Never let me down again. *Managing Leisure, 12*(2–3), 120–142. https://doi.org/10.1080/13606710701339322

Behr, A., Negus, K., & Street, J. (2017). The sampling continuum: Musical aesthetics and ethics in the age of digital production. *Journal for Cultural Research, 21*(3), 223–240. https://doi.org/10.1080/14797585.2017.1338277

bell, A. P., Bonin, D., Pethrick, H., Antwi-Nsiah, A., & Matterson, B. (2020). Hacking, disability, and music education. *International Journal of Music Education, 38*(4), 657–672. https://doi.org/10.1177/0255761420930428

Benedict, C., & O'Leary, J. (2019). Reconceptualizing "music making:" Music technology and freedom in the age of neoliberalism. *Action, Criticism, and Theory for Music Education, 18*(1), 26–43. http://doi.org/10.22176/act18.1.26

Bennett, S. (2017, October 18–21). Audio archive preservation challenges and pedagogical opportunities: School of music replayed [Paper Presentation No. 9815]. In *143rd convention of the Audio Engineering* Society. Audio Engineering Society. https://aes2.org/publications/elibrary-page/?id=19212

Blake, A. (2010). Ethical and cultural issues in the digital era. In A. Bayley (Ed.), *Recorded music: Performance, culture and technology* (pp. 52–67). Cambridge University Press.

Bowman, W. (2020). Reconceiving music and music education as ethical practices. *Revista Da Abem*, *28*(44), 162–176. http://doi.org/10.33054/ABEM20202809

Brett, T. (2016). Virtual drumming: A history of electronic percussion. In R. Hartenberger (Ed.), *The Cambridge companion to percussion*(pp. 82–94). Cambridge University Press. https://doi.org/10.1017/CBO9781316145074.007

Brixen, E. (2014). Pushing the limits. *Journal of the Audio Engineering Society*, *62*(7/8), 563–564.

Burkart, P. (2010). *Music and cyberliberties*. Wesleyan University Press.

Butler, M. J. (2006). *Unlocking the groove: Rhythm, meter, and musical design in electronic dance music*. Indiana University Press.

Cayari, C. (2020). Popular practices for online musicking and performance: Developing creative dispositions for music education and the Internet. *Journal of Popular Music Education*. Advance online publication. https://doi.org/10.1386/jpme_00018_1

Cheng, W. J. (2014). *Sound play: Video games and the musical imagination*. Oxford University Press.

Curzi, S. A. (2020). *Lilacs: Digital songs and poems for voice, clarinet, percussion, electric guitar,and electronics, and ethical considerations for the design and documentation of wearable technologies, responsive textiles, and haptic sound art* [Unpublished doctoral dissertation, Duke University].

D'Agostino, M. E. (2020). Reclaiming and preserving traditional music: Aesthetics, ethics and technology. *Organised Sound*, *25*(1), 106–115. https://doi.org/10.1017/S1355771819000505

Donoughue, P. (2018, December 28). Dead musicians are touring again, as holograms. It's tricky – technologically and legally. *ABC News*. www.abc.net.au/news/2018-12-29/hologram-technology-letting-dead-musicians-tour-again/10600996

Drott, E. (2018). Music as a technology of surveillance. *Journal of the Society for American Music*, *12*(3), 233–267. https://doi.org/10.1017/S1752196318000196

Dunmade, I. (2013). Environmental profile assessment of a plastic framed tambourine musical instrument – A lifecycle approach. *Resources and Environment*, *3*(5), 129–134. https://doi.org/10.5923/j.re.20130305.03

Elliott, D. J. (2020). Eudaimonia and well doing: Implications for music education. In G. D. Smith & M. Silverman (Eds.), *Eudaimonia: Perspectives for music learning* (pp. 107–120). Routledge.

Elliott, D. J. & Silverman, M. (2015). *Music matters: A philosophy of music education* (2nd ed.). Oxford University Press.

Frisk, H. (2020). Aesthetics, interaction and machine improvisation. *Organised Sound*, *25*(1), 33–40. https://doi.org/10.1017/S135577181900044X

Frith, S. (1986). Art versus technology: The strange case of popular music. *Media, Culture &Society*, *8*(3), 263–279. https://doi.org/10.1177%2F016344386008003002

Gilman, L., & Fenn, J. (2019). *Handbook for folklore and ethnomusicology*. Indiana University Press.

Good-Perkins, E. (2021). *Culturally sustaining pedagogies in music education: Expanding culturally responsive teaching to sustain diverse musical cultures and identities*. Routledge.

Green, T., Sinclair, G., & Tinson, J. (2016). Do they know it's CSR at all? An exploration of socially responsible music consumption. *Journal of Business Ethics*, *138*(2), 231–246. https://doi.org/10.1007/s10551-015-2582-8

Grzegorzewska, P. (2020). *What is the value of Open Source? Preliminary results of the Commission's study*. Open Source Observatory. https://joinup.ec.europa.eu/collection/open-source-observatory-osor/news/first-results-study-impact-open-source?platform=hootsuite

Hampton-Sosa, W. (2017). An exploration of essential factors that influence music streaming adoption and the intention to engage in digital piracy. *International Journal of Electronic Commerce Studies*, *8*(1), 97–134. https://doi.org/10.7903/ijecs.1458

Herbert, M. (2011). *Manifesto*. https://matthewherbert.com/about-contact/manifesto/

Hesmondhalgh, D. (2006). Digital sampling and cultural inequality. *Social &Legal Studies*, *15*(1), 53–75. https://doi.org/10.1177/0964663906060973

Holm-Hudson, K. (1997). Quotation and context: Sampling and John Oswald's plunderphonics. *Leonardo Music Journal*, *7*, 17–25. https://doi.org/10/c7srr7

Holzapfel, A., Sturm, B. L., & Coeckelbergh, M. (2018). Ethical dimensions of music information retrieval technology. *Transactions of the International Society for Music Information Retrieval*, *1*(1), 44–55. http://doi.org/10.5334/tismir.13

Huff, C. (2003). Unintentional power in the design of computing systems. In T. W. Ward & S. Rogerson (Eds.), *Computer ethics and professional responsibility*(pp. 98–106). Wiley-Blackwell.

Kirn, P. (2021). MIDI 2.0 in a DAW – MultitrackStudio adds MPE and new MIDI standard. *CDM*. https://cdm.link/2021/03/midi-2-0-in-a-daw-multitrackstudio-adds-mpe-and-new-midi-standard

Kosteletos, G., & Georgaki, A. (2014, September 14–20). From digital 'echoes' to virtual 'ethos': Ethical aspects of music technology [conference paper]. In A. Georgaki & G. Kouroupetroglou (Eds.), *Proceedings of the joint 40th international computer music conference and 11th sound and music computing conference, Athens, Greece* (pp. 193–200). International Computer Music Association.

LaBelle, B. (2010). *Acoustic territories: Sound culture and everyday life.* Continuum.

Landy, L., Hall, R., & Uwins, M. (2013). Widening participation in electroacoustic music: The EARS 2 pedagogical initiatives. *Organised Sound, 18*(2), 108–123. https://doi.org/10.1017/S1355771813000034

Langroudi, G., Jordanous, A., & Li, L. (2020, May 20–21). Music emotion capture: Ethical issues around emotion-based music generation [poster session]. In *Brain. Cognition. Emotions. Music.* 20–21 May 2020.

Mager, G. E. (2015, August 26–28). Legal and ethical issues regarding unpaid internships [paper presentation no. 13]. In *Proceedings of the 26th UK Audio Engineering Society conference* (pp. 78–81). University of Glasgow.

McCartney, A. (2016). Ethical questions about working with soundscapes. *Organised Sound, 21*(2), 160–165. https://doi.org/10.1017/S135577181600008X

Murray, L. (2013, July 3–5). With my own ears: The ethics of sound in non-fiction film and TV. In T. Lee, K. Trees & R. Desai (Eds.), *Referred proceedings of the Australian and New Zealand Communication Association conference.* Australian and Aotearoa New Zealand Communication Association.

New Interfaces for Musical Expression. (2020, November 18). *NIME principles & code of practice on ethical research.* https://nime.org/ethics

Oliver, M. (2009). *Understanding disability: From theory to practice.* Palgrave Macmillan.

Oswald, J. (1985). Plunderphonics, or audio piracy as a compositional prerogative. In *Originally Presented at the wired society electro-acoustic conference,* Toronto. http://www.plunderphonics.com/xhtml/xplunder.html

Oswald, J. (2004). Bettered by the borrower: The ethics of musical debt. In C. Cox & D. Warner (Eds.), *Audio culture: Readings in modern music* (pp. 131–137). Continuum Publishing Group.

Porcello, T. (1991). The ethics of digital audio-sampling: Engineers' discourse. *Popular Music, 10*(1), 69–84.

Purves, R. (2018). Technology and the educator. In G. McPherson & G. Welch (Eds.), *Creativities, technologies, and media in music learning and teaching* (pp. 143–161). Oxford University Press.

Purves, R., & Himonides, E. (2021). Acquiring skills in music technology. In A. Creech, D. Hodges & S. Hallam (Eds.), *Routledge international handbook of music psychology in education and the community* (pp. 217–235). Routledge.

Randall, R. (2016). A case for musical privacy. In R. Purcell & R. Randall (Eds.), *21st century perspectives on music, technology, and culture. Pop music, culture and identity.* Palgrave Macmillan. https://doi.org/10.1057/9781137497604_8

Roberts, B. A. (2009). Ethics in music education. *Canadian Music Educator, 51*(1), 18–19.

Sinclair, G., & Green, T. (2016). Download or stream? Steal or buy? Developing a typology of today's music consumer. *Journal of Consumer Behaviour, 15*(1), 3–14. https://doi.org/10.1002/cb.1526

Singleton, M. (2019, June 29). When you listen, they watch. *Billboard, 131*(16), 13–14.

Strang, G. (1970). Ethics and esthetics of computer composition. In H. Lincoln (Ed.), *The computer and music* (pp. 37–41). Cornell University Press.

Stras, L. (2015). Subhuman or superhuman?: (Musical) assistive technology, performance enhancement, and the aesthetic/moral debate. In J. Straus, B. Howe, N. Lerner & S. Jensen-Moulton (Eds.), *Oxford handbook of music & disability studies* (pp. 176–190). Oxford University Press. https://doi.org/10.1093/oxfordhb/9780199331444.013.19

Sturm, B. L. T., Iglesias, M., Ben-Tal, O., Miron, M., & Gómez, E. (2019). Artificial intelligence and music: Open questions of copyright law and engineering praxis. *Arts, 8*(3), 115. https://doi.org/10.3390/arts8030115

Teboul, E. (2017). Electronic music hardware and open design methodologies for post-optimal objects. In J. Sayers (Ed.), *Making things and drawing boundaries* (pp. 177–184). University of Minnesota Press. https://doi.org/10.5749/j.ctt1pwt6wq.22

Thibeault, M. D. (2012). From compliance to creative rights in music education: Rethinking intellectual property in the age of new media. *Music Education Research, 14*(1), 103–117. https://doi.org/10.1080/14613808.2012.657165

Thorgersen, K. (2012). Freedom to create in the cloud or in the open? A discussion of two options for music creation with digital tools at no cost. *Journal of Music, Technology and Education, 5*(2), 133–144. https://doi.org/10.1386/jmte.5.2.133_1

Tomatz, D. (1989, June). Technology in music: Cultural, artistic and ethical implications. In *Proceedings of the 64th annual meeting of the National Association of Schools of Music (no. 77), Reston, Virginia* (pp. 67–69). National Association of Schools of Music.

Van Tuyl, L. (1991, February 11). Issues of music ethics grow with advancing technology. *The Christian Science Monitor*, p. 10.

Voss, G. (2013). Gaming, texting, learning? Teaching engineering ethics through students' lived experiences with technology. *Science and Engineering Ethics, 19*(3), 1375–1393. https://doi.org/10.1007/s11948-012-9368-5

Wallaszkovits, N. (2018). Between standards and arts: Digitisation and restoration of audio material – a balancing act between authenticity and manipulation? *Journal of New Music Research, 47*(4), 285–290. http://doi.org/10.1080/09298215.2018.1514058

Warren, J. R. (2014). *Music and ethical responsibility*. Cambridge University Press.

Woolley, D. J. (2015). The association of moral development and moral intensity with music piracy. *Ethics and Information Technology, 17*(3), 211–218. https://doi.org/10.1007/s10676-015-9376-7

Wu, W. P., & Yang, H. L. (2013). A comparative study of college students' ethical perception concerning internet piracy. *Qual Quant, 47*, 111–120. https://doi.org/10.1007/s11135-011-9506-1

13 Acoustic Ecology

Exploring the Role of Sound and Technology in Understanding Climate Change

Leah Barclay

Listening to Changing Environments

Climate change is rapidly affecting some of the most vulnerable communities and ecosystems on earth – from remote islands and coral reefs in the Pacific to fragile rainforests in the Peruvian Amazon. Throughout 2020, the COVID-19 global pandemic has impacted lives around the world and disrupted and disconnected our relationship with the natural environment. While some impacts have been considered positive for climate action (reduction of anthropogenic noise and pollution with less travel), negative environmental consequences are inevitable for vulnerable communities (Diffenbaugh et al., 2020). The pandemic has triggered a global crisis with social, cultural and ecological impact, but it has not shifted the urgency of climate action and the critical need to make significant changes across the planet.

The evidence remains clear, with 97% of scientists agreeing that human influence is the dominant cause of global warming (Cook et al., 2013). However, it is complex to directly attribute changes in biodiversity to human activities (Thompson, 2003). We still know very little about the interconnected nature of our terrestrial and aquatic ecosystems and are challenged with ways to measure spatial and temporal changes over time. Many ecosystems across the planet still lack basic species inventories, and locations that have been studied are often only brief snapshots in time, using varied methods for biodiversity estimates which make future comparisons extremely difficult. Conventional environmental monitoring is regarded as highly invasive and constrained to restricted areas, infrequent time intervals and manual processing of observations which can generate biased results (Linke et al., 2018). We urgently need more effective methods to protect and conserve vulnerable environments and provide accurate information about ecosystem health.

Audio recordings of the environment provide a transformational opportunity to understand and document the temporal and spatial complexities of changing environments through accessible and non-invasive acoustic sensors. Recent advancements in digital technology and innovations in hardware and software mean that acoustic monitoring is now an accessible, affordable and viable method for measuring ecological changes and monitoring biodiversity (Deichmann et al., 2018). The resulting digital audio recordings can be used to estimate species abundance and population density, environmental changes over time and calculating acoustic proxies for metrics of biodiversity (Browning et al., 2017). The scientific field of acoustic monitoring has been historically defined as 'bioacoustics', with a specific focus on animal communication or sounds produced by wildlife (Krause, 1987). The term 'ecoacoustics' has recently been adopted to define a new interdisciplinary field that studies sound along a broad range of spatial and temporal scales to understand environmental changes (Sueur & Farina, 2015).

DOI: 10.4324/9781003041474-17

The scholars who pioneered ecoacoustics, including Stuart Gage and Bernie Krause, believe that 'sound is the heartbeat of the biosphere' and highlights the places on Earth where life exists. They believe that if we can measure this heartbeat, we can determine the condition of the biosphere (Farina & Gage, 2017). Ecoacoustics evolved from studies on natural and anthropogenic sounds and their relationship with the environment and increasing scientific interest in environmental sound as a non-invasive proxy for monitoring environmental changes (Towsey et al., 2014). Ecoacoustics calls for greater collaboration with other disciplines including electronics, remote sensing, big data, humanities and social sciences (Sueur & Farina, 2015). Despite being a relatively new scientific technique, there is clear evidence that measuring the acoustic diversity at a site provides information on biological diversity and the health of an ecosystem (Farina et al., 2017, Fuller et al., 2015; Sueur et al., 2008; Tucker et al., 2014; Deichmann et al., 2017; Staaterman et al., 2017). Advances in computing technology now allow automated analysis of audio recordings and recognition of particular species (Duan et al., 2011) resulting in real-time acoustic monitoring and automated species identification becoming increasingly popular (Aide et al., 2013). The advent of automated acoustic sensors is 'revolutionising environmental monitoring and leading to [a] new thrust in environmental research and education, including ecological forecasting' (Farina & Gage, 2017, p. 9).

Audio recordings of the environment are particularly valuable in ecosystems that are difficult to survey visually, such as dense rainforests or echolocating bats at night (Barlow et al., 2015). In aquatic ecosystems, sound enables continuous observations where species are notoriously challenging to monitor (Desjonquères et al., 2015). Acoustic monitoring is well established in the marine environments for whale song (Tavolga, 2012) and has been employed for monitoring fish in tropical coastal habitats (Staaterman et al., 2017). Acoustic monitoring has been effective in exploring the temporal and spatial variation in coral reefs and predicting certain aspects of coral reef communities and their physical characteristics (Nedelec et al., 2015). Ecoacoustics is now advancing in the freshwater realm, with evidence that audio recordings can substantially mitigate the effort, expense and invasive nature of traditional freshwater monitoring techniques (Linke et al., 2018; Barclay et al., 2020). Recent research on freshwater ecoacoustics has included characterisations of sounds that can offer the basis for automatic detection algorithms, which include Gottesman et al. (2018) and Desjonquères et al. (2015)'s catalogues of aquatic insect and physicochemical sounds. Other recent studies have characterised calls by piranhas in Peru (Rountree et al., 2019) and estimated the population of spadefoot toads based on the acoustic temporal patterns in a target frequency band (Dutilleux & Curé, 2018). Linke et al. (2018a) examined a series of long-duration freshwater recordings and discovered changes in the underwater insect chorus shifting with moonlight and directly correlating with lunar patterns.

The increased engagement in marine and freshwater ecoacoustics builds on a large body of rigorous studies in terrestrial ecosystems. Acoustics are standardised and respected methods for monitoring bird populations (Dawson & Efford, 2009), and ecoacoustics has been used effectively in a diversity of terrestrial settings, including estimating the presence and abundance of African forest elephants in Central Africa (Wrege et al., 2017). It has been used to detect invasive pest insects (Mankin et al., 2017) and is now commonly used to monitor illegal activity such as chainsaws or gunshots in remote rainforests (Astaras et al., 2015). Recent research has also demonstrated the value of sound in the plant world with evidence that plants emit sound and can detect and respond to the sounds of their environments (Gagliano, 2018b). New discoveries are published regularly and engagement in the field of ecoacoustics is increasing at a rapid pace globally.

The ability for audio recordings to be collected from many places simultaneously but analysed remotely at a later date makes it a valuable tool for rapid inventory work (Sueur et al., 2008; Ribeiro et al., 2017). Acoustic monitoring equipment has historically been expensive, reducing the accessibility for large-scale research, but various devices are now available to offer low-cost alternatives. One of the most popular recent additions, the AudioMoth, is a low-cost full-spectrum acoustic sensor that is the size of a credit card and can operate for long durations in the field. The AudioMoth can effectively capture acoustic data from remote locations and has made adopting ecoacoustics methods accessible for communities who found previous acoustic sensors cost-prohibitive (Hill et al., 2019).

The collection of data using acoustic sensors does not require specific scientific knowledge or skills – meaning the deployment and management of acoustic monitoring can be conducted by community members and returned to a central repository for analysis. This provides a viable and accessible way to engage local communities in global conservation efforts and directly participate in local research that will assist in advancing this field. While the ecoacoustics research to date has provided valuable evidence on the critical importance of this research for managing our ecosystems into the future, there is still a significant amount of work required before it is a standardised and accessible technique for species identification and analysing acoustic complexity as a proxy for biodiversity. It is important to note that while ecoacoustics is primarily concerned with the role of sound in our environment, listening has not played an active role in many existing studies. Acoustic sensors are often deployed in the field by scientists at predetermined locations and analysed using automated algorithms. The resulting data is produced without drawing on the incredible capacity of our auditory perception. Active listening and our comprehension of the acoustic data can inform every stage of the process and dramatically increase our abilities to collect precise information – from selecting locations in the field to deploying acoustic equipment and analysing the resulting audio recordings. The existing automated analysis techniques operating in time or frequency domains may be insensitive to the dynamic patterns of interaction in the soundscape (Eldridge et al., 2016), and these could be improved by drawing on our auditory perception in the creation of new analytical methods that suggest clear opportunities for the specialist skills of music technologists.

Listening to the state of the environment as a method for understanding the planet is not a new proposition – ecoacoustics draws on the well-established interdisciplinary field of acoustic ecology founded by R. Murray Schafer in the late 1960s in Canada. Schafer's premise was that we should attempt to hear the acoustic environment as music and we should take responsibility for its composition (Schafer, 1977). Schafer was a passionate scholar and educator and advocated strongly for integrating listening skills and 'sonological competence' into the school curriculum (Wrightson, 2000). Schafer launched the *World Soundscape Project* with his founding colleagues Hildegard Westerkamp and Barry Truax in the late 1960s at Simon Fraser University in Vancouver. Schafer's book *The Tuning of the World* (1977) documents these activities and remains an essential resource on acoustic ecology that has inspired a wider spectrum of composers, music technologists and artists globally.

Ecological sound artists emerging from the acoustic ecology movement have propelled many of the most significant discoveries that have informed the development of ecoacoustics. They understand the technology required and recognise that sound can engage communities and listeners at a deeper, more attuned level and encourage a connection and respect for the environment. Creative explorations and immersive sonic experiences can transport listeners to a place and time and evoke empathetic and philosophical responses to climate change that can inspire ecological action (Monacchi, 2013; Burtner, 2011). Ecological sound art can create metaphors to help us connect with environmental issues on a deeper and more personal level. The field can also inspire awareness of and respect for invisible or inaccessible areas of the environment and facilitate a heightened knowledge for changing ecosystems (Gilmurray, 2017). When listening to ecological sound art, Salomé Voegelin (2014) believes we become submerged is a 'sonic possible world' and our personal listening experience can inspire us to think differently about the environment.

Perhaps the most powerful aspect of ecological sound art is its ability to inspire environmental empathy through listening and feeling connected to an ecosystem and the species that inhabit it. Evolutionary ecologist Monica Gagliano believes that the missing link in many responses to climate action is environmental empathy and our capacity to recognise the planet and its many life forms as more than 'elusive entities to be objectified' (Gagliano, 2018a). Gagliano believes that the environmental guilt associated with the framing of the Anthropocene is counterproductive and focuses on our dominion over the environment. This aligns with Nancy Knowlton's call that we must inspire a sense of hope and earth optimism to respond to our current ecological crisis (Knowlton, 2018) and Boulton's (2016) belief that we need a new climate narrative that engages and inspires our sensory abilities. Climate action requires much more than ecological thinking: we need to inspire communities to reimagine alternative futures and actively engage in the protection and conservation of vulnerable ecosystems.

Ecoacoustics has propelled the scientific value of sound as a measure for environmental health and has the capacity to expand into a truly interdisciplinary endeavour by embracing the foundations of acoustic ecology and the possibilities of listening to engage global communities in responding to environmental change. While there are tensions in terminology amongst scholars in the field, all share the fundamental mission of understanding the role of sound in the environment. Differences between acoustic ecology and ecoacoustics are however evident in field recording approaches, particularly the role of human perception in the process. Ecoacoustic recordings are generally referred to as passive acoustic monitoring, or PAM, and captured remotely at multiple sites over a broad range of spatial and temporal scales. These studies are designed to generate large databases of recordings, often over weeks or months, and require computational analysis as listening is not feasible with large datasets. These analytical techniques function more effectively on mono recordings, and the logistics of long-term monitoring mean monophonic and low sampling rates are very common, as the power consumption and data storage required for high-fidelity recordings is usually not viable for long-term monitoring (Barclay & Gifford, 2017). Field recording approaches in ecological sound art and acoustic ecology tend to focus on capturing high-quality audio with multi-channel techniques including ambisonic (capturing a full sphere of sound) now being very common. These recordings are designed for active listening and intended to engage our auditory perception, whereas ecoacoustics studies are focused on quantifying scientific evidence and removing subjective perception. Both approaches can benefit from more interdisciplinary exchange and both have clear pathways to engage the skills of sound technologists in advancing the field work, education, industry engagement, software and hardware.

As a Transdisciplinary Field

This research adopts acoustic ecology as the umbrella term for a transdisciplinary field embracing the artistic and scientific possibilities of listening to the environment and encouraging and facilitating collaborations. In the context of Australia, acoustic ecology has evolved across the country as a highly interdisciplinary, dynamic field with increased engagement across environmental sciences, architecture, health, digital technology, creative arts and humanities. The last decade has seen a strong emergence of socially engaged practice and sonic activism, along with a rapid increase in education and academic research, with large-scale projects supported by competitive national funding. These have recently included *The Acoustic Observatory* – a continental-scale acoustic sensor network recording for a five-year period with 400 continuously operating acoustic recorders collecting sound data across multiple Australian ecosystems. Key acoustic ecology scholars in Australia including percussionist Vanessa Tomlinson believe that compositions that intentionally interact with the environment change the way we listen and leave markers of cultural, social and environmental conditions at particular junctures in time. She suggests that this sound work is well placed to reawaken our custodianship of the land and assist us in shaping our future (Tomlinson, 2019). Australian composer Ros Bandt is widely regarded as a sonic pioneer of acoustic ecology and founded 'The Acoustic Sanctuary' – a remote property in Fryerstown, Victoria, that has evolved over two decades as a dedicated place for listening, a place to contemplate our sonic habitat and a sound laboratory for her innovative and interdisciplinary creative practice. Bandt's work calls for a deeper understanding and respect for our sonic heritage and further engagement with sound culture across Australia (Bandt, 2019).

These scholars and many more operate under the banner of the Australian Forum for Acoustic Ecology (AFAE), an organisation that represents artists, scientists, scholars and those with a personal and professional interest in our sonic environment. The AFAE brings together people who aim to promote a culture of listening to strengthen and enhance the value of acoustic ecology in Australia. This includes increased engagement with climate activism and fields such as environmental sciences, urban design and architecture. The AFAE respects and acknowledges Indigenous knowledge systems and communities who have listened to and lived sustainability with the environment for over 60,000 years. The AFAE is an affiliate organisation of the World Forum for Acoustic Ecology (WFAE), the largest international acoustic ecology initiative that links like-minded groups from around the world.

Organisations such as the WFAE have proven to be effective in engaging communities and actively promoting awareness about our changing soundscapes. Other collectives, such as the *World Listening Project*, have also been successful in promoting engagement in acoustic ecology, with the most significant initiative being *World Listening Day*, an annual global event hosted on July 18 (R. Murray Schafer's birthday) that attracts hundreds of participants from across the world for collaborative projects, concerts, sound walks and educational initiatives exploring the value of listening and acoustic ecology. *The Global Sustainable Soundscapes Network* (soundscapenetwork.org) was created in 2011 by Bryan Pijanowski and Catherine Guastavino with a grant from the National Science Foundation (USA) to bring together landscape ecologists, conservation biologists and acoustic ecologists to coordinate international research projects and collaborations. Sound art organisations including *Ear to the Earth (eartotheearth.org)*, founded by the president of the *Electronic Music Foundation*, Joel Chadabe in New York, have also acted as a catalyst in inspiring composers, sound artists and music technologists to consider the role their practice can play in climate action. When initiating *Ear to the Earth*, Chadabe believed that the artistic practices of electroacoustic music composers were rooted in the idea that new technologies can produce sounds used to communicate core messages, including information about the state of our environment. He claimed that this work could communicate ideas that relate more closely to life than those communicated through traditional musical forms, and he called for composers to think of themselves as 'leaders in a magnificent revolution rather than the defenders of an isolated and besieged avant-garde' (Chadabe, 2011). The most significant activity of *Ear to the Earth* was an annual festival in New York City. While the organisation is no longer operational, Chadabe (1938–2021) continued to advocate for the role sound artists and music technologists can play in environmental engagement until his death in May 2021.

Electroacoustic composers and ecological sound artists have regularly diversified their practice to include education, industry engagement and environmental communication activities in response to climate action. Argentinean/Canadian composer Ricardo Dal Farra founded the Balance-Unbalance International Conference series in 2010 to explore how artists can participate in the challenges of our ecological crisis and launched a global sound art competition in partnership with the *Red Cross/Red Crescent Climate Centre* as part of the conference series. The project has attracted hundreds of submissions from across the world, and the sonic art resulting from this initiative has been used by the Red Cross in events, field activities and engagement campaigns. Composer and clarinetist David Rothenberg performs with the sounds of insects, birds and whales and has documented his process in publications including *Why Birds Sing* (2005), *Thousand Mile Whale Song* (2008) and *Bug Music* (2014), which have served as valuable resources for musicians interested in the soundscapes of the natural world and are also accessible for general readers. In a similar vein, Bernie Krause has invested considerable time in science communication and established *Wild Sanctuary* (wildsanctuary.com) to record, research, archive and disseminate the sounds of the natural world. The initiative includes regular media engagement, outreach activities, education programs, creative works and acclaimed books including *Voices of the Wild* (2015) and *The Great Animal Orchestra* (2012).

British composer Rob Mackay has developed many creative projects and community engagement initiatives around acoustic ecology and environmental sound art. He is passionate about building links between art and science and explores how we can connect to the natural world through sound and music. In his large-scale interdisciplinary project 'Following the Flight of the Monarchs', he brings together artists, scientists and conservationists to connect ecosystems and communities along the migration routes of monarch butterflies as they travel the 3,000-mile journey between Mexico and Canada each year. This project has resulted in scientific research, touring installations, live performances and a highly engaging radio feature on BBC Radio 3. He has also collaborated on projects such as 'Red River: Listening to a Polluted River', an 18-month research project funded by the UK Arts and Humanities Research Council led by Dr John Wedgwood Clarke. This project has included soundscapes, poetry, community events, workshops and showcases at conferences including COP26 (Climate Change Conference) in Glasgow in 2021.

Acoustic ecology pioneer and soundscape composer Hildegard Westerkamp believes that creative works that make the issues facing our planet audible can inspire listeners to engage and take action. She believes composers have the skills and expertise to make a significant contribution to climate action and by posing the question 'can soundscape composition initiate ecological change?', she has inspired a generation of composers to actively explore the links between acoustic ecology, soundscape composition and environmental action (Westerkamp, 2002). Annea Lockwood is an internationally respected composer who is renowned for her Sound Maps of river systems that have been exhibited throughout the world. These sound installations act as both an acoustic representation and artistic interpretation with social, political, ecological and sonic explorations on river systems including the Hudson, Danube and Housatonic (Lockwood, 2004, 2007). These works evolved from Lockwood's *River Archive*, which she began in the 1960s, to capture recordings of rivers, streams and springs. This sound archive pioneered what we now call an ecoacoustic approach and was the first to focus on recording river soundscapes, although there were existing sound archives focused on cataloguing individual species. With so much scientific research focusing on framing ecoacoustics as a new and emerging field, it is important to acknowledge the work of composers who have developed these techniques, pioneered audio technologies and paved the way by actively listening to the environment.

Immersive Recording Techniques

Deep in the Bosavi rainforest of Papua New Guinea, anthropologist and sound artist Steven Feld explored various immersive recording techniques to capture the soundscapes of a day in the life of the Kaluli people. The resulting composition, *Voices of the Rainforest* (1991), is an aural immersion into the rainforest with wildlife, waterfalls and environmental soundscapes intertwined with Kaluli voices, songs and culture (Feld, 1996). Feld developed a close relationship to the local community through his fieldwork in Bosavi from 1975 to 2000 and observed unique connections between sound and the environment that led him to coin the term acoustemology. Acoustemology refers to sound as a way of knowing and being in the world, and Feld suggests it is a generative concept rather than prescriptive (Rice & Feld, 2020). For the 25th anniversary of *Voices of the Rainforest*, Feld released a new version in 7.1 surround sound with an accompanying experimental documentary created in collaboration with filmmaker Jeremiah Ra Richards. The documentary immerses audiences in the visual and sonic world of the Bosavi rainforest and outlines the long-term positive impacts this project has had on the local community.

Sound artist and composer David Dunn believes that the most important thing he can do as a composer 'is listen to nature's changing messages and pass them along' (Zuckerman, 2006). Dunn's *The Sound of Light in Trees* (2006) is a work that draws on recordings of the pine bark beetle – an invasive insect that has destroyed large populations of pine trees in New Mexico. During his field work and listening experiments, Dunn discovered that playing the recordings back to the beetles disorientated them and could shut down their reproductive cycle. This discovery resulted in further collaborations with scientists and a patented sonic device to disrupt the bark beetle populations and conserve the pine trees (Rappaport, 2017). Norwegian sound artist Jana Winderen has also been responsible for sonic discoveries that have assisted scientific research with her work exploring ecosystems that are difficult for humans to access, such as the deep sea and polar ice. Winderen's underwater recordings at Lindaspollen north of Bergen captured the sounds of pistol shrimp in the region, revealing the shrimp had moved further north (Rudi, 2011). This discovery resulted in the album *The Noisiest Guys on the Planet*, released in 2009.

Incorporating Activism and Education

Composers such as Alaskan-born Matthew Burtner have extended their compositional and music technology skills to include activism, education and establishing organisations to facilitate greater engagement in our sonic environment. In 2008, Burtner created *Eco Sono*, an activist network designed to advocate environmental preservation through experimental sound art. One of *Eco Sono*'s main activities has been with field institutes that invite emerging artists to deepen their practice in various environments. Burtner believes that

> by creating responsible interactions between the natural world and audiences, those involved may come to think in new ways about the environment. They may convince others of the need for sustainable practices, or they may join preservationist societies and activism networks.
>
> (Burtner, 2011)

His creative practice and research encourage composers and music technologists to push the boundaries of their work and actively engage with the natural world.

David Monachi's *Fragments of Extinction* was initiated in 2001 with the intention of recording the world's undisturbed primary equatorial forests to highlight disappearing soundscapes (Monacchi, 2013). Monacchi is an Italian composer, researcher and multidisciplinarian who is pioneering new ecoacoustic compositional approaches based on 3D soundscape (ambisonic) recordings of ecosystems to foster discussion on the biodiversity crisis. His recordings have captured sound portraits of circadian cycles and provided evidence on the systemic behaviour of sound in rainforest ecosystems (Monacchi, 2013). *Fragments of Extinction* has evolved into a non-profit organisation that works in collaboration with artists, scientists and sound engineers to produce immersive installations. The intention of these immersive experiences is to increase public engagement and scientific knowledge of the acoustic biodiversity of equatorial rainforests (Monacchi, 2016). The soundscapes are recorded in high-definition ambisonics and ideally diffused in Monacchi's ecoacoustic theatre that enables a 3D reconstruction of the sonic environments. Monacchi believes we are losing a 'sonic heritage of millions of years of evolution' (Monacchi, 2016), and the ongoing ecocide is silencing soundscapes that must be documented and preserved.

The artists featured present a snapshot of a large body of work emerging in acoustic ecology and ecological sound art. These projects share a similar mission of drawing wider attention and awareness to our changing sonic environment and are all initiated by composers and sound artists who are working at the intersection of art, science, technology, activism and education to inspire connection with major ecosystems across our planet through sound and technology.

Biosphere Soundscapes

Interdisciplinary acoustic ecology research in Australia led to the development of *Biosphere Soundscapes* – a large-scale international research project that was conceived in 2011 and launched on World Listening Day 2012 in Queensland, Australia, in the Noosa Biosphere Reserve. The project studies and records the changing soundscapes of UNESCO biosphere reserves and has a strong focus on education, community engagement and industry partnerships to advance the field of acoustic ecology (Barclay & Gifford, 2017). The initial phase of the project had an explicit education focus to explore the artistic and scientific possibilities of accessible audio recording technologies and acoustic ecology in connecting and empowering local and global communities of UNESCO biosphere reserves.

Biosphere reserves are sites designated by UNESCO for the conservation of biological and cultural diversity. They are considered learning laboratories for sustainable development and ideal sites for testing and exploring interdisciplinary approaches to managing and understanding ecosystems. The World Network of Biosphere Reserves currently includes

727 sites across 131 countries and actively encourages collaboration and knowledge sharing related to climate action and environmental management. Biosphere reserves are ideal sites for acoustic ecology research, and the network has been highly supportive of the Biosphere Soundscapes project.

Biosphere Soundscapes was designed to work at the intersection of art and science, with the audio recordings providing scientific data for biodiversity analysis to advance the field of ecoacoustics in addition to providing source material creative works that bring awareness to these environments. The intention was to create a dialogue between scientific and artistic perspectives and ensure the practice of listening was considered in scientific studies. The mission of the program is to inspire communities across the world to listen to the environment and explore the value of sound as a measure for social, cultural and environmental health in UNESCO biosphere reserves. This mission has been explored through various programs within the project that focus on education, including immersive workshops residencies with artists and scientists in biosphere reserves, research laboratories, intensive masterclasses, virtual education programs and a diversity of creative projects spanning four continents. The education programs have introduced accessible audio recording technologies to local communities and resulted in multiple research projects across the planet that have documented changing soundscapes.

Biosphere Soundscapes has focused on advancing the field of acoustic ecology as an accessible, inclusive, interdisciplinary field that can assist local communities in biodiversity monitoring and understanding the environment in deeper and more attuned ways (Barclay & Gifford, 2017). The project has been flexible and responsive to the needs of collaborating communities and has developed and encouraged appropriate protocols for field recording, which always involve seeking permission to record from traditional custodians and respecting Indigenous knowledge systems and protocols in local environments. The project has acted as a catalyst for bringing diverse voices together and highlighting the critical importance of Indigenous approaches in environmental management.

Biosphere Soundscapes draws on interdisciplinary knowledge, emerging science, new technology and responsive community engagement to explore the social, cultural and ecological soundscapes of biosphere reserves. The project has successfully delivered workshops, education programs, acoustic monitoring and large-scale research projects in over 20 biosphere reserves. In the context of UNESCO biosphere reserves that seek to reconcile the conservation of cultural and biological diversity, acoustic ecology offers valuable tools to understand environmental and cultural changes with new technology and creative experiences. Biosphere Soundscapes has focused on positioning acoustic ecology as a way to understand and document the rapid changes taking place in a diversity of ecosystems. The project is fundamentally focused on promoting the value of listening to the environment from artistic and scientific perspectives and encouraging engagement through education, partnerships and collaboration.

Listening to Country

This approach to acoustic ecology can also be applied in a broader interdisciplinary context. *Listening to Country* is an arts-led research project exploring the value of acoustic ecology in promoting cultural connection, maintenance and wellbeing among Aboriginal and Torres Strait Islander women in prison who are experiencing separation from family, culture and country. The project began in 2018 with a pilot phase in Brisbane Women's Correctional Centre (BWCC) in Queensland, Australia, where an interdisciplinary team of researchers worked with incarcerated women to produce a one-hour immersive audio work based on field recordings of natural environments (of Country). The pilot was built on several years' engagement with BWCC delivering participatory workshops and the decision to engage with acoustic ecology came from a direct request from a group of Aboriginal women at BWCC to create a culturally relevant relaxation soundscape – a sound recording for the purpose of reducing stress and connecting to country (Woodland et al., 2019). The women reflected that they had access to nature CDs in prison that were provided for relaxation, but these recordings did not feel culturally relevant or sound like the places that made them feel connected to Country. The pilot for *Listening to Country* was supported with a grant from the Lowitja Institute for Aboriginal and Torres Strait Islander Health Research the project team consists of two Aboriginal (Dr Bianca Beetson and Dr Vick Saunders) and two non-Aboriginal researchers (Dr Leah Barclay and Dr Sarah Woodland). The BWCC pilot was also supported by two Aboriginal Elders, Aunty Melita Orcher and Aunty Estelle Sandow from the Brisbane Council of Elders, who work as volunteers in Queensland prisons to reconnect incarcerated Aboriginal men, women and young people with family, country and culture.

Aboriginal and Torres Strait Islander women are the fastest-growing prison population in Australia. The majority are mothers, experiencing the trauma associated with separation from family, community and country. Existing prison programs and workshops do not traditionally address the specific needs of Indigenous women, particularly when connection to country is regarded as central to Indigenous wellbeing. Recent research has demonstrated there is a demand for holistic, innovative and flexible approaches to engage and support women in prison (Kendall et al., 2019). Acoustic ecology and listening to the environment are valuable ways to strengthen connections to place and Country. *Listening to Country* is a creative approach to promoting wellbeing, and the process of developing the immersive audio work with the women was underpinned by a number of key principles and processes. Acoustic ecology was the foundation for producing the work, and for understanding the connections between listening to environmental soundscapes and the wellbeing of individuals and communities. The women were inspired by the possibilities of sound in understanding the health of the environment and engaged in listening to various ecosystems during the workshops.

The workshops introduced acoustic ecology to incorporate other understandings around the value of listening, including Steven Feld's 'acoustomology' (Feld, 1996) and 'deep listening' from Pauline Oliveros, where sound facilities expanded consciousness and healing with transformational changes in the body and mind (Oliveros, 2005). From an Indigenous perspective, the workshops were grounded in the idea of dadirri – a term that comes from the Ngan'gikurunggurr and Ngen'giwumirri languages of the Aboriginal peoples of the Daly River region (Northern Territory, Australia) to encourage the idea of deep listening to the world around us. Aboriginal healer Miriam-Rose Ungunmerr (2017) introduced dadirri as a practice that involves whole body listening or listening with more than the ear, which aligns with Pauline Oliveros' and Hildegard Westerkamp's perspectives on acoustic ecology. The workshop process involved listening to environmental soundscapes from local places, talking about what feelings and memories these evoked and then exploring what sounds made the women feel connected to Country, or their 'belonging place'. It was important to include the broader idea of belonging for those women who did not know their country or ancestry (Woodland et al., 2019).

The second phase of the project involved field work, visiting the locations the women selected to record the environments and the specific sounds they had requested during the workshops. This included familiar sounds, such as laughing kookaburras by a river, a dawn chorus in the rainforest or a dusk soundscape of insects with a crackling campfire. The field recordings were collected from 15 locations across South East Queensland and edited into short soundscapes for the second phase of workshops in the prison. These workshops involved listening, reflecting and collaborative composition with the field recordings. In addition to the soundscapes, the women wrote and recorded poetry in the prison and included the sounds of their heartbeats and footsteps in the composition to personalise the final piece. The composition was constructed through graphic scores (the team were unable to bring a laptop into the prison for security reasons), which created some tension during the creative process. This tension was also amplified through the industrial soundscape of the prison, where alarms, slamming doors and constant distractions made facilitating the process of deep listening challenging at times. The team were exploring the idea of using sound intentionally to promote 'acoustic agency' (Rice, 2016), where participants might take control of the sonic environment and resist the oppressive industrial soundscapes of the prison. The consistent engagement with listening during the workshops had an obvious positive impact on the participants, and the women described the final soundscape they created as making them forget they were in prison and feel 'spiritually alive, calm, relaxed and free' (Woodland et al., 2019).

Listening to Country demonstrates the potential for acoustic ecology and music technology to be used for healing and rehabilitation in prisons and beyond. The research team are planning to expand the program to other prisons and explore how the project might be transferable into a number of different wellbeing contexts, including with at-risk youth, Elders/seniors off Country in care, women transitioning from prison to the community and hospitals. The next phase will include capacity building and education, where Indigenous youth will be trained in environmental field recording and acoustic ecology and invited to assist in workshop facilitation. The intention is also that the capacity building programs will empower communities to engage with local conservation through acoustic ecology and provide pathways for workshop participants to engage with environmental management and caring for Country programs that could increase their skills and opportunities for professional employment in the health or environment sector.

Acoustic Ecology Futures

The examples highlighted in this chapter focus on projects and practitioners who are exploring the possibilities of sound and technology in addressing some of the most critical issues of our time. The composers and sound artists featured are actively working with community and industry to facilitate education and engagement with the field of acoustic ecology. These projects leverage music technology to encourage connections between art and science to mobilise communities to listen, connect and collaborate. The increased scientific interest in acoustic ecology and the emergence of ecoacoustics have provided an important opportunity for the field to expand and reinvigorate. Advancements in audio technologies mean it is now accessible and affordable to develop large-scale initiatives and engage remote communities in the process. Ecological sound art has acted as a catalyst to promote a wider understanding and awareness around the value of sound to monitor the health of the environment. It is evident that interdisciplinary approaches are critical to advancing this field, and this research calls for further collaborations between artists, scientists, technologists and communities to record, document and share the changing soundscapes of the planet to help us understand and respond to climate change.

For emerging music technologists interested in engaging in this field – an excellent first step is researching local environments and conservation organisations who could act as partners and collaborators in your field recording or ecological sound art projects. Engaging with local knowledge holders is critical to understanding the environment you are recording, and it is always encouraged to seek permission from Indigenous communities where the recording is taking place, if possible. For more experienced music technologists – there are various opportunities to engage with advancing the field, which include assisting in the development of autonomous sensor networks and developing more effective and robust analytical methods and signal processing tools. The acoustic ecology community is actively developing global audio repositories, open-source projects for audio hardware and software, real-time monitoring with live streaming audio and networked sensors for rapid computational analysis. There is further work to be done around standardised protocols for acoustic data and there is a need for increased audio recordings and contributions to central repositories so acoustic ecology and ecoacoustics can be adopted for global monitoring programmes and projects.

Despite the ecological crisis and the urgency of climate change, it is an exciting time to engage with acoustic ecology and contribute towards a field that has the potential to make a real difference. There are many opportunities for specialists in music technology to work directly with community and industry to advance the development of the technologies, methods and approaches currently needed. The opportunities for acoustic ecology in the future cross into a truly interdisciplinary context, bringing together Indigenous knowledge systems, biological sciences, computational technology, engineering, big data, arts and humanities to explore the ways we can use sound and technology to understand the planet. From embodied and immersive solo field recording expeditions to large-scale remote sensing, acoustic ecology promotes the value of listening and the aesthetic properties of sound as a way to inspire environmental empathy while also recognising acoustic data as a measure for ecological health. The rapid advancement of this field encourages collaboration and calls for creative ideas to preserve and understand vulnerable ecosystems across the planet through sound.

References

Aide, T. M., Corrada-Bravo, C., Campos-Cerqueira, M., Milan, C., Vega, G., & Alvarez, R. (2013). Real-time bioacoustics monitoring and automated species identification. *PeerJ*, *1*, e103.

Astaras, C., Macdonald, D. W., Wrege, P., & Linder, J. M. (2015). Darwin Initiative Annual Report: Improving anti-poaching patrol evaluation and design in African rainforests.

Aubin, T., & Jouventin, P. (2002). How to vocally identify kin in a crowd: The penguin model. *Advances in the Study of Behavior*, *31*, 243–277.

Bandt, R. (2019). The acoustic sanctuary: A dedicated listening place. *Soundscape: The Journal of Acoustic Ecology*, *17*(1), 11–18.

Barclay, L., & Gifford, T. (2017). Acoustic ecology in UNESCO biosphere reserves. In *The international journal of UNESCO biosphere reserves. V1 (1)*. Viewscape Publishing.

Barclay, L., Gifford, T., & Linke, S. (2020). Interdisciplinary approaches to freshwater ecoacoustics. *Freshwater Science*, *39*(2), 356–361. https://doi.org/10.1086/709130

Barlow, K. E., Briggs, P. A., Haysom, K. A., Hutson, A. M., Lechiara, N. L., Racey, P. A., Walsh, A. L., & Langton, S. D. (2015). Citizen science reveals trends in bat populations: The National Bat Monitoring Programme in Great Britain. *Biological Conservation*, *182*, 14–26.

Boulton, E. (2016). Climate change as a "hyperobject": A critical review of Timothy Morton's reframing narrative. *Wiley Interdisciplinary Reviews:Climate Change*, *7*(5), 772–785. https://doi.org/10.1002/wcc.410

Browning, E., Gibb, R., Glover-Kapfer, P., & Jones, K. E. (2017). Passive acoustic monitoring in ecology and conservation. *WWF Conservation Technology Series*, *1*(2). WWF-UK.

Burtner, M. (2011). EcoSono: Adventures in interactive ecoacoustics in the world. *Organised Sound*, *16*(3), 234–244. https://doi.org/10.1017/s1355771811000240

Carlyle, A. (2019). The god's eye and the buffalo's breath. In *Presentation at WFAE viseau, Portugal 2015*. http://invisibleplaces.org/2014/pdf/ip2014-carlyle.pdf

Chadabe, J. (2011). A call for avant-garde composers to make their work known to a larger public. *Musicworks, 111*(6).

Cook, J., Nuccitelli, D., Green, S. A., Richardson, M., Winkler, B., Painting, R., Way, R., Jacobs, P., & Skuce, A. (2013). Quantifying the consensus on anthropogenic global warming in the scientific literature. *Environmental Research Letters, 8*(2), 024024. https://doi.org/10.1088/1748-9326/8/2/024024

Dawson, D. K., & Efford, M. G. (2009). Bird population density estimated from acoustic signals. *Journal of Applied Ecology, 46*, 1201–1209. https://doi.org/10.1111/j.1365-2664.2009.01731.x

Deichmann, J. L., Acevedo-Charry, O., Barclay, L., Burivalova, Z., Campos-Cerqueira, M., d'Horta, F., Game, E., Gottesman, B., Hart, P., Kalan, A., Linke, S., Nascimento, L., Staaterman, E., & Aide, T. (2018). It's time to listen: There is much to be learned from the sounds of tropical ecosystems. *Biotropica, 50*, 719–178.

Deichmann, J. L., Hernández-Serna, A., Delgado, J. A., Campos-Cerqueira, M., & Aide, T. M. (2017). Soundscape analysis and acoustic monitoring document impacts of natural gas exploration on biodiversity in a tropical forest. *Ecological Indicators, 74*, 39–48.

Desjonquères, C., Rybak, F., Depraetere, M., Gasc, A., Le Viol, I., Pavoine, S., & Sueur, J. (2015). First description of underwater acoustic diversity in three temperate ponds. *PeerJ, 3*, e1393. https://doi.org/10.7717/peerj.1393

Diffenbaugh, N. S., Field, C. B., Appel, E. A., & Azevedo, I. L. (2020). The COVID-19 lockdowns: A window into the Earth System. *Nature Reviews Earth & Environment, 1*, 470–481.

Duan, S., Towsey, M., Zhang, J., Truskinger, A., Wimmer, J., & Roe, P. (2011). Acoustic component detection for automatic species recognition in environmental monitoring. In*2011 seventh international conference on intelligent sensors,sensor networks and information processing* (ISSNIP) (pp. 514–519).

Dutilleux, G., & Curé, C. (2018). A software detector for monitoring endangered common spadefoot toad (Pelobates fuscus) populations. In *Proceedings from the 10th international conference on ecological informatics*, Jena, Germany.

Eldridge, A., Casey, M., Moscoso, P., & Peck, M. (2016). A new method for ecoacoustics? Toward the extraction and evaluation of ecologically-meaningful soundscape components using sparse coding methods. *PeerJ, 4*, e2108. http://doi.org/10.7717/peerj.2108

Farina, A., & Gage, S. (2017). *Ecoacoustics: The ecological role of sound*. Wiley.

Feld, S. (1996). Waterfalls of song: An acoustemology of place resounding in Bosavi, Papua New Guinea. In S. Feld & K. H. Basso (Eds.), *Senses of place*. School of American Research Press.

Fuller, S., Axel, A. C., Tucker, D., & Gage, S. H. (2015). Connecting soundscape to landscape: Which acoustic index best describes landscape configuration? *Ecological Indicators, 58*, 207–215.

Gagliano, M. (2018a). Planetary health: Are we part of the problem or part of the solution? *Challenges, 9*(2), 38. https://doi.org/10.3390/challe9020038

Gagliano, M. (2018b). *Thus spoke the plant: A remarkable journey of groundbreakingscientific discoveries and personal encounters with plants* (Illustrated ed.). North Atlantic Books.

Gilmurray, J. (2017). Ecological sound art: Steps towards a new field. *Organised Sound, 22*(1), 32–41. http://doi.org/10.1017/S1355771816000315

Gottesman, B. L., Francomano, D., Zhao, Z., Bellisario, K., Ghadiri, M., Broadhead, T., Gasc, A., & Pijanowski, B. C. (2018). Acoustic monitoring reveals diversity and surprising dynamics in tropical freshwater soundscapes. *Freshwater Biology, 65*(1), 117–132. https://doi.org/10.1111/fwb.13096

Hill, A., Prince, P., Snaddon, J., Doncaster, C. P., & Rogers, A. (2019). AudioMoth: A low-cost acoustic device for monitoring biodiversity and the environment. *HardwareX, 6*. https://doi.org/10.1016/j.ohx.2019.e00073

Kendall, S., Lighton, S., Sherwood, J., Baldry, E., & Sullivan, E. (2019). Holistic conceptualizations of health by incarcerated aboriginal women in New South Wales, Australia. *Qualitative Health Research, 29*(11), 1549–1565. https://doi.org/10.1177/1049732319846162

Knowlton, N. (2018). Earth optimism – recapturing the positive. *Oryx, 53*(1), 1–2. https://doi.org/10.1017/s0030605318001333

Krause, B. (1987). Bioacoustics, habitat ambience in ecological balance. *Whole Earth Review, 57*, 14–18.

Linke, S., Decker, E., Gifford, T., & Desjonquères, C. (2018a). Diurnal variation in freshwater ecoacoustics: Implications for site-level sampling design. *Freshwater Biology, 65*(1), 86–95. https://doi.org/10.1111/fwb.13227

Linke, S., Gifford, T., Desjonquères, C., Tonolla, D., Aubin, T., Barclay, L., Karaconstantis, C., Kennard, M., Rybak, F., & Sueur, J. (2018). Continuous monitoring of freshwater environments using underwater passive acoustics. *Frontiers in Ecology and the Environment, 16* (4), 231–238.

Lockwood, A. (2004). Sound mapping the Danube River from the Black Forest to the Black Sea: Progress report, 2001–2003. *Soundscape – The Journal of Acoustic Ecology, 5*, 32–34.

Lockwood, A. (2007). What is a river? *Soundscape – The Journal of Acoustic Ecology, 7*, 43–44.

Mankin Xie, J., Towsey, M., Zhu, M., Zhang, J., & Roe, P. (2017). An intelligent system for estimating frog community calling activity and species richness. *Ecological Indicators, 82,* 13–22.

Monacchi, D. (2013). Fragments of extinction – An eco-acoustic music project on primary rainforest biodiversity. *Leonardo Music Journal, 23*(Sound Art), 23–25. ISAST, The MIT Press.

Monacchi, D. (2016). A philosophy of eco-acoustics in the interdisciplinary project fragments of extinction. In F. Bianchi & V. J. Manzo (Eds.), *Environmental sound artists.* Oxford University Press.

Nedelec, S. L., Simpson, S. D., Holderied, M., Radford, A. N., Lecellier, G., & Radford, C., (2015). Soundscapes and living communities in coral reefs: Temporal and spatial variation. *Marine Ecology Progress Series, 524,* 125–135.

Oliveros, P. (2005). *Deep listening: A composer's sound practice.* iUniverse.

Rappaport, S. (2017). Music professor receives patent to help fight bark beetles ravaging Western forests. *UC Santa Cruz News.* https://news.ucsc.edu/2017/02/bark-beetles-dunn.html

Ribeiro, J. W., Sugai, L. S. M., & Campos-Cerqueira, M. (2017). Passive acoustic monitoring as a complementary strategy to assess biodiversity in the Brazilian Amazonia. *Biodiversity and Conservation, 26,* 2999–3002.

Rice, T. (2016). Sounds inside: Prison, prisoners and acoustical agency. *Sound Studies, 2*(1), 6–20. https://doi.org/10.1080/20551940.2016.1214455

Rice, T., & Feld, S. (2020). Questioning acoustemology: An interview with Steven Feld. *Sound Studies,* 1–14. https://doi.org/10.1080/20551940.2020.1831154

Rountree, R. A., Bolgan, M., & Juanes, F. (2019). How can we understand freshwater soundscapes without fish sound descriptions? *Fisheries, 44*(3), 137–143. https://doi.org/10.1002/fsh.10190

Rudi, J. (2011). Out into the sound of what we don't know – an interview with Jana Winderen. In *Soundscape in the arts ed.* Joran Rudi. Oslo, NOTAM.

Schafer, R. M. (1977). *The tuning of the world.* Random House.

Staaterman, E., Ogburn, M. B., Altieri, A. H., Brandl, S. J., Whippo, R., Seemann, J., Goodison, M., & Duffy, J. E. (2017). Bioacoustic measurements complement visual biodiversity surveys: Preliminary evidence from four shallow marine habitats. *Marine Ecology Progress Series, 575,* 207–215.

Sueur, J., & Farina, A. (2015). Ecoacoustics: The ecological investigation and interpretation of environmental sound. *Biosemiotics.* http://doi.org/10.1007/s12304-015-9248-x

Sueur, J., Pavoine, S., Hamerlynck, O., & Duvail, S. (2008). Rapid acoustic survey for biodiversity appraisal. *PLoS ONE, 3,* e4065.

Tavolga, W. N. (2012). Listening backward: Early days of marine bioacoustics. In A. N. Popper & A. D. Hawkins (Eds.), *The effects of noise on aquatic life.* Springer-Verlag.

Thompson, W. L. (2003). *Sampling rare or elusive species: Concepts, designs and techniques for estimating population parameters.* Island Press.

Tomlinson, V. (2019). Intersecting place, environment, sound, and music. *Soundscape: The Journal of Acoustic Ecology, 17*(1), 19–26.

Towsey, M., Parsons, S., & Sueur, J. (2014). Ecology and acoustics at a large scale. *Ecological Informatics, 21,* 1–3.

Tucker, D., Gage, S. H., Williamson, I., & Fuller, S. (2014). Linking ecological condition and the soundscape in fragmented Australian forests. *Landscape Ecology, 29,* 745–758.

Ungunmerr, M. (2017). To be listened to in her teaching: Dadirri: Inner deep listening and quiet still awareness. *EarthSong Journal: Perspectives in Ecology, Spirituality and Education, 3*(4), 14–15.

Voegelin, S. (2014). *Sonic possible worlds: Hearing the continuum of sound.* Bloomsbury Academic.

Westerkamp, H. (2002). Linking soundscape composition and acoustic ecology. *Organised Sound, 7*(1), 51–56. http://doi.org/10.1017/S1355771802001085

Woodland, S., Saunders, V., Beetson, B., & Barclay, L. (2019). Listening to country: Exploring the value of acoustic ecology with Aboriginal and Torres Strait Islander women in prison. *Soundscape: The Journal of Acoustic Ecology, 17*(1), 41–44.

Wrege, P. H., Rowland, E. D., Keen, S., & Shiu, Y. (2017). Acoustic monitoring for conservation in tropical forests: Examples from forest elephants. *Methods in Ecology and Evolution, 8,* 1292–1301.

Wrightson, K. (2000). An introduction to acoustic ecology. *Soundscape, The Journal of Acoustic Ecology, 1*(1), 10–13.

Zuckerman, A. (2006, August 25). Music for greens. *New York Magazine.* https://nymag.com/guides/fallpreview/2006/classicaldance/19745/

14 Generative AI and Music Composition

Robert Laidlow

Introduction

Artificial intelligence. What do you imagine when you hear those words? For many, visions of robots, spaceships, and distant sci-fi worlds are conjured. For others, perhaps those who keep up with the newspaper's 'Technology' section, it might mean self-driving cars, targeted social media advertising, or their phone's facial recognition software. For a fast-growing group of musicians and other artists, it represents testing the boundaries of their work using algorithms that can feel truly collaborative, interactive, and even creative.

Clearly, the term *artificial intelligence* (AI) means many things to many people. Setting aside the term's use in fiction and sensationalist media articles, AI in a research context usually means the design of algorithms that, through statistical methods, can 'learn' how to mimic human intelligence.[1] The vast majority of AI research,[2] including the algorithms discussed in this chapter, are developed for very specific tasks; their understanding of the world narrowed to only a few specific parameters. This contrasts with the field of *artificial general intelligence* (AGI), which is concerned with creating more generalised intelligence. This distinction is very important to remember: while many things are called artificial intelligence, almost none of them are intended to be, or have the possibility to be, sentient entities.

There are several distinct methodologies that have been developed over the last fifty years to create artificial intelligence, and all of them have been tried to some extent with music (Fernández & Vico, 2013). In recent years, research in music as well as most other disciplines has focussed on the subfield of machine learning. *Machine learning* specialises in algorithms that learn through experience: a dataset is provided (the 'training data') and the algorithm learns by training on this data. It will then complete a task, and if it does not complete the task according to a certain standard, it will alter some of the mathematical functions it uses to analyse the dataset and try again. This is the area upon which this chapter will focus, and in this context the terms *artificial intelligence* and *machine learning* can be treated as synonymous. The machine learning process requires both computer code, which is usually created using the Python programming language and widely available libraries of mathematical functions (see Figure 14.1 for an example),[3] and physical hardware which requires most importantly one or more graphical processing unit(s) that can complete the task at hand.

The relatively small intersection of machine learning and music is much too large to satisfactorily surmise here. Machine learning is being used effectively to automatically classify music by genre (Bahuleyan, 2018), identify individual instruments in polyphonic music (Han et al., 2017), create mappings between gestures and sound (Fiebrink & Cook, 2010), and extract contextual information from music automatically, such as tempo (Böck et al.,

DOI: 10.4324/9781003041474-18

2015). In this chapter, however, I am principally concerned with machine learning algorithms that can *generate* new music in various ways.

Fundamentally, there are currently two popular methods of programming intelligent algorithms that create music. An algorithm might be audio-generative, meaning that it generates raw sound files (usually WAV format). Alternatively, it might be symbolic-generative, where its outputs are more like a musical score (usually MIDI format). How the differences between these methods can be creatively exploited will be discussed later – but it is important to note that they also have significant crossover. Most algorithms in both categories utilise *recurrent neural networks* (RNN), or an architecture that is adapted from an RNN. This is because RNNs are well suited to generating material that evolves over time (such as music or text). Both audio- and symbolic-generative algorithms have difficulty maintaining long-term coherence in a piece of music – a problem that is potentially tied to musical time existing in many reference frames simultaneously.

Recently, there have been several defining advancements in the audio-generative domain that have attracted the attention of musicians across the world, and the field is becoming increasingly active. In 2016, DeepMind released WaveNet (Van den Oord et al., 2016), a neural network capable of producing audio on a sample-by-sample basis which has since proved popular amongst composers. SampleRNN (Mehri et al., 2017) marked an improvement on WaveNet in terms of required computational resources as well as more flexibility for the user. This development led to its use by a number of artists, such as the group Dadabots, who produce endless heavy metal music livestreamed to YouTube™. In 2020, SampleRNN was reimplemented and released by PRiSM (Melen et al., 2020) to be more flexible, intuitive, and usable by musicians without programming experience. Also in 2020, OpenAI published Jukebox (Dhariwal et al., 2020), which remains one of the most accomplished algorithms yet developed in the audio-generative domain, able to create coherent songs (complete with original lyrics) up to a length of several minutes. (By contrast, WaveNet is capable of only a few seconds without changing genre, instrumentation, or style.) While these algorithms remain the most popular and influential, many artists have also created their own bespoke neural networks either from scratch or through adapting existing work. Examples include Holly Herndon in her 2019 album *PROTO*, Jennifer Walshe and Memo Atken in their 2018 work *Ultrachunk*, and Robert Thomas, who collaborated with a large team of machine learning experts on a performance projected onto the outside of the Walt Disney Concert Hall.

Symbolic-generative machine learning algorithms have also gained ground in recent years, although there appear to be fewer composers utilising them as part of the creative process. Developing their PerformanceRNN (Oore et al., 2018) and Music Transformer (Huang et al., 2018) models, Google's Magenta lab (https://magenta.tensorflow.org/) have made efforts to allow their work to be widely applicable and available, both as an open source TensorFlow (an open source library for training neural networks) library for easy use in Python and JavaScript for those wishing to implement the code themselves and through a number of interactive web-based interfaces. They have also made available a downloadable Magenta toolkit and released a model that can assist a composer by completing partial musical scores (Huang et al., 2019). However, FolkRNN (Hallström et al., 2019) remains one of the most popular web-based RNNs for composers to explore. It is trained on a dataset of folk music from the UK, Ireland, and Scandanavia. Compositional applications include Oded Ben-Tal's 'Bastard Tunes' and the transcriptions of Torbjorn Hultmark. OpenAI's MuseNet (Payne, 2019), also a music transformer, is the current standard for long-term coherence in symbolic-generative algorithms. Users of MuseNet are able to produce pieces of music several minutes in length and can plausibly emulate the styles and musical fingerprints of composers across disciplines and time.

Case Studies

Machine learning is not the general artificial intelligence of the kind seen in sci-fi movies – you cannot converse with it as you might with a human collaborator. Nor can it intentionally suggest directions for a piece of music, nor directly engage with drama, narrative, language, or any other critical elements of music that are not directly represented in its dataset. What it does offer is a vantage point that is quite unlike collaborating with other humans or utilising top-down algorithms. Studying how artificial intelligence learns alongside working with the music it generates can lead to a new realm of musical understanding. Machine learning as a creative tool is rooted in the complex relationship between impossibly subjective human art and a machine that learns through patterns, logic, and mathematical functions.

A machine learning algorithm can generate music either as a sound file (audio-generative machine learning) or as notation (symbolic-generative machine learning), but in either case, the algorithm has no concept that it is generating music – rather, it is attempting to optimise a mathematical function (the 'cost function', defined in the algorithms code) by iteratively generating outputs and comparing them to the training data provided. The human user can guide the algorithm through their choice of training data, cost function, and other elements of the algorithm's coded structure. This requires a certain level of technical knowledge; therefore, this area of composition often depends upon collaboration with data scientists, or at a minimum, using code others have designed. These collaborations can serve to inform a composer's methodology, yet sometimes the most rewarding results are those artefacts that the original programmer might least expect or desire. Happily, the machine learning community generally takes an open-source approach to research; algorithms are often freely available to copy, test, and modify, providing the user has the necessary technical experience and computational resources.

The following studies of my own work focus on different approaches to composition using machine learning. Each methodology treats working with machine learning as though it is an exercise in translation; algorithms can generate complex music endlessly and it is the role of the composer in this situation to determine what, if any, meaning these generations can hold and how best to translate that into their own practice. Unlike a linguistic translation, however, the source (machine learning-generated music) does not inherently have any purpose or meaning, and so the composer's interpretation cannot be argued to be incorrect. As a result, the musical implications and the potential for exploration of its outputs are often as important as the sounds it generates. New developments will quickly outdate many of the algorithms discussed here, but the building blocks of learning to collaborate with intelligent technology may continue to generate fruitful results in the future.

These case studies comprise music that is written for live, human performers, with or without an accompanying electronics part, and in a physical space with an audience. They are the result of my position as PRiSM (Centre for Practice & Research in Science & Music) Doctoral Researcher in AI-Assisted Music at the Royal Northern College of Music and funded by the Arts and Humanities Research Council. My PhD studentship is in association with the BBC Philharmonic Orchestra, with whom I have a collaborative relationship exploring the potential of artificial intelligence for classical music.

The discussion will focus on how I have used symbolic- and audio-generative neural networks across four examples of my music. The specific works that will be discussed within the context of these two approaches are:

1. *Three Entistatios* (Laidlow, 2019b) for twelve players from the BBC Philharmonic Orchestra[4];
2. *Alter* (Laidlow, 2019a) for mezzo-soprano and ensemble commissioned by the Barbican Centre for the event 'Ada Lovelace: Imagining The Analytical Engine' (PRiSM commission[5]);
3. *Turing Test//Prelude* (Laidlow, 2019c) for harpsichord, composed for the event 'The Eternal Golden Braid' with Marcus du Sautoy at the Barbican Centre;
4. *Silicon* (Laidlow, 2020) for the BBC Philharmonic Orchestra.

Case Study: Symbolic-Generative Machine Learning

Symbolic-generative algorithms are currently uniquely well-placed to employ as a tool when working as a composer whose music will end up as notated material to be interpreted by live performers. Due to MIDI files acting as training data for symbolic-generative music algorithms, symbolic-generative algorithms are necessarily focussed upon those elements of music well-represented by Western notation: harmony, melody, and rhythm. They have no direct reference point through which to understand timbre, performance technique, expression, rubato, or any other musical element not described clearly by score-based notation. This makes symbolic-generative machine learning next to useless for exploring an AI's approach to those latter elements, but extremely potent to explore the former. Symbolic-generative networks reach a level of fluency and conviction in these elements far more quickly and efficiently than their audio-generative counterparts, which, despite being more computationally expensive in addition to training and generation time periods an order of magnitude longer, seldom reach a comparable level of apparently genuine understanding in these areas of music.

When combined with a specific dataset with which the composer is already familiar, it is relatively simple to determine what exactly the model has learned from the dataset, how easily it has learned it, and what elements of notated music elude even the most sophisticated model. This is the approach I have taken in several projects through training an artificial intelligence network on my own music. My compositional work often emerges through considering how to recontextualise artificial intelligence technology. That is, instead of acting as a force for automation and replacement, it manifests through creative augmentation and collaboration. Indeed, it is more often about artificial intelligence than a creation from it. While each composition necessarily has a distinct creative process, Figure 14.2 shows a general blueprint that roughly captures the main elements of my workflow for some of the works discussed in this chapter.

During the composition of *Three Entistatios*, I worked with the MuseNet transformer (information on which can be found at https://openai.com/blog/musenet), which is a general-purpose large-scale model trained on many thousands of MIDI files. I, along with its programmer, Christine Payne, fine-tuned this network on a dataset comprised of my own works, which was much smaller. The resultant model could generate symbolic output in a style it deemed similar or indistinguishable from my own, yet it did not need to rely only on that small dataset to learn the 'rules' of music.

Examining the results of this model is like wandering through a house of mirrors: musical reflections abound. Some compositional techniques I use in my work (i.e., those that the network appeared to easily learn) were replicated and magnified in its generations. With much of my compositional work drawing upon my jazz training, particularly in the construction of vertical harmony and individual melodic lines, the model recognised this very quickly and its outputs often had distinct jazz-based elements. This is an advantage of the general-purpose but fine-tuned approach; once the network identified a jazz-like tendency in my small dataset, it appeared to me to delve into the much larger reserves of its general training which contained much more jazz. Therefore, it could include elements of jazz in its output without directly copying my specific techniques; it was aping the process, not the final result.

Examination also surfaced another easily identifiable trait of my music: chord rotation. Chord rotation is an approach to harmony used notably by Stravinsky in his late serialist works – although my approach, which detaches the technique from its twelve-tone syntax, is more similar to that of composer Oliver Knussen (Anderson, 2002). This technique transposes a chord n times around a given pitch, where n is the number of pitches in the chord. Thus, the given pitch can remain static but its harmonic function within this rotating context changes. As this technique is pattern-based, it was hardly surprising that the artificial intelligence network could learn and utilise it. In another sense, since this technique will not have appeared in the general-purpose training data, it is remarkable that this understanding of non-tonal pitch-based harmony could emerge from studying my music alone.

The focus on certain musical elements while excluding others which are equally or more important is considered a teething problem by many researchers in the field of AI composition. As an artist, however, I am not looking for an algorithm that can generate meaningful music by itself. In fact, algorithms that have fundamental flaws in their approach to music are much more valuable. Approaching and overcoming the shortcomings of machine learning offers the composer new perspectives on the fundamentals of music. Perhaps nowhere is this clearer than in the area of structural coherence. The inability to compose coherent music beyond 60 seconds remains a persistent issue that many researchers are working to moderate in the code itself.

Through these recent musical works, I have developed three broad strategies that aim to either transform this 'bug' into a positive feature of music co-created with artificial intelligence or mitigate it through compositional solutions: Interlocking; Collaging; and Hidden Layers. Each of these strategies will be examined further in this section.

Interlocking

One successful approach to addressing the limited capability of machine learning in creating music that is coherent over a relatively long period of time is the method of 'interlocking' musical phrases. It refers to the practice of interweaving entire blocks of material composed alternately by myself and by the neural network. This is the primary focus of the second movement of *Three Entistatios*. Figures 14.1a and 14.1b show the initial phrase I provided the network, followed by its response, which I then orchestrated for the ensemble. I would then continue this response and compose the next phrase or section of music myself, before providing this new music to the algorithm as another 'initial phrase'. In this way, the model was never allowed to compose 'freely' but instead was always instructed to continue a given prompt, and that prompt was always the entirety of the piece until that point.

Machine learning response

Initial prompt

'De-orchestrated'

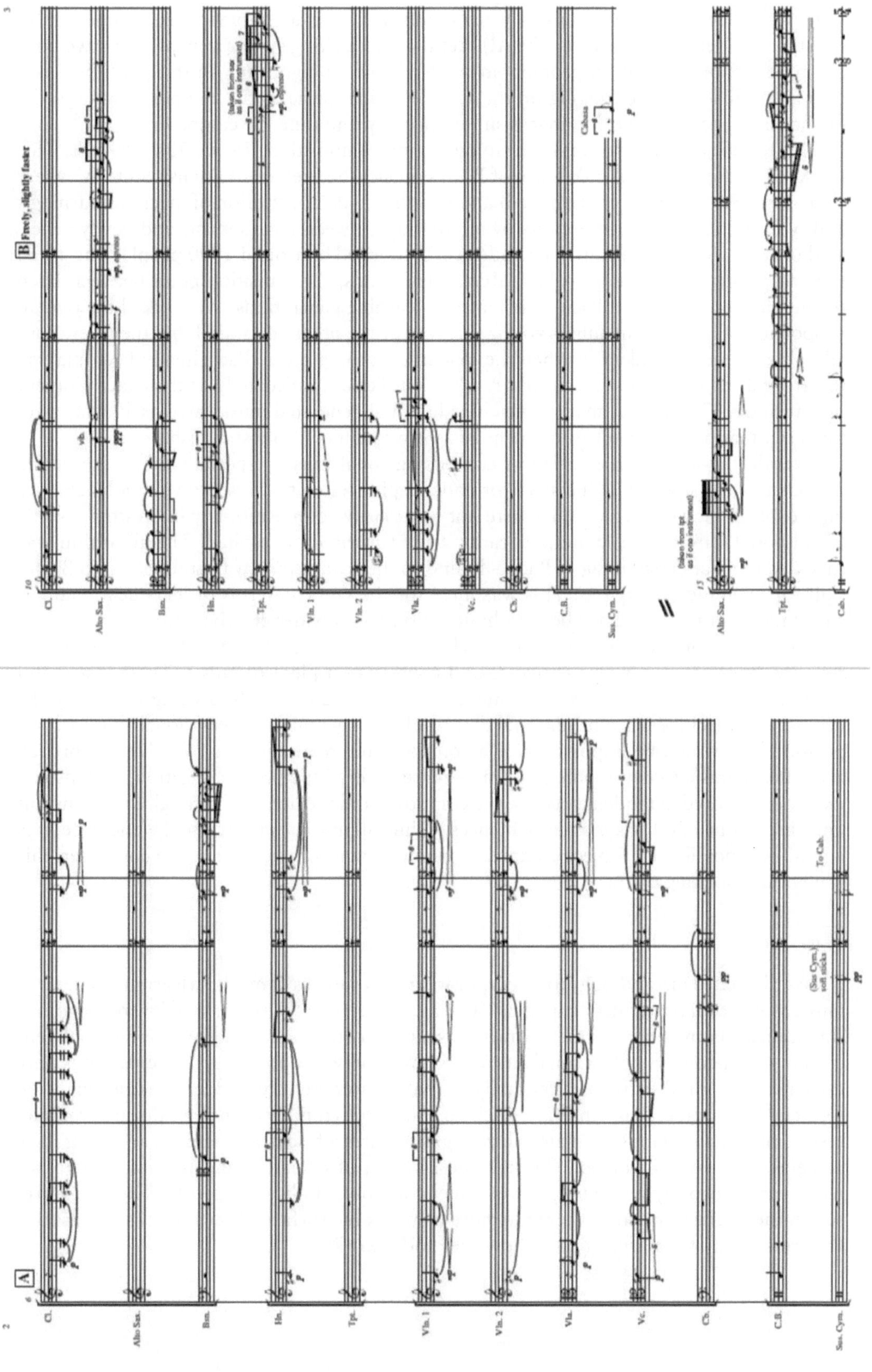

Figure 14.1 (b) Machine learning response orchestrated and developed.

In *Three Entistatios*, all music is being composed, or is attempted to be composed, 'in my style' (i.e., either by me or by the AI). Yet the interlocking system demands that we both compose responses to given prompts in the 'style' of an algorithm. In this way there is a distinct feedback loop occurring on the surface of the music as the composer imitates the methodology of the algorithm that is simultaneously imitating the composer.

This technique was also employed to create my composition, *Turing Test//Prelude*. This work was composed atop a skeleton of Bach's music (the Prelude to English Suite IV where some sections of music were removed) and served as a demonstration of machine learning's ability to imitate human composers by alternating between Bach's music and newly generated outputs to fill in the gaps. The audience, comprised of around 1000 people, was asked to guess (using two-sided signs held above their heads) the transition point between Bach the human composer, and Bach-style machine learning generations. We tracked the overall proportion of audience members voting one way or the other and found that they were usually able to correctly identify when the machine learning music had already been playing for around ten or more seconds, but rarely identified it immediately at the exact moment of transition. This implies that the machine learning-generated music gave itself away over time, but that on a moment-to-moment basis it was difficult to distinguish.[6]

Overall, the algorithm excelled at composing tonal music, especially when the points of change were selected as the starts or ends of phrases or to coincide with cadences (see Figure 14.2). However, the results were not necessarily compositionally interesting – while it composed sensible music, outputs rarely truly surprised or inspired. The algorithm was shackled to its understanding of Bach – bound to these limits in a way antithetical to Bach's skill for breaking boundaries. This was ideal for the work in terms of its educational circumstance, but it would have been of limited utility in a wider creative context.

Interlocking provides a unique approach to composition, where the composer can plan roughly, but not exactly, the structure and content of a piece of music. There is a useful tension between trying to steer the music in a certain direction and being driven by the decisions of machine-learning material that results in a genuine conversational style of composition that would be impossible for a composer to create on their own. This approach also allows music to develop in real-time – there is very little pre-composition, and instead ideas are explored in tandem between the composer and the network through their constant finishing of one another's musical sentences. While all music can surprise the audience, it is arguably impossible for a piece composed on one's own to truly surprise the composer: this is what interlocking offers.

Collaging

A second, related methodology for incorporating discrete cells of machine learning-generated music is what I have termed 'collaging'. Collaging refers to the practice of layering outputs simultaneously in order to create a meta-texture of combined sound. Any individual generation might contain only a small clue as to how a network processes music, and it is only through mass aural or theoretical analysis that a more nuanced understanding might be formed. As a comparison, while interlocking encourages this aural analysis through the successive placement of musical material, collaging creates a fascinating and engaging paradox of being both hyper-complex (through the layering of disparate and unrelated material) while simultaneously clarifying how a model composes. Judicious use of collaging can result in the strange situation where the more complex the surface of the music is, the greater the opportunity for clarification of how the model works.

Figure 14.2 Turing Test/Prelude 2 score evidencing the general blueprint that roughly captures the main elements of workflow for works discussed in this chapter.

The intention behind my first movement of *Three Entistatios* was to create a collage soundscape utilising, and responding to, the very beginning of a neural network's training process. Initial use of collaging and analysis of symbolic outputs produced at this stage revealed musical features inherent to the model, including tonal and harmonic stagnation, melodic meandering, indiscriminate use of long silences, phrases or individual notes repeated endlessly, stylistic disparity between generations, and occasional complete overfitting (where the model simply reproduced music from its dataset verbatim, like an accidental quotation). After identification, these features were exacerbated through the integration into the texture of newly composed musical cells. Each cell (AI- or human composed) was edited to have a unique duration in seconds and a unique orchestration which highlighted the variance and unpredictability of the network's generations. The result was a carefully crafted collage which, while informed by and comprised of mostly machine-learning generated material, was enhanced through manual composition. Figure 14.3a shows the collaging of four distinct cells (in the woodwind, brass, bass, and percussion), which serves to highlight the model's tendency to repeat itself. While the cells are very different in musical content, there is a sense of stagnation emergent from repeated notes in the bass, percussion, horn, and trumpet.

The collaging approach can be used in other contexts. For example, the final section of *Alter* collages generations from a fully trained model attempting to compose in the style of Schumann, but responding to a prompt composed by me (see Figure 14.4). While the features of the model that become audible through collaging are quite different to *Three Entistatios*, the method works equally well.

Both compositional methodologies discussed so far have focussed on incorporating machine learning-generated material more or less in its generated form. While there is always some editing and structural change, the benefits of these approaches lie in showcasing and magnifying the unique qualities of this material. Most of the current symbolic-generative networks, however, including those used in these case studies, cannot usefully provide material created for specific instruments. Thus, the question of orchestrating this material must always be addressed by the composer alone. Many algorithms convert the entire dataset into simple strings of data that are detached from their original instrumental home. The outputs of these algorithms are usually interpreted as 'piano' when realised by a computer, but in reality they are written for no instrument and represent abstract music.

Even algorithms that attempt to retain instrumental information throughout the training process cannot usefully orchestrate material. Symbolic neural networks lack first-hand understanding of the physical sound of an instrument and its critical overtone series–which is vital to their distinct timbres and therefore to the decision-making employed by composers. These algorithms also approach generating music in prescriptive ways (even if their process requires analysis to understand), often either instrument by instrument or in terms of vertical harmony. Effective orchestration needs careful thought regarding both dimensions, and others such as surprise and musical memory, simultaneously. This is not to say an AI can never create novel, exciting, and creative orchestrations, but rather that orchestration is not always a priority in algorithms concentrating on harmonic, melodic, and structural learning. Therefore, even when using an algorithm that can nominally write for instruments, I would usually choose to receive the output as abstract music before orchestrating it myself. For example, to facilitate the interlocking during the second movement of *Three Entistatios*, I would 'un-orchestrate' my music to its most simple form, receive MuseNet generations in that same format, then orchestrate that material for the full ensemble (see Figures 14.1a and 14.1b).

Figure 14.3.1 The collaging approach with the untrained model.

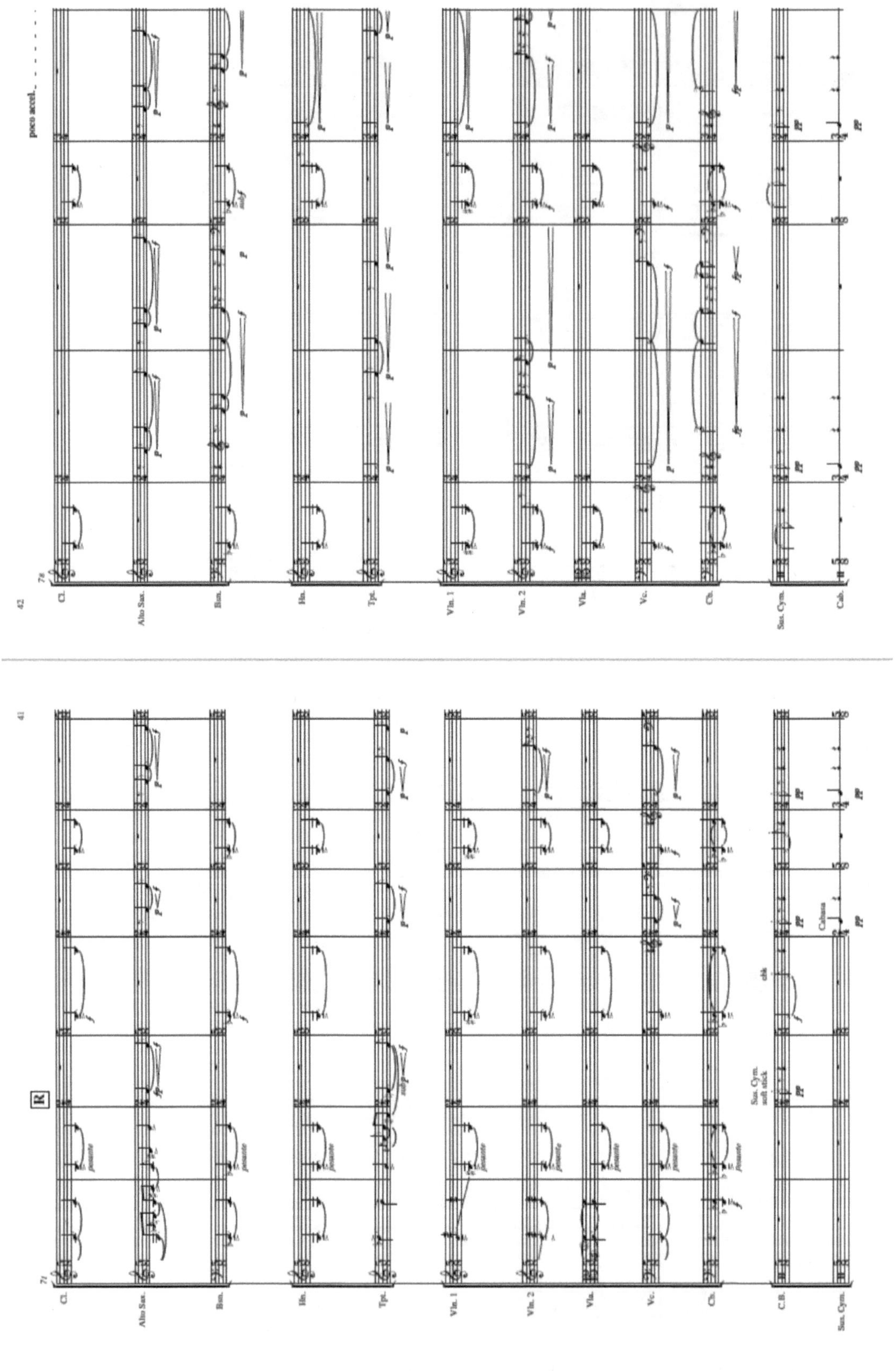

Figure 14.3.3 ... of the alternating structure of human and AI repetition and the repeats on a phrase-by-phrase level.

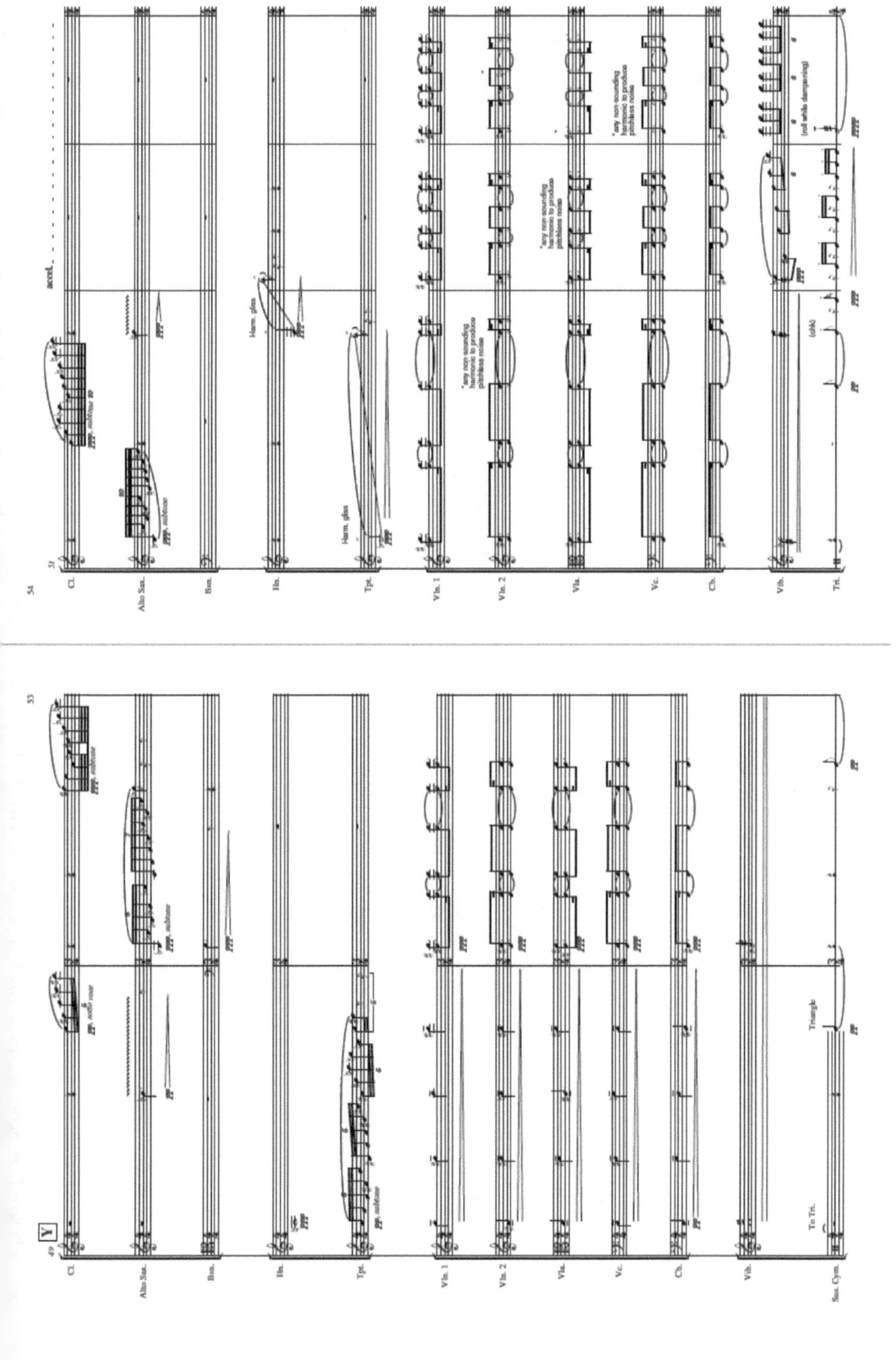

Figure 14.3.3 Sample of output with twenty-note cell repeated twenty times, each iteration faster than the last.

Figure 14.4 Score sample of the final section of *Alter* (by Robert Laidlow) evidencing collages generations from a fully-trained model attempting to

Hidden Layers

Interlocking and collaging both utilise machine learning-generated music on the surface of the music. However, this material also has an important role to play in the planning of a work. As an analogy, if a musical composition was building a house, we can imagine it to have layers analogous to foundations, cement, and floorboards. All are important, but not all are visible in the end. In the case of my music, pieces usually pass through several layers of structural sketching before developing a harmonic framework and thematic material. These layers can be repeated, edited, discarded, and replaced several times before they finally give rise to the musical surface. I refer to the process of using artificial intelligence to replace one of these stages as creating 'hidden layers'. Including a hidden layer in a work before developing it using familiar pre-compositional techniques results in the music being pushed in new directions outside of one's control while at the same time allowing the composer to retain absolute control over the fine detail of the music. Where the interlock forces the composer to adopt a spontaneous relationship to composition, taking each generation as it comes, by comparison the hidden layer encourages and rewards careful planning and exploration.

The harmonic landscape of *Alter* demonstrates this technique across the entire composition. Early in the compositional process, I set the model the task of completing different prompts in various styles. Stripping the resultant outputs to what I perceived to be their basic harmonic components, I found a satisfying harmonic framework that had the potential to drive the work forwards. This framework was then developed over the course of *Alter*. As a result, every moment in the piece stems from these initial generations, yet throughout most of the piece there are very few literal machine learning-generated notes.

Alternatively, *Three Entistatios* utilises a hidden layer at a more conceptual stage of composition. A striking quality of the network used during the composition of this piece was its approach to repeated material, as mentioned previously. In classical music and other genres, repeats are very common but generally function in a limited number of ways. An entire section might be repeated, as in the exposition of sonata form. Or an individual phrase might be repeated, perhaps with the cadential progression of the final bar modified. Alternatively, an earlier block of music, such as a chorus in a pop song or the theme in a rondo, might return after an interlude.

It was fascinating to find that the network did not appear to learn any of these approaches to repeats but instead developed an idiosyncratic logic. Melodic and harmonic motion often became 'stuck' alternating between two distinct ideas or tones for an arbitrary period before suddenly moving on to new material. While this feature was independent of how far through the training process the model was, the way that it was realised did change. In the first movement, the collaging approach with the untrained model created a texture that was at once always moving while seemingly stuck (see Figure 14.3a). The fully trained model of the second movement was much more likely to repeat multiple bars, although not in a manner comparable to phrase-based repeats of Common Practice Era music. This movement's interlocking also produces a conceptual repeat, in that the alternating structure of human and AI is repeated many times, but there were also repeats on a phrase-by-phrase level that continued the juxtaposition of progress and stagnation found in the first movement. For example, the last few bars represent an arrival point as the music alternates between a unison pitch and a complex chord derived from the model's output (see Figure 14.3b). The final movement treats the repeat as its primary material, rather than as a technique to be applied to material. The music consists of a twenty-note cell repeated twenty times, each iteration faster than the last (see Figure 14.3c). Machine learning's consistent employment of repeats is thus transformed from a quirk to be ironed out to key musical material.

Case Study: Audio-Generative Machine Learning

An algorithm that generates raw audio tends to be an enticing prospect to the inquisitive and creative mind. Like the early stages of electronic music in centres such as IRCAM, RAI, or WDR, which produced original music using new techniques of sonic manipulation (Manning, 2004), audio-generative machine learning seems to promise wholly original sounds and timbres. These have never been heard and are waiting to be presented or exploited by the artist. It is critical that there need not be any filter between the voice of the machine and the audience; unlike the generation of symbolic notation or text, it requires no human performer to mediate its results.

Utilising recorded audio, which contains the entire spectrum of sound audible to humans, as training data is more inherently fuzzy than MIDI data. The hiss of a vinyl player, the silence that begins or ends a track, or the noise of a guitarist's fingers. are all learned by an audio-generative algorithm as diligently as the pitch and temporal content of the music. Even less obvious training factors must be considered: the distance of the microphone from the instrument and the mastering technique of the recording engineer will have a profound effect on a network's output. This is a marked contrast to the symbolic-generative algorithm, which can only learn the parametres we have chosen to be represented through MIDI data, such as pitch and rhythm. In short, an audio-generative algorithm's advantage is that it hears audio as it is, rather than through human perceptions, human filtering habits (e.g., ignoring extra-musical sounds), or human training (e.g., mentally enhancing a poor-quality recording with our imagination).

This immediacy of sound is extremely compelling, especially when composing a work that responds to artificial intelligence narratively as well as creatively, such as *Alter*. Throughout this work there is an electronic soundscape woven from samples generated by DeepMind's WaveNet. It is trained on recordings of speech. These samples were first edited to contain only the 'fuzzy', unintended artefacts – sounding like the algorithm clearing its throat, drawing a breath, or licking its lips. As the piece progressed, the algorithm was allowed to mature. This process began through forming sentences in languages that do not exist, since an audio-generative algorithm understands only the spectrographic profile of a word, not its semantic meaning. By the end of the piece, the algorithm has developed into a voice that sings an AI-generated text[7] in English, in duet with the human mezzo-soprano. The juxtaposition of audio against text, alongside symbolic-generated machine learning material performed by the ensemble, served to form an immersive tapestry, inviting the audience to imagine the mind of a machine. To achieve such a goal, one needs to hear machine learning-generated material in a more direct way than the subjective and embodied interpretation of human performers can provide.

Within audio-generative algorithms, an area of great potential is that of style transfer. Style transfer is the focus of the second movement of *Silicon* for orchestra. This AI compositional process involves extracting the style of a 'source' and applying it to the content of a 'target'. An example is the recent trend of animating deceased actors in modern films. The dimension of time (compared to a static visual artwork) and the haziness of what constitutes musical 'style' and 'content' makes symbolic music one of the most challenging areas to develop style transfer, but it has seen success in generating new timbres utilising elements of two or more existing sounds. This is because, while it does exist in time, a timbre can be represented as a spectrogram featuring time as an axis and therefore generated by algorithms designed for images.

Audio style transfer was immediately attractive as a companion to the orchestra, which remains the richest source of colour in live classical music. Through incorporating machine learning, it was possible to turn the ensemble and concert hall into a quasi-laboratory. Here the composer and audience can audibly examine experiments in colour, texture, and sound quality against the yardstick of the traditional live performers. Giving control of the algorithm to an orchestral musician through a user interface operated by piano keyboard was essential for this idea.[8] An algorithm cannot currently achieve the level of temporal, dynamic, and expressive sensitivity shared by interacting musicians. Even if it could, allowing the performer autonomy over elements of the sound was essential to the work's focus on machine learning augmenting creativity, not replacing it. It is artistically appealing to challenge such an institution with this technology while preserving the elements that make the orchestra so powerful: communal music-making, common purpose, and clear technical ability. In this case, the orchestral musician's approach to music-making within an ensemble remains the same, but the resulting sound is completely original.

Silicon also draws from style transfer on a deep structural level, utilising a hidden layer that responds to this technique. A fascinating aspect of visual style transfer is the ability to apply a learned style to any target, or many targets in succession. This was well-demonstrated in an early paper which applied the movements of a source dancer to the bodies of other target humans, essentially creating fake videos of these targets when moving (Chan et al., 2018).

The distillation of a source to its most basic components like this is enlightening, intriguing, and unexpectedly alien. There is a tendency to believe intelligent algorithms function like humans because we instruct them to create outputs that resemble human creations. Seeing an algorithm cycle capriciously through different targets shatters this illusion and aims to place the viewer in an uncomfortable uncanny valley. The metaphorical hood has been lifted, and it becomes plain that the neural network knows only numbers, functions, and vectors. An algorithm views output that changes the dance's target every second as perfectly natural – after all, the underlying probabilities do not change, just the way that they are realised. But the emotional difference to a human viewer could be immense, drastically redefining the meaning we draw from such a performance.

It is this unnatural blurring of surface level that informs *Silicon*'s hidden layer. Its underlying skeleton was composed to the work akin to the source of a style transfer algorithm, as performed on the instrument described earlier. This source was then exploded out compositionally into the style of several different target genres, with sudden shifts between the targets becoming exponentially more frequent. It is hoped that this approach will mean any individual moment of the piece is stylistically coherent but taken as a whole, the work subverts the idea of genre.

The Future of AI Composition

This chapter has examined the current possibilities of artificial intelligence as a means of creative augmentation, but it leaves the question of what is the future of this technology in industry, especially when it is no longer novel?

A wider focus on collaboration may provide an answer. Most compositional work in this field involves utilising other peoples' algorithms, which were not necessarily intended to be compositional aids. Developing methodologies to 'hack' existing neural networks can be creatively stimulating, as shown in this chapter's case studies. However, there is room for more bespoke tools that focus only on one or two areas of the compositional process. An example might be an algorithm that offers possible orchestrations of music provided to it, which could be useful both for the professional and the student or amateur composer. Another example might be a network that can produce audio when provided with a textual description by a user. This interaction between music and text algorithms seems a prime area for research, given their shared features and similar architectures. Pieces created with such algorithms would not need to be concerned with machine learning from a philosophical point of view, only using it from a practical perspective. The more music *uses* AI without being *about* AI, the more this technology will transcend its current period of novelty and become a permanent addition to the artist's general toolkit, just as the microphone, computer, and Internet have before.

Moderate use of artificial intelligence during the creative process can encourage the composer to act as curator and listener in addition to creator. Selecting from a wide range of AI-generated outputs before structuring, layering, adapting, and orchestrating them blurs the distinction between composer and audience, providing a middle ground where the artist is both listening and composing. Delving further into this aspect of machine learning and music will inevitably lead to the breakdown of some barriers between traditionally separate genres. For example, composers usually write in a style and context with which they are familiar. However, it is perfectly imaginable that a composer operating, for example, outside of contemporary classical music could utilise the algorithm fine-tuned on my music and therefore engage with their own work in a fresh way, informed by the model's generations.

In an educational setting, judicious use of algorithms could focus students' attention on specific areas of the compositional process or be employed as tools to generate endless exercises and points of discussion. These bespoke neural networks could be employed very early in a student's development, allowing them to create a fully-fledged piece from an initial idea, long before they would have the technical skill to do so through teaching and practice alone. This could provide positive reinforcement for a student who might otherwise have given up – consequently, they could learn to rely less on less on artificial intelligence to produce works of which they are proud. Or it might encourage a new generation of composers who do not see any difference between composing with or without an intelligent algorithm alongside them. Consider someone who is learning to code while learning to write music. Both skills develop in tandem: would a student see a difference between music they have written with pencil and manuscript paper, and music created by an algorithm they invented? Would an audience?

For such a thought to become reality, there are issues separate to technical challenges that must be addressed. The field of AI ethics (see Chapter 12), even in the small area of AI and music, has grown substantially in recent years as machine learning has become more effective and reliable. In my personal work, the following ethical questions become integral considerations: when, if ever, should AI fully replace human musicians?; how does composing alongside AI challenge the notion of authorship?; and how can this technology be accessible to those without the privileged access to resources and institutional support?

Accessibility

It is important that this technology becomes more accessible to those without the resources and expertise that is currently necessary to use artificial intelligence. If the future of music and AI remains in the hands of a small number of institutions and highly trained individuals, the lion's share of potential creative and educational uses will be stifled and economic and geographic boundaries imposed. Electronic music provides an interesting parallel here: while there is now certainly a large degree of technological democratisation compared to the period of its gestation between 1950 and 1980 (anybody can use a digital audio workstation for free on their computer), the performance of many large-scale electronic works that require more than standard speakers or headphones is still often generally restricted to institutions and venues with the necessary expensive equipment or space to house an installation.

There is also the issue of expertise: machine learning is complex and requires detailed knowledge of one or more programming languages to even attempt. My experience of working with generous experts who are willing to create custom interfaces for me is not enough; this must become standard practice for AI and music researchers if they want their algorithms to be creatively useful for those outside of academia and computer science.

If the resources, expertise, and training data necessary to use machine learning are hidden behind paywalls and accessible only to those with advanced skills, it will risk remaining completely inaccessible to those who might use it to create the most exciting work. This can be avoided through responsible scholarship, awareness of potential ethical issues, and the development of outward-facing technology that is created to assist artists and students.

Conclusion

I have argued that artificial intelligence can be employed in myriad guises as an assistant, inspiration, or springboard for the work of human artists. Furthermore, the subjective and creative nature of composing music may act to protect artists from automation in a way that other careers are not; there is rarely a 'right answer'. This does not, however, mean that musicians are at no risk of replacement; it simply makes it likely that any wholesale replacement of humans will be undertaken in pursuit of financial, rather than creative, gains. Here the allure is that eventually algorithms will be able to generate music more quickly and cheaply than human artists. The question of replacement is therefore: *in which situations* will it be profitable to fully automate the creative process? The answer may arise from learning how much audiences require a perceived personal connection with a composer to derive value from a work and can be elucidated in further artistic questions: How does a piece in a classical concert differ from the music in a video game? What about the music that accompanies an advert, or plays in an elevator?

While people have always made a distinction between music they feel does or does not have value, we may soon have to decide collectively which music we will accept as having absolutely no connection to a human composer. At the same time, it is possible some of these decisions will happen behind closed doors, without audience knowledge. Artificial intelligence might become a natural part of streamlining the music production process, blurring the line between computer and composer. It might also be employed by streaming services as a cost-cutting measure to covertly phase out human artists on their playlists. The rapid development of machine learning capabilities, far exceeding the notorious Moore's Law of computer power (AI Index Steering Committee, 2019), shows that this potential monopolisation of certain areas of the music industry may be alarmingly close.

What is certain is that artificial intelligence will irrevocably alter the world's creative landscape in years to come. The very real possibility of automation and replacement of human musicians in some areas of music exists in tandem with the potential of this technology to democratise the creative process and unlock new realms of creativity and collaboration.

Acknowledgements

The cases outlined in this chapter were funded by the Arts and Humanities Research Council.

Notes

1. This accurate definition of artificial intelligence was generated using OpenAI's GPT-3 model.
2. This chapter was accepted in 2021.
3. To experiment with the audio-generative machine learning algorithm in Figure 14.1:

   https://colab.research.google.com/gist/relativeflux/10573e9e1b10b1ff45e3a00099259741/prism-samplernn.ipynb

4. Recording found at https://www.youtube.com/watch?v=839rF8pucmY
5. Recording found at https://www.youtube.com/watch?v=L1mQGaNmfUM
6. In the original performance at the Barbican Centre, the audience was able to see the proportion of other audience members voting for "Bach" or "Bach-style AI", which likely influenced some members and makes the data problematic in terms of statistical analysis. The experiment was intended to be thought-provoking instead of scientifically rigorous. Similar results were found in two subsequent performances of *Turing Test//Prelude*.
7. *Alter*'s text was entirely generated by machine learning. The generations of each section were primed by the section(s) that preceded it, which kept the work consistent. The piece's first and second sections are generated by PRiSM researcher David de Roure using the Word-RNN algorithm, though there was a considerable amount of cherry-picking to create a text that is singable. The text in the third section is generated by GPT-2 (Radford et al., 2019). These generations are not cherry-picked. Usually, GPT-2 produces sensible output, veering towards the safe 'article' or 'conversation' style of text. Priming it with the output from another algorithm appeared to push it in a direction which was more artistically exciting. GPT-2 generations clearly expand the themes of self-awareness and self-doubt that were present in the cherry-picked Word-RNN outputs.
8. To achieve this I adapted, with PRiSM researcher Professor David de Roure, Google Magenta's NSynth Super. NSynth is a style transfer-like algorithm that intelligently morphs timbre; NSynth Super is an intuitive user interface that allows the algorithm to be played through a keyboard without the need for computers.

References

AI Index Steering Committee. (2019). *The AI index 2019 annual report*. Human-Centered AI Institute, Stanford University.

Anderson, J. (2002). Harmonic practices in Oliver Knussen's music since 1988: Part I. In *Tempo, New Series, No. 221* (pp. 2–13).

Bahuleyan, H. (2018). Music genre classification using machine learning techniques. *arXiv:1804. 01149 [cs.SD]*.

Böck, S., Krebs, F., & Widmer, G. (2015). Accurate tempo estimation based on recurrent neural networks and resonating comb filters. In *Proceedings of the 16th international society for music information retrieval conference, ISMIR, Málaga, Spain* (pp. 625–631).

Chan, C., Ginosar, S., Zhou, T., & Efros, A. A. (2018). Everybody dance now. *arXiv:1808.07371 [cs.GR]*.

Dhariwal, P., Jun, H., Payne, C., Wook Kim, J., Radford, A., Sutskever, I. (2020). Jukebox: A generative model for music. *arXiv:2005.00341v1 [eess.AS]*.

Fernández, J. D., & Vico, F. (2013). AI methods in algorithmic composition: A comprehensive survey. *Journal of Artificial Intelligence Research*, 48(1), 513–582.

Fiebrink, R., & Cook, P. R. (2010). The Wekinator: A system for real-time, interactive machine learning in music. In *Proceedings of the eleventh international society for music information retrieval conference*.

Hallström, E., Mossmyr, S., Sturm, B., Vegeborn, V., & Wedin, J. (2019). From jigs and reels to schottisar och polskor: Generating scandinavian-like folk music with deep recurrent networks. In *Sound and music computing 2019*. http://urn.kb.se/resolve?urn=urn:nbn:se:kth:diva-248982

Han, Y., Kim, J., & Lee, K. (2017). Deep convolutional neural networks for predominant instrument recognition in polyphonic music. *IEEE/ACM Transactions on Audio, Speech and Language processing (TASLP)*, 25(1), 208–221.

Huang, C. A., Vaswani, A., Uszkoreit, J., Shazeer, N., Simon, I., Hawthorne, C., Dai, A. M., Hoffman, M. D., Dinculescu, M., & Eck, D. (2018). Music transformer: Generating music with long-term structure. *arXiv:1809.04281v3 [cs.LG]*.

Huang, C.-Z. A., Cooijmans, T., Roberts, A., Courville, A., & Eck, D. (2019). Counterpoint by convolution. *arXiv:1903.07227 [cs.LG]*.

Laidlow, R. (2019a). *Alter* [Chamber ensemble score]. Self-Published.

Laidlow, R. (2019b). *Three entistatios* [Chamber ensemble score]. Self-Published.

Laidlow, R. (2019c). *Turing test//Prelude* [Harpsichord score]. Self-Published.

Laidlow, R. (2020). *Silicon* [Symphony orchestra score]. Self-Published.

Manning, P. (2004). *Electronic and computer music*. Oxford University Press.

Mehri, S., Kumar, K., Gulrajani, I., Kumar, R., Jain, S., Sotelo, J., Courville, A., & Bengio, Y. (2017). SampleRNN: An unconditional end-to-end neural audio generation model. *arXiv:1612.07837v2 [cs.SD]*.

Melen, C., Salem, S., de Roure, D., & Howard, E. (2020). PRiSM SampleRNN *RNCM PRiSM blog and released*. https://github.com/rncm-prism/prism-samplernn

Oore, S., Simon, I., Dieleman, S., Eck, D., & Simonyan, K. (2018). This time with feeling: Learning expressive musical performance. *arXiv:1808.03715 [cs.SD]*.

Payne, C. (2019, April 25). MuseNet. *OpenAI*. openai.com/blog/musenet

Radford, A., Wu, J., Child, R., Luan, D., Amodei, D., & Sutskever, I. (2019, February 24). Language models are unsupervised multitask learners. *OpenAI*.

Van den Oord, A., Dielemann, S., Zen, H., Simonyan, K., Vinyals, O., Graves, A., Kalchbrenner, N., Senior, A., & Kavukcuoglu, K. (2016). WaveNet: A generative model for raw audio. *arXiv:1609.03499v2 [cs.SD]*.

15 Exploring Links Between Music and Science-Informed Play in Primary and Secondary Education

Evangelos Himonides, Ross Purves and Nicolas Gold

Introduction

Most modern educational theories and praxes see exploration and experimentation as key components of effective learning and development. This is also widely evident within formal and other-than-formal music education (Green, 2017). In traversing novel ways to introduce such notions within a music learning context, a plethora of creative approaches have been taken by researchers internationally, varying from the use of novel digital tools (Jordà et al., 2007), nano-scale materials (Petersen et al., 2015), spaces (Zanolla et al., 2013; Mandanici, 2015), language activities (Hess, 2021), making (Chen & Lo, 2019), body movement (Long, 2006), project management (Himonides, 2013), sports (Cabane et al., 2016), painting (Nijs, 2018), programming (Brown, 2007), live coding (Burnard et al., 2016), music creation (Barbancho et al., 2023), and collaborative synergies (Himonides et al., in preparation; Bell et al., 2020). Similarly, recent work by the authors (Gold et al., 2022; Himonides et al., 2020) looked at software engineering and other technical concepts and how we might use construction toys and music to help young people develop skills within a conventional music education classroom context. This led to a number of realisations regarding the beneficial omnidirectional interplay between technology, music, and engineering (both physical as well as software) and how core principles within each context could bring valuable insights to the development of skills and understanding.

In this chapter, we share experiences and present findings from a short-scale, exploratory funded case-study with participatory research components, where pupils in an English secondary school participated in creative exploration of instrument making, collaborative project management, musical performance, and rehearsal of instrument making principles within both the acoustic and digital domains. We emphasise the benefits of gradual and gentle introduction of the student participants to principles of instrument making, facilitated by the creation of 'simple' instruments, and critical reflective assessment of the challenges and caveats of undertaking the construction of somewhat more complex instruments.

Many educators regard construction blocks, such as LEGO, as a familiar, open-ended exploratory and playful learning tool. Such thinking underpins the LEGO Serious Play (LSP) methodology, used worldwide by educators, trainers, designers, and business professionals (Purves, 2019; Gauntlett, 2010).

DOI: 10.4324/9781003041474-19

Baratè et al. (2017) articulate a series of advantages of the use of LEGO in the kinds of activities we describe, which are echoed throughout the literature in this area:

- Gamification approaches foster learner engagement and motivation;
- LEGO bricks are familiar and comfortable for learners from an early age. The complexity of constructions using them scales well to learners of different ages and experiences;
- The characteristics of bricks, e.g. shape, colour, position can all be 'reconfigured' to have meaning within the particular problem-solving activity.
- LEGO is a good tool for 'algomotric' learning (Bellettini et al., 2014; Baratè et al., 2017) projects because of its open-ended nature.

Hood and Hood's (2005) fieldwork highlighted the high levels of engagement, creativity, and comfort that stemmed from LEGO-based computing education – a further advantage is that it is relatively low-cost and that the absence of traditional forms of 'technology' may liberate learners from feelings of intimidation.

Moreover, since LEGO is understood to be a 'toy', it is not typically regarded as a threatening or unfamiliar tool even amongst very young learners (MacPherson, 2015). As a result, it affords group cooperation from the outset (Oestermeier et al., 2015). These same qualities of LEGO have appealed to researchers working in music and computer science, as well as in interdisciplinary educational projects spanning both areas. As Kurkovsky et al. (2019) note, 'As a tangible manipulative, LEGO works well to support designing hands-on case studies that mix studying software engineering concepts with the elements of team building and playful creativity' (p. 218). On the other hand, Hood and Hood (2005) also found that some teachers were unfamiliar with LEGO, either as a toy or a learning resource, which could lead to hesitancy in its adoption within educational activities.

LEGO to Learn Coding

Since the beginning of the LEGO group in the 1930s and the subsequent introduction of the 'automatic binding bricks' (i.e. the first kind of what we now call 'typical LEGO bricks'), a number of different products have been developed within this system with different foci, from agriculture, to urban life, the natural world, fantasy, science fiction, but also engineering and robotics (LEGO Systems A/S, 2023). Although Mindstorms itself was not introduced until circa 2008, Hood and Hood (2005) distinguised between this type of tool and the actual use of traditional LEGO bricks to teach programming. A somewhat more recent product by LEGO combines these approaches: LEGO Education's *Coding Express* (kit reference 45025) is aimed at primary-aged children. According to Ralli (2018), this kit uses a train-based metaphor to model a range of fundamental programming concepts including sequencing, looping, and conditional statements. A series of five special bricks can be used to control aspects of models otherwise constructed out of 234 DUPLO bricks. Initial product evaluations by Ralli (2018) suggested that Coding Express is capable of conveying these kinds of programming concepts to children aged between three and eight, when supported by adult guidance. Ralli concluded that 'the focus on learning through play is developmentally appropriate for the toy's targeted audience and will appeal to adults. Coding Express is an affordable, accessible, and enjoyable way to explore foundational coding concepts with young children' (2018, para. 8). Barbancho et al. (2023) offer creative examples of employing customised approaches beyond LEGO's own kits.

Hood and Hood (2005) explored the use of LEGO as a medium for teaching computer programming concepts with learners of different ages, including both schoolteachers and their pupils. Their research identified high levels of engagement, creativity, familiarity, and comfort with the tools and reported that LEGO also has the advantage that it is relatively low-cost, arguing that both basic and more advanced concepts can be taught through their LEGO-based method. Their work led to the development of a 'programming language' based around the type of brick and its colour and location on a baseplate, somewhat akin to a low-level machine language. Hood and Hood (ibid.) have used this language as the basis of team-based programming activities, whereby members of the team tend to adopt different roles in the task. These different perspectives, combined with the inherent motivation typically associated with LEGO play, not to mention the discussion that the activities generated, often led to successful debugging procedures when problems were encountered.

Although located within higher age groups, Kurkovsky et al. (2019) offer interesting observations regarding the use of LEGO in supporting the teaching of software engineering. They explored how LEGO could be used in specifying requirements in teaching university students about software engineering tasks. This allowed the identification of active learning scenarios as being closer to what students will encounter in the 'real world' than lecture-style education in this area. In this context, Kurkowsky et al. (ibid.) suggested that teamwork can help learning for the same reason. They claim that adding play to this is important because it has connotations of being 'just a game', a context where there is lack of 'failure' (or at least, where failure is acceptable), and of being voluntary. Drawing on Kurkovsky's earlier (2015) work, they suggest that LEGO can be used to represent abstract concepts such as programming code or software subsystems to mix software-engineering learning with creativity and team-building.

LEGO to Learn Music

In further exploring the use of LEGO outside of the stereotypical 'play-room', a number of recent investigations have been conducted by educators and researchers worldwide. Creative work at New York University, led by Alex Ruthmann in the NYU Design Lab (Learning Music Through Play, 2020), presented interesting findings from introducing LEGO and design to collaboratively design new experiences for 'teachers, students, audiences together'. This work was intended to illustrate a way of playing/engaging with LEGO as a process to engage students and teachers

> with a design process to self identify, to identify audiences, develop empathy, to go through a process of raising different end-users' needs and wants and gains and pains, so you can come to a design solution that meets the needs for everybody.
>
> (ibid., 2020)

A plethora of resources (e.g., TINKAMO,[1] a 'rapid prototyping environment for building interactive controllers and instruments') have since been made available on the lab's official website (https://musedlab.org/). The spirit of 'play' in fostering creative praxis is also evident within the mainstream professional world of the 'music industry'. For example, famous producer and musician Mark Ronson, in a recorded video interview available on the official LEGO YouTube channel,[2] posits that "Play is kind of at the heart of anything creative, you know, certainly at that jumping-off point of inspiration" (00:16–00:23). In that video, Ronson uses the placement and manipulation of LEGO blocks as a metaphor for how he approaches developing material for a new track. Similar approaches have become somewhat mainstream in modern classrooms, using a plethora of tools that enable 'block-based' or loop-based music composition (Kuhn & Hein, 2021). Other commonalities between LEGO blocks and fundamental musical concepts have been explored by pedagogues in supporting musical development. An example is work by Sara Mullett (2017), which discusses a creative approach to use LEGO as an 'excellent way to teach rhythm and notation'. She calls this approach '[LEGO] beats music manipulatives', essentially capitalising on the parallels between music note durations and the standardised sizes (i.e., lengths) of different LEGO bricks. Cademartori (2016) uses a similar, somewhat augmented approach, using the *Lego Movie Music Maker*, which is a tool based on the popular *Lego Movie*. Students are able to 'drop [LEGO bricks] onto a blank staff and depending on the colo[u]r or size of the [LEGO], it will change the sounds or duration respectively' (para. 2).

Work at the Intersection of Construction, Coding/Electronics, and Music

An example of early innovation at the interface between music, computer, electronics, and construction kits was, among others, the Musical Instrument Construction Kit (MICK) (Thibault, 2001; Thibault et al., 2003), an MEng project undertaken at the Lifelong Kindergarten Group at the MIT Media Lab. This project was inspired by constructionist principles, perhaps unsurprising given this institution's close association with Papert and Resnick, but also earlier work advocating the use of constructionism in fostering learning through experimentation. This might, also somewhat unsurprisingly, dovetail with the role that the MIT Media Lab has played in the development of the LEGO robotics platform. Similar exciting work can be witnessed in near geographical proximity to MIT, at the Tufts' Center for Engineering Education and Outreach (CEEO). According to their online nomenclature, the CEEO is 'an interdisciplinary center dedicated to creating the next generation of problem solvers, kindergarten through college, through engineering education'.[3] The CEEO offers a number of activities and workshops that aspire to emphasise social interactions just as much as engineering with a focus on tackling open-ended engineering design challenges. Construction blocks, such as LEGO, are oft-used tools for the delivery of these workshops.

Legato is an online tool developed by Baratè et al. (2017, 2019) using standard web development tools, in tandem with the Web MIDI API in order to produce sounds using a standard web browser. According to the authors, this tool is "'based on the metaphor of building blocks, whose characteristics (e.g., position in space, shape, and colo[u]r) can be associated with basic music parameters (e.g., pitch, rhythm, and timbre)' (2017, p. 227). Similarly, Grønbæk et al. (2016) presented their creative solution called 'hitmachine', which 'empowers children to make music through building physical, shared interactive instruments from Lego Mindstorms™ and playing them to a beat' (p. 1). The authors evaluated their creative approach in a four-day workshop with 150 children participants aged between 3 and 13 years of age and offered suggestions for effective approaches when designing interventions for group music making to:

> consider when designing for collective music making. This includes designing for multiple access points and spatial orientation of these, designing for sense of impact as well as sense of control, and giving careful consideration to how the spatial configuration of technological art[i]facts and furniture can provide opportunities for social interaction.
>
> (p. 10)

The LEGO instruments envisaged by Jakobsen et al. (2016) were intended to afford new forms of musical expression. From the aforementioned workshops from which Grønbæk et al. (2016) drew findings, Jakobsen et al. (2016) looked at the concept of open-ended constructive play and explored how these workshops enabled the children to build their own instruments from LEGO and perform together in pairs. Again, the instruments were more properly described as interfaces, featuring LEGO EV3 sensors which trigger high-quality audio samples on linked iPads. Using multimodal data collection (i.e., video capture, photographs of instruments, participant and teacher feedback, researcher fieldnotes), the researchers were able to conclude that the tools empowered 'children to collectively make expressive music without the need for prior musical skills' (2016, p. 46).

Other research has explored musical representation with LEGO and LEGO-inspired interfaces. MacPherson (2015), Baratè et al. (2017), and Ludovico et al. (2017) employ 'LEGO Musical Notation' (LMN), an alternative system of musical notation based on the inherent standardised qualities of LEGO.

Baratè et al. (2017) highlight the computational parallels of this representation, pointing out that informatics teaching can benefit from interdisciplinary activities, with 'non-technical working examples drawing from a wide spectrum of subjects' (p. 1335). Their proposed workshops are underpinned by the pedagogical concept of 'algomotricity', whereby learners explore problems in practical 'unplugged' contexts before transferring their conceptual learning to the computer. The focus is on guided discovery learning, where learners are encouraged to manipulate LEGO bricks to form an expressive musical notation system, then to use this to encode a series of musical examples. According to the researchers, algomotric activities enable learners to confront 'several scientific aspects, such as the ability to abstract from experience, to formally describe a problem-solving process, and to test the validity of the latter' (p. 1334). Oestermeier et al. (2015) present a smart table application in the form of a grid-based music sequencer. Musical material is 'entered' onto the grid by positioning LEGO blocks on the table's surface. LEGO was chosen for its tactile qualities and its scalability; both simple and more complex structures can be developed, and compositional operations like copy/paste and flip, reverse, and rotate can easily be achieved with direct manipulation of bricks on the surface.

The representational power of building with LEGO has also been explored in music education workshops conducted by Ruthmann (2011). Here, LEGO was used to draw out parallels between design and architectural thinking and music compositional thinking. Workshop participants were encouraged to consider how 'the reflective conversation with materials over the course of the experience influence[d] their anxiety, creative freedom, and self-efficacy' (p. 1).

Case Studies

The literature highlights the educative potential of the synergies between LEGO, music, and computational thinking. The case study research conducted (Gold et al., 2022) combined many aspects of these studies. For instance, LEGO is valued both for its playful, tactile, and familiar qualities but also because it offers a strong technical medium for computer music interfaces. As in several of the studies reviewed, our participatory research workshops sought to balance the exploration of design and building constraints with problem-solving, creativity, and musical expression. Moreover, like Jakobsen et al. (2016), we undertook multimodal data collection, following our initial exploration of suitable instrument designs, in order to capture the inherent richness of classroom-based, hands-on learning activities.

We had a number of aims for our small-scale investigations (Gold et al., 2022), partly motivated by Wing's (2006) argument for pre-college student exposure to 'computational thinking' (i.e., beyond programming). We designed our activities whilst sensitive to the fact that in order to be able to scale up coding skills we needed to educate in concepts such as modularization, abstraction, interfacing, and considering trade-offs in a final design. The final workshop designs included creating music and musical instruments, both acoustic and digital. We wanted to explore the effectiveness of adopting an interdisciplinary strategy to the technical education aspects and assess the logistical and practical challenges of doing so. The ultimate 'aspired deliverable' for the students was a 'blended' musical instrument that bridged the acoustic and digital worlds in an attempt to approximate the mechanical properties of a traditional piano. The phylogenetic 'journey' of this instrument-making exploration, but also the rationale and experience-led choices that informed our designs are further unpacked hereafter.

Case Study 1: Prototyping a LEGO Guitar

To develop a feasible, realistic, and engaging musically driven experience for students, and given the criticality of the properties of materials used in lutherie, understanding materials (i.e., both in general and applied to a particular problem) is an important first step in using it for practical applications. To this end, prior to the workshop stage of our work, we explored the affordance of LEGO for instrument design for ourselves, designing and creating a small 'guitar' to understand the kinds of issues that we expected to find but for which we anticipated that practical experience would be further illuminating.

Since we were particularly concerned with concepts involving subsystems and separating concerns, we considered as an example the multiple modular subsystems involved in guitar lutherie (e.g., the neck, tuner, body, fretboard, soundbox), each of which can be designed separately and cohesively (e.g., the neck must have certain properties of dimension and strength but these are independent (i.e., 'hidden') from other parts of the guitar; the body is not inherently concerned with the strength of the neck). However, when considering overall 'system' design, these sub-systems must also integrate to form a coherent whole, and thus their interfaces and coupling must also be considered. When each is thought of wholly in isolation this could lead to failure or over-engineering (e.g., at the body-neck interface). Thus, multi-level thinking and trade-offs are needed during the neck design (i.e., an illustration of Dijkstra's (1982) concept of separation of concerns: 'being one-and multiple-track minded simultaneously' (p. 1)). Our primary focus remained on the strength of the component, but this could not be totally at the expense of considering how the neck would interact with the body and transmit that strength across the interface. Likewise, when considering the body and focusing primarily on its properties (e.g., shape, comfort) one could not ignore the body-neck interface and the constraints and trade-offs this brings. For example, one might conceive of a body and neck design that are each strong but have little coupling, thus necessitating a very strong interface (i.e., like a glued or bolted neck in traditional guitar lutherie – difficult to achieve in LEGO), or one might choose to compromise slightly the cohesiveness of the body, and bring the neck through it (i.e., more like a 'plank' guitar design), the trade-off perhaps occurring between quality of sound and ease of construction and stiffness.

This design exploration helped us to understand the likely challenges that students might encounter in constructing instruments solely from LEGO. To further inform our work, we then constructed a small 'guitar' using the modern LEGO Technic system. This meant that we were primarily working in the 'studless' paradigm, thought to be more challenging in general than 'studful' building (Kmieć, 2016), but with the potential for stronger and lighter structures. Unlike the traditional LEGO brick that has studs on top, permitting its connection to other bricks and plates, studless parts are connected using pins. This was a helpful exercise as it exposed a range of issues that might otherwise only have been discovered later. Some issues we expected: for example, the difficulty of stiffening the neck of the guitar (a role normally fulfilled by a truss rod in traditional lutherie) to counteract the tension of the strings. The neck of the guitar was constructed using a stack of frames (element 4539880) pinned with high-friction pins (elements 4121715 and 4514553). Although multiple pins secure each frame to its neighbours, the cumulative effect of the minute tolerances that permit the insertion and removal of pins led to considerable flex in the neck in multiple dimensions once multiplied to the scale of even a reduced-length neck. We tried various approaches for strengthening the neck including reinforcing it with beams (e.g., element 4542573) internally and/or externally, running perpendicular to the 'grain' of the frame joins. We also experimented with triangular reinforcement, similar to planar trusses as described by Kmieć (2016). None of these solutions were sufficient to give confidence that the neck would remain sufficiently stable, and any external solution disturbed the external line of the neck to the degree that it would be uncomfortable to play.

Three solutions were ultimately adopted together, two in the construction and one in the design. Internal bracing was retained and combined with a modified base-plate element (element 6139364). We observed that the hole spacing on the side of the neck was compatible with the stud pattern on the baseplate. The plate was cut into strips of the correct width on a bandsaw, allowing the strips to be attached into the side of the neck over a long run of frames. Baseplates of this type are flexible in response to bending forces perpendicular to their main plane, but rigidly resist skewing forces in that plane. As such, when attached to the neck in this way, the large number of connection points, combined with the rigidity of the part itself, strongly resists flex in the neck. These two construction techniques permit a relatively rigid neck.

To further minimise the bending force exerted by the strings, we reduced the number of strings to three and strung them through the hollow centre of the neck and around a roller bridge, rather than only on its top surface. The strings in effect thus exert a counter-balanced compression force on both sides of the front face of the neck, rather than an unbalanced force on one side only. Although these measures create only a minimal bend optically, the effect of bending can be heard in the string tuning as the tensions are altered.

We also addressed the challenge of attaching the neck to the body, resulting in a through-body design similar to that of a semi-hollow body guitar where the body in effect surrounds a 'plank' on which the fingerboard is mounted and that the body encloses. In our design, the body plays no acoustic role and thus is skeletal and intended to permit the guitar to be held and rested more easily than the simple plank alone would permit. We also encountered unexpected issues such as the difficulty of integrating multiple instances of a good standalone design for a geared continuous string tuner into the confined mounting points at the end of the neck. This is a problem not just of space, but of available points for attachment.

Constructing the guitar illustrated well the concepts to which we aimed to sensitise the students. The interaction of decisions and trade-offs was also nicely shown; number of strings was traded for stiffness, quality of tuner traded for successful integration, and acoustic resonance traded for simpler construction. However, whilst constructing a guitar was a useful exercise in exploring the affordance of LEGO, it was a complex, costly, and

Figure 15.1 Guitar prototype.

time-consuming construction, and we judged it unsuitable for direct classroom use. We drew on this learning to develop more appropriately scaled challenges and simpler instruments for the workshop sessions.

Case Study 2: Classroom Based Pilot

Our small-scale participatory research project (presented in Gold et al., 2022 with detail of ethical approval obtained) involved secondary school students in a state school in England, UK. With the support of the school's management and staff, we conducted three interactive sessions.

The first session dealt with constructing a range of simple instruments from LEGO bricks and various other components. The second focused on constructing a pre-designed instrument for which we had compiled detailed instructions. Finally, in the third session, students explored extending this pre-designed instrument to include a digital interface. To collect data from our student participants, we used self-reflective notes and journals. We also recorded anonymous quotations from participating pupils and teachers as the sessions unfolded and recorded photographic and video evidence. We obtained qualitative textual data from plenary sessions with our student participants, and a follow-up interview with a member of staff who had supported the sessions. For the delivery of the interactive workshops, we had set the school's music classroom up in a number of 'island tables'. Each table was covered in an absorbent tablecloth to help reduce the sound of LEGO being handled by the participants across the different 'stations', therefore reducing noise spillage between stations and allowing for clearer communication between our participants (Jensen et al, 2018). All tables were 'equipped' with two cases (plastic hardware sorting, stackable cases featuring different compartments) filled with LEGO blocks and other LEGO components.

Our participants' first task was to work in groups, but with the objective of creating their own simple shaker-inspired musical instrument, using whatever component struck their fancy. Once all participants had completed their own shaker designs, we encouraged them to consider modified designs and explore/experiment with different construction methods, but also different sound production methods (e.g., using beaters, gears, or rubber bands). We also encouraged pupils to be critical about the actual acoustic properties of their instrument and try to gauge the instrument's performance in a live performance context, within a loud room (i.e., where many other instruments would be played in concert). We concluded that session with a live music "jam" (i.e., an impromptu live music improvisation session) of a simple salsa rhythm, accompanied by electric piano, flute, and electric guitar. This interactive musical experience was reported to have been a very exciting conclusion to the first practical session (Gold et al., 2022).

Given our experiences with the design and implementation of the LEGO guitar (see previous section), we designed the second practical workshop around the construction of a piano-like musical instrument. In actuality, this design is somewhat closer to a traditional Zimbabwean mbira musical instrument, consisting of a 'box'-like component that acts like the resonator and amplifier of the notes produced by plucked lamellae of different length (so that a different note/frequency can be produced). For our simple design, we introduced only three tines. We produced high-resolution photographic step-by-step assembly instructions for all construction stages and made available printed copies of these instructions on each station. Once all groups/teams had successfully constructed their initial designs, we aimed to introduce an 'upgrade' to these 'systems' by introducing the development of triggers for the three tines; somewhat similar to what the keys of a piano do. Once that stage was completed, the third and final session involved relinquishing the acoustic soundbox 'module' and using the previously constructed 'triggers' in order to control LEGO sensors that were connected to a RaspberryPi single-board computer running SonicPi (a programming language developed by Sam Aaron, centred on live music making using coding – see Burnard et al., 2016; Aaron, 2023). The RaspberryPi boards were all connected to a set of miniature speakers, therefore allowing the trigger/computer/speaker designs to form a self-contained musical instrument.

A number of exciting findings arose from the three intensive workshop sessions (Himonides et al., 2020; Gold et al., 2022). Perhaps surprisingly, what the research team was seing as the most exciting part of the tripartite practical experience (i.e., the final digital instrument) was not what the overwhelming majority of the participants reported. Approximately seventy percent of all young participants reported that they enjoyed the first free-flowing practical session the most (i.e., the construction of the simple shakers). In looking through participants' feedback forms and session notes, 'fun', 'choice', and 'imagination' were the dominant themes connected to their experiences from the first session. A minority of the participants did report, though, that they much preferred dealing with the fully structured experience by following the clearly compiled assembly instructions. What was reported in the participants' feedback forms was that the diminished risk of failure and certainty that following the instructions faithfully would lead to a guaranteed result was appreciated and reduced anxiety.

We certainly felt that further exploration would be necessary in order to introduce more excitement in the second and third parts of this structured intervention whilst continuing to offer a scaffolded pathway that could still effectively introduce the somewhat nuanced new concepts of software engineering and design. Participants' valuable feedback suggested that there was a need for perseverance and sharp focus and attention to the intricate details of the final designs. Classroom management and concerns about potential lack of engagement were shared by staff prior to conducting the workshops. It was therefore a very positive outcome to witness that all adult facilitators had expressed genuine surprise and admiration about how highly engaged all student participants had been throughout the delivery of the workshops and how all pupils engaged in creative synergy with genuine personal interest and investment in working with their peers collaboratively.

Additionally, it was interesting to see that – although the team had invested a significant amount of time in sourcing adequate numbers of LEGO components per design station – some groups reported that they had run out of vital components. On-the-fly problem-solving, also confirmed by later inspection of the multimodal datasets, suggested that at certain junctures, some components had been used erroneously (i.e., in place of other similar-looking ones). This suggests that in future workshops, particular attention is required in offering additional clarity about the use of specific components.

In general, feedback regarding the structure, administration, delivery, timings, and balance between musical and practical activities for the workshops was quite positive and the team felt that only minor modifications would need to be performed for future iterations. The teacher felt that a demonstration of the final digital instruments at the beginning of the workshops could trigger greater enthusiasm and engagement in the third session.

The school management were keen to publicise their pupils' and school's participation in the project, offering strong evidence of the broader perception of value in the work and the positive experiences and outcomes for the student participants.

Figure 15.2 Pupil instruments.

Discussion

It is valuable to note that, based on the multifaceted analyses of the complex datasets that the team recorded, what different student participants 'took out of' their participation in this tripartite project was not necessarily what the research team had intended as the primary objective of the project. Although the rehearsal (and perhaps learning) of key software engineering concepts using LEGO and music were central to the workshops, individual pupils reported to have benefited variably (and in their own way) in all three interwoven worlds of music, design/engineering, and computing. Additionally, the very notion of 'having fun' whilst having a meaningfully collaborative and creative experience was reported as a central outcome by many, perhaps somewhat out of conformity to traditional educational praxis where a tangible/concrete educational objective is hoped to be achieved, hopefully in a positive/fun way.

Our work suggests that it is possible to generate a wide range of LEGO instruments from small, simple kits, offering opportunities for making and group-musicking in education without such substantial financial or temporal investment. Subsequent to the workshops described earlier, we further explored the potential for constructing instruments from kit-books such as *Gear Bots* (Klutz, 2020), which has 62 LEGO elements, and *Crazy Action Contraptions* (Stillinger, 2008), which has over 100 elements. With the *Gear Bots* parts we were able to construct eight instruments including an 'unreliable' drummer, several variants of a 'shaft' shaker, 'striker' instruments, and a simple two-'note' piano. These would provide opportunities to experiment with determinism and non-determinism, mechanism, pitch, and robustness. Some instruments could be constructed by following book instructions, either partly or in full (with subsequent augmentation), while others required free-building. With the *Crazy Action Contraptions* parts, we produced a further nine instruments including a ratcheted spinner, cabasa-style percussion, a low-frequency 'oscillator' (in several variants), a simple 'harp' with different pitches, several box-style shakers, and a pitched 'glockenspiel' style instrument. The point is not that these specific kits are required, simply that complex construction kits are not necessarily required to undertake simple instrument building in LEGO: with a degree of ingenuity, even very small and simple kits can be used.

This work echoes, and perhaps amplifies, previous work that celebrates the need for transdisciplinary dialogue in questioning 'how music needs to be learnt' and 'what a musician needs to look like' (see among others Williams and Webster's (2022) work on 'multimusical' or 'bimusical' selves and technology, Savage's (2012) views on digital 'expats', Himonides' (2012) views on the misunderstanding of music-technology-education, and Obodaru's (2012) work on 'alternative selves').

Although not novel, this is perhaps one additional reminder that learning is not 'one', is not 'static', and is not 'universal'. It is therefore germane to facilitate person- and context-sensitive learning in ways that foster individuality, difference, personality, and celebrate people's individual cravings, creativities, needs, aspirations, but also moods and personal circumstances. The analyses of the multimodal datasets and recorded feedback from this short-scale empirical work suggest that working at the intersection of engineering/construction, music, and software engineering renders the ground fertile for meaningful and creative synergies and effective learning. We believe that this has very strong future potential and suggest that further research would be welcome in gaining greater and more critical understanding of how this can be put to use more effectively.

Notes

LEGO® and DUPLO® are a trademark of the LEGO Group of companies which does not sponsor, authorise, or endorse this work.

"UCL research team prototype 'guitar'" by Himonides, Gold, and Purves is licensed under CC BY 4.0 (https://creativecommons.org/licenses/by/4.0/)."

"A selection of pupil-built instruments from UCL's activity" by Himonides, Gold, and Purves is licensed under CC BY 4.0 (https://creativecommons.org/licenses/by/4.0/)."

Notes

1. https://musedlab.org/tinkamo
2. https://www.youtube.com/watch?v=xWdSRaFVyoY
3. https://ceeo.tufts.edu/about

References

Aaron, S. (2023). *Sonic Pi – The live coding music synth for everyone.* Retrieved October 11, 2023, from https://sonic-pi.net/

Baratè, A., Ludovico, L. A., & Malchiodi, D. (2017). Fostering computational thinking in primary school through a LEGO-based music notation. *Procedia Computer Science, 112*, 1334–1344.

Baratè, A., Ludovico, L. A., & Mauro, D. A. (2019). A web prototype to teach music and computational thinking through building blocks. In *Proceedings of the 14th international audio mostly conference: A journey in sound* (pp. 227–230). Association for Computing Machinery. https://doi.org/10.1145/3356590.3356625

Barbancho, A. M., Tardón, L. J., & Barbancho, I. (2023). Building music with Lego bricks and Raspberry Pi. *Multimedia Tools and Applications.* https://doi.org/10.1007/s11042-023-15902-z

Bell, A. P., Bonin, D., Pethrick, H., Antwi-Nsiah, A., & Matterson, B. (2020). Hacking, disability, and music education. *International Journal of Music Education, 38*(4), 657–672.

Bellettini, C., Lonati, V., Malchiodi, D., Monga, M., Morpurgo, A., Torelli, M., & Zecca, L. (2014). Extracurricular activities for improving the perception of informatics in secondary schools. In Y. Gülbahar & E. Karataş (Eds.), *Informatics in schools. Teaching and learning perspectives* (pp. 161–172). Springer International Publishing. https://doi.org/10.1007/978-3-319-09958-3_15

Brown, A. R. (2007). *Computers in music education: Amplifying musicality.* Routledge.

Burnard, P., Florack, F., Blackwell, A. F., Aaron, S., & Philbin, C. A. (2016). Learning from live coding. In A. King, E. Himonides & S. A. Ruthmann (Eds.), *The Routledge companion to music, technology, and education.* Routledge Handbooks Online. https://doi.org/10.4324/9781315686431.ch4

Cabane, C., Hille, A., & Lechner, M. (2016). Mozart or Pelé? The effects of adolescents' participation in music and sports. *Labour Economics, 41*, 90–103. https://doi.org/10.1016/j.labeco.2016.05.012

Cademartori, F. (2016 July 22). *Lego rhythms unit.* Retrieved October 7, 2023, from A Sound Mind: A 21st Century Music Ed Blog website https://asoundmind.edublogs.org/2016/07/22/lego-rhythms-unit/

Chen, C. W. J., & Lo, K. M. J. (2019). From teacher-designer to student-researcher: A study of attitude change regarding creativity in STEAM education by using Makey Makey as a platform for human-centred design instrument. *Journal for STEM Education Research, 2*, 75–91.

Dijkstra, E. W. (1982). On the role of scientific thought. In E. W. Dijkstra (Ed.), *Selected writings on computing: A personal perspective* (pp. 60–66). Springer. https://doi.org/10.1007/978-1-4612-5695-3_12

Gauntlett, D. (2010). *The open source LEGO serious play manual.* http://www.davidgauntlett.com/wp-content/uploads/2013/04/LEGO_SERIOUS_PLAY_OpenSource_14mb.pdf

Gold, N. E., Purves, R., & Himonides, E. (2022). Playing, constructionism, and music in early-stage software engineering education. *Multidisciplinary Journal for Education, Social and Technological Sciences, 9*(1), 14–38. https://doi.org/10.4995/muse.2022.16453

Green, L. (2017). *Music, informal learning and the school: A new classroom pedagogy*. Routledge. https://doi.org/10.4324/9781315248523

Grønbæk, J. E., Jakobsen, K. B., Petersen, M. G., Rasmussen, M. K., Winge, J., & Stougaard, J. (2016). Designing for children's collective music making: How spatial orientation and configuration matter. In *Proceedings of the 9th Nordic conference on human-computer interaction* (pp. 1–10). Association for Computing Machinery. https://doi.org/10.1145/2971485.2971552

Hess, J. (2021). "Putting a face on it": The trouble with storytelling for social justice in music education. *Philosophy of Music Education Review*, 29(1), 67–87.

Himonides, E. et al. (in preparation). Hackathon as collaborative research informed praxis in music education: Experiences from the 'The Accessible Instrument Challenge'.

Himonides, E. (2012). The misunderstanding of music-technology-education: A meta perspective. In G. E. McPherson & G. F. Welch (Eds.), *The Oxford handbook of music education* (Vol. 2). Oxford University Press. https://doi.org/10.1093/oxfordhb/9780199928019.013.0029_update_001

Himonides, E. (2013). Technology enhanced learning in the 21st century: The ethos of OPEN SoundS. In G. Fiocchetta (Ed.), *OPEN SoundS: Peer education on the internet for social sounds* (pp. 285–292). Editoriale Anicia Srl.

Himonides, E., Purves, R., & Gold, N. (2020). Building a bridge between software engineering and music with construction blocks: A pilot project. *Media Journal in Music Education*. http://www.mjme.net/

Hood, C. S., & Hood, D. J. (2005). Teaching programming and language concepts using LEGOs®. In *Proceedings of the 10th annual SIGCSE conference on innovation and technology in computer science education* (pp. 19–23). https://doi.org/10.1145/1067445.1067454

Jakobsen, K. B., Stougaard, J., Petersen, M. G., Winge, J., Grønbæk, J. E., & Rasmussen, M. K. (2016). Expressivity in open-ended constructive play: Building and playing musical lego instruments. In *Proceedings of the 15th international conference on interaction design and children* (pp. 46–57). Association for Computing Machinery. https://doi.org/10.1145/2930674.2930683

Jensen, C. N., Seager, T. P., & Cook-Davis, A. (2018). LEGO® serious PLAY® in multidisciplinary student teams. *International Journal of Management and Applied Research*, 5(4), 264–280. https://doi.org/10.18646/2056.54.18-020

Jordà, S., Geiger, G., Alonso, M., & Kaltenbrunner, M. (2007). The reactable: Exploring the synergy between live music performance and tabletop tangible interfaces. In *Proceedings of the 1st international conference on tangible and embedded interaction*, pp. 139–146. Association for Computing Machinery: New York, NY.

Klutz (2020). *Gear Bots*. Klutz (Scholastic Inc.). ISBN: 978-1-338-60345-3

Kmieć, P. S. (2016). *Unofficial LEGO technic builder's guide* (2nd ed.). No Starch Press, Incorporated.

Kuhn, W., & Hein, E. (2021). *Electronic music school: A contemporary approach to teaching musical creativity*. Oxford University Press.

Kurkovsky, S. (2015). Teaching software engineering with LEGO serious play. In *Proceedings of the 2015 ACM conference on innovation and technology in computer science education*(pp. 213–218). https://doi.org/10/gfxh6x

Kurkovsky, S., Ludi, S., & Clark, L. (2019). Active learning with LEGO for software requirements. In *Proceedings of the 50th ACM technical symposium on computer science education* (pp. 218–224). ACM. https://doi.org/10.1145/3287324.3287444

Learning Music Through Play. (2020). *Interview with Dr.Alex Ruthmann*. https://www.youtube.com/watch?v=EvkKf_Mm_ho

LEGO System A/S. (2023). *LEGO® History – LEGO.com US*. Retrieved October 13, 2023, from https://www.lego.com/en-us/history/

Long, M. M. (2006). Stamping, clapping and chanting: An ancient learning pathway? *Educate~*, 3(1), 11–25.

Ludovico, L. A., Malchiodi, D., & Zecca, L. (2017). A multimodal LEGO®-based learning activity mixing musical notation and computer programming. In *Proceedings of the 1st ACM SIGCHI international workshop on multimodal interaction for education* (pp. 44–48). Association for Computing Machinery. https://doi.org/10.1145/3139513.3139519

MacPherson, T. (2015). Using LEGO to create a visual tool to show the relationship between different notes. St George players. *Rhythmic Notation in Lego*. http://stgeorgeplayers.com.au/rhythmic-notation-in-lego/

Mandanici, M. (2015). Interactive spaces: Models and algorithms for reality-based music applications. In *Proceedings of the 2015 international conference on interactive tabletops & surfaces –ITS '15* (pp. 451–456). https://doi.org/10.1145/2817721.2820986

Mullett, S. (2017, April 3). *Lego beats music manipulatives.* Retrieved October 7, 2023, from Let's Play Music website https://www.letsplaykidsmusic.com/lego-beats-music-manipulatives/

Nijs, L. (2018). Dalcroze meets technology: Integrating music, movement and visuals with the Music Paint Machine. *Music Education Research, 20*(2), 163–183. https://doi.org/10.1080/14613808.2017.1312323

Obodaru, O. (2012). The self not taken: How alternative selves develop and how they influence our professional lives. *The Academy of Management Review, 37*(1), 34–57.

Oestermeier, U., Mock, P., Edelmann, J., & Gerjets, P (2015, June 21–24). LEGO music: Learning composition with bricks. In *Proceedings of the 14th international conference on interaction design and children, Boston, Massachusetts* (pp. 283–286).

Petersen, M. G., Rasmussen, M. K., & Jakobsen, K. B. (2015). Framing open-ended and constructive play with emerging interactive materials. In *Proceedings of the 14th international conference on interaction design and children* (pp. 150–159). Association for Computing Machinery. https://doi.org/10.1145/2771839.2771855

Purves, R. (2019, December 3). *Using LEGO to teach academic writing skills.* Retrieved October 11, 2023, from UCL Teaching & Learning website https://www.ucl.ac.uk/teaching-learning/case-studies/2019/dec/using-lego-teach-academic-writing-skills

Ralli, J. (2018). *Get on board with LEGO's coding express|Tech Review|School Library Journal.* Retrieved October 1, 2023, from https://www.slj.com/story/get-on-express-train-coding-tech-review

Ruthmann, S. A. (2011). Learning to teach composing with LEGO: A hands-on workshop exploring the affordances and constraints of compositional task design and assessment. In *Proceedings of the seventh international research in music education conference University of Exeter, Exeter, UK.*

Savage, J. (2012). Driving forward technology's imprint on music education. In G. E. McPherson & G. F. Welch (Eds.), *The Oxford handbook of music education* (Vol. 2). Oxford University Press. https://doi.org/10.1093/oxfordhb/9780199928019.013.0032

Stillinger, D. (2008). *Crazy action contraptions.* Klutz (Scholastic Inc.). ISBN: 978-1-59174-769-7

Thibault, S. H. (2001). *MICK: A design environment for musical instruments* [Thesis, Massachusetts Institute of Technology, Massachusetts Institute of Technology]. https://dspace.mit.edu/handle/1721.1/86843

Thibault, S. H., Lyon, C., Dekoli, M., & Mikhak, B. (2003). MICK: A constructionist toolkit for music education. *Submitted as a Long Paper in CHI.* https://pubs.media.mit.edu/?section=docdetail&id=210180&collection=Media+Lab&filtercollection=Media&Lab

Williams, D. B., & Webster, P. R. (2022). *Experiencing music technology* (4th ed., New to this ed.). Oxford University Press.

Wing, J. M. (2006). Computational thinking. *Communications of the ACM, 49*(3), 33–35.

Zanolla, S., Canazza, S., Rodà, A., Camurri, A., & Volpe, G. (2013). Entertaining listening by means of the Stanza Logo-Motoria: An interactive multimodal environment. *Entertainment Computing, 4*(3), 213–220. https://doi.org/10.1016/j.entcom.2013.02.001

16 Future Directions

Artificial Intelligence, Immersive Learning and Online Learning

Carol Johnson and Andrew King

Introduction

There are many technologies that can support and aid educators and students in learning about music and music performance. While there are many technologies available, how the technology is integrated into music learning is an important point for educators. For example, we know from the various chapters that contribute to this volume, as well as from complimentary research in music education, that technology has become an integrated part of music learning. Music education has a strong foundation of scholarship that outlines strategies and approaches for effective music learning. As authors and researchers in the field of music education technology, we believe that technology should be used to support the extension of effective music learning and therefore is considered within the alignment of music education research.

Therefore, as we look forward to the future of music technology innovation and its implications for music education, we acknowledge that we must continue to use and build upon the depth of knowledge and research that has paved the way for the application of new ideas in music teaching and learning. It is from this standpoint that this chapter explores the opportunities and challenges of current and future technologies that are yet to be explored in depth. Specifically, this chapter will highlight music learning potential including: the future of online music learning; immersive music learning; motion-capture technology; and hologram technology. The chapter concludes with a short discussion on the areas for further research within the parameters of innovations in music education technology.

Building a Learning Future with Artificial Intelligence (AI)

Our students are navigating a world of technology that is rapidly increasing within both their personal and educational environments. The use of AI has moved from supporting spell checking in a text program (e.g., Grammarly, Microsoft Editor), to immersive exploration of the ocean with augmented reality (Clarke, 2023), to real-world self-driving cars with companies such as Wayve (Huddleston, 2023). While the road to autonomous driving software that supports navigating London's streets to deliver groceries is not yet realized, the current ability of the technology is bringing further questions regarding to what extent AI may be part of our personal and educational lives in the very near future, and the ethical questions this raises. AI has the potential to positively impact our learning experiences through immersive digital worlds (i.e., augmented reality, mixed reality, and virtual reality) as well as our real world.

DOI: 10.4324/9781003041474-20

Many see the benefits of AI in our personal lives and educational lives in the forms of financial savings. In an interview with Alex Kendall, CEO of Wayve, Kendall tells Huddleston (2023) that the adoption of AI systems in autonomous cars "lets you build vehicles that are affordable, that don't have hundreds of thousands of dollars of sense and [computer power] on them". In the education domain, we can now use the generative AI software to *create* a beginner lesson plan on topics from music composition to writing software code; the user is sent back a response within seconds within the application's response field with a list of learning objectives, potential practical activities, and a step-by-step teaching plan. Whether these would be useful in student learning needs to be explored.

Generative AI software can "generate humanlike text based on a given prompt or context. It can be used for a variety of natural language processing tasks, such as text completion, conversation generation, and language translation" (Baidoo-Anu & Ansah, 2023, p. 4). The processes involved include accessing vast stores of data/information to generate human-like text through its machine learning programming. Specific to ChatGPT, it is "able to understand human language as it is spoken and written, allowing it to understand the worded information it is fed, and what to spit back out" (Hughes, n.d.). Using its machine learning drawing upon 175 billion parameters described by Hughes (n.d.), users can request the chatbot to craft poems, texts, formulas, computer code, or even (re)search the Internet.

This type of emerging technology is evolving rapidly in education and touted as a time management tool – and creating epistemological questions across the education landscape from authorship to the user's learning development. Lodge et al. (2023) highlight how generative AI works:

> Generative AI such as ChatGPT does not work in the way that a calculator works. A calculator performs the calculations required to reach an answer; this is important. Generative AI does not perform calculations, it does not go through the learning, it does not engage in thinking. ChatGPT and similar tools make predictions; they guess.
>
> (Lodge et al., 2023, p. 3)

While the predictions are statistically accurate, there are epistemic educational concerns we must investigate as educational researchers: How are students learning to learn when using technology-enhanced learning environments? And how can TEL be used for meaningful learning?

As educational researchers, we are aware of the need for students to construct their knowledge (i.e., theory of constructivism) and to develop knowledge and skills in their social world (i.e., social constructivism). However, when students use generative AI to complete a task, the software itself goes from question input to response output. The response is created within milliseconds and does not walk the user through the steps toward the answer – it simply feeds the answer back to the user. From an educational point of view, this type of knowledge exchange (or rather, *knowledge oracle*) has the potential, over continued use without educational guidance, to limit the development of its users in terms of critical thinking skills, language development, independent creativity, and ethical decision making. Furthermore, errors from the technology itself through *chatbot hallucinations* (Knight, 2023) can create fake information in their response to the questions being asked by the user. Although OpenAI recently announced that its chatbot can now "access the Internet in real time and provide direct links to its sources" (Ortiz, 2023), the potential for the hallucinations may not be fully resolvable.

Music-specific and industry-driven developments in AI will begin to shape curriculum and support for educators and students. Laidlow in Chapter 14 discusses symbolic-generative machine learning and audio-generative machine learning. Avdeeff (2019) provides an overview of the first AI-human collaborated album, *Hello World*. Using technology developed by Sony called *Flow Machines*, we can start to see how AI is influencing the world of popular music production. King in Chapter 10 also discusses advances in *Intelligent Music Production* (IMP) tools that are already commercially available for music production. These tools appear to be aimed at AI as an assistive tool to support the creative process. Whether this is assisting with the dynamic levels and tonal qualities of a song or instrument track or creating melodies for a harmonic structure provided by the human musician the possibilities to support the creative process are becoming a reality. Where the agency resides in terms of the technology or the human – or somewhere in between – is a matter for debate. Many of these tools provide solutions that are straightforward to edit. For example, *Flow Machine* will allow a user to change the pitch and duration of a note once the AI has created the melody. How these tools are used will be key for both industry and educators. Understanding how to compose a melody will be a key component for many music curricula that focus on creativity. If AI can provide an assistive solution, will this be the way for students to compose music for commercial projects? Many composers may recoil at the idea of leaving this part of their work to an AI, while some in the world of computer-based music may already be embracing this technology and utilizing its potential. Some of the producers in Chapter 10 discussed the issues of commercial pressures and having to work at a pace assisted by digital technology. The ease of these types of solutions could mean composers working within certain projects to rely on this assistive AI approach. What this means for skills-based training and the necessary expert knowledge will become a point of contention.

The challenges facing technology-enabled learning (TEL) use among all levels of students does not mean we forbid its use in the classroom. Instead, through a learning (and research) posture, we can investigate how we can effectively design and support our students – from K-12 and up into graduate programs – and support our teachers with evidence-based teaching technology-enabled learning design principles and models to appropriately prepare for current and future technologies. A recent statement by A/P Sam Illingworth from Edinburgh Napier University effectively sums up the task of educators and educational researchers: "These are things that have the potential to reduce workload and improve efficiency, our responsibility as educators is to decide how to utilise it" (Hughes, n.d.).

There are three key areas for research that will support the development of meaningful and effective use of today's technology-enabled learning (TEL) education:

1. *Exploring of Supportive Teaching Models for Implementing TEL in Education*

In terms of exploration of educational technologies in music teaching, Webster and Williams identified four opportunities for maintaining the use and advancement of music technology. These include:

1. To experiment with application, tutorial, and software development;
2. As personal professional tools;
3. In support of instruction, integration into teaching, the classroom, and the curriculum; and
4. To encourage student use of technology as integral to their learning and professional development (Webster & Williams, 2018, p. 22).

2. *Identification of Digital Literacy Skills for Music Skill Advancement*

The foundations of digital literacy (i.e., skills competencies and epistemic considerations) can be used for the development of initial topic inquiries and support user time management. However, in an educational context, the use of these types of technology tools without foundations in digital literacy (i.e., skills, competencies, and epistemological considerations) could lead to decreased critical thinking skills, lower language development, limited independent creativity, ethical deviations for the user (e.g., identifying generated text as written by the user), and overall dependence on technology for music making. Given the focused human creativity aspect in music making, additional research in this field is required to support the sustainability of music education.

3. *Exploration of Immersive Technologies for the Development of Musical Skills*

When considering the purpose for the inclusion of technology, many music researchers have explored how technology can support student motivation and enhancement of practice (see Chapter 3), improvement of music listening and analyses through music technology and performative dialogues (see Chapter 7), and overall supportive feedback loops for learning (see Chapter 4).

As we consider the development of technology that includes evaluation for learner scaffolding (e.g., Auralia or Musition, as highlighted in the Section 2 opener), much of the technology has begun to integrate AI at some level. Whether it is AI technology to provide musicians with in-depth performance evaluations (e.g., pitch, note errors, and rhythmic accuracy) or hologram technology to depict an artist singing or playing (see https://www.youtube.com/watch?v=PObUosg5ZUg for Whitney Houston's UK hologram stage tour), we are on the cusp of immersive technology integration within the music learning environment. With the technology providing three-dimensional lifelike images and sound, the learning experience will soon be one of connectedness and sense of presence for the students, as well as the potential of autonomous teaching scenarios.

At the core, immersive learning with technology allows for the learner to engage in artificial, simulated activities, events, or worlds, that allows the user to have *authentic* real-world experiences. The most common immersive technology is virtual reality (VR), with its requirement of a VR headset to bring the user into a fully immersive sight and sound experience. Additional body technology opens the potential for the user to create instruments and perform on any musical stage (or even a planet).

Immersive technologies also have the potential to enhance our real world with additional digital content viewed through augmented reality glasses or screens. Augmented reality has the potential to support musicians' mobility as well as performance posture and stage presence. Current examples of spatiality in dance using augmented reality can be found abundantly across the Internet.

By combining augmented reality and virtual reality, mixed reality has the potential to provide music students with music tuition using three-dimensional digital visualizations that enable the student to experience a *teacher presence* that goes beyond the two-dimensional monitor used in online lessons. This technology has already been used for more than ten years on music tours (i.e., Whitney Houston's UK hologram stage tour), as well as being a focal point at the London Theatre while hosting the 90-minute ABBA Voyage concert performance (https://abbavoyage.com/theconcert/). Recorded with the use of motion-capture technology, the blended music concert stage of real-life and digital images may have a concerted effect on how we teach and learn music in the future. Beyond the current concert stage, there is an exploration of this technology to support musicians' physical health when playing/performing, as well as developing our understanding of performance technique.

Future of Online Music Learning

Online music teaching has been used since at least the mid-2000s to support music education for students in rural areas, students requiring flexibility of attendance, as well as supporting students who have varied learning needs (Johnson, 2022). As we move beyond the pandemic, many new technologies have been advanced, including the elimination of latency through music software like Real Time Audio (www.realtimeaudio.com), LoLA (Low Latency Network, available across the United Kingdom), as well as other apps like Jamkazam (https://jamkazam.com/). Unfortunately, not all higher education music faculties have explored the use of these technologies, with Australia universities arriving late to the adoption of online music classes in higher education (Johnson & Cheok, 2022). Some of these issues may be related to implementation and cost.

When looking into the challenges of teaching music online (i.e., teaching music lessons online, teaching academic music subjects online, etc.), many of the challenges can be mitigated through careful online instructional design and the use of online music pedagogical approaches. As noted in the article by King et al. (2019), online teaching for young students requires teachers to have access to the necessary technology and be informed in effective online music teaching practices. Today, these practices are being shared and developed by those in academic research, as well as on-the-ground practitioners, like online music instructors on the YouTube Music Repo (2020) videos.

There may also be opportunities that have been developed by industry for students to collaborate in online learning. Online tools, like *Source-Connect, Landr,* or *Audiomovers,* that facilitate creative practice online may become more affordable as the technology develops. This could facilitate collaboration away from the classroom and maybe even create global opportunities for different schools and colleges to co-produce music.

Using educational technology supports for students requires adaptation to traditional music pedagogy, potentially encouraging a more sustainable future for some aspects of education. While not every instructor may be ready or willing to take up new pedagogical approaches, the inclusion of AI in learning, immersive learning (i.e., XR, VR, AR, etc.), and other innovative teaching approaches are being utilized in education. It poses the following questions: how will the field of music education be prepared to advance and prepare music students for their teaching futures? And how can we provide students with opportunities to learn through effective online music learning?

Concluding Remarks

Dorfman (2022) outlines that there are important considerations when we look to implement technology and technology policy into music education classes. Being open to considering how teachers may feel with their worlds being disrupted by technology is not only integral for those developing the technology policies, but it also becomes the case that those implementing the policy must show how they are supporting teachers' use of technology in meaningful ways and that they are not overwhelmed by the changes.

While many academics use technology in their teaching, we often assume that our students are well prepared and have the technological know-how to effectively support their learning. Prior to the 2020 pandemic, Webster and Williams (2018) identified that educators in Higher Education had minimal (or limited) provision to support students with appropriate training in music technology. In addition, for teacher education Bauer and Dammers (2016) suggested that less than fifty percent of surveyed programs had students taking part in a music technology course during their music education program.

It has been suggested that as a consequence of the pandemic, the technology skills and proficiencies of students (and instructors) made large advancements (Joseph & Lennox, 2021). We are aware that not all instructors feel comfortable or proficient (i.e. have self-efficacy) at consistently using technology in their music teaching (Sarikaya, 2022). However, this volume demonstrates that technology can be effectively integrated into music learning to prepare music students for a future of music innovation.

References

Avdeeff, M. (2019). Artificial Intelligence & Popular Music: SKYGGE, Flow Machines, and the Audio Uncanny Valley. *Arts*, 8(4), 130. https://doi.org/10.3390/arts8040130

Baidoo-Anu, D., & Ansah, L. O. (2023). Education in the era of generative artificial intelligence (AI): Understanding the potential benefits of ChatGPT in promoting teaching and learning. *Journal of AI*, 7(1), 52–62.

Bauer, W. I., & Dammers, R. J. (2016). Technology in music teacher education: A national survey. *Research Perspectives in Music Education*, 18(1), 2–15.

Clark, M. (2023, January 13). Seeing the sea in 4D with ocean explorer. *CSIRO*. https://www.csiro.au/en/news/all/articles/2023/january/ocean-explorer

Dorfman, J. (2022). *Theory and practice of technology-based music instruction* (2nd ed.). Oxford University Press.

Huddleston, T. (2023, August 28). 29-year-old's self driving car startup was born in a garage – now it has Bill Gates' attend and a $1 billion valuation. *Make It: CNBC*. https://www.cnbc.com/2023/08/18/how-ai-boom-helped-billion-dollar-self-driving-car-startup-wayve-grow.html

Hughes, A. (n.d.). *ChatGPT: Everything you need to know about OpenAI's GPT-4 tool*. https://www.sciencefocus.com/future-technology/gpt-3

Johnson, C. (2022). *A framework for teaching music online in higher education*. Bloomsbury Publications. https://doi.org/10.5040/9781350201880

Johnson, C., & Cheok, T. (2022). The Australian landscape of online bachelor music courses pre-COVID-19. *International Journal on Innovations in Online Ed*, 5(4), 1–18. https://doi.org/10.1615/IntJInnovOnlineEdu.2022045717

Joseph, D., & Lennox, L. (2021). Twists, turns and thrills during COVID-19: Music teaching and practice in Australia. *Music Education Research*, 23(2), 241–255. https://doi.org/10.1080/14613808.2021.1906852

King, A., Prior, H., & Waddington-Jones, C. (2019). Connect resound: Using online technology to deliver music education to remote communities. *Journal of Music, Technology & Education*, 12(2), 201–217. https://doi.org/10.1386/jmte_00006_1

Knight, W. (2023, October 5). *Chatbot hallucinations are poisoning web search*. Wired. https://www.wired.com/story/fast-forward-chatbot-hallucinations-are-poisoning-web-search/

Lodge, J. M., Thompson, K., & Corrin, L. (2023). Mapping out a research agenda for generative artificial intelligence in tertiary education. *Australasian Journal of Educational Technology*, 39(1), 1–8.

Ortiz, R. (2023, September 23). ChatGPT can finally access the internet in real time, but there's a catch. *ZDNET*. https://www.zdnet.com/article/chatgpt-can-finally-access-the-internet-in-real-time-but-theres-a-catch/

Sarikaya, M. (2022). An investigation of music teachers' perceived self-efficacy for technology integration. *International Journal of Technology in Education and Science*, 6(2), 204–217. https://doi.org/10.46328/ijtes.369

Webster, P., & Williams, D. (2018). Technology's role for achieving creativity, diversity and integration in the American undergraduate music curriculum: Some theoretical, historical and practical perspectives. *Journal of Music, Technology & Education*, 11(1), 5–36.

Index